Social Studies Instruction

PRENTICE-HALL INTERNATIONAL, INC., *London*
PRENTICE-HALL OF AUSTRALIA, PTY., LTD., *Sydney*
PRENTICE-HALL OF CANADA, LTD., *Toronto*
PRENTICE-HALL FRANCE, S.A.R.L., *Paris*
PRENTICE-HALL OF JAPAN, INC., *Tokyo*
PRENTICE-HALL DE MEXICO, S.A., *Mexico City*

Social Studies Instruction

Third Edition

Organizing, Teaching, and Supervising
Social Studies in Secondary Schools

MAURICE P. MOFFATT

Montclair State College
Montclair, New Jersey

Prentice-Hall, Inc.
Englewood Cliffs, New Jersey

To the Memory of
My Mother
Catherine M. Moffatt

Preface

In preparing the third edition, the author has given considerable thought to the challenges and trends in education. An intensive study was made of the growing importance of the social studies and social sciences in the secondary school curriculum. A constant supply of new knowledge is steadily enriching this subject-matter area. The current decades have been characterized by rapid change, a surge of technological and scientific progress which holds implications for society and our present civilization. Thus, effective education at the secondary level, and especially a productive social studies curriculum, can provide youth with a foundation for fostering competent citizenship in a democratic society. Young people are being helped to meet their needs and at the same time are acquiring knowledge, skills, and understandings so essential for effective living in a changing society. An awareness of the responsibilities and challenges facing the individual in our complex world are of utmost importance.

Considerable research and experimentation, through education, has revealed and will continue to reveal new approaches, methods, procedures, and techniques for teaching the social studies. The social studies teacher must be aware of the importance of content as it is related to methodology and experiences in the learning process. He also must be competent in handling new ideas, materials, and equipment required in today's instructional scheme.

This volume, it is hoped, will aid the prospective teacher as well as the experienced teacher in guiding the education of youth and meeting their needs in our secondary schools. The author has been mindful of the actual teaching-learning situation and has employed recent research, the best modern theory and concrete experiences with newer and more democratic teaching procedures.

The reception of the two previous editions of *Social Studies Instruction* as a guide to the prospective teacher has attested to its practical value. The author hopes that the third edition, which treats new instructional materials in a functional and practical manner, will prove equally useful. Both teachers and students have made constructive suggestions, and the roles of these two groups in the learning process have been emphasized.

As in the two previous editions, many new ideas, influences, and visions have been incorporated in the body of the book. The author has drawn upon his own writings, experiences, and activities as a teacher and supervisor in various kinds of schools and at different levels of instruction. New chapters dealing with the process of culture, developing economic competence, block-time classes and the core program, and a social studies prospectus have been added. Other chapters have been enriched with new materials to bring them in line with current trends. The author has attempted to stress the importance of content, information, and acquiring knowledge through the use of functional experiences. The importance of acquiring skills and developing proper attitudes and understandings has been included in the objectives and units found in the text.

Acknowledgment and appreciation are due many people who helped make this book possible. Mr. Frank S. Kelland, the geographer, and Miss Emma Fantone, Coordinator, Audio-Visual Center, Montclair State College, have been especially helpful. Mr. David N. Alloway, a colleague in the Social Studies Department, made valuable contributions. Miss Wahnetah Brummett read the entire manuscript and made many valuable and worthwhile suggestions. Mrs. Mary Hellman, Reference Librarian at Montclair State College, aided materially with the library chapter. Mrs. Marion Siegeltuch and Miss Elsie Gibson, reference librarians, gave valuable assistance as did Miss Claire M. Merlehan of the library staff, Montclair State College, Montclair, New Jersey. Appreciation is extended to Mr. Vincent A. D'Arrigo of Prentice-Hall, Inc., for his valuable assistance in the production of the book.

Many educational associations, school systems, publishers, and business organizations have granted permission to reproduce material. Credit is given for their material where it is reproduced, and appreciation is expressed here.

Maurice P. Moffatt

Contents

Chapter One

A Social Studies Prospectus

The advancing frontiers in our contemporary world present a challenge for the social sciences. It is through the store of knowledge derived from research in the social sciences that the individual is aided in better understanding the nature, scope, and workings of society. We are living in times of change which present issues and problems for which we turn to the social sciences for understanding. The responsibilities of the individual in a culture affected by dynamic changes calls for effectively educated citizens functioning in a free democratic society. The changing and emerging needs of our society necessitate the constant evaluation of educational needs.

One of the characteristics of a dynamic society is that its frontiers are constantly changing. The frontier of today becomes the familiar territory of tomorrow. The very effort of mobilizing energies for constructive tasks in one decade may inhibit creativity in another. The correctives of one age may become the roadblocks of another. Thus, the rewards and esteem which we attach to the fields in which we have been most successful may inhibit the development of talent in other highly important areas. We must recognize that one important factor in the unwillingness of youth to undertake certain critical tasks is due to a rather severe imbalance inherent in our current system of incentives. The skills which we need most critically today are not necessarily those that we reward most highly.[1]

---

[1] Rockefeller Brothers Fund, Inc., *The Pursuit of Excellence: Education and the Future of America* (Garden City, N.Y.: Doubleday & Company, Inc., 1958), p. 12. © 1958 by Rockefeller Brothers Fund, Inc. (as it appears in Prospect for America. © 1961). Reprinted by permission of Doubleday & Company, Inc.

1

Looking ahead

Secondary education and especially the social studies have a major responsibility in helping youth to understand today's world and to prepare for the future. Any attempt to estimate the future needs of society demands serious consideration and evaluation since society's needs have changed so markedly in recent decades. In the period ahead we will no doubt continue to experience the effects of the growth of science and technology upon the nation and the world. This single factor alone should provide a vast amount of change for civilization. Other emerging factors, large in scope, will be deeply charged with many innovations.

The rapidly increasing mobile population coupled with increased urbanization will continue to influence the social and economic aspects of society. The implications of automation and the creation of new industries will play an important role in tomorrow's world. The utilization of the fruits of scientific progress will become more pronounced in the decades ahead. Furthermore, new technologies will undoubtedly furnish an increased amount of leisure time for the individual. Increased competence and a greater breadth in skill and knowledge will become a premium in most types of endeavor. The following excerpt will further amplify the scope of changes to be expected.

New sources of power and automation are raising standards of living and increasing leisure. Higher levels of competence and greater flexibility are being demanded of workers. There is need for more technicians, engineers, scientists, managers, and professional workers. The greatest demands are at the highest levels of competence.

Advances in mass communication, increased standardization and homogeneity, and ideological conflict have brought increased pressures toward conformity at a time when increased individuality and creativity are needed. The rapidity of change is almost catastrophic. Social institutions and value standards have difficulty in coping with the increased power and material wealth produced by scientific and technological advances. The separation between the generations is becoming wider and communication between adults and the young is becoming more difficult.[2]

The changing scene in American civilization with its implications for education are clearly expressed as follows:

In order to appraise the opportunities and requirements faced by education, it is essential to review certain basic changes and movements which characterize contemporary American society. Among these factors which condition America's future are (1) an ongoing scientific and technological revolution;

---

[2] I. J. Quillen, "The Education of Teachers: Quest for Quality," *The Education of the Teachers—Curriculum Programs*, National Commission on Teacher Education and Professional Standards (Washington, D.C.: National Education Association, 1959), p. 32.

(2) a contracting world of complex international relations; (3) a world-wide population growth of unprecedented proportions; (4) the penetrating influence of public policy on all phases of life; (5) changing economic structures and patterns; (6) the emergence of the behavioral sciences and the advancing frontiers of all the social disciplines, and (7) conflicts in values and ethics. These areas of basic change in American life must be viewed in relation to the traditional values of a free society, but they are the determinants of education in the future and the sources of current confusion, controversy, and creativity.[3]

The significance of education

Secondary education is charged with the assignment of helping to build competence for individuals who will take their place in society. A wider knowledge of the workings of our economic, social, and political activities will be a necessary requirement for living in a society charged with advancing scientific and technological achievement. Furthermore, a broader understanding of our ever-shrinking world will be necessary to understand contemporary civilization with its various cultures.

Students will be called upon to meet new problems, make important decisions and face the challenges of change in their future daily living. Many young people will leave the high school to seek their full share of higher education.

Education is important in any modern society, whatever its political or economic forms. But a society such as ours, dedicated to the worth of the individual, committed to the nurture of free, rational, and responsible men and women, has special reasons for valuing education. Our deepest convictions impel us to foster individual fulfillment. We wish each one to achieve the promise that is in him. We wish each one to be worthy of a free society, and capable of strengthening a free society.

Education is essential not only to individual fulfillment but to the vitality of our national life. The vigor of our free institutions depends upon educated men and women at every level of the society. And at this moment in history, free institutions are on trial.[4]

In conclusion as we survey the dynamic changes sweeping the world, it is imperative that the social studies curriculum keep pace with our new age. The impact of communication along with the scientific revolution is constant in our American culture. The social studies program at the secondary level becomes a vehicle by which the student is provided an opportunity to continue his intellectual growth. An important aspect of our complex society is the effect upon the individual of the vast amount of increasingly abundant and pertinent knowledge.

---

[3] National Commission on the Social Studies, *Curriculum Planning in American Schools: The Social Studies* (Washington, D.C.: National Council for the Social Studies, 1958), p. 1.

[4] J. W. Gardner, "National Goals in Education," in *Goals for Americans* by The American Assembly (Englewood Cliffs, N.J.: Prentice-Hall, Inc.), p. 81. © 1960.

Knowledge acquired by the social scientist using specific methods, a pioneering spirit, and some creative initiative can assist in the educative process. The utilization of new information, skills, and challenging ideas can do much to meeting the needs, problems, interests, and goals of youth.

The following chart is designed to illustrate the interrelationships between the social sciences and the social studies and how they fit together in our civilization. It also illustrates the flow of concepts and ideas that we should endeavor to communicate to the secondary school student through the social studies program. Finally it shows how these must focus in order to bring about the desired competencies and effective citizenship our culture expects of its citizens.

NEW HORIZONS FOR THE SOCIAL SCIENCES AND THE SOCIAL STUDIES

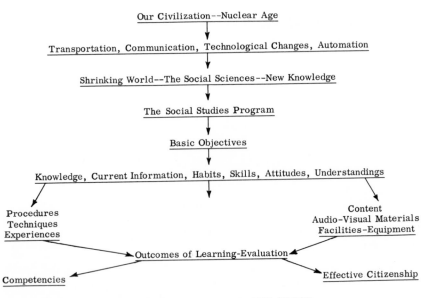

A SOCIAL STUDIES PROGRAM FOR YOUTH

Bibliography

Educational Policies Commission, *The Central Purpose of American Education.* Washington, D.C.: National Education Association, 1961.

Patterson, F., ed., *Citizenship and a Free Society: Education for the Future,* Thirtieth Yearbook of the National Council for the Social Studies. Washington, D.C.: National Education Association, 1960.

President's Commission on National Goals, *Goals for Americans.* Englewood Cliffs, N.J.: Prentice-Hall, Inc., 1960.

Rockefeller Brothers Fund, *The Pursuit of Excellence: Education and the Future of America,* Report V, The Special Studies Project. Garden City, N.Y.: Doubleday & Company, Inc., 1958.

Chapter Two

The Social Studies
and Secondary Education

The social studies has a dynamic role to assume in the secondary school curriculum that provides a sound foundation for living in the increasingly complex world. This field of instruction has much to contribute to the education of today's youth. Through research in the social sciences, the social studies has provided a vast reservoir of knowledge for effective learning about contemporary society. Pertinent information dealing with the political, social, economic, and cultural aspects of our nation and the world is important for a better understanding of civilization. History alone carries many memories that furnish the rich story of our cherished American heritage. Effective living in a society charged with rapid changes places a premium upon an educated and informed citizenry. For this reason secondary education should help to meet the needs of youth and those of our dynamic society.

In meeting the demands of education the social studies and other subject matter areas of the curriculum should greatly contribute to the fulfillment of the purposes of the school and the goals of education.

Central purpose of the school

Considerable thought has been given to the nature of our educational structure at all levels. In recent decades, much study has been directed toward the learner, curriculum, and society. The following materials have stressed the significance of the school:

velops the rational potentials of its people, along with their intuitive and aes-

The individual with developed rational powers can share deeply in the freedoms his society offers and can contribute most to the preservation of those freedoms. At the same time, he will have the best chance of understanding and contributing to the great events of his time. And the society which best de-thetic capabilities, will have the best chance of flourishing in the future. To help every person develop those powers is therefore a profoundly important objective and one which increases in importance with the passage of time. By pursuing this objective, the school can enhance spiritual and aesthetic values and the other cardinal purposes which it has traditionally served and must continue to serve.

The purpose which runs through and strengthens all other educational purposes—the common thread of education—is the development of the ability to think. This is the central purpose to which the school must be oriented if it is to accomplish either its traditional tasks or those newly accentuated by recent changes in the world. To say that it is central is not to say that it is the sole purpose or in all circumstances the most important purpose, but that it must be a pervasive concern in the work of the school. Many agencies contribute to achieving educational objectives, but this particular objective will not be generally attained unless the school focuses on it. In this context, therefore, the development of every student's rational powers must be recognized as centrally important.[1]

Stating the purposes of education

The purposes of education and those especially related to the secondary level serve as guides for building educational programs. They are framed in terms of what is expected to be desirable outcomes of education, and stem from deep considerations of the growth or education of the individual.

Following are the fundamental purposes of education as stated by one school system:

To develop and maintain physical and mental health; to develop competency in the fundamental tools of learning, traditionally called the 3R's; to think critically and act responsibly; to develop and strengthen home and family life; to respect, understand, and live well with others; to develop moral and spiritual values; to understand and to cope with the physical world; to grow in appreciation of the arts and in desire and ability to express oneself creatively through various media; to develop interest and skill in worth-while leisure-time activities; to develop understanding of and respect for the cultural heritage; to develop the knowledge, skills, attitudes, and understanding essential for earning a living; to develop consumer effectiveness; and to appreciate the duties, responsibilities, and privileges of citizenship.[2]

---

[1] Educational Policies Commission, *The Central Purpose of American Education* (Washington, D.C.: National Education Association, 1961), pp. 11-12.

[2] *World Geography*, Curriculum Bulletin No. 13 (Cincinnati, Ohio: Board of Education, 1958), p. 17.

There is a definite need to clarify and evaluate the purposes of any program whether it be at the local or state level. Any revision should be in terms of current trends and future expectations in education.

Society's needs and youth

Youth should understand the demands and needs of a world highly charged with technological change and new scientific progress. He must adjust to the emerging responsibilities that will be his in a society with constantly pressing needs and wants. The immediate needs in youth's environment and how they are coped with has a high priority for youth's consideration.

The essentials for a proper mastery of one's goals call for effective skills developed through a school program.

Our mobile and technological society is characterized by fast-paced changes. Thus secondary education must focus attention and place value upon living and working in our times. This calls for the acquisition of flexible and functional skills, understanding civic and national responsibilities and privileges, fostering creativity in terms of thinking and activity, comprehending community and family living in our complex society, practicing effective decision-making, applying economic intelligence, developing competencies that correspond with the needs of industry, business, and the professions. The future and the present will require the individual to be mature in judgment and action so as to adjust in a world of change with all its economic and social implications.

The curriculum and youth

The curriculum should have directives to assist youth in finding new areas of usefulness. Since the implications of change are so great the secondary school should develop a curriculum geared to the times. A dynamic program should have as a major objective the equipping of youth with knowledge, skills, and experiences that will aid him in meeting new problems and reaching satisfactory solutions.

A modern curriculum must be flexible enough to meet rapid change and must point toward future trends in society as well as to the needs of youth. It must be sensitive to the challenges presented by various factors in the world. The task ahead is that of building an effective curriculum with selective content that will provide an abundance of sound educational experiences. Any worthwhile instructional program must be geared for our times and must provide knowledge for youth as he moves forward in a democratic society.

The Social Sciences and the Social Studies

The social sciences

The social sciences have much source material to contribute to our instructional program at the secondary school level. They are the compilation of all previous knowledge concerning man and society. This vast storehouse can have tremendous value for study in our times. Today's civilization with all its complexities needs the fruits of the social sciences for clarification. The social sciences are affected by constant changes similar to the dynamics of contemporary society.

The social sciences are disciplines which are concerned with the relationships of human beings with each other and with their natural environment. They include such areas as history, economics, political science, anthropology, sociology, and geography. The social sciences present the story of human affairs from the past to our contemporary life. The history and culture of our own state and immediate community are encompassed in the social sciences.

The social sciences furnish much of the content for the social studies field. The historical, social, political, and economic materials offer a reliable source for gathering valuable knowledge. Such areas as political science, economics, history, sociology, and the semisocial sciences are fruitful for research and study. The subject matter can be analyzed and used in understanding trends, solving problems, and revealing the past as a means toward better understanding of the present. Understanding the social sciences gives a broader knowledge and a more complete picture of the growth of modern civilization.

The social studies

The social studies draw substantially from the resources of the social science disciplines with some refinements for instructional uses. This field has a definite relationship for the individual to the development, structure and functioning of society.

The social studies program as generally considered includes history, geography, civics, modern problems, contemporary affairs, and current events. A greater importance is being placed upon community resources and functional experiences of youth in our society. Each area of the social studies has something to contribute to the total aims of education. For example, one of the chief aims of education is social competence. Its purpose is to develop the minds and character of our students so that they will realize the true meaning of democratic living in modern society. Scientific and technical skill may be valuable, but social competence is of great importance in the development of good, effective citizens. Emphasis is placed upon people and the world in which they live. The art of effective living is an art to which the social studies contribute understanding.

Some definitions of the terminology used in the social studies field may be helpful at this point. The *social sciences* are those areas of knowledge dealing with man and society in the development of civilization; the *social studies* may be considered in terms of knowledge drawn from the social sciences and contemporary life for instructional purposes in aiding youth to understand the growth of modern civilization. The *social studies* field is that area which aids youth through sound knowledge, information, and the functional experiences which are essential to the building of basic values, desirable habits, accepted attitudes, and worthwhile skills basic to effective citizenship.

The term *social education* is used interchangeably by some writers with *social studies*. However, the former term is of more recent usage and covers a broader scope of activities that contribute to the student's social learning. Thus, *social learning* encompasses the social growth of the student gained by his experiences in the school and elsewhere in society. *Social living* permeates the experiences in the school and aids the student in making satisfactory adjustments in his everyday world. *Citizenship* or citizenship education when emphasized in connection with the social studies is concerned with the function of effective living in our modern democratic society. *History* constitutes the flow of events that comprise our past and contemporary civilization. *Geography* is the study and interpretation of the distribution of the physical and cultural features on the surface of the earth.

The social science categories

The following statements provide an excellent overview of the categories of the social sciences. This should furnish a greater insight into the social sciences as they relate to a social studies program.

The more purely social-science disciplines include:

1. *Political Science,* the study of the theory and practice of institutions of control or government of the organized community
2. *Economics,* the study of the theory and practice of the ways in which groups of men extract or grow raw materials, process them and make goods and services, and distribute them to satisfy human wants

3. *History,* the study of the record of man's past in all the basic human activities
4. *Jurisprudence,* the study of the theory and practice of law
5. *Anthropology,* the study of the customs, habits, attitudes, and institutions of men in cultural evolution
6. *Penology,* the study of crime, its punishment, and the management of prisons
7. *Sociology,* the study of the totality of the basic human activities in communities

The four semisocial sciences are:

1. *Ethics,* the study of the standards for judging the rightness or wrongness of human conduct in communities
2. *Education,* the study of the process by which communities enculturate their young for perpetuation and improvement of the culture and the individual
3. *Philosophy,* the study of the principles which underlie all human behavior
4. *Social psychology,* the study of the behavior of the individual and of groups as they react in groups

The *Encyclopedia* [*of the Social Sciences*] still further lists five disciplines which are more accurately classified as natural sciences or humanities but which have significant implications for the social sciences:

1. *Biology,* those aspects that have social content, such as eugenics
2. *Geography,* those aspects that deal with man living in his physical environment
3. *Medicine,* those aspects that have to do with the social causes and management of health or lack of health
4. *Linguistics,* those aspects of comparative language that show the history of development of societies of men
5. *Art,* the study of man's efforts to interfere with nature for his own ends[3]

Social studies development in secondary education

In reviewing the development of secondary education in America, one can note the growth of the social studies in the curriculum. The contributions of conferences and committees, the work of historians and educators, the results of studies and experimentations, and the dynamic changes in our society have all done much to map the course of the social studies field. The term "social studies" was officially adopted in 1916 by the Committee on Social Studies of the Commission on the Reorganiza-

---

[3] P. A. Hanna, "Generalizations and Universal Values: Their Implications for the Social-Studies Program," *Social Studies in the Elementary School,* National Society for the Study of Education, 56th Yearbook, Part II (Chicago: The University of Chicago Press, 1957), chap. II, pp. 30-31. Quoted by permission of the Society.

tion of Secondary Education of the National Education Association. The Committee defined the term:

> The social studies are understood to be those whose subject matter relates directly to the organization and development of human society, and to man as a member of social groups.[4]

The aims of the social studies were explained in some detail. The committee declared that although all studies have a social aim, the social studies have a certain special content of information bearing on questions affecting society. The indirect effect of all studies in school progress is "social efficiency," yet social studies have a more direct bearing on this than others in the curriculum.

Since the Committee approved the term "social studies" and clarified its meaning, numerous changes have been made in the social subjects as they were taught in the secondary school. Programs have been revised and reorganized, and much of the content of the older subjects has been modified. The social studies curriculum was treated in some detail in the *Fourteenth Yearbook* of the Department of Superintendence published in 1936. Emphasis was placed upon the factors conditioning the social studies and the nature and organization of the social studies program. Another milestone in the progress of the study of social studies was the founding of the publication, *Social Education*, in 1937 by the National Council for Social Studies.

Today the National Council for the Social Studies is a department of the National Education Association. It serves as the professional organization of the teachers of social studies. The publications of the National Council for the Social Studies have contributed much to the field of social studies.

The social studies and secondary education

The social studies program is a segment of the secondary school curriculum. It serves as a type of "core" in the content alignment. A major objective of secondary education and the social studies instruction is the development of an effective citizenry.

The secondary school must serve a dual role. It must contribute to the development of basic citizenship beliefs and skills and also promote the individual's unique abilities. Although both functions contribute ultimately to the same goal, a better society, they are not always cultivated by the same process or experience and the school must organize its program to further both ends.[5]

---

[4] *The Social Studies in Secondary Education,* United States Bureau of Education, Bulletin 1916, No. 28 (Washington, D.C.: Government Printing Office, 1928), p. 1.

[5] Association for Supervision and Curriculum Development, *The High School We Need* (Washington, D.C.: The Association, a department of the National Education Association, 1959), p. 5.

There need be no inconsistency, however, between the goal of social education for all students and the development of special social competence among the academically talented. Although the skills of citizenship are essential to all functioning members of a democracy, gifted youth are in a position to exert special influence in society either as leaders or as followers. The social studies should help to prepare them for this role by providing learning opportunities that will tap both their intellectual and their leadership potential.[6]

This important aim of competent citizenship should be considered as a major goal for the entire curriculum areas at the secondary level.

The Purposes of Education in our Democracy

The *Cardinal Principles of Secondary Education* state the general objectives of our educational structure.[7] These objectives included: health, command of fundamental processes, vocational efficiency, good citizenship, worthy home membership, worthy use of leisure time, and ethical character.

The Educational Policies Commission, later, in 1938, listed four main categories relating to the everyday life pattern of an educated citizen. The four groups are identified as:
1. The objectives of self-realization
2. The objectives of human relationship
3. The objectives of economic efficiency
4. The objectives of civic responsibility[8]

Meeting the needs of youth

Education for All American Youth,[9] issued by the Educational Policies Commission in 1944, gave further educational directives which have since been organized in terms of youth needs. The needs as outlined below have a direct influence upon the curriculum.

---

[6] M. M. Klein, *Social Studies for the Academically Talented Student in the Secondary School* (Washington, D.C.: National Education Association, 1960), p. 10. With the permission of the author.

[7] Commission on the Reorganization of Secondary Education, *Cardinal Principles of Secondary Education,* U.S. Office of Education Bulletin No. 35 (Washington, D.C., 1918), pp. 11-15.

[8] Educational Policies Commission, *The Purposes of Education in American Democracy* (Washington, D.C.: National Education Association, 1938), pp. 51-123.

[9] Educational Policies Commission, *Education for All American Youth* (Washington, D.C.: National Education Association, 1944).

A. The imperative needs of youth

All youth have certain educational needs in common. All parents can agree that the school should meet these needs, which become the modern goals of education.

1. All youth need to develop saleable skills and those understandings and attitudes that make the worker an intelligent and productive participant in economic life. To this end, most youth need supervised work experience as well as education in the skills and knowledge of their occupations.
2. All youth need to develop and maintain good health and physical fitness and mental health.
3. All youth need to understand the rights and duties of the citizen of a democratic society, and to be diligent and competent in the performance of their obligations as members of the community and citizens of the state and nation, and to have an understanding of the nations and peoples of the world.
4. All youth need to understand the significance of the family for the individual and society and the conditions conducive to successful family life.
5. All youth need to know how to purchase and use goods and services intelligently, understanding both the values received by the consumer and the economic consequences of their acts.
6. All youth need to understand the methods of science, the influence of science on human life, and the main scientific facts concerning the nature of the world and of man.
7. All youth need opportunities to develop their capacities to appreciate beauty, in literature, art, music, and nature.
8. All youth need to be able to use their leisure time well and to budget it wisely, balancing activities that yield satisfactions to the individual with those that are socially useful.
9. All youth need to develop respect for other persons, to grow in their insight into ethical values and principles, to be able to live and work cooperatively with others, and to grow in the moral and spiritual values of life.
10. All youth need to grow in their ability to think rationally, to express their thoughts clearly, and to read and listen with understanding.[10]

A look ahead

No doubt the secondary school of tomorrow, like the curriculum, will change to meet the needs of students and the demands of society. This will hold true for the social studies program. Secondary education is charged with the development of appropriate skills, attitudes, understandings, values, and knowledge so essential for living in a democratic society. Flexibility will characterize the entire program to provide those

---

[10] *Planning for American Youth* (Washington, D.C.: National Association of Secondary School Principals, 1951), p. 20. Reprinted by permission of the National Association of Secondary School Principals.

varied experiences to meet the capacities, needs and talents of each student in the developmental process. Experimentation and research should aid educators in providing youth with the competencies for meeting the challenges of our dynamic society. Learning will be enriched through the use of various materials, methods, and equipment by the competent teacher in the secondary school.

Long-range planning is essential for introducing new ideas, techniques, practices, and programs. Thought should be given to education beyond the secondary level. This calls for an evaluation by society and each community of the present facilities providing education for our youth. As we plan ahead, an inventory of plant facilities, community resources, laboratories, staff membership, and libraries are essential to providing a more effective education at the secondary level.

Conclusion

The social studies have assumed an important role in the education of students in our modern secondary school curriculum. The social sciences, with their vast resources of organized knowledge and thought about human affairs, have contributed much to our present social studies structure. The structure of the current social studies offerings can furnish much worthwhile knowledge in the realm of secondary education. It follows that the social studies program in the secondary school curriculum shall be focused toward the needs of youth and furthering their maximum growth. A sound knowledge of America's heritage and of the ideals of democracy and good citizenship are a significant phase of this education. The development of working skills, good habits, proper attitudes, and sound knowledge is stressed.

Bibliography

Beard, C. A., *The Nature of the Social Sciences,* Report of the Commission on the Social Studies of the American Historical Association, Part VI. New York: Charles Scribner's Sons, 1934.

Chase, F. S. and H. A. Anderson, *The High School in a New Era.* Chicago: University of Chicago Press, 1959.

Price, R. A., ed., *New Viewpoints in the Social Sciences,* Twenty-eighth Yearbook of the National Council for the Social Studies. Washington, D.C.: National Education Association, 1958.

Stiles, L. J., L. E. McCleary, and R. C. Turnbaugh, *Secondary Education in the United States.* New York: Harcourt, Brace & World, Inc., 1962.

Taylor, L. O., D. R. McMahill, and B. L. Taylor, *The American Secondary School.* New York: Appleton-Century-Crofts, Inc., 1960.

Chapter Three

Developing a Social Studies Program

The social studies program occupies a major segment in the secondary school curriculum. This field deals with the drama of life and all its ramifications. Similar to the social sciences, the social studies is concerned with human relationships, with attention focused upon man and his environmental society. Therefore, the significance of this content area is most apparent in the contemporary educational structure.

The social studies program is an avenue for fostering attitudes, skills, understandings, and competencies that are so essential to effective everyday living. A purposeful program must be comprehensive and current in structure to achieve its desired objectives. Constant evaluation is necessary for the improvement of the social studies program. This requires intensive study utilizing recent research and experimental findings that provide new vision for improving instruction and making needed program changes. New frontiers emerging in society necessitate that sound planning and adequate resources play a significant role in developing programs.

Continuous program improvement

The need of an organized procedure for program improvement presents a challenge to both teachers and curriculum-makers. These educators will continue to draft an instructional plan through the utilization of new ideas and viewpoints. This calls for an intelligent approach to the influence of change upon society and the accompanying new responsibilities for education.

Curriculum improvement comes through answering questions in three fundamental areas. First, what does the nature of our society imply for the development of its future citizens? Second, what should be the role of the school in this development? Third, what does our knowledge of the nature of the learner and of the learning process indicate for the most effective performance of this role?[1]

The dynamic rate of change as contrasted with the past will no doubt weigh heavily in developing a flexible social studies program suited for meeting the new needs of an expanding society. Furthermore, the responsibilities of citizenship demand an alert individual who is constantly sensitive to events occurring in his environment. This requires the individual to read intelligently and to keep alert to new trends. Developing an educational program which encourages these traits can be one of the goals for instructional improvement.

Objectives of the Social Studies

The objectives of the social studies program are usually stated in terms of knowledge, understanding, skills, habits, and attitudes, as illustrated by the following example:[2]

The basic purpose of the social studies program is to provide the motivation, understanding, knowledge, and skills necessary for informed and active citizenship in the United States of America. Ideally, each pupil who completes the program should understand the basic principles upon which his nation functions and should be motivated to support these principles actively as a patriotic, participating citizen. The selection of social science materials for inclusion in the school curriculum is made with this purpose in mind. The social studies program is intended to offer opportunities for each pupil to develop:

1. Knowledge of the physical aspects of the world and how such physical factors as climate and topography affect the lives of people in various regions
2. Knowledge and understanding of how various groups of people have developed social institutions suited to their needs and how various peoples have met the problems encountered in developing their respective cultures and civilizations
3. Knowledge and understanding of the historical backgrounds of the

---

[1] Association for Supervision and Curriculum Development, *Research for Curriculum Improvement* (Washington, D.C.: The Association, a department of the National Education Association, 1957), p. 14.

[2] State Curriculum Commission, *Social Studies Framework for the Public Schools of California* (Sacramento, California: State Department of Education, 1962), p. 7.

government and institutions developed by the people of the United States and of the social, economic, and political problems faced by this country and its people during the past two centuries

4. Understanding of and a loyalty to the principles upon which the government of the United States is based

5. Understanding of the problems faced by the United States in its role as a leading world power, both at home and abroad

6. Certain skills, habits, and attitudes essential to good citizenship in a democratic republic. These include the personal skills needed by each individual to make use of the varied sources of information commonly available in the social science fields. In addition, skills and attitudes are included which are requisite to life in a society in which each citizen is expected to work cooperatively with others and to assume the proper obligations of citizenship.

Characteristics of a social studies program

In stating the general objectives for a social studies program, attention should be given to developing effective living in a free democratic society. Although the entire curriculum shares in providing the essentials of general education for youth, the specific goals of the social studies are significant in building the foundation for perpetuating our way of life.

It should prove profitable to establish guidelines which express those characteristics that lend themselves to the building of a modern social studies program. From this sound approach the objectives can be framed for those courses that comprise the main body of social studies instruction. The purposes or goals agreed upon should furnish direction for an effective social studies program within the scope of the secondary school curriculum. It is effective if:

1. It is based upon the spiritual, moral, intellectual, emotional, and physical development of the individual and upon the needs of the society in which he is a member.

2. It applies the best available information about the learning process and its relation to the development of children and youth, and it challenges the capabilities of each individual.

3. It emphasizes American values and provides individuals with continuous opportunity to experience democratic living.

4. It emphasizes the importance of moral and spiritual ethics and provides for the acquisition of those ethical values cherished in the American culture.

5. It promotes particularly the dignity of man and the ideal in our free society that people of all races and creeds shall have equal opportunities to excel.

6. It gives attention to current and persistent problems and utilizes contributions from the social sciences, as well as knowledge of the past, in formulating suggested solutions for those problems.

7. It stimulates creative thinking and reasoned action based upon an objective study of controversial issues.

8. It provides many opportunities for individuals and groups to use problem-solving techniques and to develop skills for effective thinking.

9. It provides a series of experiences which help individuals understand and appreciate that the rights and privileges of American society entail attendant responsibilities and duties.
10. It balances the contributions of the several social sciences and emphasizes the interrelatedness of social, political, economic, and spiritual forces in the United States and in the world.
11. It emphasizes the fact that democracy is a process through which ideas and institutions are submitted to public discussion and debate and it places value on the contributions of Americans to the development of their traditions.
12. It develops understanding and appreciation of other peoples and ways of life and of the reciprocal contributions to civilization made by individuals and groups of our own and other nations.
13. It illustrates how science and technology have made peoples of the world increasingly interdependent and have, at the same time, created many social, economic, and political problems that are international in scope.
14. It promotes an awareness of basic human needs and the development of skills and attitudes that enable individuals to contribute positively towards improved human relations in family, school, and communities.
15. It gives adequate attention to the development of the varied skills and competencies that are required for effective citizenship in a republic.
16. It utilizes and interrelates other areas of the curriculum in order to further its purposes.
17. It provides for continuous evaluation of the achievements and progress of individuals in terms of behaviors, understandings, competencies, values, and attitudes.
18. It is flexible enough to meet the individual differences of pupils in varying environments, yet maintains a continuity of purpose and content that gives direction to the program at all levels.
19. It develops from kindergarten through the fourteenth grade, reinforcing and expanding content, skills, and attitudes at each level, and it encourages an appropriate variety of emphases and approaches to learning at different educational levels.
20. It provides for revisions to incorporate new research findings and to meet the emerging demands of our changing society and of the individuals therein.
21. It is taught by persons who have the breadth and depth of preparation that will enable them to teach effectively the wide range of topics which comprise the social studies.[3]

Programs in Operation

New York[4]

The program of social studies comprises many types of experiences which lead to growth in knowledge and to understanding of the world about us. An important objective of the social studies program also involves appreciation of

[3] *Report of the State Central Committee On Social Studies to the California State Curriculum Commission* (Sacramento, California: State Department of Education, 1961), pp. 6-7.
[4] *Social Studies 7, 8, 9: A Syllabus for Junior High Schools* (Albany, N.Y.: State Department of Education, 1961), pp. 2-5.

the American heritage, the American way of life and the responsibilities of good citizenship.

Pupils in the early secondary school years are generally eager for participation in school and community citizenship projects. They are interested in the heroes of the past and present, in the local community, the State and the Nation. On these interests, teachers are encouraged to build instructional programs that will help to develop ideals of American citizenship. While courses of study and instructional materials are necessary tools, the skill and enthusiasm of the teacher are vital in creating responsible citizenship.

Social Studies

Grades 7, 8, 9

Seventh Grade—Our Community and State

Begins with local school and community and features New York State history, geography and government.

    I. Geographic Features of New York State
    II. History of New York State to 1865
    III. New York State History since 1865
    IV. Government of New York State
    V. The Empire State Today
    VI. Geography and Growth of Our Local Community
    VII. Our Community Today

Eighth Grade—United States History

Chronological study of the United States History. Emphasis on dramatic events and colorful personalities in the nation's past.

    I. Our Country—The Land and People Today
    II. Exploration and Colonization
    III. The Colonial Period
    IV. Formation of the New Nation
    V. Early Years of the 19th Century
    VI. Division and Reunion
    VII. The End of the Century
    VIII. The United States as a World Power
    IX. The United States as a World Leader
    X. Trends in the United States since World War I
    XI. The American Heritage and Our National Security

Ninth Grade—The Economic World

The American economic system and the human geography of the interdependent world, with stress on the pupil's role as a consumer, as a worker, as a citizen.

    I. Geography of the "Shrinking World"
    II. Western Europe
    III. The U.S.S.R. and Eastern Europe
    IV. North Africa and Southwest Asia
    V. Africa South of the Sahara
    VI. China, Japan, and Korea
    VII. South and Southeast Asia

VIII. Australia, New Zealand, and Oceania
 IX. Latin America
  X. Canada
 XI. The United States
XII. The Interdependent World
XIII. Occupations
XIV. The American Consumer
 XV. The United States Citizen in an Interdependent World

World History[5]

Tenth Grade—The organization is chronological and largely Europe-centered.

  I. Introduction to World History (Two to three weeks)
 II. Medieval Background to Modern Europe
III. Beginnings of Modern Times
 IV. Revolt against Absolutism
  V. The Industrial and Agricultural Revolutions—Twin Revolutions
 VI. Growth of Democracy and Nationalism in Europe
VII. Spread of European Civilization
VIII. Background and Aftermath of the First World War
 IX. Between the Two World Wars
  X. The Second World War
 XI. The Postwar World

American History[6]

Eleventh and Twelfth Grades—Two-year Course

This course is recommended for use in all schools because it affords opportunity for providing an enriched and meaningful study of American history and government.

As a guide in estimating the number of days that can be scheduled for the topics in the two-year course, it is suggested that by the end of the first semester the class should have progressed through topic V, and at the end of the first year through topic IX. In the second year the class may complete topics X-XIV by the end of the first semester, with the second half of the year to spend largely on topics XV-XX, devoted to fundamental issues of present-day American life.

Introduction: The Age of Exploration and Discovery (1450-1600)

  I. The Period of Colonization (1600-1763)
 II. Establishing the Nation (1756-83)
III. The Constitution of the United States
 IV. The Constitution and Government of New York State
  V. Development of the New Nation (1789-1816)

❊　❊　❊

---

[5] *Citizenship Education 10, 11, 12: A Syllabus for Senior High Schools* (Albany, N.Y.: State Department of Education, 1958), p. 53.
　[6] *Ibid.*, p. 15.

VI. Upsurge of Nationalism (1816-40)
VII. Intensification of Sectionalism (1840-60)
VIII. The Civil War and Reconstruction Era (1860-76)
IX. Progress of the Reunited Nation (1876-1900)

* * *

X. The United States, a World Power (1900-20)
XI. The United States between Two World Wars (1920-39)
XII. World War II (1939-45)
XIII. The Postwar Years (1945-the present)
XIV. The American Ideal of Freedom and Self-Government

* * *

XV. Agriculture in the United States
XVI. Conservation of Natural Resources
XVII. Business and Industry in the United States
XVIII. Labor-Management Relations
XIX. Taxation and Finance
XX. International Relations

California[7]

Grade 7—Life in the World Today: The Mediterranean Area and the Middle East; Europe and the European Backgrounds of the United States

Grade 8—The United States and Our Heritage

Grade 9—History of Western European Civilization: Its Social, Economic, and Political Characteristics; Its Present Position in the World

Grade 10—The New Nations and Economically Underdeveloped Countries of Asia, Africa, and Latin America; The Communist Countries and the Challenge of Totalitarianism to the Free World

Grade 11—The United States: Its Development; Its Emergence as a World Power; The Contemporary Scene

Grade 12—Government in the United States and Problems of Democracy

Secondary-school curriculum and the social studies

Planning and developing a secondary-school curriculum is an important process in terms of the trends in our current society. The function of secondary education in the space age will be charged with the responsibility of developing competent individuals for living in a democratic society. Continuous educational research and experiments will produce new ideas which will have a direct bearing upon future instructional programs, procedures, facilities, materials, content, and evaluation

---

[7] State Curriculum Commission, *Social Studies Framework for the Public Schools of California* (Sacramento, California: State Department of Education, 1962), pp. 6-7.

techniques. These findings will suggest new approaches to learning, and in turn will be felt in the social studies program as well as throughout the entire curriculum. A challenge to develop new ways to more effective instruction will be met through a dynamic curriculum.

The problem of curriculum design

The selection and organization of content in the various courses offered at the secondary level is an important item when considering balance in the curriculum.

In the process of selecting and organizing curriculum content three positions are explained as follows:

1. Selecting content in terms of logically developed bodies of subject matter
2. Selecting and organizing curriculum content around the immediate interests and concerns of students
3. Selecting content to include provisions for dealing with subject matter, the learner and society.[8]

In the treatment of the last listed position, it is interesting to note the following:

Points of view in favor of this approach to the selection of curriculum content include: (a) the curriculum is developed to provide not only for the interests and concerns of the learner, but as well for the attitudes, understandings and skills needed for effective living in our changing society; (b) the curriculum is up-to-date; and (c) the curriculum is lifelike, drawing upon all fields of subject matter to deal with personal and social concerns.

In opposition, it may be asked: Is there a guarantee that our cultural heritage will be explored in an adequate manner? Do we have teachers qualified to utilize this approach to curriculum development? Will the community accept a departure from a subject-centered basis for selecting content and organizing the curriculum?

Whatever the answers may be, it is certain that we have gone beyond the idea of concentrating upon knowledge set-out-to-be-learned; that we have gone beyond the idea of depending upon the apparent interests of the learner as a sole criterion for the selection of content; and that we have gone beyond the idea of selecting content only in terms of social issues and social situations. Today, any consideration of content selection must include provisions for dealing with subject matter, the learner and society—all as one and each interacting to effect desired modifications of behavior.[9]

To keep the curriculum up-to-date and dynamic it is necessary that we constantly evaluate it and make changes when deemed essential. This

---

[8] Adapted from Gordon Gardner, Leonard Grindstaff, and Evelyn Wenzel, "Balance and the Selection of Content." Association for Supervision and Curriculum Development, *Balance in the Curriculum,* 1961 Yearbook (Washington, D.C.: National Education Association, 1961), pp. 119-122.

[9] *Ibid.*

demands the inculcation of new knowledge and fresh skills in the instructional program to keep pace with trends and change.

Types of programs

In general the types or patterns of curriculum organization, like the courses, have undergone change at the secondary level. The subject-centered program has long dominated the curriculum, and the transition to other patterns has been gradual. However, this type of pattern may encompass separate subjects on related fields such as history, geography, and civics. The experience-centered program focuses more attention upon the group's needs and interests. The broad content or areas curriculum may include different subject fields. The core curriculum or unified program tends to utilize content from various areas when a particular problem is studied. All have specific features or variations in providing experiences for youth through the use of selected content in the teaching-learning process. In connection with programs we have also various types of core arrangements in block-time classes:

> Some major types of curriculum organization are identified as: (1) the organization by *separate subjects* (2) by *subject fields* or groups *of related subjects* (3) in terms of *broad areas that cut across subject fields* and (4) from the *needs or problems faced by the group,* broadly interpreted. Each of these types of design is planned to achieve certain specific values.[10]

A study of curriculum bulletins will reveal interesting arrangements of units and activities for a particular course in a social studies program. These resource guides provide direction for pupil-teacher planning in the study of various topics and problems.

Fusion, correlation, and integration

Literature relating to organizing the curriculum contains such terminology as *fusion, correlation,* and *integration.* These terms relate to the arrangement of content in the curriculum and should not be thought of as types of curricular organization.

Fusion refers to the organization, for instructional purposes, of content from several subject areas into a unified course. Such an arrangement ignores the conventional barriers or boundaries between existing subjects; for example, in the social studies curriculum, history, geography, and civics are frequently united at the junior high level into one course.

---

[10] F. B. Stratemeyer and others, *Developing a Curriculum for Modern Living* (2nd ed.; New York: Bureau of Publications, Teachers College, Columbia University, 1957), p. 87.

Correlation considers the systematic and continued association or relation of one subject to another, keeping the subject at the high school level. This planned arrangement deals with a common topic or area of interest.

Integration is more difficult to define since more confusion exists in reference to its use, both in the social studies and in the secondary school curriculum. Some writers use integration merely in reference to degree. Integration, as applied to subject matter, is generally accepted as a median between correlation and fusion; that is, as a process that cuts across subject boundaries more freely than is done in correlation in order to place greater stress on inter-relationships.

When organizing the materials, experiences, and themes for the social studies program, one is reminded of a larger unified block of work. The subjects in the social studies field permeate other areas of the secondary curriculum and supply rich sources of content for the changing needs of the program. Let us now examine some types of programs in order to understand the attempts to reorganize courses at the secondary level.

Revising the curriculum and the social studies program

Curriculum revision is essential to meet the needs of youth and the demands on our educational structure. Changes in society call for a program which emphasizes the aspects of functional living. The task of improving the instructional program involves the cooperative efforts of administrators, supervisors, teachers, consultants, subject-matter specialists, students, parents, and community personnel or laymen. Many school systems have established a committee or curriculum council for studying possible improvement in their program. Such a project becomes an exploratory venture for those participating. Each individual should understand the nature of the planning process and the work to be accomplished. Dynamic leadership by the chairman is most essential to provide positive direction in curriculum reform. The secondary school principal and the chairman of the social studies department must be aware of the need for improving the present curriculum, and must display impelling leadership. Plans should be formulated only after research findings are assembled and thoroughly studied.

The builders of instructional programs realize that education must keep pace with changes in society.

Society and contemporary life outside of the school can and do act as guides to curriculum development. Society provides the framework within which children and youth live and learn, and inevitably affects what they bring to school, and the ways in which they put their school experiences to work. The kind of society from which learners come points to the values they must live by as they share with others the task of building their country and their world. A study of society can indicate the understandings and competencies children and youth are likely to need just as it can bring into focus the problems with which they are dealing and with which they will have to cope. An examination of society also suggests the environments out of which come the citizens who mold the world of today and tomorrow. Cultural values, societal needs, and learners' backgrounds serve as guides to curriculum development.[11]

Some guidelines for modern and effective curriculum study are:

1. Examine recent professional literature, current developments in education and especially those findings relating to curriculum trends. Analyze research efforts in the social sciences and experimental results in the social studies field as they relate to the existing curriculum.
2. Study the student body, the community, contemporary society as it relates to the state, country, and world scene in the light of the type of reforms to be undertaken.
3. Establish a philosophy and formulate definite educational goals and objectives.
4. Establish an outline of the basic needs which the particular program will be expected to achieve. This can be done through pre-planning, in view of the proposed changes, after careful study of the materials assembled for this program.
5. Consider the proper choice of materials, instructional tools, learning experiences and the type of instruction expected to be achieved in the new program.
6. Formulate an evaluation structure in order to examine the features of the program and allow for any changes deemed advisable after some initial usage. The final program should be flexible enough to meet future needs.

Studies of the curriculum

Considerable attention has been given to the study of the secondary curriculum as well as to the social studies offerings. Various groups have examined the changes in our society as they relate to the construction of a modern program for the secondary schools, and have reviewed the major disciplines of the social sciences in terms of new materials for the various grade-levels of learning in a social studies program. Such reports furnish pertinent knowledge for enrichment of instructional programs. Curriculum committees preparing courses of study will find these reports an aid when applying a suggested framework for developing course guides. In this manner some direction is provided for change and improvement in a social studies curriculum.

---

[11] *Ibid.*, p. 26.

The significance of textbooks

The textbook is a significant instructional aid in providing a stockpile of materials for developing a social studies curriculum. The application of the textbook by teachers in the learning process has a great bearing on the information presented in a specific course. Furthermore, the textbook carries a considerable influence in developing a course of study. Authors as well as publishers are interested in providing textbooks that are in line with modern curriculum and course trends. No doubt the contents reflect the outcomes of surveys and reports and new horizons in the educational scheme. A textbook should reflect pertinent resource content and new information for enriching instruction. It is by far more inclusive in scope and treatment than an instructional guide.

The modern teacher utilizes the textbook and other supplementary resources with discretion in helping students plan and organize their learning experiences. Many teachers and curriculum builders employ the textbook in developing units and themes. The teacher himself should comprehend the worth of the textbook for instructional purposes and for organizing materials in the process of planning a program.

Guides to improvement of instruction

Instructional or teaching guides serve as a handbook for teachers of social studies. They usually state the function of the particular bulletin, a philosophy of the program, and a list of objectives. The general purpose of a guide is to assist teachers and to provide direction in planning an effective social studies program. Some of the current guides for teaching the social studies at the secondary level present an overview of the program for specific grades. Lists of units are outlined with suggested problems, topics, questions, learning experiences, and activities. Some include suggested techniques, evaluation procedures, and bibliographies. Since instructional guides represent the fruits of study, experimentation, new knowledge, and emerging practices in modern education, they can prove valuable to both teachers and supervisors for program revision or planning a new curriculum.

Selecting a social studies textbook

It is important to use care and good judgment in the selection of textbooks. The responsibility for selection of textbooks may be delegated to an individual teacher or to a committee of teachers. In the latter case, the committee should be composed of from three to seven members. The committee chairman may be a teacher or the head of the department. The effectiveness of the committee's work depends upon the competence of the individual members, the time allowed them to complete their task, and the motivation provided by the leader. Whether textbooks are selected by an individual or by a committee, two major processes may be described.

It is essential in the first place that a check list of criteria be drawn up to judge and evaluate books. This check list may be constructed by the committee to meet the specific needs of the classes in social studies. The list should be sufficiently comprehensive and objective, and designed for particular needs. Each item in judging can be given appropriate weight in the scale of 100 on the check list.

All textbooks available in the field of study may be thoughtfully examined, and sample review copies are frequently procurable from publishers. It is easy to note books that are inappropriate or that do not conform to objective standards. One may ask if the textbook is sufficiently recent, if it includes whatever is essential and pertinent in today's curriculum, and if it conforms to the present needs of the course of study. It is well to inquire if the vocabulary is within the range of students' abilities. Sometimes the mechanical make-up of the book is unacceptable, or the book is too high in price. One has to ask if the textbook is sectional or biased in viewpoint. Then, in rating the textbook on the basis of comparative study, it becomes plain what the score of the book reviewed is. Should there be doubt as to the worth of the two or three top selections, these alternates may be tried out in class over sufficient intervals. Teachers in different classes may use the recommended textbooks, or certain chapters or units, during the term and submit a report to the school administration and textbook committee. Naturally, they will be influenced by the use of illustrations or color, attractive, readable typography, grade of paper, the system of presentation of topics, and many other considerations. One textbook cannot be best in all features, but the one with most elements of value can be found.

Check list for social studies textbooks

Accurate and objective evaluation of textbooks is difficult and time-consuming. Perhaps the most difficult of the four processes is the construction of a valid check list which meets specific needs and upon which the entire committee can agree. Many excellent check lists are available which can be studied and adapted for use by the committee. It can be stated that, up to a point, the greater the time spent upon the thoughtful planning of the check list, the greater will be the time ultimately saved in actual evaluation. A check list is offered here as a simple and practical guide for use in the selection of any kind of social studies textbook.

Title .... Subject ....

Author .... Arrangement ....

Date .... Edition .... Grade Level ....

Publisher .... Price ....

Remarks ....

....

Authority (analysis of author's qualifications)

    1. Position
    2. Training and experience
    3. Relationship to secondary education
    4. Knowledge of the social studies field

General appearance (attractiveness)

    1. Size
    2. Binding
    3. Paper
    4. Type
    5. Margins
    6. Illustrations

Organization and presentation

    1. Purpose
    2. Sequence of material
    3. Length of chapters, units, or sections
    4. Number and nature of subdivisions
    5. Accuracy of material
    6. Literary style and vocabulary
    7. Completeness and utility of table of contents
    8. List of maps and illustrations
    9. Kind, completeness, and utility of index
    10. Appendices and bibliographies

Illustrative material (number, size, clarity, accuracy)

    1. Illustrations
    2. Maps
    3. Charts
    4. Graphs
    5. Cartoons

Instructional aids (at the end of each chapter or unit)

    1. Lists of questions
    2. Vocabulary list
    3. Projects and activities
    4. Problems for research
    5. Topics for reports and debates
    6. Identification lists
    7. Pupil reading lists

Suggestions for using the check list

The heading includes such items as "arrangement," "date," "edition," and "grade level," in addition to the items of identification, to facilitate the preliminary elimination. Thus, it can be seen at a glance which textbooks conform to the course of study and the grade level as well as which are sufficiently recent for the purpose. It is suggested that three symbols or degrees of rank be assigned for use with this check list and that the list be mimeographed with the same number of suitably labeled columns placed at the right. For example, the headings may be "excellent," "satisfactory," and "unsatisfactory," or any symbols arbitrarily chosen to indicate such rank. The number of columns can be increased to include four or five possible ratings. However, the use of only three is specifically recommended since this number will tend to encourage more thoughtful and careful ratings, will eliminate more readily, and will facilitate comparison of results. The method of scoring by placing check marks in the proper columns instead of by the writing in of scores or symbols will also facilitate comparison and tabulation of results.

After the check list has been agreed upon, each member of the committee should spend sufficient time in careful study to familiarize himself with the various items. It will be of great assistance to the inexperienced teacher if he can choose two or three satisfactory textbooks already in use in his classes for actual rating on the check list. He will thus gain in experience, judgment, and confidence, and his contribution to the committee will be of greater value.

All members of the committee should endeavor to avoid snap judgments on any item. Much information can be quickly and easily obtained if the teacher knows where and how to look for it. One source of information that is too frequently overlooked is the author's preface or introduction, in which he usually states the purpose of the book, the use for which it is intended, the method of arrangement chosen, the reasons for the choice, and a description of the outstanding features of the book.

Trends in social studies instruction

Considerable thought and study are being given to the social studies program at the secondary level. This may entail a revision of the existing program with the view of including new courses and the reorganization of the present offerings. Education for the space-age and that of automation must be geared to change. Automation is already having an important impact upon society. The astounding scientific achievement of today and tomorrow will have a tremendous influence upon civilization.

A greater use of audio-visual materials is evident; the library with its various resources is becoming the real heart of the curriculum; newer methods and procedures including team teaching is being practiced and is in the experimental process in our schools; increased attention is being given to the gifted and academically talented student; advanced placement programs are increasing; such content areas as economics, sociology, and geography are receiving greater attention; a considerable use is being made of community resources in the instructional program; evaluation techniques and the guiding of today's youth toward effective citizenship is of major importance. These are but a few of the activities in secondary education.

Conclusion

The social studies program is a major part of the total secondary school curriculum. It does not stand still but moves forward to meet new challenges presented by a dynamic society in today's world. Much of the content of the social studies is based on student-experiences in the process of "growing up" or in the sphere of life itself. The patterns of organization will vary from system to system and among the states. Change in many instances is a slow process; however, trends indicate a shift from the traditional subject-dominated organization to a modern approach for meeting the needs of youth. Content boundaries have been somewhat removed, and the recognized areas are being integrated to a good advantage.

Curriculum improvement trends indicate some reorganization toward a core, unified, and fused type of course. More attention is given to the individual learner, his needs, interests, and problems encountered in the growth process. The organization of materials into well-planned units that will provide a wealth of experience is important. It is the responsibility of each school system to evaluate and develop a curriculum suited to meet the needs of youth in the particular community. More attention should be given to the establishment of a continuous curriculum improvement program with all individuals sharing in the project.

Bibliography

Aldrich, J. C., ed., *Social Studies for the Junior High School: Programs for Grades Seven, Eight, and Nine,* Curriculum Series No. VI, rev. ed., Washington, D.C.: National Education Association, 1957.

Association for Supervision and Curriculum Development, *Balance in the Curriculum,* 1961 Yearbook. Washington, D.C.: National Education Association, 1961.

————, *New Insights and the Curriculum,* 1963 Yearbook. Washington, D.C.: National Education Association, 1963.

Johns, E., ed., *Social Studies in the Senior High School: Programs for Grades Ten, Eleven, and Twelve,* Curriculum Series No. VI. Washington, D.C.: National Education Association, 1953.

Price, R. A., ed., *New Viewpoints in the Social Sciences,* Twenty-eighth Yearbook of the National Council for the Social Studies. Washington, D.C.: National Education Association, 1958.

Pritzkan, P. T., *Dynamics of Curriculum Improvement.* Englewood Cliffs, N.J.: Prentice-Hall, Inc., 1959.

Wiles, K., *The Changing Curriculum of the American High School.* Englewood Cliffs, N.J.: Prentice-Hall, Inc., 1963.

Chapter Four

Block-time Classes
and the Core Program

There are various types of core arrangements and block-time classes in operation at the junior and senior high school levels. The arrangements and nomenclature differ with the schools, and frequently the terms seem to overlap or to be used interchangeably. The author or school system must define the usage of the terms, especially the terminology applied to core. The following distinctions are stated for classification.

Block-time Classes. All classes which meet for a block of time of two or more class periods and combine or replace two or more subjects that are required of all pupils and would ordinarily be taught separately.

Core Classes. Classes having the block-time organizational pattern and which also unify or fuse their content around units or problems which may be either subject-centered or experience-centered.[1]

Terminology and combinations in block-time classes

Some of the terms or names applied by school systems to block-time classes are the following: core, unified studies, block class, self-contained classroom, basic education, general education, common learnings, and social living.

[1] G. S. Wright, *Block-Time Classes and the Core Program,* Office of Education Bulletin 1958, No. 6 (Washington, D.C.: Department of Health, Education, and Welfare, 1958), p. ix.

In an examination of the content combinations utilized in the block-time classes, we find such subject matter areas as: English and social studies; English, social studies, and science; social studies and mathematics; social studies and science; and science and mathematics.

It is interesting to note that some school systems which have the block-time arrangement never progress to initiating a core program. Usually the block-time classes utilize the same hourly schedule as do the single subject classes which they replace.

Some features of block-of-time

Our professional literature contains many interesting accounts pertinent to block-of-time classes. These studies explain the characteristics, features, problems, and values relative to the block-of-time plan. It is not the purpose of this discussion to delve into these features in extensive detail, but some of the more salient features will be touched upon.

The Teacher—It is interesting to note some of the desirable or essential teacher requirements. Naturally teaching experience is important as is a thorough knowledge of the content areas, especially the language arts and social studies since this combination seems to be prevalent. An understanding of and a deep interest in adolescents is essential, and the ability to assume guidance responsibilities is a major aspect of the plan. The personality of the teacher is of paramount importance and should include such characteristics as sympathy, enthusiasm, and friendliness. The teacher should have considerable background experience as well as an understanding of the skill of effective planning and organizing of instructional materials, activities, and procedures. He must possess a degree of flexibility and be capable of doing research and carrying out some experimentation in the teaching-learning process.

Some problems—The major problems or deterrents to such a plan are: lack of trained instructional staff for the operation of the plan, insufficient learning materials including audio-visual aids, lack of suitable equipment, facilities, and space to operate effectively, and the difficulty of including such a plan in the existing regular program.

Some advantages—The chief advantages claimed by the block-of-time in the learning experiences are:

1. A pupil can know well one teacher and a teacher easily can learn more about a given pupil.
2. The learning situation profits from increased laboratory work, more effective field trips, better use of audio-visual materials, and enhanced opportunities to practice desired skills and to develop appropriate attitudes and appreciations.
3. Learners are more inclined to acquire more knowledge of self as well as skills in group processes and human relations.

4. Improvement in thinking skills is more likely to occur as the concept of pupil-teacher planning is explored and implemented.
5. Fruitful guidance opportunities multiply and pupils more readily work toward a philosophy of life.
6. Concepts of democratic living come alive as they broaden and become more deeply embedded in the minds of pupils.
7. Integration of learning experiences is enhanced as subject barriers fade away and language arts and reading, for example, in part become important to *all* teachers.[2]

The block-of-time classes usually are found in the seventh, eighth, and ninth grades in the junior high school, and vary in structure with each school. The following recommendation by James Bryant Conant is significant in the light of block-of-time teaching.

To my mind, there should be a block of time set aside, at least in grade 7, in which one teacher has the same pupils for two or more periods, generally in English and social studies. Otherwise, grades 7, 8, and 9 should be departmentalized; that is to say, pupils should have specialist teachers in each of the subject-matter fields.

Block-time teaching is a controversial subject among educators. Generally speaking, however, even the opponents admit it may have advantages if teachers equally qualified in two subjects can be found. Thoroughly *competent* and *enthusiastic* teachers are essential for its successful operation. I do not recommend it above grade 8 except in very special circumstances.

My reason for advocating block-time teaching is simply to enable one teacher to know his pupils well because of the fact that he meets fewer of them for a longer period of time. As a consequence, he is in a position to counsel pupils who have been accustomed to the personal and solicitous attention of an elementary school teacher. In the absence of block-time, special efforts to provide this attention should be made through other means, notably through the homeroom teacher and guidance personnel. In other words, there should be a smooth transition for the pupil from the self-contained classroom with one teacher in the elementary school to the departmentalized situation with many teachers in the secondary school.

The block-time teaching I am discussing need not break down subject-matter lines. Occasionally, one finds a school in which offers to integrate or fuse subjects are successfully made. These "core" programs are oriented to the problems of young adolescents and involve considerable teacher-pupil planning. Many schools that had these programs within a block of time have now given them up and teach two separate subjects instead. Though I am not opposed to experimentation with the core approach, I must make it plain that my advocacy of block-time teaching does not presuppose an endorsement of core teaching. Sometimes the meaning of these terms is not clear.[3]

With these introductory remarks let us turn directly to the core program and the features that comprise it.

---

[2] M. D. Baughman, *Block-of-Time Scheduling Practices in Junior High Schools*, The Junior High School Principals' Association and the Junior High School Association of Illinois (Urbana, Ill.: University of Illinois Press, 1960), p. 35.

[3] J. B. Conant, *Recommendations for Education in the Junior High School Years* (Princeton, N.J.: Educational Testing Service, 1960), pp. 22-23.

Assumptions underlying the core curriculum

It would be well to review some of the assumptions which have led to the development of core programs and, further, which distinguish core classes from traditional secondary school classes:

Learning takes place more effectively when the learner shares in deciding what will happen to him in school.

The present interests and concerns of pupils are important and worthy of attention in curricular planning.

Classroom teachers can and should take responsibility for group guidance. This guidance should include helping each student better to understand his strengths, weaknesses, interests and purposes—and how these relate to each other.

The responsibility of the school extends beyond the mastery of subject matter and academic skills. All students should be assisted in developing attitudes and interpersonal skills which are consistent with the democratic ideal and which will lead to improvement of our democratic society.

Experiences and learning characteristics of each student are unique. Therefore, all classroom practices should be designed to challenge each pupil to work up to his optimum capacity. Standards, evaluation procedures, and day-to-day operation of classes must give adequate recognition to individual differences.

Most adolescent youngsters are capable of assuming much more responsibility in self-direction and self-discipline than they are usually given or allowed in secondary schools.

The subject matter of the school should center on real-life problems both because learning takes place more effectively in this fashion and also because schools have not given adequate attention in the past to their role as agents of social improvement.[4]

Examples of core program

The following examples of the core program provide a foundation for learning about this type of curriculum arrangement. It should be noted that the theme and units are designed to meet a specific need or purpose of the school system. The planning committee for a core program guide should give considerable thought to the existing curriculum and the needs of the student body of the particular school system. This is particularly true of students at the junior high school level.

The interests of junior high school pupils are many and transitory. His attention span is regulated by the intensity of his interests. He is curious. He wants to know about things and why they are as they are. This is a time of

---

[4] Delmo Della-Dora, "The Self-contained Unit in Action in the Junior High School," Association for Supervision and Curriculum Development, *The Self-Contained Classroom* (Washington, D.C.: National Education Association, 1960), pp. 78-79.

exploration and self-discovery—a time that provides a stimulating challenge to his teachers.

In planning instruction for junior high school class, educators must be highly sensitive to the physiological, social, and emotional changes of pupils. Learning activities must be geared to these changes and must be designed to help pupils accomplish their developmental tasks. Perhaps there is no place in the school program where greater variety of learning activities is more essential, or more possible, than in the junior high school.[5]

In the core program the teacher must focus considerable attention upon the learners in the teaching-learning process.

The educator today must have firm grasp of the subject matter he is to teach and knowledge about the forces operating in today's world. He must also understand the learners in his class at their particular stages of development and in relation to the culture in which they live. Recent research has increased greatly our knowledge about human growth and development and has given us much scientific information about human variability. Research on human learning and human behavior is giving us new insight into the way children learn and into the effect of the self concept upon learning. The self, according to perceptual psychology, determines what we see, what we hear, and what we learn.[6]

Pennsbury Core Program[7]

The core program embodies a daily three-period block-of-time, broadfields combination of English, social studies, and core activities; and the scheduling of twelve additional periods weekly for the study of those subjects termed resource areas; mathematics, science, art, music, home economics, and industrial arts. In all instruction there is much emphasis upon pupil-teacher planning, flexibility of subject boundary lines, the problem-solving approach to learning, and the guidance of every individual so that he may become a worthwhile member of society in every way.

The central theme of this program, which covers two years of work, is Community Living. During these two years the pupils first study their own community and their country, and then set up and organize a hypothetical model community. Problem areas, allocated to the different grades, are as follows:

Grade 7   Getting Acquainted
          Taking a Look at Life in Pennsbury
          Surveying Life in These United States

Grade 8   Locating a Model Community
          Selecting a Suitable Government for our Community
          Zoning the Model Community

[5] *The Pennsbury Core Program—A Tentative Guide in Grades Seven and Eight* (Fallsington, Pennsylvania: The Pennsbury Schools, 1959), p. 45.

[6] Lavone Hanna, "Meeting the Challenge," Association for Supervision and Curriculum Development, *What Are the Sources of the Curriculum? A Symposium* (Washington, D.C.: National Education Association, 1962), p. 55.

[7] *The Pennsbury Core Program—A Tentative Guide in Grades Seven and Eight* (Fallsington, Pennsylvania: The Pennsbury Schools, 1959), pp. iii-iiia.

Choosing a Vocation and an Avocation
Building and Furnishing a Model Home
Examination of Problems Peculiar to Community Life

Objectives of the Pennsbury Core Program

I. Teacher Objectives
   1. To place more emphasis on the learner than on the subject
   2. To encourage planning by pupils and teacher around a center of interest
   3. To utilize all types of experiences as avenues of learning
   4. To relax classroom tensions by bringing all children into the co-operative effort
   5. To broaden the interests and expand the horizons of all pupils

II. Pupil Objectives
   1. To learn to share individual interests and experiences with others
   2. To learn to share cooperatively in group understandings
   3. To have an opportunity to feel a sense of accomplishment
   4. To feel adequate in those skills which are needed on the level of the experience and maturity of the individual
   5. To learn to identify group problems, as well as personal problems, and intelligently seek their solution
   6. To develop techniques of independent research
   7. To develop critical thinking and problem-solving techniques by the functional use of reading, writing, speaking and listening skills
   8. To develop intellectual curiosity
   9. To learn to stick to the task in hand until a degree of accomplishment has been reached
   10. To render service to the school and community of which the student is a member

Probably the most outstanding feature of the core program at Pennsbury is its faculty organization. Grade level meetings of all teachers working with particular groups of students are scheduled during each day so that maximum planning, integration, communication, and guidance can take place. Thus, the mathematics, science, art, music, home economics, and industrial arts teachers join with the core teachers in planning their teaching around the skills required to solve the problems under consideration.

The key words which describe core classes are *teacher-pupil planning, group and individual guidance, content which cuts across traditional subject matter lines and relates to present needs of students,* and *an extended period of time.* At least one more key phrase is needed to characterize the activities in core classes and that is *continuous evaluation.*[8]

---

[8] Delmo Della-Dora, "The Self-contained Unit in Action in the Junior High School," Association for Supervision and Curriculum, *The Self-Contained Classroom* (Washington, D.C.: National Education Association, 1960), p. 70.

Ohio State University School Core Program

Another interesting development of the core program is that of the University School. It was built around problem areas related to the concerns of young people. These specific features for grades seven through nine included:

A. Personal Living (problems related to growing up)
B. Personal-Social Living (problems related to living with others)
C. Social-Civic-Economic Living (problems of living in and understanding society.[9]

The staff, after considerable study of the school's philsosphy, child growth and development, and the social concerns impinging on the individual in our society, listed the problem areas or recommended units as follows:

1. Problems of School Living
2. Problems of Healthful Living
3. Problems of Communication
4. Problems of Government
5. Problems of Producer-Consumer Economics
6. Problems of Conservation of Resources
7. Problems of Values and Beliefs
8. Problems of Human Behavior (Understanding Self and Others)
9. Problems of Conflicting Ideologies
10. Problems of Education
11. Problems of Occupations (Selection and Preparation for)
12. Problems of a Developing Cultural Heritage
13. Problems of Social Relationships in a Rapidly Changing Society
14. Problems of Living in the Atomic Age[10]

Social studies in a core program

The social studies field and the knowledge derived from the social science disciplines play a significant role in most types of the core arrangement as well as in block-time classes. One of the principal objectives of these techniques is to teach various subjects in relation to other subjects—in other words, no single subject is taught in isolation.

A study of the community, local history, geography, government, and the natural resources are all phases of society in which people live and work. When a group of secondary school students studies the problems

---

[9] Faculty of the University School, *A Description of Curricular Experiences—the Upper School* (Columbus, Ohio: The Ohio State University School, 1952), p. 12.
[10] Faculty of the University School, The Ohio State University, *A Description of Curricular Experiences, Grades 7-12* (Columbus, Ohio: The Ohio State University School, 1956), pp. 17-18.

and needs of a community, learning takes place both in the classroom and out in the community; the students are learning about living in their own area, and as a result acquire valuable training in citizenship. Like the social studies, the core course utilizes the materials of the library, audio-visual materials, and the human and natural resources of the community. The process of educating youth for effective democratic daily living in our contemporary society presents a challenge for the builders of our secondary curriculum. The nature and purpose of a modern program carries the responsibility of developing effective types of skill, knowledge, appreciations and understandings for the students. The general educational structure for meeting common needs, interests, and problems of the immediate society for the learners through functional experiences is most essential for responsible citizenship. Such a program draws its resources from various subject matter areas.

The curriculum and the core program

A continuous curriculum reorganization and evaluation of the existing programs and courses has received considerable attention. In fact, new objectives and improved programs are the order of the times. Dynamic changes in society, a vast new supply of knowledge, and new approaches to the learning process are a part of the emerging pattern.

The curriculum, therefore, to be functional, it is thought, must center around the problems of personal and social needs necessary to provide those behavioral competencies essential to successful democratic living. Problem solving becomes the basic media of individual and group procedures involved in class-school activities. Obviously, such an approach to curriculum planning will make areas of life activities the bases of curriculum organizational patterns in preference to a curriculum organization based upon traditional school subjects. It also involves greater integrating within the curriculum, and the consequent organization of class periods into larger units of time-blocks of 2-3 hours. The recognition of guidance, broadly understood, as an integral function of education made necessary by this new conception of learning and the curriculum requires a new concept of teaching; suggesting the need for greater continuity of contact between teacher and pupil, teacher-pupil cooperative planning as basic to genuine problem solving procedures and to modern theories of motivation in learning, greater attention to individual difficulties both in learning abilities and in the environment background experiences the pupils bring to a given learning situation.

At the present time there has been only one major attempt to formulate an organization of a consistent curriculum pattern based upon the theory of experience learning, and which endeavors to include the features of modern education and curriculum emphasis outlined above as natural corollaries of that learning theory. This pattern of curriculum organization is generally known as the Core Curriculum. One division of this curriculum organization, called the Core Program, is devoted to the development of the common competencies—

sometimes called Common Learnings needed by all citizens. The other division is devoted to the development of the special competencies of pupils, sometimes called Special Interests, which are based upon the recognition of individual differences in interests and abilities.[11]

Types of core programs

In order to comprehend the meaning of a core program, we should turn our study to the following definition:

The core program, then refers to the total organizational activities of the part of the school curriculum devoted to the determination of the personal and social competencies needed by all, and the procedures, materials, and facilities by which the school assures the adequacy of the learning experiences essential to the development of the competencies.[12]

Alberty gives an excellent analysis of programs designed to meet the needs of adolescents. He lists the following:

Type-One Core: Program design based upon separate subjects, each taught independently

Type-Two Core: Program design based upon informal correlation of subjects

Type-Three Core: Program design based upon systematic correlation

Type-Four Core: Program design based upon fusion or unification of fields of knowledge

Type-Five Core: Program design based upon a preplanned structure determined by adolescent needs

Type-Six Core: Program design based exclusively upon teacher-student planning[13]

These programs indicate the trends of thought in designing a curriculum that will attempt to meet the needs of youth.

Advantages of the core

It is most important to understand the general purpose and nature of the core. In this manner teachers are in a better position to plan and evaluate the teaching-learning process. Some of the chief advantages are:

1. The core is in harmony with the best we know about the nature of learning.

---

[11] N. L. Bossing, "The Core Idea in the Junior High School," *The High School Journal*, ILIII, No. 4 (January 1960), 127-128.

[12] R. C. Faunce and N. L. Bossing, *Developing the Core Curriculum* (2nd ed.; Englewood Cliffs, N.J.: Prentice-Hall, Inc., 1958), p. 57.

[13] H. Alberty, "Designing Programs to Meet the Common Needs of Youth," *Adapting the Secondary-School Program to the Needs of Youth*, National Society for the Study of Education, 52nd Yearbook, Part I (Chicago: The University of Chicago Press, 1953), chap. VII, pp. 120-140. Quoted by permission of the Society.

2. The core centers around vital problems of personal and social concern to the learner.
3. The core with its problem-centered emphasis through experience learning, provides a superior opportunity for pupils to learn such essential social skills as cooperative planning and working together.
4. The core makes possible greater attention to the individual differences of children.
5. The use of the multiple period now commonly associated with the core organization combined with the emphasis upon personal-social problems as basic in the core, provides an excellent opportunity for the teacher to exercise the guidance function now accepted as the central activity of learning.
6. The life-like activities and purposeful atmosphere of the core curriculum are most conducive to the serious motivation of pupils, and thus to a lessened concern of the school with disciplinary problems.
7. The core curriculum provides for a natural integration of school, home, and community living.
8. The core concept makes the so-called extracurricular activities a natural, integral part of the curriculum.
9. In the core concept teachers take on a new status.
10. The core curriculum provides the theoretical bases favorable to the establishment of rapport and cooperative efforts within the school staff.[14]

Guidance by the core teacher

The core teacher has an excellent opportunity to provide both individual and group guidance in the learning process. Furthermore, each teacher can develop his own particular techniques in the role of providing helpful assistance to students.

The core program which by its very nature is concerned largely with the personal-social development of boys and girls carries much of the guidance function of the school. Both directly and indirectly the core program seeks to help adolescents with their developmental tasks and their adjustments to the complex society in which we live. Engaging the attention of core classes are such units as healthful living, self-understanding, family relationships, getting along with others, and choosing a vocation. Also, the problem-solving method of core, with its opportunities for teacher-pupil planning, making choices, and working in small groups, gives daily or frequent experience in democratic living, choosing values, gaining self-confidence, learning correct behavior in social situations, respecting the contributions of others, and critical thinking. Group guidance is thus inherent in the core program.

Individual guidance likewise has its place in the core class. In the longer block of time, the core teacher becomes better acquainted with the child than can single-subject teachers; he observes him in both social and work situations. The teacher checks his observations against the individual's cumulative record and he confers with parents. He finds time during the block class while groups

---

[14] R. C. Faunce and N. L. Bossing, *Developing the Core Curriculum* (2nd ed.; Englewood Cliffs, N.J.: Prentice-Hall, Inc., 1958), pp. 61-64.

are at work—or in special periods designated for guidance if the school is one which provides such periods—to talk with him individually about his interests and concerns. He makes himself approachable. Of course, the teacher's effectiveness in guidance depends very largely upon the extent to which he is able to use what he has learned about the child in conjunction with his knowledge both of child growth and development and of society to help the child develop to his fullest potential.[15]

The teacher a co-worker

The core teacher as a planner is concerned with the learners, for the creative process of learning evolves around the learner and his environment. In the process of selecting problems for investigation the teacher must look ahead to the organizational procedure. It must also be remembered that functional learning is a product of the student's active participation in the teaching-learning situation. The teacher serves as a builder, director, and evaluator in both cooperative planning and in the active meaningful learning process. He aids the group in interpreting new experiences as they relate to the familiar learning in studying a particular topic or problem. This calls for effective communication in the avenues of learning if the established goals are to be achieved and the learners' needs are to be met effectively. Considerable attention is given to the learning experiences that students may in some way relate to their own special interests.

The teacher utilizing problem-solving techniques can direct many experiences toward creative activities for the learners. Such opportunities provide the learner with an incentive to explore and develop some new interests. In this manner learning becomes a series of forward moving experiences. These students are being challenged each day by the world in which they live and grow.

The library and resource materials

The core programs utilize a wide variety of library materials. The objectives and methods applicable for core courses necessitate the variety of instructional resources. The school library in reality becomes a laboratory for learning where exploration and research activities furnish students with essential information and knowledge. The librarian becomes a key person serving as a consultant for both teachers and learners.

Many of the basic skills and appreciations related to the core are broadened through the functional learning experiences provided in the

---

[15] G. S. Wright, *Block-Time Classes and the Core Program*, Office of Education, Bulletin No. 6 (Washington, D.C.: Department of Health, Education, and Welfare, 1958), pp. 49-50.

library. The learner has an opportunity to explore ideas and interests, and to develop worthwhile appreciations by consulting several sources in his work.

The teacher, librarian, and learners cooperate in an efficient manner through understanding the general purposes of the library as it serves the core program. The librarian can furnish optimum service when the teachers make known their plans for teaching various units or topics. Some advanced cooperative planning can clarify purposes to be achieved and will facilitate a more effective application of needed materials. A librarian can aid the core teacher in innumerable ways in improving a program.

The core teacher and the librarian form an effective team for fostering the student's information-gathering skills and for encouraging him to solve his problems through research. Reading for reference as well as for pleasure is also stressed.

Unit for study

The organization of effective units for instructional purposes is the goal of every teacher. The trend seems to be toward a more complete study of some particular problem or topic. The broader units provide for the greater use and wider variety of materials and facilities. Learning activities and functional experiences are developed in the instructional scheme. Teachers usually consider the practical values and aspects when selecting materials to be employed in the unit. Selected units can be used with satisfactory results throughout the course at the secondary level.

Planning the units or problems

When choosing problems for study in the core program, the teacher will profit greatly from a preliminary exploration of the various facets of a tentative problem for study. When the teacher and students finally select a problem, the teacher who has made previous research can move forward readily with the work. The teacher and students through co-operative planning must feel the value or importance of the problem to be investigated. Will the problem present sufficient challenge so that the group can generate the essential interest to move ahead in meeting a possible solution? Does it meet the immediate needs, and is it geared to the ability of the students? In the process of preplanning the teacher no doubt would examine the available resources for exploring the particular type of problem. If so, the students can discuss the possible avenues for research, desirable activities, and worthwhile experiences that might be employed in the learning process.

Activities and experiences

Some of the procedures, techniques, and activities utilized in the conventional programs are applicable in the core program. It is most important that each student participate in some aspect of the study. Will the theme or topic arouse curiosity, stimulate thought, stir the imagination, foster thinking, and develop the creative skill of the group? Both individual and group activity should be stressed in order to provide breadth and opportunity for the ideas and interests expressed by the students. The planning sessions and discussions can help to clarify the established purposes and illuminate the main strands for possible investigation and exploration into the new frontiers of knowledge. In the learning process, understandings will be acquired and the student's personality developed. Acquiring various types of skills should provide the student with the essential tools to use in meeting the problems of everyday living and for successful group participation. Thus learning to live and work cooperatively and effectively with a group can bring satisfaction to the student.

Some of the various activities and learning experiences may include: discussions, debates, dramatizations, interviews, field trips; drawing graphs, charts, and maps; writing letters, stories, summaries, and research findings; building tack-board displays and murals; collecting materials for scrapbooks; viewing films, and listening to resource speakers. Furthermore, the usual culminating activities pertaining to a unit or problem are a part of the total experience.

The various committees have an opportunity to share their research findings with the group. They may employ some type of audio-visual materials to amplify the problem. These selected reports furnish the students with a chance to test their skills, ideas, and assumptions. Also the other members of the group have the opportunity to ask questions for clarification or to gain further information about the topic. Such procedures in presenting information lends itself to a free exchange of experiences and opens the way to further study and investigation.

The learners and the core

It is most important that the core teacher provide for the slow as well as the more capable learners. This aspect of instruction is a vital factor in a core program.

Basic principles for teaching slow and rapid learners have been defined through scientific educational research. The paragraphs which follow outline some of the important principles which must guide the education of these children.

Instruction must be differentiated so that both the slow and the rapid learners have the fullest opportunities for the maximum development of their abilities.

The slow learner needs to become self-reliant and to feel himself an important, accepted member of the group. The rapid learner needs to learn to take the initiative, to adjust to and feel secure in different situations, and to realize and accept his responsibility for the welfare and progress of the total group.

Activities for the slow learner must be varied and adequately brief in scope and area.

Activities for the rapid learner must be varied, intensive in scope and duration, and stress creativity.

The slow learner must have sequential individuated instruction, purposeful drill, and continuous practice in reading—for information and for enjoyment.

The rapid learner's innate ability and intellectual curiosity must be utilized in leading him to read widely. He must be given training so that he can develop and employ skills in using a variety of reading sources and techniques.

The work of the core class affords a functional setting for learning and practicing reading. Pupils read for orientation to their problems and for information to help solve their problems; pupils read novels, plays, short stories, poems, and essays for enjoyment and for understanding. They read for details, for instructions, for ideas, and for appreciation. Core activities arouse the children's interest in words and in communicating ideas, as they read and write about their own experiences. The core teacher works to develop in pupils increased ability in using the skills of reading in such things as drawing inferences and making generalizations.[16]

The learners profit from their planning, sharing, evaluating, and working as members of small groups and committees. In the informal and formal discussions pertinent to a topic, the chairman assumes an important role. The leader of any group can be helpful by keeping the individual members aware of the task at hand. He can see that the group is working toward the solution of a particular problem or the study of a selected issue. He can see that each individual has an opportunity to express his views and thereby contribute to the thinking of the group. Cooperation and a spirit of achievement are essential aspects for any group activity.

Evaluation in the core program

Evaluation programs of the core curriculum are needed to provide evidence that the objectives are realized. Many of these outcomes concern intangibles difficult to evaluate. The core teacher has many techniques for measuring the growth of the individual and the group.

---

[16] *Developing A Core Program in the Junior High School Grades*, Curriculum Bulletin No. 12 (New York: Board of Education, 1957-58 Series), pp. 101-103.

Obviously evaluation involves more than tests and examinations to measure subject-matter achievement. Complete understanding involves determining that quantitative aspect, together with the qualitative aspect of personality and growth change. The following evaluative criteria are all available for use or are being used currently in William Penn:

I. Subject-matter Measurement or Quantitative Evaluation
   A. Standardized tests are administered either by the guidance department, with the aid of teachers, or by the teachers themselves.
   B. Teacher-constructed Tests
      Test construction requires careful planning and a great deal of prior thought.

II. Understanding Individual Differences and Behavior or Qualitative Evaluation
   A. Controlled observation is applicable when pupils are working on a project in a classroom situation.
   B. Informal observation is applicable to a wide variety of classroom situations.
   C. Anecdotal records are cumulative notes kept on each pupil's behavior and expression.
   D. Sociograms are useful in revealing the social structure of a class and the relations of the pupils with each other.
   E. Conferences and interviews are especially useful as a vis-à-vis means of evaluation.
   F. Self and peer evaluation will also help the teacher to evaluate and to understand pupil growth and development.
   G. Informal contact affords the teacher the opportunity to observe pupils in everyday social situations in the corridors, the library, the dining room, and the auditorium.

III. Total Personality Evaluation
   Without a doubt, various standardized and teacher-constructed tests lend themselves to an evaluation of the behaviorial aspects of a pupil's total personality as well as to the measure of subject matter.
   A. Individual project evaluation includes the observation of the pupil performing the tasks involved in completing the project and the final evaluation of the finished product.
   B. Group project evaluation covers the same topics and areas as individual projects but provides the added dimension of cooperation.
   C. Discussions and oral reports also fit into the broad area of evaluating the total personality.
   D. Cumulative records are an important means of evaluating individual differences.[17]

Some core program findings

The various studies and research information provides some interesting insights into the core arrangement.

[17] *The Pennsbury Core Program—A Tentative Guide in Grades Seven and Eight* (Fallsington, Pennsylvania: The Pennsbury Schools, 1959), pp. 59-63.

a. The number of core programs is increasing.
b. The pupils enrolled in core programs either showed more than the expected gain or made scores as high as, or higher than, those made by pupils enrolled in conventional programs in the fields of reading, language arts, social studies, arithmetic, and work-study skills.
c. The pupils enrolled in core curriculums made less than the usual gain or made scores lower than pupils in conventional curriculums in language arts, social studies, and work-study skills.
d. Pupils enrolled in core programs were likely to be better adjusted personally and socially than pupils enrolled in conventional programs.
e. There are no research data available to indicate the degree to which pupils in core programs develop social skills, although informal observations suggest that the core is more effective than the conventional in this respect.
f. On the basis of pencil and paper tests, pupils enrolled in core programs appeared to take a more democratic position toward social goals and policies than did pupils in conventional programs.
g. There was no evidence that pupils enrolled in core programs were more interested in social problems and conditions, or were better able to apply facts and value judgments to the solutions of such problems, than were pupils in conventional programs.
h. There was no evidence that experience in a core program is a handicap to success in college. Rather evidence suggested that students who had experienced core programs had somewhat better chances of success than those who followed the conventional pattern of preparation.[18]

Suggestions for a core program

To make any type of program succeed, there must be a wholehearted spirit of cooperation among teachers, administrators, students, and parents. A thorough study of the problem should be made before embarking upon such a program. It might well begin with a small unit of teachers working together experimentally. Conferences and workshops with teachers in other schools similarly engaged will prove valuable to all. The progress and problems of such an experimental group should be the subject of discussion in all curriculum meetings. At some general meetings, a consultant who is an authority in the field should be invited to discuss problems and to make suggestions.

It is imperative that adequate equipment and materials be available for the proper functioning of a core program. A list of some of the essential facilities for a core program might include: a laboratory type of classroom with movable furniture, adequate tackboard and chalkboard space,

---

[18] J. M. Michelson, "What Does Research Say about the Effectiveness of the Core Curriculum?" *School Review,* LXV, No. 2 (Summer 1957), 157. Copyright by The University of Chicago.

filing cabinets and storage space, construction equipment and tools, a plentiful supply of audio-visual materials and proper equipment, a well-stocked library, and various materials for testing and evaluating. Well-planned field trips are of considerable value in such a program. The teacher's needs include professional journals, methods books, source books, resource units, newspapers, and contemporary materials.

Conclusion

The development of both block-time and core classes has been discussed in terms of their structure and place in the modern education program. Each has specific features that are advantageous in attempting to meet the needs and interests of youth at the junior high school level. This type of instructional pattern and the selected theme may vary with the school system. Much of the success of the introduction and the implementation of such a program will depend to a large extent upon the complete cooperation of the administration and teachers.

To move from the familiar methods to something new is challenging for all who are involved. Guidance opportunities are broadened to the extent that each teacher gets to know his students better. Education becomes functional and meaningful to the student. The development of block-time and core classes in the future will necessitate familiarizing teachers, through education, with this type of program. The block-time classes and core program has something to offer in the ways of meeting the needs of youth.

Bibliography

Alberty, H. B. and E. Elberty, *Reorganizing the High School Curriculum*, 3rd ed. New York: The Macmillan Company, 1962.

Faunce, R. C. and N. L. Bossing, *Developing the Core Curriculum*, 2nd ed. Englewood Cliffs, N.J.: Prentice-Hall, Inc., 1958.

Faunce, R. C. and M. L. Clute, *Teaching and Learning in the Junior High School*. Belmont, Calif.: Wadsworth Publishing Company, Inc., 1961.

Lurry, L. L. and E. J. Alberty, *Developing a High School Core Program*. New York: The Macmillan Company, 1957.

Van Til, G. F., G. F. Vars, and J. H. Lounsbury, *Modern Education for the Junior High School Years*. New York: Bobbs-Merrill Company, Inc., 1961.

Wright, G. S., *Block-Time Classes and the Core Program in the Junior High School*, Bulletin 1958, No. 6. Washington, D.C.: Federal Security Agency, Office of Education, 1958.

Zapf, R. M., *Democratic Processes in Secondary School*. Englewood Cliffs, N.J.: Prentice-Hall, Inc., 1959.

Chapter Five

The Learner in the Program

The modern secondary school has assumed a major responsibility for the education of American youth. Education at this level places considerable focus upon the learner and his ability to achieve and accomplish to the fullest. The purpose of the selected courses in the curriculum, in general, is to aid youth in becoming effective citizens. This training in essential skills should further the learner's competence in coping with the ever-present problems in our rapidly changing society and complex world. The social studies program is designed to carry its share of the responsibility for the education of young people to meet the challenges of our free democratic society and contribute to building responsible citizens.

Contemporary educational practices necessitate that the teacher acquire a knowledge of the students in his classes. This should be accomplished at the earliest possible stage of the instruction of a particular group of learners. The teacher can examine the various available sources for obtaining information about each individual learner. This should provide some basic background knowledge that will prove helpful. Through the avenue of observing and working with the learners, the teacher gains much firsthand knowledge. This information can be profitable in developing in the learner the skills, understanding, and attitudes so essential for effective living.

The Nature and Needs
of the Learners

The teacher who has a knowledge and understanding of the youth he teaches will enhance the general achievement of his group. He must know the physical, mental, social, and emotional characteristics of youth in order to direct more fully their growth and development. The teacher can gain practical knowledge by observing and studying young people. Sharing the interests, feelings, and desires of the learners is a most compensating experience.

In the following arrangement, the physical, mental, social, and emotional aspects of adolescent growth and development are grouped.

Physical Development[1]

Ages 15, 16, 17, and 18

Growth Rate. At 16 to 18 maturity in height and weight is almost achieved. •Sex differences in the rate and timing of physical growth exist. •Characteristic bodily proportions are developed such as high waistline, high hipline, broad shoulders, long arms and legs, and large hands and feet.

Maturation Level. By the last year in high school, a few boys have achieved the psychological maturity of the girls. •Both are developing adult sexual characteristics. Girls tend to mature about 1 or 2 years earlier than boys. Both are concerned about changes taking place in their own bodies; for example, most boys begin to shave, and girls are concerned with the size of their hips and breasts.

Muscular Development. Some expend much more energy than is advisable. •Boys at this period gain greatly in muscular strength. •The pupils' physical coordination and dexterity equals or exceeds that of most adults. •They participate more in such individual sports as tennis, swimming, and golf. Most boys still prefer group games.

Dentition. Interest in the appearance of teeth; time is devoted to their care.

Organic Development. The growth of the heart often lags behind that of the arteries and so heart strain by overexercise is possible. Sometimes pupils experience faintness, heart palpitations, and digestive disturbances. •Pupils are relatively free from infection. •They continue to have large appetites. •Girls have relatively little menstrual pain, although some discomfort may be felt. Irregularity causes some unnecessary concern. Failure to begin menstruation by 18 is not unnatural, but often causes anxiety. •Interest is centered on physical development—girls because of weight and figure—boys so that they will be in condition for athletics.

---

[1] *Social Studies Grades 7 and 8,* Curriculum Bulletin No. 10 (Cincinnati, Ohio, Board of Education, 1958), pp. 7-16.

Mental Development

Ages 15, 16, 17, and 18

Space, Time, and Number Concepts. Pupils of this age demonstrate increasing interest and ability to utilize these concepts in discussing the larger social, economic, and political issues of the day.

Personal and Impersonal Interests. They seek to establish themselves as independent and mature persons; in doing this, they often develop a highly critical attitude toward themselves and their endeavors. •They usually are interested in personal appearance. •They sometimes develop religious doubts; but these are not deepseated or of long duration. •They are developing a sensitivity to the opposite sex and begin to think seriously of the qualities desired in a prospective mate. •There is an increased desire for successful human relationships.

Realistic and Imaginative Interests. Emphasis is upon a realistic approach in facing crucial problems of living; they attack their problems with more directness than previously. •They are deepening their interests in aesthetic and intellectual activities; their interest is centered upon vocational plans, the development of a talent, or the pursuit of a hobby. •They seek work outside the home to supplement allowances. •It is a period of faith in social progress and their ability to participate.

Ability to Make Comparisons and See Absurdities. There is increased ability to see differences and incongruities between abstract words.

Ability to See Causal Relationships. They recognize that the data for solving the problems of a society come from both the past and the present, and can be used in drawing conclusions concerning the future. •They exhibit a growing comprehension of the larger social, economic, and political issues of the day.

Ability to Generalize and Make Judgments. Young people of these ages form opinions on general social matters such as war, crime, and birth control, but their opinions still reflect their family pattern of belief.

Attention Span. This is increasingly dependent upon the person's choice of and interest in the situation.

Language Development. There is greater facility in expressing ideas. •There is an increased ability to recognize the importance of abstract connecting words in the comprehension of a sentence. •They are more capable of intellectualizing their experiences than at earlier levels. •Boys' reading preferences shift from adventure stories to stories of real exploits. Girls perfer current light fiction.

Social Development

Ages 15, 16, 17, and 18

Methods of Social Contact. Pupils desire to follow patterns in much of their social life. •Some endeavor to achieve status through competition with others in the group. •They have keen interest in obscene stories and jokes, and they have desire to indulge in vulgar language; these are means of gaining prestige. •They attack problems and difficulties with more directness than previously. •Immature boys and girls tend to explore personal relationships vicariously, in fiction or biography and in the movies. They often find ideal persons whom they admire and respect.

Race Attitudes. Pupils begin to build personal philosophies in which basic principles appear. •The opinions of boys and girls still reflect the family pattern of belief.

Nature of Social Values. Many of the social values held by these young people are still superficial. "Good looks," poise in social behavior, and financial standing are still important social criteria. •Pupils are interested in learning about the ways of the world and curious about the intricacies of personal relationships. Their ability to understand other people's attitudes and to arrive at more stable relationships with them is improving.

Extent of Social Interest. Pupils begin to realize mutual obligations and responsibilities of persons in social relationships. •They become more distinctly aware of the importance of the community because it provides jobs, recreation, and social opportunities. •Usually a growing comprehension of the larger social, economic, and political issues of the day is exhibited. •They realize that the data for solving problems of society come both from the past and the present and can be used in drawing conclusions concerning the future. •They believe that human life can be bettered, and many of them accept responsibilities and privileges of social progress.

Response to Authority. Pupils desire to achieve status as individuals outside of the family, and to be as acceptable as possible to their peers in both individual and group relationships. •They shift from desiring family protection to wanting to give protection. •They are highly sensitive to the reactions of their parents, despite their carefully camouflaged feelings toward them. They spasmodically accept and reject parents and teachers. •They often seek some adult person as a confidant. •They gradually withdraw their role as recipients of parental affection and guidance, and refuse to accept the hitherto established forms of family behavior. They bitterly resent parents not permitting them to grow up. •These young people dream of being absolutely independent, as they imagine adults are. •They usually conform to the customs of a self-selected group, and follow adolescent fads.

Sex Grouping. Pupils desire to have friends of the opposite sex and to date. •Girls of this group are more secure if accepted by a select group, not everyone. Boys are somewhat afraid to go with girls who do not have prestige, for fear of losing their own status. •This is a period of love affairs and cliques. Friendships, also, tend to become more lasting. •Occasionally they fall in love with older members of the opposite sex. Boys, however, are most often attracted to girls somewhat younger than themselves. •They frequently revert to friendships with their own sex if they experience disappointment in heterosexual attachments.

Emotional Development

Ages 15, 16, 17, and 18

Sources of Conflicts. Some of these young people feel awkward and embarrassed because of increasing size, skin eruptions, and body odors. •They often have conflicts with younger children in the family because of the differences in social standards. •A good deal of insecurity is shown in a highly critical attitude during this period. They are critical of themselves, of their family, of their school, of their church, and of their possessions. •Pupils of these ages frequently raise questions regarding religion. •They develop greater family consciousness, and are often embarrassed or ashamed of parents who have not made a success of their marriage or business affairs. •They fear to appear "peculiar," different, or conspicuous in any way. They want to be adequate, both mentally and physically, in terms of the standards of their group. •Many are investigating ways of financing their college careers. •In their striving to be independent they may even accept blind-alley jobs. •They are disposed to feel inadequate as they face decisions of far-reaching importance in such areas as further education, vocations, sex, marriage, and religion.

Range of Feeling. They have decided likes and dislikes. •They deeply resent parents who do not allow them to grow up. •They dream of being absolutely independent as adults. •Religious feelings and high ideals are a paramount concern.

Provision for individual differences

The problems of individual differences are commonly met through the organization of the school program and by the teacher as the key builder of the curriculum. Administrators, supervisors, and teachers are generally interested in identifying and providing for individual differences so that every student can derive satisfaction from his learning experiences. The teacher is continuously confronted with a range of differences among students. For this reason the teacher cannot expect the same degree of achievement from each one.

The following is an excellent example of how a secondary school attempts to meet the problem of individual differences:

The problem of individual differences is exceedingly important and has a vital bearing on course offerings, materials of instruction, and teaching procedures. Since pupils of all levels of ability—gifted, average and slow—attend the same school and take required courses, each must be given work which he can accomplish and which at the same time presents a challenge to him. Grouping pupils in required courses according to interest, ability, achievement and ambitions for the future is practiced whenever feasible, to provide for individual differences. Under such a plan flexibility in scheduling classes is imperative. One pupil may be pursuing advanced work in mathematics and remedial work in college preparatory English. Grouping is based upon the individual pupil's pattern of capacities in specific subjects. Each year the pupil's individual program is evaluated. This process of evaluation and periodic review of elective courses helps pupils and parents to regard the curriculum as an individualized program for particular needs. Effective guidance, counseling, and conferences with the pupil and parent are essential for this type of individual programming.[2]

---

[2] *Program of Study for the Madison High Schools Grades Ten, Eleven, Twelve* (Madison, Wis.: Madison Public Schools, 1961), p. 1.

The teacher and individual differences

The social studies teacher accepts the challenge of individual differences and in his own particular way moves to meet the problem while working with students. There is no one special method or formula for a teacher to follow in coping with this problem during the instructional process. The experienced teacher no doubt through simple experimentation, planning, and the application of a variety of techniques has adjusted to individual differences in his own program while working with groups. The author has found that during the planning, introduction, and development of a unit, a considerable knowledge can be gained of the needs, interests, purposes, and differences of the students. Today's teacher utilizes his own knowledge of the units and problems to be studied, together with selected procedures, techniques, and effective skills, along with all the available resources and materials in making the study both interesting and effective for a given group.

It is encouraging to find that a teacher can actually gain from working with students in the following manner: individual conferences, discussions, reports, evaluation of individual work or committee projects, utilizing simple tests and finding the student's strengths and weaknesses in the instructional program. In this manner the teacher is in a better position effectively to guide and plan for both individual and group work. The careful selection of functional experiences and practical activities is especially important while working with slow groups. When the students are aware of what is expected of them and when they understand the proper application of essential skills, a measure of success can be expected. However, the teacher must be always alert and ready to alter his plans and follow new avenues in making the proper adjustment to meeting individual differences.

The beginning teacher can acquire a better understanding of his groups from the following sources; cumulative records, which reveal much factual information; direct observations of the student in the learning process; discussions with the guidance director and other school personnel; parent-teacher conferences; student's work both oral and written; tests, questionnaires, and checklists, all of which can supply much significant information.

The gifted and talented student

Modern education at the secondary level is aware of the responsibility of identifying and providing adequate and new instructional programs for the gifted and talented youth. Various techniques and procedures are utilized in the identification process.

A number of school systems have established systematic programs for the identification of gifted youth. Many of these screening programs have been introduced in the elementary schools and there are a few secondary schools which are introducing similar selection procedures. Additional identification techniques are used in some secondary schools to discover the ablest pupils in both academic and nonacademic areas. A few schools have prepared departmental files of pupils who have been identified as possessing unusual talent in particular subject fields.[3]

In the social studies field efforts have been made to challenge the talents of the gifted students.

Although the skills of citizenship are essential to all functioning members of a democracy, gifted youth are in a position to exert special influence in society either as leaders or as followers. The social studies should help to prepare them for this role by providing learning opportunities that will tap both their intellectual and their leadership potential.

Academically talented students, because of their more acute perceptions and keener insights, should be particularly trained to understand and analyze the values, judgments, and attitudes that underlie American society and to recognize and comprehend the attitudes and values of cultures other than their own.

The intellectual endowment of academically talented students permits them to acquire more than usual factual mastery of the social world around them. The content of their social studies education should be modified to provide them with greater knowledge of the present and of the historical past, both as an aid to understanding contemporary culture and as a discipline through which they may refine their judgments and enlarge their appreciations.

Intellectually gifted students are better prepared to deal with generalizations, abstractions, and relationships than less gifted youngsters; and their social studies instruction should correspondingly place greater emphasis on ideas, concepts, and theories than on mere factual content.[4]

Some school systems have attempted to handle the problem of improving the instructional program for talented students through enrichment classes. Advanced placement programs and honors class arrangements for the talented students working as a group utilize materials and problems in such a way as to provide greater depth and greater challenge for these groups. These more capable students can do broader research, more intensive reading, employ more reference sources, explore more fully a problem or topic, write more comprehensive term papers or reports, and employ greater background knowledge in solving a particular problem. At the same time these students are building proper attitudes,

---

[3] L. S. Michael and other contributors, "Secondary School Programs," *Education for the Gifted,* National Society for the Study of Education, 57th Yearbook, Part II (Chicago: The University of Chicago Press, 1958), chap. XII, p. 264. Quoted by permission of the Society.

[4] M. M. Klein, *Social Studies for the Academically Talented Student in the Secondary School,* National Council for the Social Studies, (Washington, D.C.: 1960), pp. 10-11.

increasing understandings, sharpening effective skills, widening interests, and learning the values of cooperation and competent citizenship through planning, organizing, presenting, discussing, and evaluating broader learning experiences in the instructional process.

The competency of the teacher

Directing the program for a group of talented students is of major importance. Adequate teaching experience, a broad background of content, effective command of methods and procedures, and an understanding of the needs of today's youth are basic.

Teachers working with the academically talented in social studies should have a scholarly knowledge of their subject or area, be liberally educated, have a deep understanding of the nature of learning and the learning process, a brief in and an understanding of the needs of academically talented students, and a keen desire to teach such students; they should also have grappled with the philosophical problems of the meaning and purpose of education and have a knowledge of the history of American education. As indicated earlier, such teachers should also have to an exceptional degree, a good mind, broad intellectual curiosity, creativeness, energy, enthusiasm, emotional balance, a deep interest in students and a sense of humor.[5]

Any program for guiding the development of talented students requires a plentiful supply of interesting reading materials, reference books, magazines, pamphlets, booklets, newspapers, and government and business publications. Mass media, audio-visual materials and equipment, and resource people should also be utilized. In the planning process, the librarian and the teacher should work closely in the choice of instructional materials. Cooperation between the teacher and the librarian should continue as the study of a problem progresses and reaches a conclusion. The enthusiastic teacher must be alert to meet the needs, interests, and individual differences through attractive assignments, selected readings, and suitable independent research for the students.

Slow learning groups

School systems have various methods for identifying the slow learner. Special instruction is provided for the slow learner as well as for the talented student. This calls for grouping students according to ability. The identification and careful selection of slow-learner groups at the

---

[5] *The Identification and Education of the Academically Talented Student in the American Secondary School,* Conference Report (Washington, D.C.: National Education Association, 1958), pp. 120-121.

junior and senior high school levels is an important function of the school administration. A variety of tests may be employed. Each student's academic record is carefully evaluated. All available reports from guidance counselors, home room teachers, special supervisors, and parents should be taken into consideration. The grouping is usually made on the basis of similar abilities and other educational needs. If homogeneous grouping exists, students develop and progress at their normal level of ability. Slow learners or basic groups are expected to participate in and enjoy the various activities in the school program.

As has been stressed in this chapter, the selection of an experienced and understanding teacher is especially important for such a group. The application of proper teaching procedures, the selection of desirable instructional materials and appropriate content contributes to the proper classroom atmosphere and will determine to a large measure the outcome and success of the instructional program.

Conant takes into consideration the slow learner at the secondary level.

Those in the ninth grade of the school who read at a level of the sixth grade or below should be given special consideration. These pupils should be instructed in English and the required social studies by special teachers who are interested in working with such students and who are sympathetic to their problems. Remedial reading should be part of the work, and special types of textbooks should be provided. The elective programs of these pupils should be directed toward simple vocational work, and they should be kept out of the regular vocational programs for boys, the distributive education program, and the regular commercial program for girls. These students should not be confused with mentally retarded students. The education of the mentally retarded is a special problem which in some states is also handled in the regular high school through special instruction and the use of special state funds.[6]

The good teacher with a friendly spirit and a sincere interest can through encouragement help to build confidence for a slow group. If given that chance for achievement within their abilities, the group can experience much satisfaction. The program of instruction should be geared within their interests and capacities. The helpfulness of the teacher can do much to foster the growth and development of the slow learners. The need for security, recognition, success, and satisfaction from the learning experiences is a significant factor in directing the learning processes of the slow groups.

In the final analysis the importance of the teacher as a guide, friend, leader, and provider of direction in the teaching-learning process for the slow groups must receive due consideration if the challenge for learning is to be accomplished.

---

[6] J. B. Conant, *The American High School Today* (New York: McGraw-Hill Book Company, Inc., 1959), p. 55.

The slow learner

The slow learner may be defined as that individual whose ability to grasp intellectual knowledge is below that of the average learner when measured by standardized intelligence tests. He is, with the exception of intellectual capacity, much like the other students in his group. He has needs, interests, and problems. He, like other students, learns through group, as well as individual, experiences. The slow learners as a rule are not slow in all types of activities; in fact, they may be somewhat rapid in certain areas of learning. For example, a slow learner may be quite skilled in activities that require considerable mechanical skill.

Slow learners, with their limited intellectual ability, are able to learn if teachers supply them with reading materials suitable for their level, worthwhile activities, and interesting experiences. One of the common problems at the secondary level is the inability of the student to read adequately and to make normal progress in this area of achievement. To overcome this weakness the teacher must ascertain the student's chief interests and locate materials for him which will interest him and at the same time provide him with some growth in reading.

Some school systems are meeting the problem of educating slow learners by establishing a special educational program for them. By grouping students with similar educational abilities, some of the real needs of youth can be satisfied. The grouping of slow learners is determined in many cases by the particular local situation, and is accomplished either in a regular classroom group made up of ability levels of students, or in a special group composed of all slow learners. In a heterogeneous group, the slow learner gains richness in experiences through aiding and sharing in cooperative activities. Such an arrangement calls for effective planning so that each student grows in accomplishment as well as in confidence. Careful planning for a composite grouping is necessary so that each student regardless of his level of ability, will have a sense of security within the group. For example, slow learners may be assigned such duties as painting murals, arranging the bulletin board display, taking the class roll, helping the teacher with the arrangement of furniture, and sharing in the construction of the program that the group is to follow. The more intellectual tasks may be assigned to the other members of the composite group.

Working with slow learners

The slow learner needs work that he can do satisfactorily. He can reach a fair degree of achievement if experiences are geared to his own needs and interests. He must be taught to understand relationships, and not be confronted with a maze of difficult content. Effective work habits are important for his progress. The student should have opportunities for practical experiences as well as self-expression. The slow learner in his own way has something to contribute in the process of group living and learning.

It is truly amazing what can be accomplished with slow learners. The students must understand what is to be accomplished in terms of their own capacities. They need meaningful learning that can be easily transferred to other situations in the everyday life of a community. In no other learning situation is the element of understanding and encouragement so essential. Slow learners need to have instilled in themselves the element of confidence in their work. A little sincere commendation for their achievements is most helpful. This provides the momentum and enthusiasm necessary to accept the challenge of new responsibilities. Tasks should be adjusted to their abilities. Units or topics should be of a shorter duration than those for the superior student. Work in the classroom should be related whenever possible to real life situations. All assignments should be clarified for the slow learner, and it is wise to have him copy assignments in his notebook. The writer has had the pleasure and satisfaction of teaching slow learners at both the junior and senior high school level and realizes the importance of giving all students a chance for successful achievement.

Subject requirements and learning procedures should be flexible rather than rigid and always subordinated to the abilities, needs, interests, and problems of the students. Manual aids are particularly helpful in instructing slow learners. These students enjoy working with their hands, doing construction as well as creative work. They learn much from the preparation necessary in the process of teacher-student planning; for example, such things as the construction of a large pictorial or physical map depicting some phase of history or society can be undertaken only after much study and discussion. Such instruction encompasses content materials as well as manual skills. Particularly in the social studies, the progress of the group in social living, and the awakening of individual pride and responsibility are of greater importance than the acquisition of much factual knowledge. The teacher should help each student to:

1. Attain his best possible development at his own rate
2. Develop his interests and skills
3. Expand his vocabulary
4. Improve his reading skill
5. Develop good work habits
6. Feel a sense of belonging, of being secure, and a spirit of recognition within the group
7. Feel that he is appreciated and a vital part of the learning process

8. See that learning is continuous, cooperative, and worthwhile
9. Meet his special needs through educational as well as vocational guidance
10. Grow socially through new and varied experiences

Guidance is essential in directing the progress of slower learners. The social studies teacher and the homeroom teacher should act as friendly advisers. Social responsibility and desirable social attitudes should be developed in the individual. A program for the slower learners' growth may include homeroom activities, clubs, special work assignments, participation in sports, and encouragment of hobby during leisure time. In this way the individual maintains a greater association with other students.

Practices used with slow learners

The following are some of the most frequently listed practices used by social studies teachers with slow learners:

1. Use current events as an important part of class work.
2. Teach pupils to use the layman's reference books: the dictionary, encyclopedia, World Almanac, etc.
3. Teach pupils how to register and vote; give experiences in studying party platforms and personal views of candidates.
4. Encourage pupils to engage in conversation in school and at home on current events, politics, government, and community affairs.
5. Encourage pupils to use references in a large library.

The five least frequently used were:

1. Supervise the planning of culminating activities by class to organize major ideas of a unit.
2. Have pupils make charts and graphs based on statistics.
3. Encourage pupils to read classics of historical significance.
4. Encourage participation in local adult movements.
5. Arrange for preparation and presentation of radio and television programs.[7]

A review of such items especially by the beginning teacher will provide excellent guides when selecting procedures for directing the learning of slow students. It is interesting to note that the study of current events was high on the list for both slow and rapid learners. The understanding of current topics is an integral part of citizenship education.

---

[7] *Teaching Rapid and Slow Learners*, U.S. Department of Health, Education and Welfare, Office of Education, Bulletin No. 5 (Washington, D.C.: Government Printing Office, 1954), pp. 32-37.

Individual differences in the social studies

The good social studies teacher identifies early the individual differences in a group and gears the work to meet the needs of each student. Some means to be used in identification are school records, interviews and observation of the learners at work. A friendly conference with a student can reveal much valuable information. The writer in working with slow students found this to be one of the most rewarding experiences as a guidance measure. In this informal manner the teacher and student get to know each other better, and this is a valuable asset in the teaching-learning process.

One of the most challenging problems in the social studies program is that of providing for the individual differences of our youth. The teacher is faced with a complicated task as each student has his own unique background pattern and capacity for learning. Providing for the range of differences among students in a group presents a challenge for the social studies teachers.

The teacher must provide work geared to the level of the slower student, but he must also insure that the talented and gifted student use his ability to capacity. To accomplish this, the teacher gears the work to meet the ability of each student in the group, and aids each individual through guidance and direction in the process of learning. Modern democratic teaching in the social studies makes provision for the uniqueness of each individual. The teacher identifies differences through observation and study, and provides for each learner so that he may gain from the instruction.

Knowing each student well and helping him to understand himself better is of prime importance in any teaching-learning situation. Likewise, the student should know his teacher well, and through this mutual friendship both can contribute to the student's growth. The student respects the teacher as a co-worker and friend. The teacher is considered the important authority in the group. He helps the students plan activities, develops functional experiences, and establishes desirable goals. When the student's interests and needs are recognized, the instruction can be pitched to the range of the individual's ability. The student can, with the proper assistance from the teacher, be channeled into the stage where he is in many cases self-directed in learning. Each individual is allowed to proceed at his own rate. Consideration is given to the student's general development and his readiness for particular study when working on a problem. His interest, skill, and ability to achieve and profit by the experience is uppermost.

Teachers of social studies know that before students can develop an accurate view of others, they first need to gain a measure of understanding about themselves. This self-understanding is usually encouraged through one or more of the following means: developing a friendly attitude between teacher and student, and a group climate which accepts differences; maintaining a variety of flexible methods in the classroom with a balance of group and individual work, and of lecture, discussion, and audio-visual presentations; offering many materials from which students may make choices in line with their interests and maturity; talking informally and individually with students; and encouraging class discussions that consider human needs and motives.

Self-understanding also comes as a teacher has short, informal talks with individual students. These individual contacts help to balance the impersonality of today's large high school, and to convince adolescents that adults are truly interested in them. In some instances these on-the-spot contacts signal to the teacher that certain students have unusually serious problems. The teacher then is able to refer them to a school counselor who offers special guidance.[8]

Principles of student growth

The understanding of youth in our social studies classes is most significant for the teacher in guiding the growth of students in the program. The following is an excellent list of selected principles that should prove helpful in guiding the teacher in his judgment:

1. School experiences should recognize the adolescent's striving to achieve independence and adult status as a normal phase of growing up.
2. School experiences should assist the adolescent in achieving a desirable relationship with his age mates of both sexes.
3. The school program should help the adolescent make adjustments to his changing body.
4. Educational experiences should give the adolescent a sense of security and satisfaction with his own development as a person.
5. The successful teacher understands that normal adolescent behavior is not necessarily desirable nor pleasing from the point of view of the teacher or the adult.
6. Teachers should face realistically the fact that an adolescent in his relations with the school and the outside world lives in a confusion of double standards.
7. Every adolescent behavior problem has a cause or causes that the school may be helping to alleviate or to aggravate.
8. Growing up is regarded as a total, unified process for the adolescent.
9. Adolescents vary in the rate at which they grow and their ultimate level of growth.[9]

[8] California Test Bureau, *Guiding Today's Youth* (Los Angeles: Los Angeles County Board of Education, 1961), pp. 195-96. Copyright © 1961 by California Test Bureau. Reprinted by permission of California Test Bureau, Del Monte Research Park, Monterey, Cal.

[9] V. E. Anderson and W. T. Gruhn, *Principles and Practices of Secondary Education* (2nd ed.; New York: The Ronald Press Company, 1962), pp. 12-17. Copyright 1962.

The teacher should understand that good working relationships with students at this stage in their education is the key to effective instruction.

Leadership ability among students

The following list should provide the teacher with insights into the student's abilities.

Which of your pupils stand out in these characteristics when compared with the rest of the class?
1. Is liked and respected by most of the members of the class?
2. Is able to influence others to work toward desirable goals?
3. Is able to influence others to work toward undesirable goals?
4. Can take charge of the group?
5. Can judge the abilities of other students and find a place for them in the group's activities?
6. Is able to figure out what is wrong with an activity and show others how to do it better?
7. Is often asked for ideas and suggestions?
8. Is looked to by others when something must be decided?
9. Seems to sense what others want, and helps them to accomplish it?
10. Is a leader in several kinds of activities?
11. Enters into activities with contagious enthusiasm?
12. Is elected to offices?[10]

The social studies teacher should find this list most helpful when observing, studying, and identifying students in a particular group. In this manner the teacher as the key person is gaining broader insights into the uniqueness of each student. Leadership abilities are essential and the teacher should help students to develop such qualities. When these characteristics are identified, they can prove useful to a teacher in planning and organizing instruction for students. It is revealing to note the real strength and ability that is illuminated in these individuals. The teacher should challenge these students with assignments and responsibilities geared to the qualities they possess. When developing projects and instituting needed research for a problem, the assistance of these students in leading committees is most essential. These leadership experiences in activities are helpful to both the individual and his own group.

The creative student

The need for encouraging creativity among students is an important responsibility of modern secondary education. Teachers should be alert to identify the creative student and foster his growth through appropriate

---

[10] R. F. DeHaan and J. Kough, *Identifying Students with Special Needs*, Secondary School Edition, I (Chicago: Science Research Associates, 1956), 33. Reprinted by permission. © 1956, Science Research Associates, Inc.

experiences. The following characteristics are most often found in the creative individual:

1. The highly creative individual values what others do not value.
2. The creative individual perceives richly, fully, and deeply.
3. The creative individual feels what others do not feel.
4. Creative individuals think in ways others do not think.
5. The creative individual is more complex as a personality than other individuals.
6. The highly creative individual tends to commit himself to a cause outside himself.
7. Highly creative individuals live more fully in the present, in the moment of "now," than other persons do.[11]

Working with learners

The social studies teacher realizes the importance of observing, knowing, and understanding the students he is working with. He provides experiences for the slow as well as the gifted learner. Learners are prone to learn in response to their immediate needs and interests. The social studies teacher frequently adapts to the range of individual differences through projects and special research assignments. All students are provided opportunities to explore and do research on specific topics geared to their abilities and interests. The teacher effectively guides individual as well as group work. He is alert to motivate whenever needed, and to encourage the student to work effectively in a cooperative manner with the group or in committees. He realizes the importance of the students' understanding themselves and making the proper adjustment to the immediate learning situation.

It is through effective planning and productive experience that the teacher develops appropriate techniques and methods suited for working with students of varying interest and abilities. The social studies teacher shows a deep interest in the work and achievement of each individual. He capitalizes upon the inherent interests of youth that have learning implications. To implement learning in the social studies program then, the teacher must begin with the learner's readiness for the work at hand, build on his previous learning experiences, and at the same time keep in mind his ability and interest. He must introduce a wide variety of audio-visual materials and various techniques to facilitate learning. With the slow learner, it will mean starting with functional experiences that have an appeal to the individual. The student should never be forced, but should be allowed to move as rapidly as his ability warrants. Vocational interests are sometimes helpful in guiding the work of the slow pupil. The

---

[11] L. M. Berman, "The Creative Student," *Wisconsin Journal of Education*, XCIV, No. 9 (April 1962), 11-12.

gifted student should be made aware of his potentialities and encouraged to develop them. He should be permitted to sample and use a great variety of materials. Those experiences and activities that foster a high degree of abstract thinking are stimulating to the gifted student.

Conclusion

The learner plays a key role in the modern educational program. This necessitates that individual differences be recognized and met in a satisfactory manner. In this way youth is given proper guidance and every opportunity to foster growth and development. The social studies teacher is sensitive to planning and developing the course work in such a flexible manner as to provide for the varying interests, needs, and talents found among students in a given group. It is interesting to note that students working together in a committee can share experiences and information related to the problem being studied.

The good teacher should be encouraged and given every opportunity to experiment with techniques, materials, and equipment that may be productive in the teaching of all youth. He should study and observe his students in order to meet effectively individual and group needs, interests, and problems. Every teacher is aware of the fact that students differ in many respects, particularly in interests and needs. The slow learner as well as the gifted youth should be encouraged and helped to grow to his fullest capacity. Consideration should be given to those productive and functional learning experiences both in the learning laboratory and the local community that challenge and motivate our youth. It is through the channels of constructive guidance and evaluation that the student is helped to achieve with success.

Today's changing society and complex world necessitate considerable study and experimentation to build a flexible and functional curriculum to meet the problems of providing for individual differences. It can be accomplished in a manner that will meet the intellectual as well as the social and emotional needs of youth. This can further provide for youth's transition from high school to college or effective living and employment in adult society.

Bibliography

Getzels, J. W. and P. W. Jackson, *Creativity and Intelligence: Explorations with Gifted Students.* New York: John Wiley & Sons, Inc., 1962.

Los Angeles County Superintendent of Schools Office, *Guiding Today's Youth.*

Del Monte Research Park, Monterey, California: California Test Bureau, 1962.

Johnson, G. O., *Education for Slow Learners*. Englewood Cliffs, N.J.: Prentice-Hall, Inc., 1963.

Kline, M. M., *Social Studies for the Academically Talented in the Secondary School*. Washington, D.C.: National Education Association, 1960.

Torrance, E. P., *Guiding Creative Talent*. Englewood Cliffs, N.J.: Prentice-Hall, Inc., 1962.

Wiles, K., *Teaching for Better Schools*, 2nd ed. Englewood Cliffs, N.J.: Prentice-Hall, Inc., 1959.

Chapter Six

The Teacher for a New Age

The modern social studies teacher is a scholarly person, alert to the changes and challenges facing civilization, and to their implications for education. These changes place a responsibility squarely upon the teacher to feel the pulse of this new era and to apply new knowledge intelligently and effectively in the learning process.

The social studies teacher serves as one of the architects in building a curriculum which will help the student to live competently. Constant alertness on the part of the teacher in using the new knowledge derived from recent research and successful experimentation is essential. The teacher is enthusiastic about his subject field, aware of the needs of youth, and constantly striving for professional growth.

New levels of excellence will come to secondary education as teachers appear in classrooms with the specific kind of understandings and skills which our dynamic time demands. These are:

1. A knowledge of a subject field to include related fields of inquiry, and an active interest in acquiring new knowledge
2. A knowledge of the process of learning and the ability to translate this knowledge into pertinent behavior in acting and reacting with students in the process of teaching
3. A knowledge of individual growth and development and the ability to provide challenges commensurate with each student's maturity, experience, background and capacity to learn

4. A knowledge of new and proven techniques, methods, and materials and the ability to recognize and utilize learning aids most suitable for specific purposes in guiding the learning process
5. A knowledge of American society, the expectations of that society for its schools, and the ability to interpret the implications of changes in society into constructive action as teacher-citizen
6. An enthusiasm for working with young people reflected in a constantly growing philosophy of education which has breadth and depth and is dedicated to the conviction that each person counts[1]

The good social studies teacher has a broad education including depth in content. He has a knowledge of specific procedures and has utilized methods during some supervised teaching experience. He has a working knowledge of our American culture and is a constant student of contemporary affairs as they relate to the nation and the world. He understands the keys to improving instruction. He makes a definite contribution to the school and the community in his own specific way.

Effective instruction

The scholar-teacher is concerned with effective instruction and learning procedures. He possesses invaluable traits of leadership, initiative, enthusiasm, cheerfulness, humor, sincerity, and patience. The teacher understands his responsibility in selecting pertinent curriculum materials for his students. He specializes in developing effective citizenship, and provides the incentive for his students to go forward into society with a feeling of confidence.

The teacher constantly extends the frontiers of learning for his students. He is aware of individual differences and provides a variety of opportunities for his students to contribute to the learning process. In this manner enthusiasm is aroused, and curiosity is so broadened as to stimulate further research. With imaginations kindled, the student is challenged to move ahead. The teacher utilizes the breadth of his knowledge together with his own physical equipment to mold an effective "teaching approach" for imparting knowledge with functional meaning. He is the efficient director of the social studies program utilizing all available tools for sound learning.

Teaching competence and effectiveness

Teaching competence is the key to effective instruction. It tends to foster steady progress and growth for the students. It entails a business-like approach to the learning process which features imagination and

---

[1] D. C. Corrigan, "Teachers For A Dynamic Age," *California Journal of Secondary Education*, XXXVII, No. 1 (January 1962), 33.

creativeness. It includes worthwhile guidance responsibilities, careful planning, productive methods, and the use of adequate evaluation techniques. The critical characteristics of an effective teacher are:[2]

Uses Effective Teaching Techniques

1. Causes learning activities to be meaningful
2. Learning activity is student centered
3. Provides for self-participation by students
4. Provides periodic evaluation of students' progress and growth
5. Has adequate lesson planning
6. Uses instructional materials and aids effectively
7. Provides varied experiences for students
8. Guidance of learning reaches individual continuously
9. Instruction materials and aids are organized and used
10. Has mastered the art of guiding learning activity effectively
11. Maintains good heat and ventilation and room environment
12. Pupils are aware of the objectives for each lesson
13. Makes assignments clear to students
14. Provides adequate provisions for student research
15. Learning program is experience centered
16. Tends to generate learning activity from interests of students
17. Obtains effective transfer from class activity to life-goals

Uses Sound and Effective psychology

1. Helps students evaluate their growth and progress
2. Always maintains dignity and integrity of students
3. Provides for individual differences effectively at all times
4. Has genuine concern for all students
5. Is sympathetic and understanding with students
6. Maintains effective discipline and class control
7. Recognizes the social and emotional needs of students
8. Paces the difficulty of learning activity effectively
9. Activity involvement used as chief means for discipline control
10. Is concerned with moral and spiritual values of students
11. Respects sacredness of individual's intimate and private life

Displays Effective Human Relations

1. Gets along well with others
2. Shows genuine warmth and respect for students and adults
3. Has personal concern for welfare of students
4. Is well liked by students
5. Participates willingly in extra- and co-curricular activities
6. Works cooperatively with others
7. Has good rapport with students at all times

---

[2] R. N. Cassel and W. L. Johns, "The Critical Characteristics of an Effective Teacher," *The Bulletin of the National Association of Secondary-School Principals,* XLIV, No. 259 (November 1960), 120-122.

8. Is well liked by colleagues
9. Is a good listener
10. Is well liked by parents of his or her students
11. Accepts recognition graciously
12. Accepts constructive criticism well
13. Does not stoop to petty "bickering"

Has Sound and Effective Community Relations

1. Interprets school program to community effectively
2. Is a good public relations agent for the school
3. Is interested in and participates in community activities
4. Works understandingly and cooperatively with parents
5. Supports and participates in parent-teacher activities
6. Makes effective use of available community resources
7. Has community belongingness and acceptance
8. Promotes the causes of education to the public

Exercises Effective Leadership

1. Uses the democratic process continuously and effectively
2. Has good leadership ability and exercises it continuously
3. Makes sound and timely decisions
4. Has good organizational ability and exercises it effectively
5. Encourages students to make their own decisions
6. Expeditiously assumes appropriate role of leader or follower
7. Carries out group decisions and school rules with dispatch
8. Sets realistic goals for students and self in teacher role
9. Sets good example for students by own behavior
10. Is willing to try new ideas that appear sound
11. Is prompt and reliable in assuming appropriate responsibility
12. Gives appropriate credit to those desiring recognition
13. Always expects the best
14. After expressing own opinions, accepts group decisions well
15. Has ability to follow through and practices it effectively
16. Has the respect of both students and colleagues

Displays Sound and Professional Bearing

1. Has teacher belongingness and identification
2. Is continuously growing professionally
3. Dresses appropriately and is well groomed
4. Speaks clearly, using good English in a well-modulated voice
5. Has a genuine acceptance of students
6. Is active on school committees
7. Thoroughly enjoys teaching
8. Has varied background and experiences
9. Own educational philosophy is in agreement with administration
10. Has a healthy regard for research findings
11. Is active in teacher workshops
12. Can admit not knowing, but always finds out the answers

The teacher and the community

The social studies teacher—and, for that matter, every secondary school teacher—has a public relations job as well as a teaching job to perform. Teaching at the secondary level keeps the teacher before the entire community. The social studies teacher is looked upon as a leader of young people and as an active member of the local community.

The teacher constantly works for the improvement of the entire school program in furthering better relationships between the school and the community and in building a cooperative spirit between the home and the school. He participates to a high degree in school and community life by supervising clubs, sports, dances, and other social functions that are outside the classroom activity. When he conducts field trips in the community, or invites resource people to speak to his groups he comes in contact with many local people. In this way he maintains relationships with the community, its agencies, and its institutions.

As a member of the parent-teacher association, the teacher attends meetings and discusses policies with parents and citizens of the community. Further contacts are made at parent-teacher conferences, athletic contests, community meetings, and other special projects.

The teacher who hopes to exert leadership in community-wide educational activities seeks to gain an understanding of the community. What type of people live there? What are their living conditions, their hopes and their goals? What groups have organized educational programs? What activities educate boys and girls incidentally? A new teacher will need to make a systematic study if he is to gain the needed information. Many teachers who have worked in the community a number of years do not know the educational forces that play on the children they teach. They, too, become more effective as they become acquainted with these forces.[3]

The teacher and guidance

In addition to teaching, the teacher serves as a guidance counselor for his pupils and their parents by helping the pupil in planning his work and in choosing a career. The social studies teacher plans, directs, and guides learning experiences and interesting activities that furnish functional knowledge for the students. Guidance becomes a definite part of building effective skills and desirable habits. The good teacher, employing a friendly approach, can materially assist the individual in developing proper attitudes, building understandings and interests, and developing

---

[3] K. Wiles, *Teaching for Better Schools* (2nd ed.; Englewood Cliffs, N.J.: Prentice-Hall, Inc., 1959), p. 263.

concepts. He employs his knowledge to the best advantage in promoting the growth of youth.

Through sincere interest, friendliness, and a helpful spirit, the teacher can assist students with their daily problems. He exhibits the emotional maturity and stability that is a tower of strength in guiding young people. The teacher in the guidance role is always optimistic and sympathetic, and employs a positive approach toward the better understanding of to-day's youth. The teacher cooperates with other school personnel, community agencies, and parents in specific matters pertaining to guidance.

The teacher has the critical role in enabling the student to achieve these successes, selecting problems which are within his grasp, providing clues and cues to their solution, suggesting alternative ways to think about them, and assessing continuously the progress of the pupil and the degree of difficulty of the problems before him. Good teaching can help students to learn to think clearly. But this can be done only by careful selection of teaching procedures deliberately adapted to each learner.

Choice as to methods and means of developing the ability to think is necessarily in the hands of the individual teacher. Professional and lay assistance may be brought into the classroom, but the intimate awareness of changes in pupils which permits evaluation of progress cannot be possessed by persons who have only limited or irregular contact with the pupils. It is therefore crucial that the teacher possess a thorough knowledge of the material to be taught, a mature mastery of a variety of teaching procedures, an understanding of his pupils, and the quality of judgment that will enable him to blend all in making decisions.[4]

The good teacher thus encourages the student to explore interesting topics and problems. He makes it possible for the learners to utilize rich materials and specific skills which will lead to fruitful experiences. This tends to provide the momentum for grappling with various types of problems in the future.

The social studies teacher has a significant role to play in the guidance of students in our secondary school. He works with students in the classroom, as a homeroom teacher, and in other activities such as sports. The teacher cooperates with the guidance counselor, parents, and supervisor in assisting students with their educational activities and problems. In this way the student is helped to know and develop his abilities and to recognize and accept his limitations.

A good guidance program should include the following basic services:

Inventory Service. Emphasis is placed upon a system of accurate and complete pupil records that accentuate the uniqueness of the individual pupil.

Information Service. Information in the areas of occupational, educational, and personal-social guidance is made available to teachers and pupils.

---

[4] Educational Policies Commission, *The Central Purpose of American Education* (Washington, D.C.: National Education Association, 1961), p. 17.

Counseling Service. For an effective program, individual counseling must be available to all pupils.

Placement Service. This service assists pupils in the selection of appropriate occupations, educational institutions, and work experiences.

Follow-up Service. A continuing follow-up of former students is one means of evaluating and improving the effectiveness of the school program.[5]

The varied skills of the guidance staff are focused upon helping teachers to: (1) increased understanding of all youth, the normal development of adolescents, and the changes and problems which growing up in today's world brings; (2) study and analysis of the particular youth in classrooms, and the community backgrounds which make the population of this school different from others; and (3) study and help with individual adolescents who do not seem to be responding to the usual services provided by the school and about whom teachers are puzzled or baffled.

These three major skills are accomplished through conferences and in-service activities with teachers, to assist them in developing competencies in observing and studying adolescents; planning and carrying out school-wide testing programs; interpreting the results and implications of test scores; compiling and using cumulative record information; studying and planning for adolescents with special needs; recognizing the special resources in school and community to meet the requirements of adolescents with exceptional needs; working with parents to understand the backgrounds of adolescents and their uniqueness, and to help parents in the guidance of young people; and knowing the community and its influences upon youth, and understanding its resources for the development and guidance of youth.

The guidance program aims to assist youth to understand themselves and their problems; enable young people to make good use of their personal and environmental resources; and help youth to make wise choices in dealing with problems of adjustment now and in the future.

These aims are accomplished through various activities: individual conferences with students, to interpret information leading to self-insight; group conferences and meetings in which such guidance information as test results and vocational opportunities is presented; individual and group conferences with parents, to help them understand their children's abilities and potentials; and organization plans for a student-teacher ratio which will enable adolescents to be known to their teachers, and which will encourage personalization of relationships.[6]

The Student Teacher

Student teaching is an important phase of the prospective teacher's preparation for entering the teaching profession. It should be a most enjoyable, profitable, and rewarding experience for the individual at the

[5]*The Curriculum in the Prince George's County Public Schools . . . A Graphic Presentation* (Upper Marlboro, Maryland: The Board of Education, 1960), p. 13.

[6] California Test Bureau, *Guiding Today's Youth* (Los Angeles: Los Angeles County Schools, 1962), pp. 334-35. Copyright © 1961 by California Test Bureau. Reprinted by permission of California Test Bureau, Del Monte Research Park, Monterey, Cal.

threshold of a teaching career. In view of this step in the initial period of his teaching career, observation is most helpful.

Value of observation

The student teacher as well as those new to the profession should devote considerable time to the observation of teaching. Watching the performance of a competent, experienced teacher constitutes a definite and important step in the training of the prospective teacher.

Teacher training institutions should establish a broad observation program including laboratory experiences for their students in addition to the observations in the laboratory school. Small groups can be taken by their supervisor to observe in different types of schools. Observations outside their major fields should be encouraged since in most cases such visits are very profitable. The prospective teacher should evaluate and engage in a little reflective thinking in the light of what he observed and compare it with the ideal learning situation. The result of such a program will find a student with a broader view of the learning situation.

Student teaching

Preliminary Observations.   After the student receives his assignment for student teaching, he will be expected to observe classes for one or two weeks before he begins his actual teaching. These observations under his cooperating teacher will be especially important to him and vital to his success as a student teacher. They should be concerned with specific details to a greater degree than were his previous observations. He must now be on the alert to notice more carefully all phases of instructional procedures and classroom management. He should study the unit being taught, discover what approach is being made by the cooperating teacher, and what techniques and activities are being applied. He should find out how and when assignments are made and the method employed in taking attendance, in passing out supplies, and in controlling light and ventilation.

The student teacher should study the pupils of the class, learn their names, and try to understand the general characteristics of each individual. He should become familiar with the layout of the classroom and the seating arrangement. He should ascertain the extent of the bulletin board space and the use being made of it, the laboratory equipment available and where it is stored, and the textbooks and supplementary books being used. During this period, the student should obtain and practice using the equipment necessary for efficient classroom organization and routine. He should help the training teacher by correcting papers; regulating light, temperature, and ventilation; and by working with individual pupils or groups.

Orientation.   Certain general principles and procedures should guide the establishment and operation of the student teaching program. It would be unfair to expect a student teacher to undertake a full schedule of classes immediately. He should never be required to handle more than three classes, and these should not be thrust upon him simultaneously. He first undertakes one class, following the procedure outlined below. At least one week should elapse before he begins his second, and another week before his third.

As a means of orienting the student teacher to the specific conditions under which he will be working, the cooperating teacher must acquaint him with all materials and tools to be used. The cooperating teachers' own semester outline or plan book should be fully explained and placed at the disposal of the student teacher in order that he may familiarize himself with the subject matter being taught in that particular course.

The student teacher should observe the work in progress for at least the first week so that he may begin making the adjustment to the teaching-learning situation.

The cooperating teacher should hold conferences with the student teacher, each day if possible, before he takes over the class. These conferences should be concerned with lesson planning, methods, the nature of the class, and the materials being used. Fundamental and definite goals should be established and made clear to the student teacher.

The major objective in this situation should be a friendly and helpful, relationship between the cooperating teacher and the student teacher.

If the teaching is to be done in a school where the pupils are not accustomed to student teachers, the cooperating teacher should prepare the class for the new situation by informing them that a student teacher will take charge for a few weeks and that he, the cooperating teacher, expects the same type of cooperation with the student teacher that they have given him.

Suggestions for the student teacher

Plan to devote your entire time to your new undertaking. Unless your schedule is so arranged that you must also take college courses simultaneously, you will be expected to be on the job during the entire school day. It is not enough to be prompt. Be early. Also be on hand after school for conferences or to assist with activities. Reduce your social activities to a minimum, watch your diet and your health, and get a good night's sleep.

Provide yourself with a notebook to be kept exclusively for a comprehensive record of your student teaching. Include in it such items as class seating chart; daily and weekly schedule; copies of your daily plan; records of all conferences, observations, criticisms, and so on.

Plan each day's lesson completely and thoroughly, including every detail. Have each plan approved by your cooperating teacher sufficiently in advance to allow you to make any necessary corrections.

Accept responsibility willingly and cheerfully. You should contribute something of value to the school. Enter into its spirit. Make yourself as useful as you can but avoid any appearance of forcing yourself or your ideas on others.

Welcome criticism and accept it graciously. Never advance alibis for your shortcomings. Make a determined effort to correct all deficiencies.

Learn to evaluate your own performance. Start by evaluating each lesson as soon as it is finished, and strive to reach the point where you can evaluate as you proceed and adjust yourself to changing conditions.

Special attention should be given to speech and diction. The importance of a well-modulated voice cannot be over-emphasized. Try to cultivate a pleasant classroom voice.

Management of classroom and equipment is an important aspect of teaching. Special attention should be given to such routine matters as lighting, ventilation, seating arrangements, and location of teaching aids.

Student teaching

When the student teacher first assumes the teaching responsibility, the cooperating teacher should assist him by making sure that all is in readiness.

The cooperating teacher must be patient. He should strive for a gradual improvement. As a general rule, one goal should be achieved before passing on to the next.

After the teaching techniques proposed by the cooperating teacher in the preliminary conferences have been mastered, the student teacher should be led to strive for procedures that are sound, creative, and imaginative.

The cooperating teacher should at all times be a teacher, philosopher, and friend. He should instill faith, self-confidence, and the feeling of freedom and independence. Once the student teacher develops the feeling of self-reliance, the way is opened for the development of leadership, cooperation, and loyalty.

Further aids for the student teacher

Student teaching can be invaluable as a training device. The student teacher can profit tremendously by following three key words; promptness, courtesy, and cooperation—promptness in arriving at school, starting the lesson on time, arriving for conferences, and submitting all plans and reports—courtesy to all whom he may meet in the course of his work; pupils, supervisors, and fellow teachers. Cooperation carries power for success in any phase of the teaching process.

Time is the most valuable thing a student teacher possesses and should be used with the fullest assurance of return. Time devoted to one's work is never lost. Every successful teacher is a busy and enthusiastic person. Ask yourself, "Am I making the most of my time?"

A sense of humor eases tension and provides for greater learning. The cheerful teacher is usually a happy and well-adjusted individual.

Friendliness, like enthusiasm, attracts pupils and fellow teachers. One can be pleasant and yet diplomatic in dealing with pupils. Stubbornness makes it difficult to deal with a person or a problem. Self-confidence and interest can do much to increase a teacher's value. The teacher who is out of step with a group's interest is lost.

If new approaches are undertaken during the practice teaching period, they should be encouraged by the supervisor. All social studies instruction should be made interesting and meaningful for the students. Be interested yourself in all phases of the work. Correlate the lesson with something the pupils are familiar with in their own lives and in which they are already interested. Always listen to suggestions from the students. Try using colorful material. Remember that history, for instance, is not all dates and names. Encourage originality as well as discussion and opinion.

For the student teacher as well as the beginning teacher pupil-teacher relationships are of major importance. The achievement of the teacher may be determined by this important factor while working with students in the various activities. It takes experience and sound reasoning to build the proper working atmosphere with students.

Skilful handling of human relations in the classroom is a many-sided activity, challenging the best efforts of the ablest teacher. He needs all the knowledge and understanding of human variation that he can get. He needs an over-all view of the range of normality as it is found both in any one stage of human development and in the sequences of development. He needs to understand that individual and group behavior is caused. He needs to develop attitudes of acceptance of individual learners as they are and, at the same time, he must seek to make them different. He needs to learn that one of the ever-present problems of the teacher is to strike a fair balance between attention to the needs of "individuals in a group" and the common needs of "a group of individuals." He needs to weigh carefully his responsibility for deciding when conformity is appropriate and desirable and when it is not; he needs also to help his students learn to form their own judgments on that point. He must carry responsibility for pupil-pupil relations as well as for pupil-teacher relationships, all involving complex interindividual and intraindividual patterns of thought and action.[7]

The teacher and discipline

The student teacher as well as the beginning teacher will through guidance and experience learn to direct the educative process. The skillful and effective teacher handles his own problems immediately in the teaching-learning process and in a very practical manner. The control of any laboratory or classroom situation is directly a part of good teacher-student relations. This connotes what is meant by a desirable learning environment. With an active and interested group any phase of discipline is kept to a minimum or is nonexistent.

The inexperienced teacher should learn always to deal with problems in an intelligent and common-sense manner. This calls for knowing the students well and showing a personal interest in each individual student. Friendliness, cooperation, and the proper guidance can foster desirable attitudes on the part of the students toward the work. The teacher furnishes the momentum and the proper motivation for students in gaining educational experiences.

The teacher allows for flexibility in the program or unit, recognizes individual differences, fosters effective skills for acquiring knowledge, and utilizes the constributions of the students to enlarge learning. In short, the good teacher tries to involve every student actively in the topic or problem being studied. The student is interested and curious to explore and think critically. With this kind of classroom atmosphere, discipline is shunted to the background and continuous learning is the outcome. Rules and harsh words are not always the answers to discipline problems. Respect, encouragement, fairness, and effective instruction are the approaches used in the modern classroom.

Supervision of the student teacher

Constructive and skilled supervision of the student teacher is essential since the future success and development of the student teacher rests upon it. The cooperating teacher is charged with the responsibility of

---

[7] E. J. Swenson, *Instruction* "Teacher Preparation," *Individualizing Instruction,* National Society for the Study of Education, 61st Yearbook, Part I (Chicago: The University of Chicago Press, 1962), chap. XV, pp. 293-294. Quoted by permission of the Society.

guiding the experiences during the student teaching period. He is a significant figure in shaping the path of the inexperienced teacher. The college supervisor in his supervising visits and conferences can provide sympathetic counsel and help to build the initial confidence that is so essential for the student teacher.

The competence developed during student teaching will in many ways shape the procedure and techniques employed by the individual in his professional career; However, experience and continuous evaluation will facilitate the teacher's growth and his future achievements in working ،with youth.

Certain basic factors must be present before the student teacher undertakes his apprenticeship.

1. A deep interest in his subject matter field, in the teaching profession, and in his desire for professional growth
2. Intellectual preparation for professional proficiency
3. Orientation to a modern teacher's actual place in the educational scheme
4. Observation of modern techniques and effective methods appropriate to the major field in which the teacher intends to teach
5. Sympathetic understanding of youth
6. An awareness of the trends and events shaping current civilization

The cooperating teacher must consider these factors in his initial appraisal of the student teacher and in providing a program for his professional growth.

The supervising or cooperating teacher can further help the beginning or student teacher in the following ways:[8]

1. He helps the beginning teacher find purpose in his teaching.
2. He furthers the beginning teacher's sensitivity to individual students and the dynamics of the classroom.
3. He enables the beginning teacher to vitalize instruction.
4. He gives the student teacher a view of teaching as learning.
5. He influences the student to act professionally.

It is through conferences, planning instruction, and observation of the student teacher in the actual teaching-learning process that the individual's work can be guided. Steady growth can be observed by the student teacher himself through the avenue of self evaluation and by the cooperating teacher's estimation of the progress being achieved. The ultimate goal is the foundation which will enable a good teacher to achieve excellence with further experience. Professional accomplishment and constant growth is a goal for the modern social studies teacher.

---

[8] J. D. McNeil, "What is the Role of the Teacher of Teachers," *CTA Journal,* LV, No. 5 (May 1959), 27-29. Reprinted with permission from *CTA Journal.* © by California Teachers Association.

Professional growth

All teachers strive for growth in their profession, the beginning as well as the experienced teacher. A good teacher takes inventory and evaluates his own growth and development. He welcomes the opportunity for improvement through those activities and experiences that are really beneficial. The social studies teacher realizes that he must be competent in his field. He must know his pupils, how to guide them and evaluate their progress. He appreciates the fact that society is ever changing and current ideas in his profession are developing newer materials and techniques. To cope with the dynamics of social studies instruction, the teacher must remain a student, an observer, a listener, an explorer, a research worker, and a cooperative individual. He must possess a "forward view" or else become lost in the rapid rate of progress in our contemporary civilization. There are various avenues to professional growth to suit the tastes of the teacher.

A program for growth

Some ideas for professional growth might include the following: an organized reading program; firsthand experimentation and research; planned travel, tours, and excursions; active participation in civic and professional organizations; attendance at conferences, workshops, institutes, educational meetings, and state and national conventions; visiting cultural centers, historical shrines, museums, public and private libraries; hobbies and leisure time activities; and further graduate work leading to an advanced degree. Space in this volume will not permit an extensive treatment of all these means for growth; however, a few may be mentioned.

Organized Professional Groups. These are local, state, regional, and national professional organizations that contribute toward the social studies teachers' professional growth. Among the national organizations of most importance to the social studies teacher are the following:

(a) *The National Education Association,* generally known as the NEA, is the largest organized group of teachers in the world. It represents the interests of teachers of the United States, formulates and coordinates educational policies, and interprets the profession to the public. A subscription to its Journal, published monthly during the school year, is included in the membership fee. It also publishes materials relating specifically to the social studies.

(b) *The National Council for the Social Studies* is the professional organization of social studies teachers. Through its series of regularly scheduled meetings, research, regular and occasional publications, and the encouragement and articulation of smaller groups, it has done much to aid the growth of social studies teachers and to improve social studies instruction. Its official journal, *Social Education*, published monthly during the school year, and its yearbooks are most helpful to teachers. In addition many other pamphlets and bulletins are published from time to time. All contain much material of practical value to the social studies teacher.

(c) *The National Council of Geography Teachers* contributes a great deal to all social studies teachers. Its official organ, *The Journal of Geography*, published monthly during the school year, contains much factual material on geography as well as practical suggestions for enrichment, units, and other professional information.

Reading Program.   Keeping informed with professional literature, and in particular that relating to the social studies field, is important for the teacher. A sweep of the field includes: professional journals, yearbooks, bulletins, reports, reported studies, biographies, methods texts, histories, and books in related fields. The literature is plentiful, and the teacher may be selective in connection with his own immediate purpose. The teacher will be his own guide to enriching his knowledge through reading.

Research Avenues.   The teacher uses research as a part of his teaching. Each teacher has in his own particular situation the opportunity to experiment and investigate various learning situations. There are many ways in which research can be applied in the social studies: curriculum evaluation and study, building units of work, developing new techniques for instruction, studying the needs and problems of pupils, the many interests, hobbies, and study habits of a particular classroom group, compiling resource guides, evaluating and studying the resources of the local community, organizing bibliographies for special topics or a course, and exploring newer evaluation techniques.

The Workshop.   Many teachers participate in workshops as a means of in-service training. This educational conference is usually conducted at a college where teachers gather to discuss problems and work with consultants. It may last a few days or a number of weeks, and a laboratory type of learning prevails. Groups may produce worthwhile materials which will prove helpful in curriculum revision. The teacher can derive valuable assistance from a workshop and improve his own instructional procedures.

Intervisitation.   Visiting other teachers and school systems is both an interesting and profitable venture. A program of intervisitation is possible in any social studies department and school program. It is always stimulating to see how other teachers teach, to observe other techniques and procedures, to compare materials, classrooms, and equipment. Such a program can be planned and conducted by the administration of a school system.

Travel. Travel is an essential experience for the social studies teacher. There are many opportunities for a teacher to enrich his education through traveling in the United States as well as in foreign countries. Guided tours of an educational nature are available in the summer for teachers who wish to combine study and travel. During recent years many countries have worked out a teacher exchange procedure with the United States whereby an American teacher may go abroad for a year of teaching, and a foreign teacher may come to America. Knowledge obtained through foreign study and travel may be developed into units of study that have a definite meaning and interest to pupils. More pupil interest will be developed if the teacher is able to talk in terms of actual travel experiences than if he has merely read up on the material being presented in class. Familiarity with historical sites, national shrines, geographical areas, and industrial sections of the country furnish both background knowledge and inspiration for the enrichment of social studies instruction. The good teacher has a desire for new knowledge and is constantly acquiring worthwhile information.

Further Study. The social studies teacher may pursue further study in his field. He can keep himself up to date on current materials and methods through occasional enrollment in extension classes or at college or university summer session. In the teaching field, emphasis is being placed currently on further study and additional degrees as a basis for promotion, and the teacher may do well to follow a definite program of graduate study.

The effectiveness of any program of professional growth on which the social studies teacher may embark will depend upon his skill and his consistency in selecting and arranging his program to suit his needs.

Department Chairman

The chairman of the social studies department must provide intelligent leadership, sympathetic guidance, and constructive assistance. Departmental relationships should be friendly, helpful, and conducive to professional growth. The modern supervisor is faced with no easy task. He must at times be an administrator, a leader, a counselor, a coordinator, a teacher, and a student.

An Administrator. The head of the department is an administrator and is responsible for carrying out the general educational policies of the school as they concern his department. His duties entail many kinds of clerical work, although he may delegate some phases of administrative detail to capable teachers. One of his most important duties is that of protecting his teachers, giving them inspiration and advice. His other responsibilities may include interviewing prospective teachers for his department, recommending the purchase of equipment and supplies, assigning classes, and arranging schedules of both teachers and pupils.

A Leader. Much has been made of the qualities of leadership. An incompetent leader can disorganize his followers and produce chaos. The schoolroom reflects the ability of a teacher in this respect: one can read the results in the aspect and demeanor of the pupils. The qualities of direction, drive, and ability to secure a following are needed by teachers, supervisors, and principals.

The department chairman must maintain the highest quality of instruction in all courses under his supervision. To achieve this end, he must furnish intellectual and professional leadership for the members of his staff by keeping informed of progress and trends in education. Among his duties as a leader may be included the arrangement of worth-while departmental meetings, the establishment and maintenance of a departmental library, and the organization of professional improvement programs. The department chairman is chosen for his integrity of character and purpose rather than because of seniority, politics, or other considerations. He is chosen because he has demonstrated his ability to get the results he has in mind. He rules not by force of authority but by securing cheerful cooperation. His pupils and fellow teachers will be inspired to take a serious view of any problems presented by him; and if the proposals of others have merit, he is quick to recognize it. Instead of exerting authority to get results quickly, he is willing to await with patience the more secure results of a gradual learning process.

A Teacher. The good supervisor should be a master teacher of students. He should carry out experimental and demonstration teaching to avoid becoming stale in his profession, and to aid his teachers by concrete examples. He should be able to supervise and direct the growth of student teachers in his department and should hold himself responsible for the orientation of each new staff member.

A Counselor. The supervisor is a counselor for his teachers. He must be ready to give assistance with their problems and to strive for practical and satisfactory solutions. He must be approachable. Teachers, students, and parents should not be discouraged from seeking his advice even on personal problems. His guidance and counsel should also be readily given to outsiders who wish help.

A Coordinator. The department chairman acts as a coordinator within his department and within the school. Within his own department, he is responsible for the coordination of instructional detail. He should set up the principles to be followed in the planning of instruction, should appoint and assist committees for the organization of course outlines, and should aid and encourage his teachers to establish uniform policies for tests, marking, written work, make-up work, and homework. Within the school, he should cooperate with other departments and the library in coordinating their separate contributions into a complete and unified whole.

A Student. The supervisor is a student of education, of his subject, and of human nature. He studies individual differences among his students and among his teachers. He travels, attends conventions, reads professional and current literature, and keeps up-to-date on local, state, national, and world affairs. He does occasional research, contributes to professional journals, and from time to time takes an extra college or university course. He learns from his teachers and from his pupils and continues to grow in his profession.

Supervision and the Teacher

The nature of supervision

Supervision is concerned with the improvement of instruction. It is a means of assistance in developing effective procedures and broadening the scope of instruction. Supervision aids teachers in evaluating their own teaching competency and growth. It is in reality a team-work type of activity among co-workers for both the beginning and the experienced teacher in professional development.

Supervision today, then, is concerned with all of the conditions of learning. It is a democratic enterprise and is rooted in the capacity of human beings for cooperation, creativity, and continuous growth. It stresses service, leadership, coordination among peers, and vision to help increase the level of aspiration for the improvement of living.[9]

Supervision is a democratic and cooperative process that entails the working with people involved in the process of education. It arises from

[9] M. E. Swearingen, *Supervision of Instruction: Foundations and Dimensions* (Boston: Allyn and Bacon, Inc., 1962), p. 25. Copyright 1962 by Allyn and Bacon, Inc. Reprinted by permission of the publisher.

educational needs and includes some major continuing functions: coordination of efforts; provision of leadership; extension of experience; stimulation of creative effort; facilitation and evaluation of change; analysis of learning situations; contribution to a body of professional knowledge; and integration of goals.[10]

New developments in education on all fronts together with the new methods, materials, and devices for learning stimulate a wide sweep of activities relative to supervision. Creativity in operation holds a key to improving instruction for today and tomorrow.

The teacher is interested in obtaining recognition and acquiring a substantial measure of achievement in his work. He enjoys a friendly and inviting atmosphere to achieve and advance his efforts. He hopes for a high degree of accomplishment in his endeavors. He wishes to contribute his share in the cooperative ventures of a group, assist in curriculum building, planning special projects and general activities of a school system. A good measure of security is a significant factor in building confidence for the teacher in his instructional situation. Effective communications and the opportunity for sharing new ideas are important considerations. An expression of appreciation for a job well done is most gratifying for the individual teacher as well as for a committee. These are some of the facets to the creative approach in supervision of the educational process through which the teacher is inspired and grows in professional competence.

Responsiblities of a supervisor

The duties of a supervisor are considerable in terms of helping teachers in the instructional process.

The main responsibilities of the supervisor may now be identified as of three kinds:

1. The responsibility to give individual help to the teacher
2. The responsibility to co-ordinate and make more available to all personnel the instructional services of the school
3. The responsibility to act as a resource person for the superintendent and other administrative personnel, as a special agent in training teachers in service, and as an interpreter of the school and its program both to school personnel and to the public[11]

Supervision in the modern sense focuses upon the improvement of the learning situation and attempts to provide a better type of education for all students. It calls for leadership, guidance, cooperation, and under-

---

[10] *Ibid.,* p. 42.

[11] J. M. Gwynn, *Theory and Practice of Supervision* (New York: Dodd, Mead & Company, Inc., 1961), p. 27. Reprinted by permission of Dodd, Mead & Company, Inc. Copyright © 1961 by Dodd, Mead & Company, Inc.

standing on the part of the supervisor, the teacher, and the learner. A good learning environment is essential if students are to reach their maximum achievement. The supervisor aids both the beginning and the experienced teacher in planning activities, building resources, selecting materials, developing units, formulating objectives, guiding students, developing experiences, directing evaluation, and facilitating growth.

Furthermore, teachers look to supervision for assistance and guidance in their work. They need and appreciate the following:

1. Some form of orientation to a new position or situation
2. Help in securing and using new instructional materials and audio-visual materials
3. Assistance in selecting and employing productive community resources for the instructional program
4. Help in handling the needs and problems of maladjusted pupils
5. Assistance in improving methods, procedures, and techniques employed in the learning process
6. Guidance in building a program for professional growth for the individual teacher
7. Direction in constructing units of work to fit the needs of a particular group of pupils
8. Access to professional literature such as journals, reports, studies, and books
9. Opportunities to observe excellence in teaching with the hope of improving their own teaching
10. Help in meeting the problem of individual differences in the groups being taught
11. Assistance in the use of the newer evaluation techniques
12. Guidance in gathering and interpreting information about each pupil

Conclusion

The modern social studies teacher is a competent educational leader in guiding the learning of youth. He is a creative and scholarly individual and assumes the all-important role of helping the student grow and achieve his established goals.

Only the learner can assure that he will learn. But the nature of the teaching-learning environment, its psychological climate, and the quality of interpersonal relationships can be determined to a great degree by the teacher and other adults whose task is to assist him. The stimulation, encouragement, enhancement, and guidance of learning are aspects of teacher leadership which, at its best, equals or exceeds any other in its requirements of personal attributes and professional competencies. The teacher is the official leader who, more than any other, is directly engaged in conducting the main business of the school—that of helping children to learn.[12]

---

[12] Association for Supervision and Curriculum Development, *Leadership for Improving Instruction,* 1960 Yearbook (Washington, D.C.: National Education Association, 1960), p. 109.

The skillful teacher effectively plans, directs, and evaluates his own work as well as that of the students. He employs a variety of modern procedures, materials, and equipment in furnishing the opportunity for his students to work in a cooperative manner, expand their interests, and improve their skills in research and in solving problems. He understands his students and provides individual guidance and encouragement whenever the occasion arises. The teacher is aware of the importance of good community, home, and school relationships. He enjoys with his students and their parents the many events and activities of the school and community. Professional growth through its many channels is a part of the teacher's own personal program. He cooperates with his colleagues and appreciates democratic supervision. The teacher, above all, remains an alert student in addition to a teacher in his profession.

Bibliography

Brown, T. J., *Student Teaching in a Secondary School.* New York: Harper & Row, Publishers, 1960.

Chandler, B. J., *Education and the Teacher.* New York: Dodd, Mead & Co., 1961.

Gwynn, J. M., *Theory and Practice of Supervision.* New York: Dodd, Mead & Co., 1961.

McGuire, V., R. B. Myers, and C. L. Durrance, *Your Student Teaching in the Secondary School.* Boston: Allyn and Bacon, Inc., 1959.

Stratemeyer, F. B. and M. Lindsey, *Working with Student Teachers.* New York: Bureau of Publications, Teachers College, Columbia University, 1958.

Townsend, E. A. and P. J. Burke, *Learning for Teachers.* New York: The Macmillan Company, 1962.

Wiles, K., *Teaching for Better Schools,* 2nd ed. Englewood Cliffs, N.J.: Prentice-Hall, Inc., 1959.

Chapter Seven

Planning the Learning Units

Effective planning for instruction in the social studies is of major importance since it assures continuity and provides direction for the teaching-learning process. It furnishes a solid foundation for the development of functional experiences for acquiring knowledge. For those who plan, it is essential that consideration be given to the purpose of education, the objectives of the social studies and the goals for developing effective citizenship. Planning furnishes the opportunity for evaluating what has transpired and provides a forward directive for new viewpoints.

One of the primary purposes of the social studies is the development of effective citizenship and teaching the student to think critically.

The security of this nation requires education for all pupils, their preparation for the duties of citizenship, and their acceptance of its opportunities and responsibilities. The teaching of the basic knowledges and skills is fundamental, but more is necessary. Civic, esthetic, moral, and spiritual values should be strengthened. Creative talents should be nurtured. Critical thinking must be fostered. Economic and vocational education must be provided. All pupils must be challenged and must be developed to the full extent of their abilities and aptitudes.[1]

---

[1] *Emphasis upon Citizenship and Patriotism, Grades Ten, Eleven, and Twelve,* Curriculum Bulletin, No. 113 (Fort Worth, Texas: Fort Worth Public Schools, 1961), p. 1.

Modern planning fosters research, generates ideas, increases efficiency and opens the door to the examination of new knowledge for instructional purposes. It provides an opportunity to use new materials and furnishes insights to the application of old materials in new and effective ways. Planning furnishes guidance for the curriculum builders and the teacher when constructing a program of study. Evaluation techniques are utilized to determine the value of materials, experiences, resources and procedures under consideration.

Kinds of planning

In terms of the social studies we can list the following types of planning; semester or year planning, unit planning that may consume a large block of time or the smaller units or unit, long range preplanning for a considerable period ahead and the daily lesson plan as a part of the unit studied. Daily lesson planning is a continuous process as the stages of the unit are being developed.

Planning for the social studies is reflected in the resource guides or curriculum handbooks. Such guides are aimed at the improvement of instruction. It involves both long-range planning, as in the course outline or the unit of instruction, and the short-term planning, as in the daily lesson plan.

Before an effective plan can be evolved for any proposed learning experience, the planner must have clearly in mind a definite idea of what he hopes to accomplish. As applied to instructional planning, these goals are usually referred to as objectives. These objectives are the outcomes—what the learners and teacher working as a team will hope to develop and achieve to their fullest.

Long range and preplanning

Good social studies teachers give considerable thought to the preplanning of their work in order to insure effective instruction to meet the needs of youth. Planning necessitates that the teacher be aware of the needs and abilities of a group in order that he may organize the learning around functional experiences to bring about desirable changes in students. Through the organizing and planning of learning activities, the teacher becomes aware of the vast content areas available in the social studies. The teacher must also give some time to research for new materials as well as to experiment with new procedures.

The building of a program or a course in the social studies to meet the needs of youth is a gradual and continuous process. It calls for much research and experimentation. The selection of content, resources, audio-visual material, and experiences to meet the grade level of the group is important. The number of units to be planned will be determined around the time factor.

With the utilization of such methods as the socialized recitation, the problem and project methods, and the laboratory method, the recognition of the desirability of using many instructional materials and resources, and the conception of democratic education as pupil-centered, the teacher becomes increasingly responsible for the organization and adaptation of content materials to fit specific situations.

Course of study and guides

The course of study or instruction guide provides a directive for the teacher. These guides may be prepared by the local school district or the state department of education. They are organized to assist the teacher in planning, organizing, and directing the learning process of his students. Guides are usually flexible and are intended chiefly to serve as a source of practical suggestions. A social studies guide or course of study has the materials organized as to units for study. Reference sources and suggested activities for learning experiences are also included. It is intended that the teacher utilize such guide materials and information to improve the instructional program.

The planning of course outlines should be based upon consideration of many factors: the needs, abilities, and interests of the students; the other courses of the social studies curriculum; the time allotment for the course; modern aims of education; current trends and objectives in similar courses; and materials and facilities actually or potentially available.

The unit

Units for learning have been classified as "Subject Matter Units" and "Experience Units"; however, more recently we have heard of "Process Units." Educational literature also lists the so-called "Resource Units," "Source Units," "Activity Units," "Problem Units," and others as patterns for organization. Trends indicate teachers are planning and utilizing more problems and questions in stating the unit theme. Units tend to be more functional for the learner, with emphasis upon worth-while experiences. Many problems studied lead directly into other similar topics, or it may happen that in the course of studying a problem the students and teacher might retitle the problem and explore in a new direction where fresh interests are revealed.

A good unit conforms to the needs, interests, abilities, and maturity level of students. It possesses intellectual and social content, is organized around a central problem, and draws upon related subject field for pertinent data. The unit has a place in the order of teaching, related to what is before and after in more or less logical continuity. Instead of a place for reciting lessons, the classroom becomes an actual laboratory for learning where work is planned and organized around functional units. The problem-solving approach is employed in all learning in order to insure behavior changes within the group. Constructing and evaluating the good unit is a cooperative student-teacher endeavor. Student-teacher relationships are thus improved by giving the student the feeling he is a co-discoverer of useful ideas and generalizations with an opportunity to make progress in the tool subjects.

The learner and the unit

Learners have much at stake in identifying, selecting, planning, and executing the unit. The learner should have actual practice in selecting problems, with guidance being supplied by the teacher. In this way he will be encouraged to do original thinking and develop skills to cope with his own needs. Research skills are sharpened and directly tied to the learning as the unit develops. Interests are enlivened when real life situations that are meaningful to the pupils comprise the experiences. It might be said that the more difficult the problems that grow out of a unit are, the more interesting it will be for rapid learners. At the same time, slower learners will progress satisfactorily with less difficult problems. Students will encounter difficulty in the process of solving a problem; they will sample many resources and will draw upon past knowledge to meet the new situation or problem. The training and rich learning through problem-solving which the student has had in the learning laboratory will aid him in developing an approach and framing his own techniques for attacking expanding problems in later life.

Planning the unit

The fact that the students are concerned with planning the unit does not relieve the teacher of the responsibility for making a detailed plan in advance. The inexperienced teacher should formulate a plan rich in every detail for any unit he proposes to teach. Only after he has thought through all details will he be able to guide the students in planning their undertaking intelligently. Although his plan should be sufficiently complete, he should not consider it inflexible. The alert teacher will no doubt consider the nature of the unit and the ability of the group to participate in the over-all planning. The students themselves, if inspired to participate wholeheartedly, will frequently have many worth-while suggestions that should be followed if possible. Some experienced teachers feel that the first stages of cooperative unit planning should not be too detailed, only a general, basic plan.

The procedure for teaching such a unit may include the introduction or beginning of the unit, the developmental process, and the concluding or culminating stage of the unit. In each step of the procedure the teacher learns much about each member of the group. The wise teacher will provide opportunities for each student to contribute and enjoy success and satisfaction from learning within the unit study. Experiences projected by students are valuable as they express their own feelings about the topic. All steps of learning utilize audio-visual materials, library sources, different procedures and activities, and evaluation techniques. It is important to see that objectives were achieved to the satisfaction of all concerned, also that rich knowledge was acquired and desirable habits, skills, and attitudes were developed.

A Unit Form

The framework or structure for organizing a unit or area of emphasis should receive due consideration. Each unit generally stresses a particular theme or topic for development in a flexible manner. The following form can serve as a guide in planning the unit.

    I. Title (theme, problem, or topic)
   II. Objectives (clearly stated and functional)
  III. Overview (interesting and stimulating)
  IV. Outline of content (well selected and functional)
   V. Activities and experiences (variety—utilizing the skills and talents of the group)
  VI. Culmination (drawing conclusions and clarifying understanding)
 VII. Evaluation (means of appraisal by appropriate devices)
VIII. Instructional Resources (reference materials, audio-visual materials and community resources)

A creative approach should be followed when building a unit of work. The skill with which the teachers carry through the original organization of the unit can be most important. Selectivity and evaluation are essential factors when building a unit—as is adaptability to the expressions of interest by the group.

Guide sheets

Guide sheets can be used as a vehicle for a group when studying a problem. These mimeographed sheets furnish an outline for the work and thereby provide some direction for the students. The title of the problem is usually stated and some guiding objectives are formulated. An introductory statement of the problem stimulates group interest and arouses curiosity. Suggested topics and questions for individual and group study are helpful as an aid to reflective thinking and research. Some teachers provide a guide sheet that contains both required and optional activities for exploration. The optional activities and suggested learning experiences related to the problem may be a means for meeting the interests of the more capable learner. Interest may be stimulated by having the group cooperatively discover other projects which they can add to the guide sheet. Teachers should see that each student is extending library and research skills. All guide sheets should be sufficiently flexible to allow for changes in the sequence of learning or for the inclusion of additional material. They aid in effective student-teacher planning and in developing good work habits and study skills. The teacher should be alert to assist students in locating and organizing information. He must see that each student utilizes his time profitably and does his planning effectively. He must assist the individual in establishing goals which he can attain through success and achievement in his work.

Planning and using resources

The challenge of selecting and planning units of work calls for a plentiful supply of resources. The modern teacher will consult many references and sources to organize materials for effective instruction on the unit or area of emphasis. He will strive to develop an adequate content outline to serve as the core of the unit. Securing and organizing learning resources that will aid the students in helping in the solving of a selected problem is an important consideration.

The teacher or a committee may be contemplating the revision of a unit or the building of a new one for a course and also to fit the needs of the students at a particular grade level. There are several sources which may aid in the planning of such a unit. The more recent instructional guides, bulletins, and courses of study for a state and a school system contain much excellent source materials. The guides for a program or a specific course usually contain a rich store of ideas, examples, and suggestions pertaining to the outline of content, suggested activities, learning experiences, procedures, primary sources, basic references, selected references and audio-visual materials. The materials contained in professional journals, yearbooks of the various professional organizations, modern textbooks, and resource units are rich in suggestions for guiding the production of a new unit.

However, the teacher should not expect that he can take a source unit of any kind and use it intact and unchanged. Each unit of instruction must be worked out by the teacher himself for a particular group. Even an original unit must be modified and revised to fit the conditions of the moment. Seldom, if ever, can the unit of the previous year be used as it stands, although it makes an excellent basis for planning. The resource unit is necessarily a more comprehensive and systematic division of subject matter that can be taught, for it represents a reservoir of materials, ideas, and general information out of which to shape a teaching unit. The resource unit is prepared by the teachers and covers a broad area, suggesting numerous possibilities for stimulating group interest. The teacher should compile all sorts of data, including bibliographies, to help him in establishing a unit of instruction. He may wish to share certain areas of his resources with the group by bibliographical lists or the assignment of selected readings.

Activities and experiences

There are many opportunities for selecting activities and worthwhile learning experiences in social studies instruction. These may be classified as individual, small group or committee, and those that include the entire group. Also there are teacher activities that include situations in which he is the center or focal point for directing learning, and the students are actively listening, observing, and learning. When studying a unit, activities fall into a sequence; unification, interest-holding, and continuity of development that relates functional experience to integrated learning. One of the principal things that the teacher must keep in mind is that activities must be related to objectives; if that relationship is not maintained, there is no direction to the learning process. Specific directions must be given by the teacher for all types of activities engaged in by the group. Following is a list of activities from which the social studies teacher and group may select those that will meet their needs: participating in group discussions, panels, debates, forums, and dramatizations; viewing films, filmstrips, slides, and television; organizing diagrams, charts, maps, models, and graphs; creating pictures, posters, poems, slogans, plays and stories; writing summaries, outlines, and notebook content; listening to lectures, music, reports, radio programs, and recordings; constructing exhibits, models, objects, and specimens; reading books, newspapers, pamphlets, and magazines; planning field trips, surveys, interviews, lectures by resource people, and assembly programs; preparing tackboard displays, murals, friezes, group newspapers, research projects, pageants, and radio scripts; evaluating individual and group progress, materials, units, issues, and problems.

Reports

Reporting to the group can be effective in the learning process, especially in presenting the results of research, study, and planning related to work in progress. If properly planned, such reports serve to enrich and enliven the learning situation, to stimulate student growth and supplement instructional materials. Both oral and written reports require research and organization before they are ready to accomplish their purpose. Presenting the report to the group gives the student excellent training in self-expression, leadership, poise, and mental alertness. Careful preparation should be made to avoid duplication and losing the group's interest. Reports will do much to balance individual student differences; those who are capable of pursuing an exhaustive search may do so, and those limited in vision are given the opportunity of selecting problems and issues that do not require extensive reading and research. The accent should always be on functional learning and student growth.

Committees and preparation

Careful planning by the teacher is essential when students select problems or topics for research and study. This entails some delineation and definition of the problem, relating it to materials being studied in the unit, and obtaining adequate and available materials for such a report. The selection of a problem can be made by the students themselves with guidance or by students and teacher cooperating for the purpose of assuring its merit. Care should be taken to see that the problem is in keeping with the committee's interests, needs, and activities. The students then plan a guide for their attack on the problem. This is an important phase of the group activity at the junior high school level. The committee assignment has some advantages over the individual assignment. In the case of the individual report, the student is confronted with the necessity of doing something for which he alone is responsible. He must gather a mass of scattered information, analyze and evaluate it, and make plans for its effective presentation. On the other hand, a committee can share the total responsibility. They enjoy working together and developing skills in social interaction. When a small group collaborates on a problem, each student undertakes a phase of the topic for study under the supervision of a leader or chairman. The teacher must evaluate each group process to assure progress in the work. The chairman may present to the teacher an outline or schedule of work. The committee members can each present a portion of the final findings.

Students who are not accustomed to organizing and presenting reports will, in the initial stages, need a considerable amount of guidance from the teacher. Their attention should be called to the probable sources of information found in the bibliography for the unit. The teacher should emphasize that newspapers, pamphlets, and periodicals should be consulted as well as reference books. One or more laboratory periods spent in the library will prove helpful for initial preparation and provide a good opportunity for individual guidance. Also references can be utilized in the classroom by the groups. Some time should be devoted to showing pupils how to organize materials and how to select and use illustrative material effectively. The development of such skills is usually retained and will pay dividends for the group. The advantages of working from an outline should be stressed, whether the report is written or presented orally from notes.

Presenting materials and discussion

Reporting the findings of research should follow proper procedures of presentation. Usually one of the committee members, acting as chairman, assumes the responsibility for planning the report. However, the teacher, as the consultant, cooperates with the leader and the committee members in directing the reporting procedure. Each report should be illustrated with outline materials written on the chalkboard, by a tackboard display, graphic materials, and if desirable by other selected audio-visual materials relating to the title of the report. The chairman should exert his leadership to see that individual efforts relate one to another, that their presentations are clear and concise and that the lesson moves along properly. Students may speak from notes but must never read their material.

Much of the responsibility for the effective presentation of materials lies with the teacher, who must create the proper climate and setting. The teacher should channel the presentation in an orderly manner and clarify materials when deemed advisable as they relate to the unit or problem studied. Inevitably much of the student's presentation and approach will depend on the example the teacher has set for the group. Students should be encouraged to gather information by note-taking in order to be prepared for the discussion and evaluation process following the presentation. Some form of summary by the chairman is a most desirable practice. The group can establish basic criteria for their evaluation if so desired. A check list may be used by the students at the junior high school level. Such a device is aimed at achieving excellence in individual and group reporting. It tends to point up the key qualities most desired in presenting material to a group. Evaluating others emphasizes standards that may be applied to themselves in analyzing and pursuing new knowledge.

Written Reports. Student reports that are presented to the class may or may not be handed in after presentation. If students are to gain practice in speaking from notes in presenting these reports, they should not be required to write out their reports in full and submit them to the teacher. However, the written report also has a definite place in social studies instruction. It is an effective method of adjusting individual differences, and this factor should be taken into consideration both in assigning the topics and in grading the reports. Subjects for the written report may range all the way from a relatively minor phase of supplementary reference to a really difficult piece of research. The written report furnishes an excellent opportunity for the gifted pupil to display his talents and use his imagination in creative self-expression through illustrative material. Requirements for the written report in advanced classes should be extended to include the proper use of footnotes, quotations, and bibliographies.

Planning the learning—"daily lesson"

Planning the Daily Lesson.   Styles in planning have changed greatly in the modern school. Time was when the written detailed "daily lesson plan" was the *sine qua non* for every teacher who hoped to satisfy a supervisor, and the "plan book" was a more important part of the teaching-learning situation than the students themselves. Long-range planning has succeeded the daily plan as a frame of reference for learning activities. The experienced teacher plans for himself rather than for the supervisor and writes as much or as little as he needs. In fact, strict adherence to a lesson plan disturbs the beginning teacher and furnishes the basis for a dull and uninteresting lesson. A guide or functional outline can be written on a few cards which the beginning teacher can refer to when necessary. This outline sketch of a lesson will give an analysis of the problem to be found in the particular unit and has to be important and relevant enough to be of concern to the class. Why it is interesting and how it fits into the program should be stated. Anticipated outcomes are also useful to the teacher. A short list of suggested questions to review the previous day's work and tie it with today's activities will afford clues of immediate value.

The "Daily Lesson" and the Unit. When the instruction in a particular course is arranged as a series of units, each "daily lesson" becomes simply a part of the larger unit. It might, therefore, seem to the beginning teacher that no further daily planning is necessary. However, the work of the unit will seldom proceed under its own power without loss of momentum, regardless of how complete the unit plan may be, unless some form of daily schedule or plan of activities is provided. This daily schedule may be noted on the guide sheet, at least tentatively, by both students and teacher as they plan for the unit. In this case, little extra daily planning on the part of the teacher will be needed beyond making sure that the cooperative schedule is working as planned. In other situations the arrangement of work for the unit may make this advance scheduling of events impractical. The teacher, then, becomes responsible for a greater amount of specific planning of the daily activities.

The traditional practice of dividing the school day into a number of separate class periods also makes it advisable for the teacher to give some previous thought to the work for each day in each of his classes. Each meeting of the social studies class is sandwiched between other classes or activities. It therefore becomes difficult for pupils to maintain proper continuity of thought and activity from one day to the next. The experienced social studies teacher usually finds that planning for some form of introduction and summary for each class period is necessary.

Daily Planning and the Student Teacher. Although for the experienced teacher the daily plan may be merely a few words to provide a guide of what he and the pupils have planned, the beginning teacher will find it necessary to write down his plan for each day's lesson in more detail. As he grows with experience, he will develop short cuts of his own in planning and his plans will steadily become less detailed. He must begin his foundation for simplified planning upon a thorough knowledge of effective planning procedures. He soon learns the success of teacher-pupil planning depends a great deal upon his own guidance of the group. He is alert and helpful whenever needed in this important process. Planning involves a blueprint, so to speak, for selecting the most appropriate activities for effective learning. It becomes a channeling process for the work and leads to accomplishing objectives and goals established and met to the satisfaction of teacher and group.

There are many reasons why the student teacher must write a more detailed plan for each day's work. Chief among these is the fact that this process gives him a chance to think through each lesson in detail. As he constructs his plan in advance, he has time to consider all the varied items that make up an effective lesson. He can go back over each detail and evaluate it, discarding or amending the learning process. As a novice at teaching, the student teacher is under a great handicap, for experience weighs heavily in guiding learning effectively. Under the pressure of fast-moving events in a daily class, inexperience makes it possible to sidetrack the novice or cause him to forget many important details. His plan should be constructed so that it will compensate for his lack of experience by enabling him to:

1. Organize and carry out classroom management and routine efficiently
2. Provide for effective use of resources and appropriate audio-visual materials
3. Make an assignment if the need be
4. Provide measures to insure student participation
5. Budget his time according to his purpose
6. Provide for smooth and orderly progress of all activities
7. Make adequate provision for individual differences
8. Allow for evaluation of the teaching-learning process in the unit

Trends in Daily Planning of the Sequence within a Unit. Modern planning and procedures stress the importance of experiences for learners in the teaching of the social studies. Selected units with well-planned activities furnish the basis for functional learning. Unit teaching has to a degree replaced the older daily assignment (textbook assignment-study and recitation) procedure. The transition from receptivity to activity in the teaching-learning process is not an easy task. It takes a little pioneering work on the part of the teacher. It can be a gradual process for those who feel students will have difficulty in making such a change in the organization of the work. In the new education, learning becomes a co-sharing process with student and teacher working together. Many teachers meet this new challenge by using the textbook but at the same time introducing topics and problems which are important for the group. The basic text is a valuable resource tool and is helpful in studying various units of work; however, the good teacher will experiment and employ procedures to meet the needs of the particular group.

Learning through cooperative planning and organization is the result of efficiently planned individual and group activities. Continuity of learning is essential if we are to meet the needs, interests, and demands of any group of learners. Fragmentary and unrelated instruction is worthless learning and lacks the "punch" that gives the pupil momentum in meeting new challenges. Good instruction is always positive, functional, and transferable to the new situation and problems. Modern planning stresses the definite organization of material and the wise choice of a unit for interesting and stimulating learning. This emphasizes adequate research or exploration and suitable opportunities for worthwhile learning.

A good lesson plan like a teaching unit provides students with opportunities and experiences for planning, investigation, research, activity, discussion, and evaluation. Factors relating to creativity, self-expression, acquisition of essential skills, selectivity and choice making, imagination, success, problem solving, ability to use tools for learning, critical reading, locating information, vocabulary study, and building appreciation are all developed and considered by the skillful teacher in the learning process.

Form of the Daily Plan. There can be no set form for a daily lesson plan. In regard to completeness and arrangement, the chief criteria to be considered are that it must be an adequate guide for the student teacher in directing the learning activities, and it must furnish the critic teacher and supervisor with a clear picture of the proposed lesson.

DAILY LESSON PLAN

SUBJECT .... DATE .... PERIOD ....

UNIT .... TOPIC ....

References, resources, and tools for learning ....

....

....

General objectives for the lesson:

Outline of content	Procedures and techniques for the teaching-learning process:
	I. Introduction (including assignment and directions for developing the work)
	II. Activities (guide problems and questions)
	III. Conclusion (a summation of the work)
	IV. Evaluation (of progress and the work in process)

Remarks: (Include the following: Was the plan successful? Did it meet the desired objectives? What was the pupil reaction? How can the work be related to new experiences?)

The daily lesson plan need not be an elaborate undertaking, but it must be direct and concise. Care must be taken in constructing the daily plan so that each day's lesson is built upon the preceding one and looks forward to the next, otherwise the instruction becomes fragmentary and isolated. The daily plan fits into the scheme of the unit and aids in giving direction for completing the unit. Each day's work must have a definite relationship to the larger unit as well as to the students' needs and interests.

The student teacher as well as the beginning teacher will no doubt make changes in the form of his plan until he feels it is the type that serves his own purpose best.

The student teacher should gain experience in planning and developing various kinds of lessons, for all types may occur from time to time regardless of the kind and extent of long-range planning. In addition, many specialized techniques are essential for the effective development of any type of lesson. In particular, the student teacher should, in all his daily planning, make definite provision for effective introductions and conclusions.

The introduction, or getting the group started in their learning, is important not only from the standpoint of success in student teaching, but also to insure interesting learning. The atmosphere, handling routine, choice of opening remarks, selecting of good review or thought questions and pertinent suggestions, the techniques planned for use in the day's activities—all are important aspects of the introduction. Building good relationships with a group is important. The way a lesson is begun will, in many cases, determine the attitude of a group toward the learning at hand. A student or the teacher may review the previous day's work as a technique in getting started. A good beginning, in the form of an appropriate and challenging introduction, will carry the work along smoothly and prevent the occurrence of many later difficulties; on the other hand, a poor beginning is a handicap even though the student-teacher redoubles his efforts for the remainder of the period. In the social studies, the introduction may well serve a dual purpose; to provide for continuity in the stream of learning and give some thought to the work that will follow. In planning for the introduction or beginning the work, the student teacher should make a constant effort to find new and varied approaches.

The concluding or summarizing activities are important in any learning situation. The inexperienced teacher often finds it hard to time the activities in a lesson. He must learn to gauge his progress and provide ample time for some conclusion and evaluation of the day's work. Every learning activity needs some form of summary, and it should occur upon the completion of the activity. Probably the most democratic and effective technique in this respect, one which the student teacher must strive to perfect, is to have students themselves make the summary as a definite part of their learning activities. It must be remembered that the more activities engaged in by a group, the more difficult it is to time and summarize.

Among the other important factors that the student teacher should consider in planning and developing a lesson are techniques and skills important for effective teaching; for instance, the planning and work session, the discussion, and other aspects of unit development. All problems and topics should challenge the desire of the pupils to do research and present their findings. There are times when some interesting event in the nation or community can be identified by the group and a problem chosen for future study.

Conclusion

Planning is a means of growth for the teacher and the student. Guidance in organizing and evaluating materials is a positive form of education. A certain amount of preplanning is important to guide the teaching-learning process in such a way that the activities will be carried to the point where functional learning is assured. Continuity of learning is achieved with flexibility as an important factor in all instruction where thoughtful planning occurs. Procedures and materials are fused to make activities meaningful in the framework of a unit. The daily plan links the parts of the unit into a concise and effective pattern for learning. The student teacher and experienced teacher will find that planning can serve many purposes in the process of helping students to grow and develop into competent and intelligent individuals.

Bibliography

Burton, W. M., *The Guidance of Learning Activities,* 3rd ed. New York: Appleton-Century-Crofts, Inc., 1962.

Clark, L. H. and I. S. Starr, *Secondary School Teaching Methods.* New York: The Macmillan Company, 1959.

Nordberg, H. O., J. M. Bradfield, and W. C. Odell, *Secondary School Teaching.* New York: The Macmillan Company, 1962.

Rivlin, H. N., *Teaching Adolescents in Secondary Schools,* 2nd ed. New York: Appleton-Century-Crofts, Inc., 1961.

Steeves, F. L., *Fundamentals of Teaching in Secondary Schools.* New York: The Odyssey Press, Inc., 1962.

Quillen, I. J. and L. A. Hanna, *Education for Social Competence,* rev. ed. Chicago: Scott, Foresman & Company, 1961.

Chapter Eight

Instructional Methods
and Techniques

Modern instructional methods, procedures, and techniques applicable to social studies instruction should aid in providing the essential avenues to effective learning. Some of the older as well as the newer practices in methodology have a role to play in learning. The vast amount of new knowledge, research findings, experimentation results, new devices and equipment, and audio-visual materials have greatly aided the teacher and student in the instructional process.

Methods may be thought of as a systematic approach to learning and the acquisition of information. It provides the teacher with the opportunity to practice and develop techniques and apply a creative approach in teaching so as to foster student growth and development.

Guilding creative talent effectively is never routine for counselors, teachers, or administrators. They are never safe in following traditional rules, strict schedules, tested and practiced methods and materials, or standard ways of assessing situations. They must continue to experiment, even when everything seems to be working well. Even the usual, unconscious kinds of self-deception may be glaringly obvious to a fully-alive, highly creative youngster. Thus, it is an understatement that successful guidance of creative talent requires qualities in counselors, teachers, and administrators which are not now very common among them.[1]

---

[1] E. P. Torrance, *Guiding Creative Talent* (Englewood Cliffs, N.J.: Prentice-Hall, Inc., 1962), p. 188.

The modern social studies teacher utilizes various methods and techniques. He plans accordingly and selects those specific teaching techniques that will best serve his immediate purpose. He realizes the necessity of adopting teaching procedures especially suitable for the particular course and the immediate group needs.

Creativeness in
Teaching Social Studies

The creativity and artistry of teaching can function at the various levels of social studies instruction. The techniques, procedures, and tools of teaching are applied with intelligence in the teaching-learning process. Educational research and experimentation are most essential if we hope to reveal a new and fresh viewpoint pertinent to the instructional sphere. The modern social studies teacher is, whenever possible, desirous of improving the methods of instruction and of enriching the materials for effective learning. Current instructional practices require that the individual think while experiencing those functional activities in the acquisition of new knowledge, understanding, and in the process of solving problems in his emerging society.

Teaching as a function

Teaching is always the implementation, directly with learners, of some kind of curriculum decision. The specific aspects of the mediating function, teaching, may be listed as:

1. Structuring and restructing a setting to make opportunities for experience available to learners
2. Pointing to possible experiences to be had in the setting created or otherwise inviting learners to avail themselves of opportunities for experience
3. Participating with an individual or group in clarifying or otherwise improving guidelines for selecting opportunities for experience
4. Serving as a model in interpersonal transactions, or otherwise fostering educative interaction among peers and people of other age groups
5. Helping an individual or group to use time, space, equipment, and materials
6. Helping an individual or group to abstract from experiences information, values, skills, and processes
7. Helping an individual or group to interpret and evaluate experiences

The mediating function, teaching, is exercised basically through communicating in verbal and nonverbal ways—offering, explaining, showing, reinforcing, raising questions.[2]

---

[2] A. Miel, ed., *Creativity in Teaching Invitations and Instances* (Belmont, Calif.: Wadsworth Publishing Company, Inc., 1961), p. 5.

The social studies teacher as a master craftsman has many opportunities to apply creativeness to the acquired skills of teaching. There are many occasions while working with youth and the wealth of available content to extend the creative urge of the learners. The teacher is employing whenever possible new ideas and exploring with different types of approaches and opportunities for helping pupils to acquire rich learnings. The best possible teaching has the threads of creativity in the selection of those functional experiences and resources for meeting the needs of youth. The procedures or techniques applied and the learning opportunities afforded are prime directives for unlocking and releasing the learner's own store of knowledge and skills that can be applied to a particular problem or topic being studied. The alert and active minds of youth provide thought that widens the horizons of learning for the individual or the group.

Developing Methods and Procedures

Specific methods and procedures applicable for social studies instruction are democratic and foster effective and new learning experiences. Current educational practices stresses flexibility in method and curriculum alike for directing and guiding learning in meeting the needs of youth. Furthermore, creative and imaginative thinking on the part of teachers can develop new ideas and techniques in the learning process that will give breadth and depth to the content being studied.

Instructional procedures should arouse critical thinking, stimulate the student's natural interests and immediate needs, and furnish a high degree of individual accomplishment, appreciation, and satisfaction in the learning. This connotes the skills and incentives so essential for independent inquiry and research. Motivation is a significant force when utilizing specific procedures in connection with students in various learning situations.

The learning experiences provided for the student are usually selected on some rational basis. Most frequently they are selected with a view toward helping the student develop some type of competence, a particular type of interest or attitude, or some other goal involving the developing of the student into a more mature and capable person. Ideally, the planner of the learning experiences will use his knowledge (or assumptions) about the previous learning of the student, his initial level of attainment, and his abilities and motivations for particular kinds of learning. He will also take into consideration the limits and opportunities provided by the particular subject area or subject matter with which he is primarily dealing. Finally, the planner (or teacher) has some idea about how learning takes place and how particular learning experiences are best developed in view of learning theory, motivational principles, and the learning characteristics of the particular group of students with whom he is working.[3]

The modern social studies teacher uses various techniques, procedures, and materials for meeting the individual differences within the group. He has an insight into the needs and interests of the learner. He has a knowledge and understanding of the abilities, attitudes, and problems of the group, and integrates counseling and guidance with the instruction. The effective teacher grasps the opportunity to use up-to-date materials and special resources that will lead to functional and worthwhile experiences.

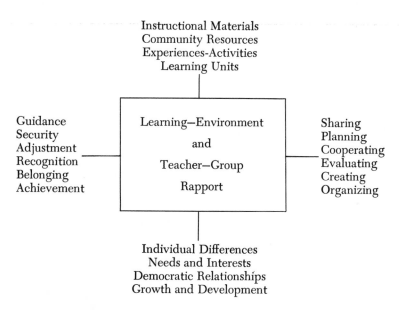

Instructional Materials
Community Resources
Experiences-Activities
Learning Units

Guidance
Security
Adjustment
Recognition
Belonging
Achievement

Learning—Environment

and

Teacher—Group

Rapport

Sharing
Planning
Cooperating
Evaluating
Creating
Organizing

Individual Differences
Needs and Interests
Democratic Relationships
Growth and Development

The Teacher-Group Relationship

The teacher in a sense exercises the basis for flexible controls in the learning situation. He acts as a consultant and guiding director in assisting individuals in the selection of resources for studying topics. He plans and motivates interesting activities in such a manner as to achieve as fully as possible the goals of the students.

[3] B. S. Bloom, "Ideas, Problems, and Methods of Inquiry," *The Integration of Educational Experiences,* National Society for the Study of Education, 57th Yearbook, Part III (Chicago: The University of Chicago Press, 1958), chap. V, p. 92. Quoted by permission of the Society.

As a group matures and learns to work as a learning team, and as it creates a climate of interdependence and reciprocal support, the members begin to communicate with one another easily and well. When they have little need to defend themselves and feel secure enough to expose their ideas and feelings to the rest of the group, the communication level in the instructional group is deep enough to permit valid feelings as well as cognitive communication. Group members seem to sense the meaning of the emotional freight-age in the words used by other members of the class.[4]

The Learner—
Setting for Learning

The following material consists of the characteristics of the learner himself, paralleled by a listing of the characteristics of a setting for learning which would fit the learner. The statements under "Setting for Learning" are directives for teaching. They might include these items:[5]

The Learner	*The Setting for Learning*
1. The learner like all living organisms, is a unitary, integrating whole.	1. The desirable setting for functional learning experiences will provide for natural integration of feeling-doing-thinking.
2. The learner, like any other living organism, seeks always to maintain equilibrium or balance.	2. Desirable learning experiences will provide opportunity for success in meeting needs and solving problems, but will also give constant challenge to go beyond immediate situations.
3. The learner is a goal-seeking organism, pursuing aims to satisfy needs, thus to maintain equilibrium.	3. The desirable setting for learning will be dominated by purposes and goals set up by the learner or learners, either by themselves or with appropriate guidance from the total group, including consultants.
4. The learner is an active, behaving, exploratory individual.	4. The setting must provide freedom to explore, to construct, to question, to differ, to make mistakes: freedom to develop creative con-

[4] J. R. Gibb, "Sociopsychological Processes of Group Instruction," *The Dynamics of Instructional Groups,* National Society for the Study of Education, 59th Yearbook, Part II (Chicago: The University of Chicago Press, 1960), chap. VI, p. 126. Quoted by permission of the Society.

[5] W. H. Burton, "Basic Principles in a Good Teaching-Learning Situation," *Phi Delta Kappan,* XXXIX (March 1958), 248.

tributions. The limits of freedom are democratic controls, rights of others, and good taste.

5. The learner has a pattern and rhythm of growth peculiar to the individual. Notable differences exist between individuals in speed of learning, energy, output, depth of feeling, facility of insight.

5. Widely varied types of learning experiences should be provided, adaptable to levels of maturity, to different rates, interests, abilities, and so forth.

6. The learner brings with him a personality, a set of aims, values, social habits.

6. The purposes and experiences established should arise out of and be continuous with the life of the learner. The family background, and social-class status, as well as the individuality of the learner, must be taken into account.

7. The learner may be quite immature in relation to one set of standards and experiences, and quite mature in relation to another.

7. Learners need sympathetic guidance while building an awareness and personality within their own experiences. They need protection from situations in which they cannot yet act intelligently; protection from fears and anxieties; protection sufficient to insure security and status on various levels; plus challenge to grow, to conquer problems, to develop self-reliance. The learner needs guidance from consultants who know and understand the problems of a growing personality; who see learning as a developmental process. Guidance must be free from domination or coercion.

8. The learner is a social animal, if normal, and naturally seeks activities involving other persons.

8. The setting must provide many varied opportunities to work in "we" relationships, developing eventually into self-directed group activity. The whole range of interactive human relationships, the cooperative group process, is essential to the new development of mature socialized personality.

The teaching-learning activities including both those for the individual and the group must be of such a nature as to stimulate interest and arouse curiosity. The teacher using a creative approach should provide an atmosphere for allowing new discoveries to develop and flourish. The learners in the proper setting and with a creative teacher have a strong desire to explore, achieve, and accomplish to the fullest in the learning process.

Methods of teaching

Method is the procedure followed by the teacher in directing the learning process. It is composed of a series of important steps placed, as the word "method" implies, in orderly, logical, and effective arrangement. Some of the steps that are an essential part of a particular method may also be found as a part of other methods. The combination of these significant elements into an effective procedure is the responsibility of the teacher. In general, method might be considered as the process of planning, guiding, sharing, and evaluating learning with a group of pupils.

There is no one best method that can be unequivocally recommended for use in teaching any specific lesson. The success of any method must be determined by its results in terms of pupil growth and development; one that is successful for one teacher is not necessarily successful for another teacher. By the same token, a method that is successful with one group of pupils is not necessarily successful when used by the same teacher with a different group of pupils, or with the same group of pupils at another time or under different conditions. Method must be both flexible and workable; it should never become stereotyped. No teacher can use the procedures of another teacher and apply them successfully until he has studied them and made certain modifications to adapt them to his own use. Method, like good teaching, requires broad general knowledge, a clear prospectus, masterful skills, a cooperative spirit, and a pleasing personality. With experience and through experimentation, the social studies teacher can become skillful in the application of method.

The creative teacher is constantly experimenting, reorganizing, and evaluating in the learning process. It is through this process that new ideas and approaches are brought into focus. This implies in a general way that in the creative process the topics, problems, resources, community, students, and teacher are involved in social studies instruction. The atmosphere or climate for learning, the physical setting, communication avenues, and the urge to be constructive and creative are essential considerations for a creative process in method.

Instructional methods or techniques may be selected to provide a particular kind of experience. Thus, some teachers have used student participation or democratic planning in a dual way: first, as an educational experience related to the development of certain objectives; secondly, as a way to share with the students the difficult job of planning a set of educational experiences designed to foster growth in such difficult areas as personality development, attitudes, and values. Similarly, extensive use of discussion procedures may have direct relevance to the achievement of citizenship and problem-solving objectives. The choice of a method of instruction is an important part of the problem of planning and organizing educational experiences, but the choice should be made in relation to the entire sequence of experiences. Seldom will the natural development of an extemporaneous discussion produce a well-organized experience; much prior planning and good leadership are necessary.[6]

The lectures in teaching

The lecture should be used with discretion at the secondary school level. The use of such a method tends to leave the students inactive, passive learners. This method is a great contrast to the other modern methods such as the problem approach where the group is active in research and in presenting information. It is difficult also for some teachers to hold the attention of a class and many students have difficulty in following the theme.

Some teachers employ a sort of *telling* approach as a means of describing and explaining materials, events, and trends. The teacher may employ lecturing for a part of the class period when introducing a unit or for summary purposes. He may at the same time utilize charts, diagrams, graphs, and outlines written on the chalkboard for the purpose of illustrating a particular point or topic. Furthermore, in answering the students' questions, a teacher may describe in an interesting manner a problem or an experience. The modern teacher is careful not to dominate the learning process. He assumes a major share of the responsibility for the planning and guiding the many activities that result in functional learning experiences for the group. He selects with care the proper techniques to meet the needs, interests, and capacities of the learners at a particular time and in a definite situation.

As we look toward the future with many young people heading for higher education, we may well re-evaluate the lecture. In advanced standing senior social studies groups at the secondary level, guest speakers, experts in the field, are a frequent adjunct in the instructional process. In utilizing the advantages of the large lecture class, the resource person presents the topic, discusses the problem area, and submits to questions. Many times these visiting lecturers can bring new and personal insights into the history and other social studies courses.

We might consider familiarizing the college-bound students with college methods and the important skill of effective notetaking. This

---

[6] P. L. Dressel, "The Meaning and Significance of Integration," *The Integration of Educational Experiences,* National Society for the Study of Education, 57th Yearbook, Part III (Chicago: The University of Chicago Press, 1958), chap. I, p. 18. Quoted by permission of the Society.

might also include up-grading the vocabulary capacity, materials, and knowledge as well as the techniques that the students will experience in the learning process while attending institutions of higher learning. This is a significant consideration and should be evaluated by those who provide instruction for seniors at the secondary level. Students must have some initial experiences in order to become accustomed to methods and techniques employed in higher education.

Seminars

A seminar method can be utilized at the secondary as well as at the college level. In the prevailing programs, advanced placement and honors classes for the gifted employ effective methods and techniques. In small groups seated around a table, the students and teacher discuss and report their research on different topics. The teacher judges the teaching situation and selects those procedures and techniques that are desirable for the occasion.

For such groups the seminars provide the setting for challenging discussions of significant topics. In such an instructional setting the students are motivated to explore, study, and evaluate pertinent information. A spirit of curiosity is constantly aroused and critical thinking is being developed. Frequently, the regular teacher and a visiting college instructor serve as a team. An effective social studies teacher utilizing such a method will be aware of the objectives of social studies instruction and also of those pertaining to effective citizenship.

Socialized recitation

As the name indicates, socialized recitation provides a greater opportunity for pupil participation than other methods. The function of the teacher is that of a guide and a consultant. It is a kind of general group discussion method with all pupils participating in a cooperative manner by making contributions, asking questions, and attempting to solve problems. It may be a method applicable to the introduction of a topic, talking over a significant event, and in the preparation for studying a problem.

The true or formal type of socialized recitation is characterized by a definite scheme of organization. For this procedure the class may be organized as a parliamentary group, with a president, a vice president, a secretary, and other special officers. The secretary will record the minutes of the discussion and write a summary of the materials included. A committee may be chosen to arrange a tackboard display relating to the topic discussed. Another group may provide the pupils with a supply of contemporary materials for the class library. A pupil may be assigned the job of obtaining films and the projection equipment for supplementary discussion of the topic. The socialized recitation is capable of achieving wholly beneficial and desirable outcomes if teacher and pupils keep the objectives in mind throughout the work.

The informal or group discussion type of socialized recitation is not so rigidly organized. The leader may be the teacher or a pupil selected by the group. The leadership may shift from one pupil to another in the course of the discussion. The informal group discussion is not a procedure or a method of teaching as much as it is a spirit, an atmosphere, a situation in which both teacher and pupils work cooperatively. The teacher is a consultant and a resource person making suggestions, giving direction and continuity, and aiding the evaluation of the discussion. The group discussion gives each pupil, in a social setting, a chance to discuss topics in a democratic manner. This type of method gives direction for developing individual competence and effective living in our secondary schools. It carries a transfer into society and out into the community where pupils are striving to achieve certain goals.

In the socialized recitation as in other methods the role of the teacher is most significant. He acts as supervisor and retains control of the learning situation. He assumes the position as a leader, consultant, planner, evaluator, and co-worker with the group. The students turn to the teacher as a resource person and seek his guidance throughout the learning and working activities. The teacher lends encouragement to the group and suggests that each individual make his contribution to the instructional sphere. The teacher in looking ahead may engage in some pre-planning, motivating, and evaluating for the individual or the group in the presentation of materials.

Advantages and values

Fortunately the true values of the socialized recitation can be achieved independently of any elaborate scheme of organization. It is the responsibility of the social studies to train pupils for participation in a social environment. Such participation implies ease and freedom in conversation, the readiness to mix in friendly groups, and the ability to work together. Thus it can be seen that the socialized situation is not essentially a procedure or a method of teaching. It is a characteristic vitally essential to the successful working out of any classroom project and to every step of the laboratory method. The socialized situation should prevail regardless of the procedure taking place—telling, problem-solving, or joint planning of work.

The current objectives of social studies instruction are so largely conceived with the development of attitudes, understandings, habits, interests, and ideals that a consideration of the values to be derived from the socialized situation should be based upon an analysis of contributions made in the attainment of the objectives in view. The chief advantages may include building leadership, stimulating interest, encouraging cooperation, providing for participation, stimulating initiative, fostering good citizenship, cultivating critical thinking, developing cooperation, and promoting tolerance and good sportsmanship.

The project method

The project method, sometimes the outgrowth of the study of a problem or topic, may be considered as an activities approach to learning, in that it provides activity for the learner as he experiences through his own obtainable goals. Pupils through their own initiative, interests, skills, and experiences may successfully achieve up to their maximum abilities. The success of any project is largely determined by the degree to which the pupils identify themselves with it and adopt it as their own. With less mature or junior high school pupils, it is relatively easy for the teacher to suggest projects in such a way that the pupils really believe that it was entirely their own idea. The mature secondary pupils are less likely to appreciate this indirect method and may, as a result, lack the genuine interest essential for its success. The social studies teacher should realize the strengths, the many possibilities, the pitfalls, and the weaknesses of the project method. He should study his group, their interests, and abilities, and use this approach to its best advantage. At the senior high school level the skillful teacher will capitalize on the interest of the group and tie old experiences with new and meaningful learning. A project may come more or less as a spontaneous outgrowth of the learning situation or some event of significant interest to the entire group. The experiences and contributions of the group should provide increased knowledge in the particular content.

The laboratory method

The laboratory method of instruction, used so successfully in the natural sciences, has been adapted for application to the social studies field with equal success. This method combines the best features of all methods in a way that makes desirable provision for individual differences, develops initiative and cooperation, and fosters growth in interests, attitudes, habits, skills, and ideals. Essentially the laboratory method is based upon problem-solving, directed or supervised study, and the socialized situation.

The ideal setting for the application of the laboratory method is, of course, the social studies laboratory. However, in schools lacking such facilities, the method can be, and has been, carried out with a high degree of success by holding one or more laboratory periods in the school library and the remainder in the social studies classroom, or by conducting all phases of activity in the classroom, with or without the use of references borrowed from the library. The laboratory method may be used for the study of an entire topic or it may deal with a subdivision of the topic. In either case, the essential features of the method, as applied to the social studies are:

A problem to be solved or a topic to be investigated.

Investigation of sources of information.

Evaluation, analysis, and conclusions.

The steps that are characteristic of the laboratory technique as applied to the social studies may be described as follows:

Delineation of the Problem or Topic. The teacher should introduce the problem or topic with appropriate remarks to stimulate pupil interest, or the problem may arise spontaneously as a result of some previous act or interest. Pupils and teacher should then discuss the major phases to be considered and how the problem may be attacked.

Planning the Working Procedure. The working procedure should be a cooperative process. Although the teacher, of necessity, has a predetermined plan in mind, to all intents and purposes the pupils themselves are working out with the teacher the complete details of procedure to be followed, including such items as probable sources of information, field trips, pupil reports, bulletin board displays, interviews, and the making of maps, charts, and graphs.

Research and Organization of Materials. The length of time devoted to this stage of the process naturally varies with the nature, scope, and significance of the problem, the intensity of investigation, and the planned working procedure. During this phase, the laboratory assumes the nature of a workshop. Students are pursuing their separate investigations and organizing their findings. Planned, purposeful freedom is the order of the day. Books, pamphlets, and periodicals are consulted; notes are taken; maps, graphs, and cartoons are drawn; committee or incidental discussions take place; and reports are written or prepared for oral presentation. Some phases of investigation may take place outside the laboratory as pupils visit the school or public library, arrange exhibits or displays, or call on prominent persons for interviews, or specific community agencies for information. The teacher's part in this scene should be that of guide, counselor, and consultant. He moves about freely among the students, noting progress, giving assistance where needed, offering suggestions and encouragement, holding conferences, and generally supervising all the activities of the pupils.

Concluding Activities.   The types of activities to be included in this step will depend upon the original plan of procedure. In general, this is the step that ties together all the separate lines of investigation. Reports are made; exhibits, displays, maps, and all special projects are presented; findings are evaluated and discussed; and results are summarized. If desired, a test is given as a means of evaluating pupil growth.

The problem method

Problem-solving occurs naturally in all subjects of the curriculum as well as in everyday life. The procedure attacks a specific situation in a scientific manner. Furthermore, the successful accomplishment of problem-solving is the goal toward which many other phases of the learning situation are directed. As distinguished from the project, the problem is characterized chiefly by mental activity, by critical thinking, and is therefore more directly applicable to the secondary school level of instruction. The steps that should be followed by the teacher in using the problem-solving process as a method of teaching follow in logical order the suggested steps outlined below:

1. Discovering, considering, discussing, selecting, and stating the problem
2. Collecting, organizing, comparing, and judging information in the light of the defined problem
3. Exploring the problem and framing some possible solutions
4. Drawing preliminary conclusions for further exploration and study
5. Evaluating findings and establishing a conclusion
6. Considering the summarization with the possibility of further study

The Problem Arises.   Problems may be introduced by the teacher or they may be proposed by members of the group. In actual practice, no doubt, some of the problems solved as a group procedure are teacher-directed. However, worthwhile pupil-inspired problems do occur with a surprising degree of frequency if the teacher is alert to the potentialities of questions spontaneously raised by the pupils. Local situations sometimes will help a teacher to decide what problems are important enough to include in the study. The good teacher will use some criteria for selecting a problem. The problem should be valuable, timely, and above all, it should impart functional learning. It should encompass the use of various content and working procedures.

Problems may serve as the integrating threads for learning experiences when the *use* rather than *knowledge* of the subject matter is stressed. The attempt to solve a problem can be a significant learning experience if the problem is of interest to the student, if the attack on the problem requires new modes of response from the student, and if the student can learn from his errors and recognizes and is rewarded for his successes. The attack on a problem can serve an integrating function when the problem requires the student to use a wide range of subject matter, different ways of viewing phenomena, and various methods of working.[7]

As a general rule, it is a part of the teacher's task to help in proposing the problem or at least to set the stage in such a manner that the pupils are sufficiently interested in the subject or topic to raise the problem themselves. There are numerous devices that may be used to create interest and stimulate thinking in the desired direction. A tackboard display, the showing of a motion picture, or a group discussion initiated by the teacher are all excellent starting points. In some situations it is entirely proper for the teacher to propose the problem by introducing it as the next in a series of problems to be considered. Classes composed of mature and superior pupils frequently prefer this procedure since they recognize that it is a tribute to their ability and to their status as young adults.

The Problem Is Defined. When the problem has been chosen, the next step is to state it so clearly and specifically that there can be no misunderstanding as to its scope and limitations. This should be a cooperative undertaking. Pupils should be allowed and encouraged to participate as extensively as possible in this step. When it has been satisfactorily defined, every precaution should be taken to keep the problem as stated before the group at all times.

Pertinent Information Is Collected. This phase of problem-solving should begin with group discussion and analysis of the problem. Various subdivisions should be outlined. The teacher should guide the process by eliciting from pupils all pertinent items of information they already possess. Plans are then made for obtaining the necessary additional information. Various types of activity are included as each individual or committee works toward a solution. The procedure followed by the pupils and teacher is essentially that described in the third step of the laboratory method.

Various Solutions Are Evaluated. Steps three and four cannot be considered completely separate entities. As pupils collect information and pursue their separate lines of investigation, it is inevitable that they will be formulating various solutions, evaluating these solutions, and either

---

[7] B. S. Bloom, "Ideas, Problems, and Methods of Inquiry," *The Integration of Educational Experiences,* National Society for the Study of Education, 57th Yearbook, Part III (Chicago: The University of Chicago Press, 1958), chap. V, p. 99. Quoted by permission of the Society.

discarding them or confirming them with additional facts. However, as these tentative solutions are presented in the form of individual or committee findings, the process continues as the group further evaluates, accepts, or rejects.

A Conclusion Is Drawn and Verified. Again, this step cannot be entirely separated from the previous step, since the processes taking place in the evaluation of the various solutions are naturally leading toward the final conclusion. Both steps four and five furnish the teacher with the opportunity of doing a masterful job of teaching, guiding thinking, and directing learning. He must be tactful in leading the group to a rejection of invalid solutions while still maintaining an attitude of respect toward these contributions. He must be skillful in the use of suggestion as a means of guiding the group toward the desired conclusion. The manner of verification will depend upon the type of problem being solved. If the problem admits of an application of the solution, this application should be made by the group as a means of verification. For some problems there will be no way of verifying the conclusions save through further study.

Values of problem-solving

Problem-solving has many values as a classroom procedure. It constitutes a realistic method for presenting the type of experience that will face the pupil throughout his career. It also gives him a chance to think, judge, compare, and select what is best. Whenever a question has to be answered, the facts have to be marshaled and directed toward solution. The individual is challenged to bring to bear all his information and experience in solving such a problem.

Application of problem-solving to the social studies

For the social studies teacher, problem-solving carries implications beyond those of a mere "method of teaching." As a teaching procedure it is inextricably involved with the broader procedure of organizing subject matter in such a way that it can be dealt with through the study of problems. Social studies materials comprise two types of problems: Those for which society has already found the solution, and those for which it has not. This fact should be considered in the application of problem-solving. Generally speaking, it may seem unreasonable to expect secondary school pupils to "solve" the problems that society has been unable to solve. However, if the values gained through the problem-solving procedure are to be carried into adult life, these "unsolved" problems furnish a vital step in the practical application of classroom procedures to real living.

Perhaps a suggestion for effective approach to these unsolved problems can be found in the customary sequence of curriculum materials. The problems that can be raised in connection with the study of history, geography, and civics are usually those that society has solved and, therefore, those for which both teachers and pupils can more easily verify their conclusions. These subjects generally occur early in the curriculum and furnish an opportunity for pupils to become proficient in the desired procedure while they are dealing with relatively easy problems. The unsolved problems of society are more likely to be raised in connection with the study of sociology, economics, and problems of democracy, subjects usually offered in the senior year. By this time, pupils who have become accustomed to the method will be ready and eager for an opportunity to work out their own solutions. The desideratum is not fact-cramming and a wide range of detailed information, but the development of an informed, critical student citizenry.

Team Teaching
and Programed Instruction

Team teaching

Team teaching is being utilized and experimented with as a procedure in the social studies at the secondary level. The students are generally placed in honors sections which vary in size. Sometimes the setting resembles that found on the college level. The facilities, methods or procedures, and audio-visual materials are usually the selection of the instructors who plan and direct the course. References include collateral readings, guide sheets, and selected bibliographies which are geared to the area being studied. The assignments, problems, research papers, and readings, are included in the requirements for the course. Some instructors may wish to utilize some of their strongest and most effective techniques. Others may revamp their methods of teaching in the advanced placement program.

Various approaches to team teaching have been experimented with. These approaches have sometimes cut across subject matter areas and included related materials or content. Attempts have been made to evaluate the advantages of the different approaches or structures utilized in team teaching. As in any method or instructional arrangement, the basic question is whether effective learning or functional experiences are being derived by the learner. It should be remembered that improved instruction is always the teacher's goal. The technique of team teaching will no doubt be explored by many schools as educational horizons are broadened.

Some advantages reported for team teaching are:[8]

1. Few pupils are limited to the instructional competence of a single teacher at a grade level or in a department at the secondary level.
2. Persons most highly qualified provide instruction to large groups, thus saving much time for the total staff which can be used for more effective planning and for instruction in smaller-than-average groups.
3. In presentations to large groups, better use is made of visual aids because more time can be devoted to the preparation of needed materials by specially-qualified team members.
4. More uniformity in instruction is achieved because all students are taught, both in the large groups and the small, by the same teachers. Sections pupils are assigned to thus make less difference than in traditionally organized schools.
5. Less repetition is required of teachers, especially at the secondary level where several sections of the same class have been traditionally assigned.
6. Teacher competencies are better utilized.
7. Better provisions are made for helpers—librarians, audio-visual experts, clerks, and the like—to do routine tasks.
8. Group size is clearly related to function. Large groups are formed for activities which are effective with large groups, and vice versa.
9. Of necessity, students assume more responsibility for their own learning. As more and more instruction is provided in large groups, a greater share of the school day is given to independent study on the part of learners.

Programed instruction

A recent development in educational methodology is programing. Programing, or programed instruction, may take the form of a "scrambled book" or a "teaching machine." Whether the teaching machine be an automatic or partially automatic device, it is simply the device into which a program is fed. The machine acts as a means, and not an end. It presents information or concepts; sometimes even guides in the development of skills, but it only presents. And what the machine presents depends entirely upon what is put into it. The program, or the programed course, is the heart of the presentation. A good program presents a stimulus to a student, provides a means of response, and then informs him of the correctness of his response. The program contains material organized in an orderly sequence, each step building on what has gone before. Thus, programing involves the process of organizing content effectively and logically. The teacher would do well to remember that his prime concern, as

---

[8] H. D. Drummond, "Team Teaching: An Assessment," *Educational Leadership,* XIX, No. 3 (December 1961), 160-165.

an educator, is with programing as a process, rather than with the teaching machine or device.

Programed instruction is a supplement to classroom instruction and not a substitute for it. Carefully prepared and selected programs help the student to master certain skills and concepts quickly and thoroughly.

No subject matter area lends itself entirely to programing, but those areas where information is precise, where concepts can be clearly formulated, and where logical progression can be established, lend themselves to programed presentation.

Techniques for Directing Learning

Social studies teachers use many techniques in guiding and directing the learning process. Some are traditional; others are new or modifications of older types. All techniques should be in line with the democratic process and relate to desired goals. Techniques are employed for getting the learning under way with guidance from the teacher. They may be applied to any subject in the social studies and should be selected as a means of serving the best purpose at a particular time with the resultant of growth for the individual.

Assignments

The modern assignment is based upon the interests, needs, and abilities of the group. Long-range projects are in direct contrast to the daily assignment of a number of pages from the text. The learner may select his own assignment after a conference with the teacher, or the group in discussion with the teacher may determine the work to be accomplished. Teachers realize the assignment must be understood by the students and presented in a way that will motivate his thinking. Each assignment, whether individualized or group, should be flexible and unified in order to relate to the general work of the problem or unit.

The current approach to the assignment stresses directed learning and cooperative planning. It comprises different variations, under any of which may be found the small group assignment, the individual assignment, and the entire group assignment. The modern assignment may begin with the long-range view that is characteristic of the unit, the problem, or the project assignment and later be broken down into shorter topical, activity, or special report assignments. In general, the distinguishing feature of the modern type of assignment, as opposed to the traditional type, is the use that is made of guide sheets, outlines, workbooks, scrapbooks, supplementary references, and various pupil activities. If a textbook is used as a basis for the assignment, the modern teacher applies wholly different methods in presenting the assignment by furnishing guide questions, specific directions, suggested study helps, and additional reference sources.

Effective learning calls for assignments that are comprehended in full by the learner. Every teacher knows that progressive improvement can be achieved with guidance and direction. The good assignment must be systematically planned and intelligently developed. The outcomes must be constructively evaluated.

Questioning

Questions are a definite part of effective learning in the social studies since they stimulate the group to think. The teacher and group in a socialized discussion find the question a challenging device for exploration and discovery.

Modern instructional procedures are such that questioning plays a far more important part than formerly. Among its chief purposes may be listed stimulation of pupil interest and curiosity about the work; motivation of the assignment; guidance and direction of the learning process; stimulation of reflective thinking; encouragement of initiative, exploration, and research; discovering of pupil interests, needs, and immediate problems; providing a stimulus for, and directing the channels of, socialized discussions; focusing attention upon important phases of the work; aid in organization of factual knowledge and experience; aid in the development of proper attitudes, appreciations, and ideals; guiding the formation of desirable habits; providing for individualized instruction; aid in developing oral expression; connecting of units of learning; furnishing drill and practice on content material; providing for review and the application of information; measuring achievement and progress; ascertaining the extent of pupil's understanding; discovering pupil weaknesses and difficulties in preparation of work; extent of behavior change and growth in the group of students.

There are certain types of questions that the beginning teacher in particular should take special care to avoid. These include catch or trick questions; most types of "discuss" questions; ambiguous and vague questions; and leading questions or questions that, either by their wording or by the teacher's expression in stating them, so unmistakably suggest the answer that pupils are led to make the correct response without any mental effort. Teachers are frequently advised to avoid the use of "yes" or "no" questions because they might limit the extent of discussion, however, this restriction should be qualified. Many instances occur in which this type of question is valid and plays an important part in the teaching-learning process. A "yes" or "no" question that causes the pupil to take a definite stand and is then followed up with one or more related questions is an excellent device for stimulating thought. The "yes" or "no" question, when properly applied to any topic about which there is certain to be a difference of opinion, and in a class that is "on its toes," will furnish the stimulus for the liveliest discussion any teacher could hope for.

The discussion of types of questions has been chiefly concerned with those demanding an answer from the pupils. However, there is another purpose of questioning in which the *stated* answer is unimportant. When questions are being employed to guide and direct the learning process, the emphasis is not upon the answer but upon the sequence of mental processes inspired by the series of questions. Thus the pupils' responses are frequently not stated but read from their expressions called forth by skillful questioning. This is true not only in the case of individualized instruction but also in instances where the entire group is being guided along an unfamiliar path. In either case, this technique calls for consummate skill on the part of the teacher.

An effective question should be definite and concise; be clearly stated; have a specific purpose; be suited to the ability and maturity of the pupils; stimulate thinking on the part of all students; relate to only one central idea; challenge and stimulate discussion; and clearly reveal a definite step forward in a progressive sequence.

Students' Questions. Students increase their learning and enlarge their experiences by asking questions about things which interest them. The skillful teacher employs any advantage to be gained from this natural tendency by exploring and building upon these revealed interests in such a way as to further their growth. Pupils' questions, even the seemingly irrelevant, should receive respectful consideration, and answers or suggestions for finding the answers should be given. Questions that have sufficient bearing upon the topic at hand may be answered by other pupils, by the teacher, or be made the basis for research. However, the latter practice should not be employed so much that a pupil hesitates to raise a question because he fears it will lead to extra work.

Many beginning teachers fear that questions will be raised that they will be unable to answer; therefore they sometimes attempt to discourage questions. This attitude is the very antithesis of good teaching. No doubt such questions will come up from time to time; however, there are many ways in which the teacher can meet them without losing the respect of the pupils. No teacher is expected to know everything. When he is faced with a question to which he does not know the answer, he should say, frankly and freely, "I do not know," or, better still, "I do not know, but let's see if we can find out." He should never attempt to bluff his way through such a situation. If the nature of the question is such that only the teacher would be able to ascertain the answer easily, he should tell his pupils that he will find out and let them know. Failure to keep such a promise is equally fatal, since pupils will interpret a broken promise as another form of bluffing. If the answer can be readily found by the pupils, he may suggest sources, or even call upon other pupils to supply the answer. Pupils, even low ability groups, possess amazing stores of facts upon the most unexpected subjects. Frequently teachers gain as much as pupils from discussions that are instituted in a cooperative spirit, and common interests are found which aid in maintaining effective pupil-teacher relationships.

Review

In modern practice, review is looked upon as a continuing process which gives direction to work. Review is a sort of analytical undertaking with the teacher and the group sharing in a cooperative manner.

Review was formerly thought to increase and stimulate learning through repetition. The teacher may use this procedure to determine not only weaknesses but also the interests, needs, and drives of pupils. Teachers realize that there is a relationship between learning ability and purposes. They are not so much concerned about covering pages of content as they are in helping pupils reach their goals. Therefore, a review may reveal the strength of the pupil to compare and relate understanding, to select and distinguish between materials used in the work. Review is an ongoing process in the activity of the modern laboratory classroom. It is a sort of evaluation on the part of the pupil or group in the learning process. It may give direction and guidance for the undertaking of a new unit of work.

The teacher should insure variety in review just as he does in any other instructional procedure. The review should never be a dull, uninteresting rehashing of facts. If pupils are to gain a new view of content in a different setting, the type of activity that is applied should be both purposeful and appropriate. In general, reviews are conducted through questions and answers. However, care should be taken to prevent this question and answer procedure from becoming a test of pupils' knowledge rather than a means of seeing the content in a different setting. Well-selected problem-type questions should be frequently used since they can be stated in a way that causes pupils to consider previously known facts as they have bearing on a new problem. Reports, summaries, and similar activities—and for younger pupils quiz games—are effective review activities. It is frequently advantageous to apply some activity that will entail both the reviewing of previous knowledge and the consultation of new sources.

Drill

Drill, rather than review, should be the term applied to repetitive procedures for the purpose of making set responses automatic: the perfection of a skill, the formation of a habit, or the fixing of specific facts for effortless recall.

The extent to which drill must be used on content materials in the social studies will depend largely upon the emphasis placed by the teacher upon the memorization and retention of facts. Many of the skills employed in the social studies can be improved through the use of drill, it is true, but also they can be acquired through practice that relates to an activity which gives meaning beyond mere drill. Some teachers feel that drill is essential in the preparation of a group for an examination and also to bind the main aspects of the content.

Workbook exercises may be used for drill and review. They are applicable to the individual and the group. Workbooks which follow the organization of the text being used make the work easier for both the teacher and the pupil.

The workbook can help to improve the techniques of lesson mastery and increase learning by means of topical reviews, as well as summaries of theme topics. A new unit or problem may be introduced or outlined in the workbook with salient facts and data emphasized for the purpose of drill work. Workbooks generally stimulate the work of the group and provide variety in activities by showing the methods used by different individuals in developing their lessons.

There is a difference of opinion among teachers and administrators concerning the merits and uses of workbooks. Some feel that they are not conducive to building good study habits and others assert that the procedure becomes too mechanical. There are those who claim that workbooks materially aid in the teaching-learning process for, as a teaching aid, they challenge the interests and abilities of all pupils.

Supervised or directed study

Modern instructional practices employing long-range planning and various methods may include, when the need arises, supervised or directed study. In the process of directing study, the teacher has many opportunities to provide instruction for developing basic skills. The teacher can give assistance to a pupil working on a problem, to a small group developing a project, and to the entire group when exploring a certain phase of a unit. The alert teacher, working with a group in the learning laboratory, helps pupils to develop good study habits, working skills, and a cooperative spirit which is conducive to learning. In the library, the teacher may assist a pupil in locating information from source materials.

Conclusion

The creative teacher applying systematic methods can do much to motivate and arouse the student to utilize skills, ideas, and research techniques to acquire, organize, and apply new knowledge effectively. He applies various procedures and techniques to relate past experiences with the new learning in an effort to enrich instruction. Thus, learning and realistic educational experiences should be so planned and directed as to build and foster future competence for the individual. Students should benefit by acquiring new procedures that should improve their competence in new experiences or in relating experiences. In the process of acquiring an education, students will be constantly called upon to solve problems. The educative process should develop and stimulate intellectual curiosity for the learner and provide the momentum for furthering the learning experiences of the individual.

Bibliography

Anderson, V. E. and W. T. Gruhn, *Principles and Practices of Secondary Education*, 2nd ed. New York: The Ronald Press Company, 1962.

Clark, L. H. and I. S. Starr, *Secondary School Teaching Methods*. New York: The Macmillan Company, 1959.

High, J., *Teaching Secondary School Social Studies*. New York: John Wiley & Sons, Inc., 1962.

Inlow, G. M., *Maturity in High School Teaching*. Englewood Cliffs, N.J.: Prentice-Hall, Inc., 1963.

Nordberg, H. O., J. M. Bradfield, and W. C. Odell, *Secondary School Teaching*. New York: The Macmillan Company, 1962.

Quillen, I. J. and L. A. Hanna, *Education for Social Competence*, rev. ed. Chicago: Scott, Foresman & Company, 1961.

Chapter Nine

Skills for Effective Learning

Students in the secondary schools should acquire basic skills for effective living. The social studies provide a proving ground for the development of these skills because of the variety of activities in which the pupils may engage. The skills and behaviors that the teacher should seek to develop in his pupils may be generally classified as follows: creative, research, communication, study, problem-solving, cooperation, planning, construction, and evaluation.

Progress in the use of these skills comes through learning experiences. The materials and procedures of the social studies foster basic skills and understandings that aid in the achievement of social competence. The needs and abilities of the pupils are always paramount in planning a program for the development and application of skills. The responsibility falls on the teacher to help the student acquire skills which will aid him in meeting problems and making sound decisions. It is essential that teachers clarify learning so that the pupil will develop competence and self-confidence. The pupil in the democratic atmosphere of the learning laboratory is using problem-solving techniques and learning skills that help him grow through individual and group work.

Principles of learning and skill development

The social studies teacher should teach skills which are useful to the learner. The improvement of instruction in any course calls for a well-planned program for teaching a skill whenever the need arises. There are certain basic skills for learning and some specific skills which relate to a particular field. For example, in the social studies it is important that the pupil develop skill in critical thinking and in solving problems. Knowing the meaning of relationships and having a sense of time sequence are important for interpreting events and for relating trends in history. We in the social studies are teaching content for the aquisition of knowledge and the building of good citizens.

Behavioral Outcomes of General Education in High School[1]

Behavioral outcomes to be sought from general education because the living of a satisfying personal life requires intellectual development toward the limit of one's capacity.

Is skillful in securing information and in organizing, evaluating, and reporting results of study and research

Illustrative Behavior

a. Decides on his purpose before planning action
b. Practices good study and other work habits when he has intricate thinking, reading, and planning to do
c. Consults some good periodicals if seeking information on political developments, foreign affairs, homemaking, scientific matters, book reviews, etc
d. Uses common sources of printed information efficiently; e.g., dictionary, encyclopedia, almanacs, telephone directory, Who's Who, Readers' Guide, and card catalog in a library
e. Can read all parts of a newspaper for needed information; e.g., weather reports, radio programs, amusements, business news, editorials, local, state, national, and international news
f. Asks questions in such a way as to secure accurate information of public services, offices, or persons likely to have special information when in need of it
g. Uses books, maps, globes, charts, timetables, and graphs of all kinds to find needed information
h. Systematizes his work in order to accomplish the things he wants to do
i. Constructs line, bar, and circle graphs, diagrams, pictographs, and statistical tables to express quantitative relationships
j. Uses the typewriter or writes well enough to meet his needs
k. Reads and interprets the graphs, charts, tables, road and other maps

---

[1] W. French and associates, *Behavioral Goals of General Education in High School* (New York: Russell Sage Foundation, 1957), pp. 92-95.

encountered in newspapers, magazines, and other popular printed matter

l. Is able to draw relevant information from several sources, correlate it, make a defensible set of conclusions, and discard what is not relevant

m. Manifests a fair knowledge of the relative reliability of various sources of information: two or more newspapers, radio and TV commentators, consumer guides, government publications

n. Develops skill in noting and recording information in outline, notes, and summary statements

o. Uses a readily acceptable footnote and bibliographical form in identifying sources of information and ideas

p. Develops listening habits that enable him to gain intended meaning

Displays an inquiring mind: is intellectually curious and industrious

Illustrative Behaviors

a. Shows by his reading, choice of TV and radio programs, attendance at lectures and by questions, his interest in at least half of the following: economic systems and economic ideologies, international relations and foreign policy, local and national politics, local community problems, religions other than his own, social relations (relations between races, ethnic groups, social class, and economic groups), in various countries, art, music, history, geographic explorations, theater, movies

b. Displays interest and asks questions in social groups where conversation is on topics in which he is interested and on which he is not informed

c. Wonders about, and forms tentative opinions concerning, some matters of a philosophical nature

d. Perseveres and carries through industriously on an intellectual task which he has accepted

e. Seeks a setting for work which is reasonably free from distraction

f. Recognizes need to apportion his time among the various legitimate demands made upon it, sets up a schedule of intellectual work for himself which is realistic, and holds himself to it

g. Follow directions intelligently

h. Endeavors to have at hand the tools and materials needed for a task

i. Makes an effort to evaluate his practices to see whether they are consistent with his goals; attempts to determine which are the means to the end he seeks

j. Takes increasing pride in his workmanship

Can learn independently and shows desire to do so

Illustrative Behaviors

a. Arranges own study plans, using school time and part of his out-of-school time

b. Can set up a procedure and carry it through for a project requiring work over a period of at least a week (research report, committee projects, etc.)

c. Can work independently and without supervision when it is appropriate to do so

d. Tries to improve his own written work by revising it so that it will convey his attention as clearly as possible
e. Formulates specific and pertinent questions as a means of seeking answers on a general topic or problem on which he is working
f. Adjusts his learning methods to the nature of the task; chooses between rote learning, practicing skills, using a procedure for applying general principles, etc.; so as to accomplish the task
g. Applies what he has learned to a new situation; e.g., setting up a job on a lathe in the machine shop, applying a science principle to personal health problems, applying a principle of grammar in a foreign language, applying the method of proof he has learned in geometry to the statements made in an advertisement, etc.
h. Faces problems connected with his work realistically and attacks any task with vigor and without urging or coaxing in spite of anticipated difficulties
i. Criticizes himself more than others and holds himself to higher standards than he expects of others
j. Dares to be different when convinced that facts warrant the position
k. Assumes responsibility for the solution of his own problems
l. Is beginning to understand the nature of intellectual freedom, and the value to society and to himself of preserving the right to seek and express what one considers to be the truth

Recognizes the importance of continuing to learn

Illustrative Behaviors

a. Sees learning as a continuous process throughout life
b. Views knowledge as exciting and worthy of further educational pursuit
c. Enjoys the process of learning and the development of skills, not just the finished product
d. Recognizes that learning occurs most effectively in terms of the individuals own effort; therefore, plans for his own growth
e. Looks forward to college or other type of post-high school education as a time when he can participate more fully in the culture, thus broadening and deepening his knowledge and insight
f. Respects scholarship for what it can do to enrich life

The Development of Skills

The social studies offer many opportunities for acquiring, developing, and strengthening essential skills for learning. Such skills as map and globe usage introduced at the elementary level reach new proportions in secondary instruction. The ability to plan, think critically, and make wise decisions in the learning process depends upon skills, insights, and the use of intelligence.

Creative thinking

The development of skills in creative thinking or problem-solving is an important aspect of secondary education. Students in the social studies classes should be provided opportunities to learn and think creatively. The following are suggestions to the teacher for developing this skill.[2]

1. Value creative thinking
2. Help students become more sensitive to environmental stimuli
3. Encourage manipulation of objects and ideas
4. Teach how to test systematically each idea
5. Develop tolerance of new ideas
6. Beware of forcing a set pattern
7. Develop a creative classroom atmosphere
8. Teach students that their ideas have value
9. Teach students skills of avoiding or coping with peer sanctions against originality without sacrificing their creativity
10. Teach students the nature of the creative process
11. Dispel the sense of awe of masterpieces
12. Encourage and evaluate self-initiated learning
13. Create "thorns in the flesh" making students aware of unsolved problems and gaps in knowledge
14. Create necessities for creative thinking
15. Provide for both active and quiet periods, recognizing that thinking is a legitimate "activity"
16. Make resources available for working out ideas
17. Encourage the habit of working out the full implications of ideas, pushing thinking as far as possible
18. Develop skills of constructive criticism—not just criticism
19. Encourage acquisition of knowledge in a variety of fields, along with a constructive attitude towards such knowledge
20. Be adventurous—spirited yourself, letting one thing lead to another, being alert to ideas when they come

The social studies teacher should consider each item in view of possible application in some phase of instruction. It should be remembered that developing creative thinking and critical thinking as well as problem-solving techniques is an important aspect of social studies instruction.

Aspects of critical thinking

Let us turn our discussion to a more concrete meaning of critical thinking.

As a root notion *critical thinking* is taken to be the *correct assessing of statements*. Since there are various kinds of statements, various relations be-

---

[2] E. P. Torrance, "Fostering Creative Thinking during the High School Years," *The High School Journal*, XLV, No. 7 (April 1962), 284-287.

tween statements and their grounds, and various stages in the process of assessment, we can expect that there will be various ways of going wrong when one attempts to think critically. The following list may be looked upon as a list of specific ways to avoid the pitfalls in assessment.

As indicated before, this list is not intended to provide mutually exclusive categories. Instead it shows common pitfalls, and items about which people are concerned. Criteria of classification are sacrificed in the interest of plausibility and intelligibility. The dimensional categories meet the criteris of classification, but sacrifice initial intuitiveness in order to do so.

Twelve aspects of critical thinking are:
1. Grasping the meaning of a statement
2. Judging whether there is ambiguity in a line of reasoning
3. Judging whether certain statements contradict each other
4. Judging whether a conclusion follows necessarily
5. Judging whether a statement is specific enough
6. Judging whether a statement is actually the application of a certain principle
7. Judging whether an observation statement is reliable
8. Judging whether an inductive conclusion is warranted
9. Judging whether the problem has been identified
10. Judging whether something is an assumption
11. Judging whether a definition is adequate
12. Judging whether a statement made by an alleged authority is acceptable

Although the root notion calls for its inclusion, the judging of value statements is deliberately excluded from the above list. This exclusion admittedly weakens the attractiveness of the presented concept, but makes it more manageable. So long as we remember that this exclusion has occurred, we should not be confused by the truncated concept. Perhaps this gap can at some future time be at least partially filled.

The exclusion of other important kinds of thinking (creative thinking, for example) from this basic concept of *critical thinking* does not imply that the others are unimportant, nor does it imply that they are separable from it in practice. This exclusion is simply the result of an attempt to focus attention on one important kind of thinking.[3]

Social studies teachers readily understand that one of the significant phases of the teaching-learning process is the development of the student's ability to think creatively and critically. Many aspects of the student's daily living and education call for sound thinking. The teacher should frame significant guide questions that will provoke critical thinking. The utilization of problems that will stir thinking and arouse thoughtful discussion will do much to improve the thinking and reasoning of the group. Furthermore, students should be guided by the teacher in framing their own questions and topics that will arouse the abilities of the students to think effectively. Well-phrased questions can lead to growth, new insights, and a sense of direction which will materially improve the students' ability to think.

---

[3] R. H. Ennis, "A Concept of Critical Thinking," *Harvard Educational Review,* XXXII, No. 1 (Winter 1962), 83-84.

Work habits and study skills

Good work habits and study skills are essential equipment for learning. Helping the student to acquire competence in these basic tools is the responsibility of the social studies teacher in all phases of his instruction. Effective planning, organization, and direction are the keys to work habits that will prove productive. Using reference materials for gathering information requires skill on the part of the learner. The students learn to use their time wisely without undue waste.

The development of study skills for a particular purpose requires certain techniques for mastery. For example, the teacher should set the stage for students to show the need for the utilization of a skill. The purpose and value of this particular type of skill should be clarified and practice provided for its use. The principles involved in improving a skill are generally acquired through specific activities. Skills properly developed can be utilized in all subject areas. It is most important that basic skills be employed at the junior high school level for furthering and enriching learning in the senior high school. Developing the essential skills including the all-important skill of problem-solving is essential in acquiring an education as well as for effective adult living.

The beginning teacher should consider the importance of the skill in a particular situation as well as the abilities of the group. Guidance and patience on the part of the teacher are essential for pupils to acquire an accepted standard in a type of skill being developed. Excessive drill can be more detrimental for a group than one may realize. The more difficult skills such as evaluation and research should be taught step by step, so the student can comprehend the full meaning, but simple skills such as map reading and interpreting graphs can be taught as a complete unit. The beginning teacher will, through experience and experimentation, develop effective procedures for profitable teaching of skills. It must be remembered that individual or even group difficulties may occur occasionally in the learning process and are handled by the skillful teacher through remedial or refresher practice. Skill-teaching in the social studies is a continuous process when studying units and solving problems. Some skills have to be clarified and readily understood by the pupils before new work is undertaken. An occasional review of skill procedures is effective in any course and with most groups.

Map skills

Map skills are sharpened with functional usage in the social studies. However, at the junior high school level it is wise to review previously acquired globe and map skills. The intelligent application of map skills is essential for richer learning and better comprehension of contemporary materials. News items tell a story and must always be geographically located to gather a fuller meaning. Areas of critical importance in the world should be located and analyzed when discussing current issues or problems.

Map skills and the ability to use, interpret, and understand social studies materials are all linked together. The teacher is alert to help students improve their skill and ability to read maps intelligently. A knowledge of the various types of maps and their effective application to learning is a necessary skill. The use of scales and grid lines, and the ability to compute distance is useful. The ability to interpret map symbols, use legends, comprehend direction, locate places and areas common to historic and geographic materials should be developed. Using longitude and latitude for location and map making is both helpful and advantageous. The skill of gathering, organizing, and evaluating information derived from various maps and map projections is a useful asset for the student.

Research skills

Research skills are important for all students in the social studies. Early in the course the skillful teacher will provide learning experiences that will develop effective research skills. Each student should learn the techniques of research as a means of solving problems. He should learn how to select, plan, organize, and present his findings in a systematic manner on a given subject. The student's interests have a great deal to do with his success and skill in doing research. Effective procedures for examining materials and sources in the study of units are essential for producing satisfactory results in learning. The ability to select pertinent material and to discard irrelevant material is essential for effective learning.

Using library materials

The ability to use library materials for learning is an important phase of modern social studies instruction. Every student should receive instruction in the effective use of the library. The amount of time teachers spend with their students on the various phases of library instruction will depend upon the provisions made by the administration and the librarian. The librarian in a series of lessons can give instruction in how to use the library resources. Even though a fairly comprehensive course in library instruction is included elsewhere in the student's course of study, the social studies teacher should constantly stress library skills and intelligent use of the library. The teacher has many opportunities for helping students to find materials from available resources to meet the work requirements. The librarian and teacher can work together to assist students with their research and to make them aware of new books and materials.

Teachers and librarians should furnish students with bibliographies of reading materials. Guidance is essential to channel these students toward desirable reading habits. The teacher, through suggestion, might occasionally read parts of a book for the purpose of stimulating interest, or give a report of a recent book. It is the duty of the secondary school to provide the basis for effective reading habits before these young people enter society. In some communities the high school reading lists are also posted in the public library where students can use them when choosing their leisure-time books.

Outlining

The volume of reading that secondary school students are required to do necessitates skill in outlining. An outline is the skeleton or framework of a written or spoken composition and serves the dual purpose of recording information clearly and aiding in the process of logical thinking. The main headings of an outline should be subdivisions of the title and should cover it in scope. Each heading of the outline should be meaningful. Repetitious or overlapping headings should be avoided. Subtopics should be clearly related to the main topic.

Outlining may be done in various ways, but the most commonly used kinds are the topical and the sentence outlines. Of these, the topical outline is the briefer, since sentence outlines must be written throughout in complete sentences. An example outline form is given on page 136.

The first word of each topic or sentence should be capitalized. In a sentence outline each topic, subtopic, or subdivision ends with a period; in a topical outline periods are unnecessary. Single subtopics or subdivisions should be avoided: if there is an A, there must be a B; if there is a 1, there must be a 2, and so on.

A good outline is consistent. If a sentence outline is being used, all topics, subtopics, and subdivisions should be complete sentences. If a topical outline is used, it should contain no complete sentences; furthermore, each topic, subtopic, or subdivision should follow as nearly as possible the same pattern—that is, all should be phrases of similar construction.

TITLE

I.
  A.
    1.
    2.
      a.
      b.
        (1)
          (a)
          (b)
        (2)
    3.
  B.
    1.
      a.
      b.
    2.
    3.
    4.
      a.
      b.
        (1)
        (2)
II.
  A. . . . And so on.

Note-taking

The ability to take useful and comprehensive notes is a valuable skill which should be developed in the social studies. Since the ability to take acceptable and worthwhile notes varies widely among students, teachers should make a definite effort to aid all students in understanding correct procedures in taking notes from lectures and oral presentations. Students need to develop the ability to recognize the principal statements of a speaker while he is speaking. The student must listen, think, and evaluate in order to write clear notes. Effective skill in note-taking can be acquired and is essential for the high school student looking ahead to college where note-taking is a major consideration. A reasonable degree of facility in outlining should precede intensive training in note-taking. Some good rules for note-taking follow.

1. System is essential. Unsystematic notes on scattered bits of paper are of little value.
2. Notes may be taken on cards or in notebooks. For general purposes, it is better to use a notebook of the loose-leaf type. Cards should be used when it will be necessary to rearrange the notes later—for instance, in the case of readings from several sources.

3. Notes on lectures, discussions, readings, and similar material should be taken in outline form in order to show the relationship of the various parts to the whole.
4. All notes must be legible. Practice writing from dictation until you have developed speed and legibility.
5. Use intelligent abbreviations, but use the same abbreviations each time you take notes.
6. Be accurate in all note-taking, particularly in the case of names, dates, references, and quotations.
7. Leave at least one margin sufficiently wide to provide space for recording supplementary or collateral information.
8. Review all notes from time to time. If necessary, expand the abbreviated notes while the material is still fresh in your memory. This will not only provide you with more useful and complete notes but will also serve to point out errors or weakness in your original procedures.

Keeping a notebook

Pupils should also learn to keep a notebook. It may seem that only pupils who are preparing for college need this skill; however, there are many situations in adult life where training in keeping a notebook will prove valuable in connection with occupational, civic, and avocational pursuits.

The notebook should be a record of the work of the class: it serves the student both as a basis for review and as a source of information. Definite minimum criteria should be established, and all students should be required to conform to these criteria. Although the teacher may require that the notebook be handed in for inspection and grading, he should remember that, in the final analysis, it is the property of the student and a reasonable degree of freedom is essential in order to encourage creativity and initiative. The students themselves should be led to set up the criteria to be followed in keeping notebooks. Among the rules which may be considered for adoption by the class as correct procedures are the following:

1. Loose-leaf notebooks of standard size should be used.
2. Each notebook should be labeled on the outside with the student's name and his homeroom.
3. Each notebook should be prefaced with a section of general information including such items as schedule, study guides, reading assignments, and so on.
4. Ink should be used in recording all materials.
5. Notebooks should be organized in sections for the various courses, with thumb guides for indicating the points of division.
6. Pages within each section should be numbered consecutively.
7. Headings should be underlined.
8. All notes should be neat and in good form with correct spelling and grammar.

9. All clippings should be pasted or stapled in place.
10. Each notebook should include a special section for each course, with a vocabulary list of new words peculiar to that course.

Written reports and term papers

Every secondary school student should acquire skill in written expression. Teachers of other subjects are too frequently inclined to relegate all responsibility for the development of such skill to the English teacher. Habits of good English can never be acquired in the English classroom alone; every teacher must be a teacher of English. Social studies materials require so much written work on the part of the students that all teachers in this field should assume a definite responsibility for aiding the English department in inculcating habits of correct usage. As a step in this direction, social studies teachers should set up minimum requirements in the matter of form, neatness, legibility, grammatical usage, spelling, clarity of expression, and vocabulary for all written work. Some instruction should also be given on proper methods of choosing a topic, limiting and defining its scope, evaluating and organizing materials, and developing ideas logically.

Requirements for written reports will necessarily vary according to the grade level of the student, the purpose for which the report is being written, and the scope of the subject. Since term papers are usually of major significance and primarily related to instruction in the senior high school, requirements should be somewhat more formal. Minimum standards might include the following:

1. All papers must be written in ink or typewritten.
2. All papers should be of a minimum length. This will vary with the maturity of the student and the significance of the paper.
3. Papers should be written on one side only with adequate margins and indentions.
4. All papers should include the following parts:
   a. A cover
   b. A title page
   c. The table of contents or an outline
   d. Footnotes in proper form for all quotations
   e. A bibliography

Summarizing

An oral or written summary is the concise statement of the main ideas or points of a discussion, a topic, or an article. The oral summary is important for concluding a lesson, a topic, or a unit: it should do more than merely review the high points of the discussion; it should tie in the ends and give a better perspective. The summary aids in complete understanding of the topic and aims toward the next undertaking. Writing summaries of materials he has read aids the pupil in cultivating the habit of careful reading and constructive writing. The following suggestions may serve as a guide for effective summarization procedure:

1. Read the material carefully and accurately.
2. Select the major points or central ideas.
3. Write these ideas in good English in your own words and style.
4. Compare your summary with the original, making sure that the true theme has not been altered or the facts distorted.
5. Revise and condense your summary if necessary.

Discussion

Discussion, a very important teaching-learning device, results when members of a group communicate their ideas and opinions on a subject of mutual interest or a common problem. Teachers of social studies have a vital responsibility in training all students in the procedure and habits of democratic argumentation and debate, through informal group discussions, the round table, the panel, the forum, and the formal debate.

The characteristics of good discussion include general participation rather than limitation to a few superior students who know how to express themselves. It is desirable to give each student a chance to have his say as well as for all to listen courteously. This discussion need not be formal and too studied. The timid member may be encouraged to say something even if it is but a single sentence. Naturally there is an organized topic, and the purpose is to exhibit the good and bad points of a matter from all sides. Here contrasted minds should meet under direction of an alert leader, keen to bring out all the qualities and talents of participants.

We define discussion as reflective thinking by two or more persons who cooperatively exchange information and ideas in an effort to solve a problem or to gain better understanding of a problem. Explicitly it means that:
1. All group members should have the opportunity to participate actively in the deliberations.
2. They should realize that they are searching for answers that have not been predetermined.
3. They should engage in problem-solving (whether the purpose is to reach a specific decision or to improve understanding) in a careful, critical and reflective manner.
4. They should carry on deliberations cooperatively.[4]

---

[4] W. M. Sattler and N. E. Miller, *Discussion and Conference* (Englewood Cliffs, N.J.: Prentice-Hall, Inc., 1954), p. 6.

Values of Discussion.   A democratic discussion is a complex process, since it means the acquisition of a number of specific, varied skills as well as certain desirable attitudes. For this reason, the social studies teacher will find it necessary to analyze his students' needs and to concentrate on a few points at a time, passing on to others when these have been dealt with. The values to be derived from discussions are important enough to justify the time spent. Experience in the various kinds of discussion should provide for pupil growth in the following: (1) effective speaking; (2) intelligent listening; (3) constructive and logical thinking with arguments based on accurate information rather than on the emotions; (4) cooperation, courtesy, and the spirit of fair play; (5) ability to take and receive criticism on an intellectual plane; (6) effective leadership; (7) ability to evaluate, organize, and present information; (8) self-confidence, self-reliance, and poise.

Debating.   All types of discussion will serve to develop the requisite skills. The debate, however, is especially effective since it is interesting to pupils and motivates them toward participation. A well-chosen program of debates should be initiated from time to time in each social studies class. Both informal and formal debates should be used. Formal debating is a parliamentary procedure. Students should, therefore, receive instruction in the rules for conducting a debate. Care must be exerted to select a problem that corresponds with the abilities of the students. The problem chosen should be timely, interesting, and stimulating to pupil growth.

In the junior high school, where debates are frequently less formal, every pupil in the group can be included in the procedure. To accomplish this objective, a greater number of speakers may be chosen for each side, the time allotted may be shortened, and all pupils may be assigned a definite part in organizing and preparing materials for presentation. In the senior high school, a more formal procedure should be followed. The number of speakers should be limited, and greater preparation is essential. For this reason it may not be practicable to assign all members of the class a part in any one debate. However, any member should feel free to make his contribution to the preparation of the speakers for either side. The teacher should guide the class in selecting, organizing, and presenting the materials and should see that the rules for conducting a debate are applied throughout.

Whether a limited number of judges is selected from the class, or the entire group votes on the outcome, the teacher should emphasize definite points to be considered in order that the decision may not be swayed by preconceived opinions.

Committee work

Committee work in the social studies furnishes excellent training in cooperative group procedures. The class is generally divided into a number of small committees, each of which chooses a chairman, or the chairman may be appointed by the teacher. Each member of the committee is responsible for a specific phase of the assignment, although the teacher can offer guidance and suggestions. The assignment may involve research work in the library, the use of reference books in the laboratory, and investigation of community resources. Each pupil shares in planning, preparing, and coordinating the work. Pupil interest should be allowed to aid in determining the phase of work each will pursue. A definite plan for checking, arranging, and evaluating the work should be established.

Upon completion the material is presented to the class in order that the entire group may benefit from each committee's findings. Any one of a number of different methods of presentation may be used, including oral or written reports, the use of visual aids, and the distribution of mimeographed materials. A discussion or question period should follow. When all committees on related assignments have reported, some form of summary should be given.

Training in committee work develops cooperation and responsibility, allows for individual differences, and provides experience in presenting information in an interesting and constructive manner.

Interviewing

Experience in interviewing is essential if secondary school pupils are to acquire social competence. The secondary school that does not take definite measures to provide this experience is neglecting its responsibility in training for life adjustment. Such training should be a part of social studies instruction through an integrated program that begins in the junior high school and is continued and expanded in the senior high school. Since it would be impossible to expect public officials or other prominent adults to submit to a constant barrage of interviews, especially by pupils who are still in the beginning and fumbling stage of practice, teachers must use much discretion in assigning such interviews. Pupils should practice in their own classroom and in other classrooms in the school by interviewing their fellow pupils and other school personnel. Only when the teacher is confident of their skill should they be allowed to interview people outside the school. The following directions should be stressed for practice interviews and should be mastered before the pupil is allowed to use the interview as a technique:

A neat appearance and good manners are vital. The pupil should be well groomed and courteous.

The interview should be brief and businesslike. The pupil should know in advance what he is going to ask and should state his questions clearly and briefly. He should listen more than he talks, and should never argue. When he has concluded the interview, he should express his thanks and leave immediately.

Note-taking should be adapted to the specific situation. If possible, no notes should be taken during the interview, for this tends to interrupt the speaker's train of thought. Notes should be written immediately afterward. However, when statistics, dates, or similar information is involved, brief notes may be jotted down at once in order to preserve accuracy.

Reading the newspaper

Some time should be spent in acquainting the pupil with skills in reading and interpreting the news. Because of individual needs and interests, it would be impossible and foolish for the teacher to force upon pupils a uniformity of interest in what is to be found in the daily newspaper. It is desirable to strive for some type of uniformity in the method used in reading, however, and it is desirable to direct pupil's choice of articles along worthwhile lines.

It would simplify the task of reading the newspaper if the teacher were to point out to the pupils the methods used by various newspapers for classifying and sectionalizing their articles. The class should become familiar with the index of the daily newspaper. Each pupil should be acquainted with the various sections of the newspapers he is to read and should become familiar with the papers' treatment of articles. If there is a section devoted to summaries of local, national, and world news, it should be brought to the attention of the pupils. This orientation to the newspaper should be conducted early in the pupil's secondary school career. Discussions on articles from various sections of the newspaper should be used to provide sufficient motivation for the perusal of these various sections.

After the orientation period, it would be well for the teacher to give certain hints to the pupil on rapid, but intelligent, reading of the news. Most news stories are written in a concise manner. Newsmen are trained to compose their material to allow for easy and quick comprehension by the reader. All well-written news articles contain the essential and meaningful facts in the introductory paragraphs. The paragraphs which follow are usually an elaboration of these facts and are more detailed in nature.

For the reader who is reading to gain a composite picture of the news, it is usually sufficient to read only the introductory paragraphs of a story.

Some newspaper articles, however, should be read in their entirety. These articles are usually written in a less formal style or are important enough to warrant full consideration by the reader. The teacher should point out the differences and set up some criteria for distinguishing between them.

The editorial page of a newspaper offers interesting and thought-provoking interpretations of the news. It is on this page that the newspaper voices its own opinions. All other pages devoted to the news should present facts objectively. This, unfortunately, is not always the case with many newspapers. It would be wise for the teacher to inform the pupil that newspapers are controlled by individuals or groups of individuals who determine the editorial policy of the paper. Sometimes this policy overflows from the editorial page into the news pages, and the result is "slanted" news, that is, news presented with the purpose of having the reader form a particular opinion. Discussions of editorial opinions of newspapers with differing stands are profitable. It is important for the teacher to urge the pupil to form his own opinion on the issues after being exposed to the various sides.

The teacher should attempt to present a comprehensive picture of the processes involved in writing about an event from the time it happens to the time it appears in print. This might be done by explaining how reporters write of local events, and correspondents and wire press services report events of a wider scope. Some mention should be made of the part which the press services play in gathering the news and relaying it to the newspapers throughout the country.

The teacher should point out the difference between factual reporting and the information printed as the opinion or statement of an individual or group on certain facts or situations. This is usually recognized by the use of quotation marks or such qualifying remarks as "Commissioner Jones stated that. . . ." This is an important distinction for the teacher to make if the pupil is to interpret the news intelligently.

After this introduction to the newspaper, the teacher should provide regular times for using the newspaper in the classroom. This is necessary for motivation and is also an essential part of the social studies curriculum.

Speaking effectively

So obvious a matter as good speech is yet in need of emphasis and discussion at this point, since many social studies teachers pay less attention to this qualification than it merits. The emphasis here is not so much on the content as on the manner of speech, the mode of delivery, enunciation, pronunciation, and volume. Good speech means control of the voice and articulation plus effective language and manipulation of ideas for clarity. This is primarily a social activity on the teacher's part, who will also set the example. To speak clearly and understandably implies that the speaker knows his topic thoroughly. He therefore does not have to search for words and has that confidence which results in an unhesitating delivery. Talks should not be long or formal but brief and adequate. The speaker should always address his remarks directly to the members of the class. Opportunities for speech improvement can be found in oral reports, panel discussions, forums, debates, and so on. The pupil should strive to develop a clear and pleasant voice, as well as a good method of presentation.

Effective listening

Effective listening is an important aspect of modern education. It is a vital communications skill as well as being a tool. The many avenues to learning demand an appreciation of the proper techniques for productive listening. The teaching-learning process involves aural activity; listening and speaking; writing and reading. As the writer or speaker anticipates attention from his listener and reader, so must the teacher train the pupil to attend to what goes on about him. Listening is one of the most difficult skills to perfect.

Radio, television, interviews, reports, and discussion all require a listening alertness on the part of both the pupil and teacher. Class reports and similar activities can be inexpensively recorded and will afford any group invaluable experience. The problem of listening attention here is solved because the pupils will enjoy listening to themselves; certainly in this type of activity the teacher can play a guiding role, pointing out weaknesses and strong points to be listened for. Thus listening becomes enjoyable, and opens new horizons for pupils. Attentive listening stimulates thinking and builds a rich store of knowledge.

Problem solving

Students should acquire skill in the techniques of problem solving. They should have a considerable amount of this experience when the teacher and group gather materials for the completion of a problem. Some guidance on the part of the teacher is necessary. In the process of recognizing and stating the problem, the pupils receive excellent training in organization. The planning, selecting, and organizing of material requires the student to use sound judgment. He must think critically when utilizing the information he has gathered for the possible solution of the problem. Learning of this type has a wide application to the problems confronted by pupils in school and in the community. Furthermore, such training has a carry-over for youth as they enter adult society.

Evaluation

Evaluation activities engaged in by the pupils are considered an integral part of the learning process. The student has many opportunities to evaluate information gathered by himself and the group. He contributes to the possible solutions of the problems studied by the group. The pupil learns a great deal about himself and his growth in terms of the goals he has established. Through evaluation the pupil learns to cooperate with the group. He learns to follow directions, accept responsibilities, and benefit by group decisions.

Gaining information from books

Since secondary school students must use books so frequently in preparation of their school, and since they should acquire habits that will serve them as adults, they should be trained in the use of books as tools. To get the best results from any tool, the user must understand it and learn to handle it efficiently. The student should be able to recognize the various parts of a book and should know what kinds of information he can expect to gain from each. Special emphasis should be placed upon the difference between the table of contents and the index and the occasions when each should be used.

The making of bibliographies

Students should acquire the ability to make comprehensive bibliographies. Both in high school and in college a bibliography is frequently required in connection with important written assignments. The student who learns to collect and arrange his sources of information efficiently will be better equipped to organize his thoughts and knowledge.

Preliminary steps in examining a subject

1. Get a general idea of its scope by reading an encyclopedia article or analyzing an elementary book on the subject.
2. Determine all possible sources of information in the libraries

available to you, by consulting (a) encyclopedias and other reference books; (b) card catalog for other books on the subject; (c) *Reader's Guide* and other indexes for articles in periodicals; (d) bibliographies found in books and articles; and (e) pamphlet file for pamphlets and clippings.

3. Examine and analyze sources that seem promising.
4. Select and make notes on all sources that are found helpful.

Since most of these steps involve the listing of sources, the student can save much time if at the outset he adopts the practice of making his notes in correct form on index cards or slips of paper. A separate card should be used for each source. This will allow sufficient space for brief notes on the value of each source and will provide for flexibility in rearrangement of items and the addition or elimination of sources. The following information should be listed on each card:

    a. Call number
    b. Author's name
    c. Title (underlined)
    d. Edition, unless the first, and volume if more than one
    e. Place of publication and publisher
    f. Date (for periodicals, list volume, number, month, and year)
    g. Any other pertinent items

When completed, the bibliography should be written or typed and appended to the report. The usual arrangement is alphabetical by author. Although there are several correct forms for bibliographical entries, the examples given below, if carefully followed, should be adequate for high school use.

Padelford, N. J. and G. A. Lincoln, *The Dynamics of International Politics.* New York: The Macmillan Company, 1962.
Moffatt, M. P., "Education and Competence," *The Journal of Educational Sociology,* XXXV (December, 1961), 189-192.

Map interpretation

Students should acquire skill in the proper use of maps and globes, since they will serve him as guides to acquiring information and knowledge of the world in which we live. The ability to use and understand geographical concepts is most important for today's youth. The social studies teacher should provide adequate instruction and appropriate activities to develop the basic map-reading skills acquired in the elementary school. Many social studies courses at the secondary level lend themselves to instruction in geography.

Skill in map reading includes: understanding symbols and their value in reading the various types of maps, understanding of direction and distance and how they are determined, determining location and making comparison to give meaning and provide understanding of a particular region.

Students learn much about the physical and economic aspects of a country by studying a map and the globe. They learn to observe more fully various geographical conditions. Both maps and globes should be used when pupils are studying a problem. In this way, distance and direction are more clearly understood. A variety of information such as population, rainfall, transportation, communication, and resources is revealed by a map. Growth in map-reading skills is an important aspect of training pupils to understand the events and trends in modern civilization.

Graphic interpretation

Reading and understanding the wide range of graphic materials used in today's society is an important skill to be emphasized in the social studies. Graphic materials include: charts, diagrams, tables, scales, cartoons, and pictures and are found in books, newspapers, and magazines. They should be studied, interpreted, and used by both pupils and teachers in the learning process.

Examples of such materials can furnish sources and information for tackboard displays, reports, researches, discussions, and summaries. A knowledge of graphic forms aids the pupil in his reading. Problems, issues, topics, and important questions are more fully understood when the interpretation is clear.

Reading, writing, and speaking

The basic skills of reading, writing, and speaking are essential to learning in the social studies. Each of these skills calls for a vocabulary that provides meaning and understanding for the learner. Such skills usually improve progressively as the pupil moves up the educational ladder.

The social studies teacher should always consider individual differences when giving directions for strengthening these particular skills. The grade level and ability of the group should be considered when planning any work. Furthermore, in making assignments that employ one such skill, discretion should be used. There are many opportunities for using these skills in oral and written reports, discussions, forums, debates, and evaluations. Every teacher should strive to improve the work of each student in the group, whether it be in gathering and organizing information, asking and answering questions, discussing and presenting materials, or planning and developing a topic.

The social studies teacher should select activities and experiences that will provide for worthwhile growth in the individual. A few suggestions might include:

1. Select interesting and timely topics for group discussion.
2. Provide a rich supply of reference materials.
3. Permit pupils to select topics that appeal to them.
4. Develop an informal atmosphere in the learning process to stimulate discussion and expression.
5. Stimulate cooperative planning and group sharing of the work as a productive approach for developing skills.
6. Encourage and furnish assistance to those students needing extra help.
7. Encourage improvement as the goal for each student and make him aware of his progress.
8. Give clear assignments which furnish a sense of direction for the group.
9. Make each student feel his responsibility for the work.
10. Stress quality rather than quantity.

Teachers must understand that the two major media in the process of social learning are through school and community experiences and language usage. This fact calls for learning activities that are productive, and readings that will build vocabularies and encourage writing.

Developing Study Techniques

One of the major responsibilities of the social studies teacher is to teach the students how to study properly. Modern instructional practices in which the pupil is actively experiencing functional learning make it essential for the teacher to provide instruction in how to study, to do research, and to develop skills that will aid the pupil in dealing with materials at hand. The student must have the interest and incentive to see the need for study. The teacher must clarify the assignment or problem and give suggestions for the pupils, so they can plan their approach to examining it thoroughly.

The social studies program calls for the study and analysis of materials and problems. The student writes reports, builds exhibits, presents research findings, participates in panel discussions, and takes tests. These activities require both study and preparation. Some groups may devote the entire period to research and guided study. The many activities engaged in by a group require the pupils to apply the habits of effective study to their everyday work. Teaching that is interesting, functional, and related to the needs of the group will, by implication, facilitate better study procedures. The alert teacher, with the help of proper evaluation techniques, can ascertain if the pupil has developed or is following desirable and effective study procedures. Remedial assistance should be given to pupils needing guidance in study techniques and learning procedures.

Schools continuing the older practice of assignment-recitation and the usual homework will require that the student follow standardized study habits in the preparation of the assignment. They should stress such fundamentals as: desirable working conditions, proper facilities, desirable study habits, and lastly readiness for the next day.

Conclusion

The teaching of skills which have a functional value in the social studies is a phase of learning that contributes to individual growth and behavior. Skills hold a definite value for the learner as he works with others in the teaching-learning process. They are the tools and machinery that facilitate learning. Furthermore, skills tend to develop social competence in the individual in his everyday life. The learner, as he masters skills, is more capable of making intelligent choices of available resources when seeking the solutions to problems that face him.

Bibliography

Carpenter, H. M., ed., *Skills in Social Studies,* National Council for the Social Studies, Twenty-fourth Yearbook. Washington, D.C.: National Education Association, 1953.

French, W. and associates, *Behavioral Goals of General Education in High School.* New York: Russell Sage Foundation, 1957.

Miel, A., ed., *Creativity in Teaching: Invitations and Instances.* Belmont, Calif.: Wadsworth Publishing Company, Inc., 1961.

Wellington, C. B. and J. Wellington, *Teaching for Critical Thinking.* New York: McGraw-Hill Book Company, Inc., 1960.

Chapter Ten

The Classroom–
A Learning Laboratory

The modern social studies classroom is a learning laboratory with a functional setting for effective instruction. No doubt the strides of new technology will influence the type of equipment and materials that will be found in the learning laboratory of the future. Some of these new devices will be considered by the teacher as a further aid in the instructional process.

The social studies curriculum calls for the utilization of new knowledge as well as appropriate facilities in the learning environment. The classroom must be adequate in size to provide for the transformation to a learning laboratory setting whenever necessary. This allows for laboratory-type teaching with its various activities and experiences participated in by the students using the newer technology and procedures. The entire learning environment should be so arranged as to encourage creative, constructive, and critical thinking. The physical equipment and resources must provide a workroom for the students, because activities and the practical solution of problems characterize every unit or topic. Newer methodology calls for appropriate facilities and classroom equipment. The social studies learning laboratory requires as much careful consideration and planning as does any other phase of the teaching-learning process.

The Classroom

The classroom has been called a learning laboratory for social studies instruction. This connotes a functional setting within which the teacher provides the essential guidance and direction for students.

The desirable type of classroom provides useful and moveable furniture, facilities, and equipment. It is so planned as to provide greater utilization and become more functional in detail as it relates to the teaching-learning process. The modern classroom should help to provide the environmental setting for instruction that furnishes opportunities for fostering student growth.

Activities

The very nature of the activities employed in today's classroom have a bearing upon its usage as a laboratory.

There is such a variety of activities used in the modern classroom that a statement on trends would undoubtedly miss some important activities. However, the following activities are either prominent today or are inherent in the experimental programs: (a) activities which bring the student in close contact with the current events, discoveries, relationships of people, and developments of science throughout the world; (b) activities involving critical thinking techniques, problem solving skills, and use of community resources; (c) activities that provide for the widespread physical and intellectual capacity of all students; (d) activities that place greater emphasis on student initiative, creativity, originality, and self direction; (e) activities that teach the democratic process through pupil-teacher planning and cooperative group activity; (f) activities which utilize the total range of audio-visual services; (g) activities involving construction and the creation of materials by students; and (h) activities which promote a wise use of leisure time.[1]

Facilities

The facilities available in the social studies classroom should be adequate to meet the demand of modern instruction. Today's classroom should be so furnished and equipped as to provide a suitable environment for an effective working situation.

The following are some of the trends that are taking place in classroom facilities:

---

[1] J. D. MacConnell and G. F. Ovard, "On Planning Academic Classrooms: General Procedures in Planning Academic Classrooms," *The American School Board Journal*, CXLIV, No. 2 (February 1962), 36.

a. Greater flexibility and portability of all room furnishings including student desks, storage cabinets, book trucks, magazine racks, folding stages, and audio-visual equipment. Such flexibility extends to more permanent fixtures through removable and interchangeable tackboard-chalkboard and other wall surfaces.
b. Expanded use of audio-visual equipment.
c. Expanded use of television as a major teaching device or tool to be used in large and small group instruction. Facilities for eventual use of commercial, community educational, and closed circuit television should be planned.
d. Greater flexibility in classroom space. This flexibility may be provided through extension. The physical facilities may be extended by utilizing other existing areas, as, library, projection rooms, and materials work centers. Proper orientation to these other facilities becomes a major consideration.[2]

This overview of the prevailing trends in classroom facilities should provide direction for teachers. As newer facilities are available for instructional purposes, the teacher can apply them to specific learning situations. The students and teacher alike will find change presents an inviting challenge. Newer devices tend to stimulate ideas, arouse curiosity, invite experimentation, and foster constructive learning activity.

Today's Social Studies Classroom

Today's planned social studies classroom has unique features and facilities for learning. It is in reality a laboratory for learning where students work and grow under the guidance of the teacher. The selected furnishings and their arrangement have a direct bearing upon the quality of results obtained. Satisfactory outcomes can be expected from any classroom situation only when adequate and comfortable working facilities prevail. It should be furnished and equipped to provide a suitable environment for the acquiring and practicing of social studies skills.

At the secondary level the social studies classroom is used as a homeroom and on occasions may be shared with teachers of other content areas. However, certain standard items of equipment are considered especially essential for social studies instruction. Light and color are a definite part of the classroom environment. Attractive colors and modern lighting design are receiving due consideration.

The modern social studies curriculum with its stated objectives, together with the methods, procedures, and activities employed by the teacher in the learning process will in a large measure determine the application of facilities, equipment and the utilization of materials. The total

---

[2] *Ibid.*

setting should provide the learners with a wide range of opportunities and a desirable working atmosphere that challenges their development. Such a climate furnishes the setting for interesting student activity which helps to build effective citizenship.

Courtesy Hanover Park High School, Hanover Park, N.J.

A MODERN SOCIAL STUDIES CLASSROOM

Special features

New features are steadily being added to the classroom. We find a built-in cabinet-sink, a library with bookshelves and bookcases, a magazine rack, a display table for special projects, display cases, a special table arrangement for conferences and committee work, a conference room, a permanent roll-up screen for projection purposes, and blackout shades. Some schools have available to all teachers a special projection room for viewing audio-visual materials. Lighting, heating, ventilation, and the choice of desirable colors for the classrooms are receiving special attention.

A conference room

A recent practical and functional addition to the social studies classroom is a conference or consultation room. It has proved to be a valuable asset for the teacher as well as the students. It can be used by a student committee in preparing an assignment. Other activities are possible here such as teacher-pupil planning, conferences, and counseling. It may also serve as a work center for the teacher. A special feature is that any activity can be in process in the conference room without disturbing the entire group.

Furniture and fixtures

The selection of suitable furniture, like other equipment, should be in line with the best educational theory and practice in the social studies field. The good teacher can put to use in the best possible way the furniture he has available. The essentials for the teaching-learning process include tables, chairs and desks, filing cabinets, bookcases, shelving, chalkboards and tackboards, globes, maps, charts, projector, recorder, radio, and television sets. In addition, for instructional purposes, books, workbooks, encyclopedias, dictionaries, and other special materials may be included.

Chalkboard.   An essential part of the social studies classroom, some chalkboards are made of green glass, a type very popular with teachers, and frequently specified in new building designs. These boards are usually located in the front of the room and are occasionally designed as sliding panels in front of lockers or storage space.

Tackboards.   This equipment, necessary in every classroom, is usually located along the side or back of the room but is often placed above the chalkboards.

Tables, Chairs, and Desks.   The new, light, and movable types provide a greater convenience for both the students and the teacher. Flexibility and usability are important factors of arrangement, especially where the core program is in operation. The individual chair and table are popular; so is the single adjustable desk-chair combination unit. Sidearm tablet chairs are usually found in the senior high school. Tables which accommodate two or three students may be joined to form a suitable committee table. Individual tables may be united for some special activities or small group arrangements. The general arrangement of the room will be determined by the teacher and students and the immediate activity for learning, such as discussions, forums, floor talks, group work, or viewing a film.

Teacher's Desk and Locker.   The teacher's desk is also movable and should be used for general administration and instruction. It should be equipped with an atlas, a desk dictionary, a World Almanac, a desk calendar, a memorandum pad, and a desk blotter. The desk top and the drawers should be kept neat and orderly, for efficient work and to set a good example. The center drawer should contain the plan book or guides, the attendance and record books, and keys. The top side drawer should contain attendance cards, report cards, excuse forms, library passes, and all other forms that are frequently used. Other drawers should be utilized for the general materials needed by the teacher in preparing his work. This procedure permits standardization, and will aid the supervisor and the substitute teacher. A personal locker for the teacher is featured in the newer classroom designs.

Storage Space. Modern social studies classroom is provided with adequate storage space. Cabinets, files, and drawers provide compartments for supplies and materials essential to the learning process. Adequate shelving for display and storage purpose can prove to be helpful. Each unit has a coat locker for students, which is concealed by doors which slide upward. In some school plants, these lockers are placed along the halls.

Cabinets and Files. Cabinets and files are essential for storing various materials that are commonly used in the learning laboratory. The social studies collection will include pamphlets, outline maps, clippings, outlines or worksheets, a picture collection, and display materials. All materials should be placed in special folders with the tabs plainly labelled.

Teachers will find it helpful to adopt and adhere to an efficient filing system in order that materials may be readily found. Students should be instructed to return all materials when they are no longer needed. Typed cards in a separate card file may be used as an index if the collection is extensive, but if an efficient filing system is used and is interspersed with sufficient cross references, the card index will be unnecessary. A suggested plan for the teacher's filing system is a scheme of subject headings similar to those used by the library. Another system might be the division of the social studies into subjects and the further subdivision of these subjects into units and topics. However, since the same clipping or picture, on transportation, for example, may be useful on occasion in geography, history, current events, or problems of democracy, it would seem that the latter method of filing would limit the over-all usefulness of the collection.

Cabinets for Miscellaneous Supplies and Tools. Since the primary purpose of the learning laboratory is constructive student activity, students must be furnished with working materials. They may include rulers, protractors, compasses, crayons or colored pencils, water colors, brushes, pen holders and nibs, erasers, scissors, and blotters. In addition, the teacher needs to keep on hand a large supply of various kinds and sizes of special papers, a sufficient amount of paste, paper clips, rubber bands, colored chalk, India ink, ink eradicator, transparent tape, drawing sets, and a stapler. All these supplies require storage space. They may be kept most efficiently in built-in cabinets with shelf or drawer space. There will frequently be unfinished maps, outlines, charts, or other work at the end of the period. For this reason it may contribute to orderly procedure if each student is provided with a folder in which to store unfinished work. These folders should be the responsibility of the students themselves and should be stored in a special cabinet for which students alone are responsible. Students might be encouraged to add suitable materials to the files for instructional purposes. An occasional inventory is profitable, and general rules for maintaining the cabinets are helpful. Students and teacher will derive a great deal of satisfaction from the orderly arrangement of materials for their work.

Maps and Globes.   Maps and globes are indispensable in all phases of the social studies, particularly in geography. Maps of various types should be available for instructional purposes. The number and kinds of maps provided may vary with the need for them, and special uses made of them, in the different courses. Good textbooks contain maps that are specifically related to the topic under consideration. However, there are certain types of wall maps that should be included in the laboratory equipment. The following is a recommended list of essential maps:

1. *Political-Physical:* World, Western Hemisphere, Eastern Hemisphere, Polar (azimuthal equidistant projection), United States, United States and Possessions, North America, South America, Europe (Modern), Africa, Asia, State, Local Community (county, township, city, or town).
2. *Historical:* One set (American series). (They tell the geographical, historical, political, and economic facts of our growth.)
3. *Slated Wall Outline Maps:* United States and the World.

Maps should be of the roll-up type and, if space permits, should be placed at the front of the room above the chalkboard. The new multiple mounting of a set of maps makes it most convenient to use them. Folding maps are very useful when a teacher is required to move to different rooms in the course of his teaching. A map display rail, usually located over the chalkboard or tackboard, can be utilized for certain types of maps. Other maps—pictorial, relief, or economic—may be added as necessary. In addition, each teacher should have a large supply of small maps for pupil use, such as outline, population, and rainfall. These may be purchased or mimeographed.

Globes.   Globes have assumed a significant role in the teaching of modern world geography. Modern geography is global geography, and essential global representations should be understood. The ability to reason geographically is important for an intelligent understanding of world society, and the student, through globes, is able to visualize world events and trends. There are various models and types of globe mountings suitable for every teaching purpose. A good, 16-inch, physical-political globe, which identifies continents, oceans, zones, meridians, parallels, and countries, is needed for every learning situation in the social studies. Project-problem globes, which are both markable and washable, have considerable utility for the study of either history or geography. The new, 12-inch, air-age globe with horizon ring mounting is most useful for demonstrating distances between areas and for teaching global relationships. Since the globe is a valid representation of the earth, it can be a very effective teaching aid for the social studies; however, it can be effective only so long as it is used.

Documents. Every social studies laboratory should have an adequate collection of authentic and significant documents. They constitute genuine sources for research purposes as well as for dramatization of historic events. Pupils should be taught how to use these documents in gathering and evaluating materials for reports, committee projects, semester papers, and dramatic presentations. For example, when studying American history, some of the fundamental sources would include copies of the Mayflower Compact, Albany Plan of Union, Declaration of Independence, Articles of Confederation, Constitution of the United States, and the Bill of Rights. The State Constitution should also be included for use in the study of local history and government. Documents specifically illustrate the actions of people and offer concrete evidence to the realistic and unimaginative students.

Duplicators. The use of duplicators in school systems and even in the social studies laboratory repays the user many times over the purchase price. Back in the days of the one-room schoolhouse, duplicators were unknown and probably would have been of little or no use to the teacher. Today, however, with the complexities of the modern school, a teacher finds duplicators invaluable in the course of the daily work. The primary advantage is, of course, its time-saving factor. However, there are many uses to which the machine may be put. Long-range assignments or guide sheets may be distributed to the classes. Outlines of current work can be duplicated, to save the students much note-taking (which incidentally also takes time away from learning). Maps, charts, graphs, cartoons, and diagrams may also be duplicated and passed to the group. Notes, bibliographies, and statistics are also included in the use of duplicated materials. All tests and short quizzes are perfect materials for the duplicator.

When preparing material for duplication, keep in mind the following points: the specific job to be done should be clearly understandable; the material should be neat, concise, interesting, and, where possible, accompanied by illustration.

Picture Collection. An appropriate picture collection is a vital part of the laboratory. It is primarily the teacher's own responsibility to initiate and maintain this collection. Each picture should be chosen either to teach a lesson or to furnish a visual image of some concrete identity. Many of these pictures may be clipped from magazines and newspapers. Postcards, posters, or travel folders may be included in the collection. Pictures not obtainable from these sources may be purchased at reasonable cost from picture publishing firms.

The pictures should be mounted on heavy paper of uniform size and kept in folders by subject. They are most easily available filed within the same folders and under the same alphabetic arrangement as the other material in the filing cabinet. However, if circumstances prevent the mounting of the pictures, it may be advisable to store the unmounted ones in large envelopes within the folder. The collection should be reviewed from time to time and all outmoded pictures discarded. The laboratory collection can be supplemented by pictures obtained from the files of the school library and the public library.

Graphic Illustrations. Applicable graphs, charts, diagrams, engravings, and prints are essential for the teaching of the social studies.

Projection Equipment and Audio-Visual Materials. Teaching aids must be made readily available for the teacher. Every school should have an effective procedure for dispensing needed materials and equipment such as an opaque projectors, motion picture projectors, film-slide projectors, recording machines, phonographs, radios, televisions, records, films, slides, and film-strips. In fact, each classroom should have a mobile projector and some of these other items. Models, specimens, and objects are valuable. Many classrooms are equipped with a two-way central sound system. In looking ahead to the application of television in the learning process, special attention should be given to the installation of this newer teaching tool. Provision should be made for adequate storage of any of these items either in the classroom or in the social studies department.

Other Items and Materials. Other helpful items should include: dictionary and stand, display cases, speaker's stand, book truck, and a typewriter.

The Learning Laboratory Library. Each learning laboratory has its own library unit with essential materials suited for the social studies at a particular learning level. In addition, the teacher and group have ready access to all materials available in the central school library. The library area has shelf space for magazine displays and open bookshelves for reference books and source materials.

The Laboratory as a Workshop. The social studies laboratory might rightfully be called a learning workshop. The integration between the laboratory and all other departments of the school is unique. For example, the laboratory and the school library provide an excellent service to the students. Reading material is placed in the laboratory for use by groups working on a particular problem; however, they are encouraged to explore supplementary material in the library. The teaching method in the laboratory encourages the reading of books, periodicals, pamphlets, bulletins, and newspapers, in addition to the use of maps, globes, slides, films, recordings, and transcriptions. When the particular unit is completed, the essential materials are returned to the library and new sources are obtained for the next topic.

This type of learning situation provides a stimulating environment, and all the pupils are given the opportunity of experiencing success, either in an individual or a group project. Students in the advanced grades may contact other departments for materials to meet their needs and interests and may communicate with agencies in the community and state.

Student Initiative in the Laboratory. A wide variety of experiences is available for pupils in the laboratory. Committees may be appointed to share in the responsibility for the room arrangement and in the selection of the projects to be studied. Each student should have the opportunity to act as program chairman and he should assume this responsibility for a definite period of time. Committees should be responsible for distributing and collecting materials, arranging equipment, organizing bulletin board displays, mimeographing materials, securing library references, welcoming guests, contacting other departments and agencies, relating community activities, arranging entertainment programs, maintaining guides for radio and television programs, and offering suggestions for improvement of the program.

Student initiative should be followed and guided in the selection of activities typical of contemporary society. Since modern education extends beyond the classroom, projects should have community significance. Group leadership and committee cooperation should dominate the laboratory. Students doing individual or group research should be encouraged to obtain source materials from commercial establishments and governmental agencies. Much valuable training can be gained through such mature correspondence. Committees should assist in selection and planning of field trips in the area.

Projects and student initiative

The encouragement of a learner in the choice of a problem or project should be a prime objective of the social studies teacher. Using the laboratory method or problem method and an adequate supply of materials and resources is a desirable approach. The teacher acts as a consultant or director when difficulties arise.

When a new unit, problem, or topic is introduced, the group might discuss what each would like to do as supplementary work. The students should be encouraged to think out their own projects, but the teacher can often suggest some activities that might appeal to the varied interests, talents, and abilities in the groups.

For example, the artistic students might draw maps or scenes of the period under discussion or write a report on the art of that time. Musically inclined students will be interested in learning about the music and musical instruments of the period. They might even wish to put on a program, singing and playing some of the songs popular in that day. Students interested in journalism might print a newspaper full of news of the period. Girls interested in homemaking could dress dolls in period clothing or start scrapbooks containing old recipes of the era being studied. Boys interested in transportation could build model vehicles and write a history of the travel during the epoch. Students might write and produce a play depicting society of the age. Similarly, a radio script could be enacted.

Committee projects should be encouraged to teach students how to work on a problem together. A large physical map or the drawing of a mural could be a committee undertaking.

There is a project to appeal to the interest of every student. The teacher might make a list of projects which could be used, and add to it when new suggestions come from the group. Teachers should always welcome any new ideas offered either by students or teachers.

Projects not only give keener interest to the text material and regular classroom work but often aid the student in finding new and fascinating hobbies. Use of projects that the individual himself suggests, heightens his enthusiasm. Projects also aid the students in gaining knowledge of how to use encyclopedias, maps, charts, graphs, reference books, and so on. This is painless teaching at its best. Projects are useful in correlating social studies with other courses.

The teacher's job in these work periods would be one of suggestion and direction, praise of the work, encouragement and help, and subtle direction in order to keep the student working toward his goal with as little waste of time and effort as possible. Project work provides the kind of social relationship in which group and teacher plan, work, study, and learn together. Each may work at his own speed and according to his own abilities, yet all feel that they are part of a unit working toward a common goal.

The classroom—a real learning laboratory

The modern social studies teacher guides and directs students in the process of effective learning in the stimulating and challenging climate of a learning laboratory. In such a friendly and yet informal type of environment, learning becomes a process of change and development in the student. Establishing and maintaining an effective learning climate in the classroom can do much to eliminate any semblance of a disciplinary situation. An interested and actively engaged group is enjoying functional learning experiences in a meaningful environment and in attractive surroundings. This becomes one of the teacher's major goals. The teacher employs individualized instruction when essential and small group activities whenever desirable or appropriate.

A plentiful supply of materials and adequate visual aids are readily available for usage. Creativity and originality are encouraged on the part of the students as they go about their work in solving problems. The use of observation and listening, along with group discussion, should do much to increase skill in communication. Realistic and functional experiences both in the classroom and the community are always a part of learning in a flexible program. In this manner the student has the opportunity to assimilate new knowledge and important information. This tends to open an avenue for the student to engage in further or new research. The teacher selects the best possible ways for meeting individual interests and needs. Each student is always given the opportunity to express his views, which are respected. Teacher-pupil planning is employed as a technique in the selection and organization of a problem for study, and in determining activities and applying appropriate evaluation measures. The best traits of appropriate citizenship are constantly practiced as a way of democratic living. In this manner the teacher and students working together in the learning laboratory are engaged in stimulating learning experiences that foster individual growth.

Conclusion

The modern functional learning laboratory is a laboratory for living and a practical workshop for learning. Materials and equipment are readily available for immediate use. Every social studies classroom should become a real learning laboratory. The furnishings and equipment can be acquired over a period of time, and many of the items can be constructed within the school at relatively small cost. If the cooperation of the students is enlisted, surprising results can be achieved as interest and enthusiasm encourage invention and originality. The real value of the learning-laboratory type of classroom can, to a degree, be judged by the accomplishments of a group. Each student may work on a special problem or project, but he relates his findings to the unit under consideration. The room itself, like all classrooms, should be as cheerful and attractive as it is possible to make it. At the same time, the primary purpose of the laboratory should not be forgotten; it should remain free from unused equipment and obsolete materials. As a learning laboratory, its purpose is to provide the setting for functional activities and worthwhile experiences that facilitate student growth through effective learning.

Bibliography

Klausmeier, H. J., *Teaching in the Secondary School*. New York: Harper & Row, Publishers, 1958.

Leese, J., K. Frasure, and M. Johnson, Jr., *The Teacher in Curriculum Making*. New York: Harper & Row, Publishers, 1961.

McKean, R. C., *Principles and Methods in Secondary Education*. New York: Charles E. Merrill Books, Inc., 1962.

National Society for the Study of Education, *The Integration of Educational Experiences,* Fifty-seventh Yearbook, Part III. Chicago: University of Chicago Press, 1958.

Noar, G., *The Junior High School Today and Tomorrow*, 2nd ed. Englewood Cliffs, N.J.: Prentice-Hall, Inc., 1961.

Wiggins, S. P., *Successful High School Teaching*. Boston: Houghton Mifflin Company, 1958.

Chapter Eleven

History–A Significant Study

History provides a recorded narrative of mankind and civilization. This formal discipline occupies an enviable position as the oldest of the social sciences. It unveils the past, illuminates the present, and focuses attention on the future path of mankind. History furnishes a priceless collection of rich stories relating to people, places, and events. It provides a chronology of the experiences of mankind portrayed as an impelling drama on the stage of life. A knowledge of the past with all its ramifications helps to furnish a better understanding of the contemporary world. History along with the other social sciences helps to provide a clear understanding of the cultural patterns of the world.

The study of history has many direct values for the student who will delve into its many pages and to absorb its rich and enlightening knowledge. New frontiers are interestingly revealed and understanding is broadened through the appreciation of history.

History and viewpoints

Various definitions and viewpoints have been expressed concerning history. Scholarly research and significant surveys have contributed new knowledge, interpretations, emphasis, and ideas. Courses in this major discipline have long been an important part of the curriculum at the college and secondary levels. The content of courses has changed and new courses have been introduced to focus attention upon specific subject matter.

Early in this century a new emphasis was directed toward the improvement of history instruction. James Harvey Robinson called for a wider conception of the subject or a new alignment of history. This broader scope of history was to include social, economic, and cultural aspects of society in addition to the political development and military treatment. Robinson published *The New History* in 1912, in which he emphasized the inclusion of a broader study of man and society in order to comprehend the past as fully as the present. The "new" history opened greater horizons for the historian and history widened its boundaries. Historical writings and textbooks soon revealed the trend toward an increased emphasis upon all aspects of life.

Since this pioneering endeavor was made, other efforts have followed which emphasized new viewpoints in history. Among these are the yearbooks of the National Council for the Social Studies, which contain excellent materials focusing upon or relating to a new viewpoint in history as well as the other social sciences.

Historical sources and values

Historical sources are classified as primary or original, and secondary. Primary sources may include written materials (books, diaries, memoirs, journals, treaties, and papers), artifacts (coins, tools, weapons, buildings, statues, and human remains), oral materials (legends, songs, and tales), and pictorial materials (maps, charts, sketches, and inscriptions). Secondary sources are those derived from primary sources (textbooks, bulletins, and reports).

The historical method should be used in evaluating materials. A critical analysis should be made to determine the authenticity of the source. The evaluation, or external criticism, should help reveal the answers to such questions as the originality of the document, its publication date, its historical accuracy, its location, and its authorship. Correct historical evaluation is indispensable for the interpretation of economic, political, and social developments. Training in the historical method provides a systematic way for pupils and college students to acquire definite knowledge.

History is the systematic narrative of the civilization and progress of man. It is no mere accumulation of facts and dates, but a living, inspiring story of man and his achievements. The study of history can easily be made a major field of interest by reason of its many interrelations. The subject gives background to the social, political, intellectual, economic, industrial, and cultural aspects of contemporary life and affairs.

History can be made to live, and it is vitally important that it be made realistic. Those events, people, conditions, and movements that made history must be visualized, known, and understood. History is changing so rapidly that all teachers must be alert to the need of acquiring new materials for instructional purposes.

History in the curriculum

The study of history is found in the elementary, secondary, and college curriculum. There are various kinds of history; political, social, economic, cultural, and intellectual. American, European, World, Latin American, Far East, Middle East, and State history are some courses commonly listed in curriculum guides or catalogues.

At the secondary level specific arrangements for history offerings are noted. American history is usually found at the eighth grade level and also at the eleventh grade. In some instances the state requirement is a two-year sequence of American history, usually found at the eleventh and twelfth grades. Some schools offer American history as a one- or two-year course. Another structure would include the state requirement of one year of American history followed by a twelfth grade problems course. The arrangement of United States History, Government, and Modern Problems can serve as an alternative two-year sequence.

World history, which has grown in popularity since World War II, is usually offered at the sophomore year either as a required course or as an elective. World history can also be an elective at other grade levels. This is a realistic course presenting the essential background materials leading to the growth of European Civilization. A unit or a separate semester course in Latin American or Hemisphere History in either the junior or the senior high school has been incorporated into some history programs.

Some states require the teaching of state history. Such a course is found at the seventh or eighth grade and may be titled *Our Community and State*. The inclusion of state history may be a specific unit on state history in connection with American history or community study.

American History

American history has a significant role in the world's development and is an important consideration in the study of civilization. Old world influences were felt in the early colonial stages of American development. It is more important that one possess knowledge of his own country's history. Furthermore, in order to comprehend the dynamics of change and to view intelligently problems related to our nation, one must have a command of the world scene. The study and teaching of American history has long been a basic part of our national educational structure. American history is taught on both the elementary and secondary level. It is chiefly placed in the fifth, eighth, and eleventh grades. The study of our nation—its origin and development—should be one of the richest, most interesting, and most challenging experiences for our youth. Good citizenship necessitates that we have a thorough knowledge of our heritage. The traditions, ideals, and premises that made America great are basic to understanding the real value of our democracy. United States history and government should be studied in a functional and informative manner.

In order to fully appreciate the present, one must have a comprehension of the past. From our nation's beginnings one can note the social and economic developments from those deep traditions and loyalties firmly planted in the past. Our heritage is a priceless one built from the work and sacrifice of our pioneers and builders who established a firm structure.

A nation's history is the record of its existence, and history is both a product and creator of national experiences. A nation's view of its own image is shaped largely by the common traditions it has developed. Narratives of struggle and crisis, heroes and heroism, courage and idealism, and problems and achievements help give the citizens of a nation common ideals, a sense of being a part of a common cause, and of having a common destiny. In highly developed contemporary cultures, national history is written and taught to the young. It is transmitted in part by parents, the mass media, cultural leaders, and by art, music, and literature, but its systematic transmission is largely the responsibility of the school.[1]

Organizational structure

The teaching of American history at the junior high school level can do much to foster the objectives of the social studies. The building of proper attitudes, appreciations, understandings, and skills is essential for effective living in a free democratic society.

The Committee on American History in Schools and Colleges made recommendations for American history courses for the junior and senior high school levels. The theme for the two were "The Building of the Nation" and "A Democratic Nation in a World Setting." The topics listed did not constitute a course of study but rather suggested content of

---

[1] I. James Quillen, "American History in the Upper Grades and Junior High School," in William H. Cartwright and Richard L. Watson, Jr., co-editors, *Interpreting and Teaching American History*, Thirty-First Yearbook of the National Council for the Social Studies (Washington, D.C.: The Council, 1961), p. 344.

significant importance at the particular learning level. The major divisions or topics recommended for the junior high school course were:[2]

1. *The American Revolution:* As the outgrowth of colonial development, with attention to outstanding military events, the government during the war, the Articles of Confederation, and the Constitution.
2. *The Rise of Industrial Northeast, Plantation South, and Free-Farm West:* With attention to the geographic and economic factors which promoted sectionalism; sectionalism versus national interests.
3. *Territorial Development, the Struggle over New States, and the Civil War:* With attention to the use and influence of public lands and to the strengthening of national unity.
4. *The Development of Waterways, Highways, Railways, and Airways, and of Domestic and International Trade:* With attention to pertinent inventions, trade routes, and the social effects of the cargoes carried.
5. *Recreation, Sport, and Social Life:* The rise of typical American games, and of resorts and vacation trips, of social clubs and organizations, of theaters, music, movies, and other commercialized amusements.
6. *The Rise and Influence of Major Communication Industries:* Postal service, press, telegraph, telephone, and radio; with attention to pertinent inventions, the industrial organization of these agencies and their cultural power.

These directives no doubt provided worthwhile guidance for teachers and builders of history courses. It could be assumed that modifications of the topics have been made by shifting emphasis and by altering time allotment to meet the needs of a social studies program.

The following are excellent examples of an eighth grade theme and an eleventh grade theme:[3]

The United States as a World Power; our State and City in Our American Democracy.

Problem I—What basic courses have impelled a continuous flow of immigrants to America?

Problem II—How did the Constitution of the United States help our nation to become strong?

Problem III—How did the United States adjust to changed conditions created by the growth of industries?

Problem IV—How did the United States rise to a world power? What part do our state and city play in our democracy?

American History—Grade Eleven

Suggestions for Teachers of American History[4]

Unit I — A New Country in a New World
Unit II — Europeans Establish an Independent Nation in the New World

[2] E. B. Westley, Director, *American History in Schools and Colleges* (New York: The Macmillan Company, 1944), p. 77. Reprinted by permission of the publisher.
[3] *Social Studies in Our Schools* (Newark, N.J.: Board of Education, 1960), p. 12.
[4] *Emphasis upon Citizenship and Patriotism—Grades Ten, Eleven, and Twelve,* Bulletin No. 113 (Fort Worth, Texas: Fort Worth Public Schools, 1961), pp. 61-100.

Unit III   The Constitution is Established
Unit IV   The New Nation Grows Strong at Home and Abroad
Unit V   Growing Democracy and Nationalism
Unit VI   The Expanding Nation is Torn Apart, Then Reunited
Unit VII   The Emergence of Modern America (1865-1900)
Unit VIII   The United States Becomes a World Power (1900-1920)
Unit IX   Prosperity and Depression (1920-1940)
Unit X   World Leadership (1940-1961)

In many cases the historical sources of the local community are plentiful and have a direct relationship to the story of our nation's history. For example, General George Washington's experiences in New Jersey during the struggle for independence is the story of local communities as they tell their share of our nation's story.

Moreover, national history is based to a large extent on generalizations formed from the study of the sources of history in localities. . . . All communities, it is apparent, have not had identical historical experiences, but each rural village or industrial city, seacoast port or plantation settlement supplies complete, convenient, and authentic materials for explaining the influence of environment on history.
. . . With imagination, based on the full utilization of local sources, teachers of American history can devise many activities in and out of the classroom to encourage historical research as well as individual expression in recreating history. Depending on the individual's interest and skills, these projects may be used to translate historical expression into words, pictures, models, maps, clothing, food, or many other devices according to the student's abilities.
Libraries, historical societies, government offices, museums and local individuals preserve the raw materials of history. . . . But most communities, both large and small, do possess documentary evidence that tells of its beginning and development, its problems and accomplishments, and that also helps to explain the ideas and concepts which we consider to be part of our history. In smaller places, historical materials may still have to be searched for and collected; in the larger, the quantity may be overwhelming. But all places provide challenges in seeking out the solution to some problem of the past.[5]

World History

World history provides a key to much essential knowledge for living in our times as well as in the future. This broad and dramatic story includes both the physical environment and the peoples who shared in the recorded pages of time. The cultures with their various aspects shed light on the actions of mankind. Both the older centers of the globe and the newer areas are important for consideration in the selection of content for the subject. The past and the present century are included in the

---

[5] William G. Tyrrell, "Local Resources for Teaching American History," in William H. Cartwright and Richard L. Watson, Jr., co-editors, *Interpreting and Teaching American History*, Thirty-First Yearbook of the National Council for the Social Studies (Washington, D.C.: The Council, 1961), pp. 417-418.

reconstructed story, called the *stream of history*, as it focuses upon the world. Since World War II certain regions of the world are receiving greater attention than previously. Furthermore, the dynamic agents of mass media, radio, and television bring the wide world to our attention as significant events occur. This avenue for learning can arouse the intellectual curiosity in relation to world affairs for both young and old alike. The individual can derive a knowledge of the events which have done much to shape the contemporary world from the study of world history. In this way the student acquires further information about the problems facing the complex world.

Objectives for world history

Some suggested objectives for a course in world history are:

1. To develop an understanding of the background and origins of present institutions and customs
2. To develop an appreciation for the values of democracy
3. To develop a sense of ethical values which are part of the heritage of civilized man
4. To awaken a realization of the ever present danger of totalitarianism to man's liberty
5. To instill an appreciation of the value of solving international disputes by peaceful means
6. To foster an understanding of the interdependence of men and of world resources and to further a knowledge of other people's cultures and an appreciation of human values
7. To develop an understanding of the importance of technology in raising living standards
8. To show the influence of Western civilization on underdeveloped parts of the world
9. To develop critical thinking, suspended judgment, objectivity, an understanding of cause and effect relationships, and research techniques
10. To show the importance of the historical method and historical evidence in problem solving
11. To foster ability to read and interpret the printed page and other mass media of communication
12. To promote skill in reading and interpreting charts, graphs, maps, and statistics[6]

World History—Grade Ten

Suggestions for Teacher of World History[7]

Unit I   The Ancient World
Unit II   Greek Civilization

---

[6] *World History for High Schools Regents Course of Study,* Bulletin No. 11 (New York, N.Y.: Board of Education, 1958-59 series), pp. 2-3. Reprinted by permission of the Board of Education of the City of New York.

[7] *Emphasis upon Citizenship and Patriotism—Grades Ten, Eleven and Twelve,* Bulletin No. 113 (Fort Worth, Texas: Fort Worth Public Schools, 1961), pp. 17-60.

Unit III   Roman Civilization
Unit IV   The Middle Ages
Unit V   The Renaissance and Reformation
Unit VI   Growth of Nationalism
Unit VII   Growth of Democracy
Unit VIII   The Industrial Revolution
Unit IX   Imperialism and the Great War
Unit X   The World since 1919

Modern World History[8]

Modern World History should precede the study of United States History and follow the study of World Geography, and should therefore be placed in the tenth grade but offered in grades ten to twelve.

Unit I—How a continuing study of peoples of the world today, their problems and aspirations, can help world understanding

Unit II—How a study of history and the social sciences can help in understanding the people and problems of the world today

Unit III—How man's way of life was changed by intellectual, political, and industrial revolution

Unit IV—How democracy, nationalism, and imperialism developed and affected men's lives during the nineteenth century

Unit V—How man's way of life was changed by wars and revolutions during the first half of the twentieth century, 1914-1946

Unit VI—How man is achieving "Horizons Unlimited," through the sciences, technology, the social sciences, and the humanities

Unit VII—How man is seeking stability and peace in a world of conflicting ideologies and nuclear dangers

When organizing units for a course in world history, flexibility should be an important consideration. Special attention should be given to discussion, vocabulary work, map and globe study, as well as written work. Opportunities for special research are especially appropriate for the more capable students. Special reports, both oral and written, relating to specific topics are both fruitful and enriching. An occasional evaluation of the course in progress can be most enlightening and productive.

Latin American or Western Hemisphere history

Either the history of Latin America or the history of the entire Western Hemisphere should provide a sound basis for an elective course. Increased emphasis upon the history and geography of the Americas is pertinent for our times.

There are many parallels and contrasts to be found between the United States and the various other countries of the Western Hemisphere.

---

[8] *Modern World History for the Secondary Schools* (Chicago, Ill.: Chicago Public Schools, 1961), pp. v-ix.

Our own development will be better understood if examined against the background of Canadian and Latin American experience. It will be seen that all countries on this side of the world went through the same process of discovery, exploration, and settlement. All the Americas had these features in common, and only with the Declaration of Independence did United States history assume its particular shape.

The course of development of these various nations of the West varied in many interesting ways, depending upon location, climate, weather, terrain, characteristics of the people, and the natural resources of the land. The emergence of the economic, social, and political patterns of life are a major part of the story. The effect of scientific and technological achievement, transportation, and communication are all tied to progress and development. The elements of trade, commerce, and a steady industrial growth all tend to bring a greater interrelation between the countries. This is especially true of the United States and Canada. The emergence of the new state of Alaska gives us a greater interest in this region. Cooperation in the light of international regulations and our common tie in a major project of transportation such as the St. Lawrence Seaway are all a part of the content of a course.

The role of education, changing cultural patterns, and the complexities of this age are significant in viewing the entire Western Hemisphere. Each of these countries has developed a special culture and has made a contribution to art, music, literature, and other areas.

The importance of including such material within the course in American history can be readily established. With the growing importance of the Latin American nations and Canada, more attention should be devoted to the history of the Americas with the purpose of adding variety to American history and providing body for world history at the senior high school level.

Such a study could serve as a one-semester elective to challenge those students in the advanced placement program. When organized on a unit basis to be included in a history or modern problems course, attention could either be placed upon Latin America or the entire Western Hemisphere. The following suggested pattern of organization may be helpful: (1) Geographical Relationships, (2) History, (3) Cultural Heritage, (4) Hemisphere Relationships, and (5) Future Trends.

Economic history

Economic history is a study of man in the process of living and earning a living—the economic institutions which he has devised to facilitate production, distribution, and exchange—and of technological progress and its impact upon civilization. It is an economic analysis and causal explanation of the actions of man in his pursuit of material things. Consequently, we study the colonial economic life of the nation, agricultural and industrial developments and changes, labor and labor-management developments and changes, labor and labor-management relations, money and banking, manufacturing, tariffs, and the regulation of business by government. Such a study attempts to throw light upon political and social happenings and aids in their interpretation. Since economic factors are closely tied to the progress of the people of any nation, an understanding of economic history and its concepts is of major importance to secondary school pupils.

Economic aspects of history should receive significant consideration since a knowledge of the history of economic growth from the simple and crude beginnings to its present state gives the pupil some of the fundamentals for understanding world events. The facts of history can be interpreted through selection and arrangement of economic data bearing on these events. Today especially history is affected by such matters that are economic by their very nature. The last seven decades naturally receive increased emphasis since great material changes in economic life have occurred with the mechanization of industry, the increase of inventions, the growth of labor unions, and the recent progress in science.

As industry has expanded and used greater and greater quantities of raw materials and minerals, the United States has looked to South America, Canada, and Africa for nickel, cobalt, iron ore, and other necessary ingredients for manufacturing. Transportation and communication have come to play an increasingly important role in economic affairs, and the manufacturing industries and the labor force have given the United States a dominant position as producers of goods and commodities. Looking to the future, the application of automation, atomic energy, and the development of new and advanced techniques of production design will have increasing implications for industry. The production of new materials in manufacturing will undoubtedly replace older types of raw materials. Trade agreements and the potential of the common market will have a widespread effect on the marketing of commodities. In fact, the impact of economic events have greatly influenced the course of history in every major country in the world. However, with progress and modern scientific achievement, the future holds the secret of further economic knowledge.

State and local history

The importance of understanding one's own state history is apparent. Such knowledge should contribute measurably to the development of competent citizenship. This precludes an overview of the historical changes relative to a particular state. An understanding of the past, the current stage, and the expectations for the future are included in the theme. The history, government, and geography of a state are fundamental in comprehending life pursuits of yesterday and today.

Much state and local history can and should be integrated with all social studies courses; and on the elementary level, particularly at the fourth grade, considerable emphasis is usually given to these materials. However, definite provision should be made for the teaching of state and local history at some point, or points, in the secondary school. Some efforts have been made at the seventh grade and as an elective semester course in the senior high school. The obvious relationship between national history, state and local history, and the present trend toward the broader view of American history, points toward the desirability and practicality of including these areas within the American history course on the junior high school level. This can be accomplished either by the inclusion of a unit dealing with state and local history within the course or the definite planned integration of state and local materials throughout the course. Some pioneering and research are essential for the organization of such a course in state history and will prove most rewarding for those teachers who will take up the challenge and carry it through to completion.

State history provides an appreciation of the heritage and industrial development of a particular state. It gives a sense of pride for those who know its outstanding personalities and historic milestones. It provides a basis for understanding the present social, economic, and political structure. It supplies a mine of source materials for intellectual appraisal. It furnishes a background for illuminating current problems on the local and state scene.

The following is a good example of a course designed for the seventh grade:

Our Community and State[9]

Topic 1   Geographic Features of New York State
Topic 2   History of New York State to 1865
Topic 3   New York State History since 1865
Topic 4   Government of New York State
Topic 5   The Empire State Today
Topic 6   Geography and Growth of Our Community
Topic 7   Our Community Today

An example of a unit dealing with state history at the eighth grade level.

---

[9] *Social Studies 7, -8, -9: A Syllabus for Junior High Schools* (Albany, N.Y.: State Department of Education, 1961), p. 3.

Missouri History and Constitution[10]

This unit is designed for two purposes: (1) as a study of the historical and geographical aspects of our great state, (2) as a means of meeting the requirement of the state law regarding the teaching of the State Constitution and institutions. The materials which are presented serve as a basis for understanding the cultural heritage and the contributions of the many people who have developed the great State of Missouri.

Outline of Content

   I. What historical factors have affected the growth of government in Missouri?
  II. How have the physical features of Missouri influenced its change and growth?
 III. How has the development of institutions and industries affected the growth of Missouri?
 IV. Who are the people from Missouri who have been leaders in our state, nation and world?
  V. Why have Missourians developed symbols to identify this state and its people?
 VI. What should we know about the principal cities of our state?
VII. Why has the historical development of Missouri made it necessary for its people to write new constitutions periodically?
VIII. How does the Missouri constitution establish the system of government?
 IX. How do the federal and state constitutions compare?
  X. What are the democratic features of our state and national constitutions?

Many interesting facts of historical value have been recorded by the pen of local historians. The past reveals a panorama of people, places, and interesting community events preserved for posterity. Museums, through their collections, provide windows for looking back at the yesterdays. Some communities or organizations may have an occasion for a bicentennial celebration and thus capture the nostalgia of a bygone era. Each county and town has significant landmarks that serve as a reminder of life in a past era. For example, a community may possess a colonial stone house which dates back two centuries and carries both cultural and educational values. Such original historic structures are valuable assets that increase in worth through each generation.

The teaching of state and local history

State and local history should be closely correlated with American history, for even state history taught independently of the national story loses much of its significance. State history should provide an understand-

---

[10] *A Guide for Social Studies Grades 7-8-9*, Publication No. 101G (Jefferson City, Missouri: State Dept. of Education, 1958), pp. 96-102.

ing of the geographic features, early settlements, historic landmarks, outstanding personalities and their contributions, natural resources, government, and social, economic, and cultural development and problems. As a general rule, the teaching of state history presents less of a problem to the teacher in the matter of organization of materials than does local history, since research within the various states has already brought to light much of the pertinent information. Quite frequently this has been incorporated into a course of study, or even a textbook, and the teacher has only to adapt it to fit the local situation and to arrange for such field trips or historical pilgrimages as are feasible. These visits should include such local scenes or landmarks as monuments, battlefields, forts, plaques, road markers, shrines, historical buildings, and the sites of pioneer industries.

With some few exceptions, notably the larger cities and those fortunate communities where historical societies have been especially active, the teaching of local history entails considerable research. It cannot be urged too strongly, however, that such research be undertaken, not only because of the significance of local history within the social studies program but also because it is vital that all existing source materials be discovered and preserved.

Local history is rich in source materials such as old newspapers, books, manuscripts, diaries, maps, albums, letters, inscriptions, gravestones, deeds, pictures, journals, and records of industrial, social, governmental, military, or other organizations. Many of these may be available in collections in local libraries or museums, both public and private, or in the community or county historical association. These collections will also include many old relics such as furniture, weapons, utensils, farm implements, tools, and other articles depicting community life of the past. The extent of such collections and the degree to which they have been arranged, documented, and catalogued will determine the facility with which they may be used in the teaching of local history.

The materials of state and local history are close at hand and within the comprehension of any pupil who knows the traditions, customs, and happenings within his area. With today's evergrowing United States, one is apt to overlook the importance of local history at hand. There are unique aspects of every community that stimulate local pride and distinguish it from other communities. Indeed, the accomplishments of the past can be made vivid by being connected with local scenes and traditions. Here the field of investigation is manageable, and the facts can be vitalized.

Necessarily, good teaching material has to be organized. We can encourage the historical societies and the museums to expand their facilities, especially those which make history readily apparent to the observer. Such local history programs have to be developed, and this takes means and resources not so often available. In one area, the telephone company each month sends out with its bills an illustrated leaflet of local history. A junior magazine might be published out of factual material adapted to the local schools. The interests of the children of the various grade levels has to be fostered. This job has to be worked into the social studies program and articulated on a firm foundation with United States and world history.

The following suggested activities in connection with the teaching of local history may be organized as either individual or group projects that will not only have value for the pupils currently participating but will also form the nucleus for a local history file of permanent value to the school and the community.

1. Collecting stories, anecdotes, poems, folklore, songs, authentic costumes, pictures, photographs, portraits, and maps
2. Compiling biographies; records of Indian life; illustrated records of all inscriptions of historical value on tombstones, monuments, markers; descriptive list of incidents and events of historical significance; list of buildings and landmarks.
3. Constructing maps and charts showing growth of community in population, area, industries, and so on
4. Dramatizing historic events; making films; recording folksongs and dances
5. Reporting interviews involving reminiscence and recollection
6. Tracing genealogies and the history of government

Community resources

Local history furnishes a dynamic approach to community study. Current educational programs stress the importance of the community as a laboratory for learning. Results show that pupils' needs are more easily met and interests are enlivened through the use of the local resources. Parents and leaders of the community are brought closer together for the benefit of all concerned. Local history is the departure for comprehending world horizons. Our daily living is enriched by a knowledge of the historical background, the geography, and the people we associate with in our own interesting community.

The local community preserves in many ways realistic evidences of the past. The preserved, restored, or reconstructed building with its period furnishings and equipment makes it possible to walk directly into the past. An increasing interest in historical preservation, at the present time, affords notable contributions to contemporary education. Student visitors to historic sites can relive the past by actually seeing how their ancestors lived, worked, played, worshipped, and also fought.[11]

---

[11] William G. Tyrrell, "Local Resources for Teaching American History," in William H. Cartwright and Richard L. Watson, Jr., co-editors, *Interpreting and Teaching American History,* Thirty-First Yearbook of the National Council for the Social Studies (Washington, D.C.: The Council, 1961), pp. 423-424.

Museums preserve other real objects that tell about the past. A simple tool can, in a clearcut way, indicate differences between hand-craftsmanship and machine production. A display of candlemolds, whale oil vessels, kerosene lamps, gas fixtures, incandescent bulbs, and fluorescent tubes explains shifts in household duties, technological improvements, and industrial expansion. The museum, however, should not merely be a storage place for a miscellaneous collection of antiquated objects. It should, instead, preserve and arrange its materials in a simple and attractive way so that the clothing, furniture, or equipment from the past will be aids to learning and will also stimulate further learning.

The use of local resources implies that the community itself, and not just the classroom, can provide a wealth of educational experiences. The visit, field trip, or more extensive journey relates evidences of the past to class activities in American history.

How shall we teach history?

It is unfortunate that a subject so alive, interesting, and revealing as history has frequently been presented to pupils in such a dry and meaningless way that it extinguishes every spark of natural interest. Three factors are essential for the effective teaching of history: a teacher who has an adequate knowledge of, and an interest in, all phases of history and who has also the desire to arouse a similar interest on the part of pupils; a wealth of interesting up-to-date reference material and teaching aids, as well as materials for collateral and supplementary reading; and an attractive, inspiring, and efficiently arranged setting.

Topics versus chronology

The topical versus the chronological method is a question in point. The teacher should not attempt to make his mind or his pupils' minds a file where names, dates, and facts are indexed without reference to their utility. A series of such detached items merely clutters the memory. With the topical method, the courses are divided into carefully organized topical units. Guidance outlines keep the pupils from being confused and help in preserving the relations of the topics to each other. It is the method of logic and unified lesson treatments, whereas the chronological series keeps things in sequence, without attempting the rounded topical method of one phase of history at a time. However, a chronological course is necessary to keep one's historical perspective, and significant dates should be kept in mind. Furthermore, the time relationship *between* dates should be noted. Names and dates can be made a dry-as-dust procedure or can be enlivened by showing the significance of important events between them.

Dates are useful and necessary, of course, and important names are needed to identify the period covered. But these are of consequence only when related and interrelated to topical areas. For example, one might divide American history for purposes of study into sections, such as:

A New World and European Contributions to American Civilization

First Period
>   Roots of American democracy and the war for Independence
>   The formation of the Union of States and the framework of democracy
>   Establishment of the American nation and its struggles for survival

Middle Period
>   Westward expansion—the effects of territorial and industrial enlargements
>   The Civil War and reconstruction period
>   Commercial and industrial expansion to 1900

Since 1900
>   Development of the United States as a world power
>   Readjustments of World War I and II
>   Signs of our times

These are broad units of work that need adequate time for treatment. They will make the pupils acquainted with important concepts and outstanding events, movements, and personages in American history. The major portion of the time may be spent on events and tendencies of the last fifty years. However, any one of the topics listed in this paragraph constitutes a grand division or comprehensive area, in which there are many sub-topics worthy of elaboration in the classroom. For example, in connection with the last fifty years, the foreign policy of the United States is full of issues to interest the pupil, and its development may be traced in its three phases of isolation, imperialism, and international cooperation.

The functional or topical plan has precedence over the chronological plan today in the eyes of some educators, although the latter avoids duplication and is easy to use with slow learners. Most textbooks follow the chronological plan of organization and are easier for high school pupils to follow. Some teachers present history chronologically and conduct reviews by topics. On the other hand, treatment of topics allows for showing cause and effect relationships that are unbroken by what intervenes instead of fragmentary portions covered by definite years. The topical method has transfer value to other subjects—science, economics, and sociology—and has the advantage of following a distinct line of thought.

History in a geographical setting

Geographical forces have worked in many ways to shape the destinies of man in various world areas. Natural resources, rivers, climate, and topography have an important bearing upon the location of settlements, the development and spread of cultures, and the building of empires. A knowledge of these geographic factors and an understanding of their influence upon man is essential to the interpretation of the development of a local community, a state, a nation, or the world.

A number of philosophical historians have pointed out the great influence of geography on American and world history. If properly used, geographic studies can arouse the interest of the pupils to a better understanding of underlying movements of history; for example, the Southern bloc, the western migration, the influence of the Mediterranean in Europe on the climate and on the temperament of nations, and the peculiar influence of Greece as a maritime and colonizing aggregate in world history. Climate, resources, and topography are some of the factors acting on populations to change their politics, culture, and social development. Such correlations make history study less dry and chronological and help fill out the outlines and amplify general statements. Of course, geography is not the prime mover of history. A country may have excellent resources and good climate and yet be occupied by backward peoples who, for ages, make no impress on history. For example, the eastern seaboard of the United States remained a wilderness for the most part until the period of the white settlement. However, environment, resources, and climate do play their part in influencing important events.

History through biography

In presenting history as a series of great movements, it is all too easy to forget that this progress was made not by impersonal "man" in one continuous struggle to achieve a faraway goal, but by many individual and entirely human personalities who struggled during their lifetimes to achieve separate and attainable goals. History can gain much in interest, color, and animation when the stories of its great men receive appropriate emphasis.

Most human beings are interested in the accounts of the successes and failures, the hopes, aspirations, and disappointments of other human beings. Young people, particularly, are inspired and motivated by a tendency toward hero-worship.

Through biography, history can capitalize on this tendency and make real the great but human men who were important historically. For many secondary school pupils, history can "come alive" in their imaginations only through the vicarious experience they gain in identifying themselves with the contemporary participants. Each generation has its leaders or famous people: statesmen, military and naval personnel, poets, scientists, inventors, artists, composers, educators, and authors. In countless instances, biography can form the connecting link between history and the pertinent geographical associations, adding reality to both. For example, the biography of John Hancock throws considerable light on the geography, as well as the business and commercial life, of colonial New England. The geographical features of Virginia may be stressed in the story of the life of George Washington. The importance of navigable rivers, upon which sailed the trading vessels of America and the Old World, may be studied. A definite program of relating the consideration of biography to the study of history can aid materially both in encouraging the habit of reading worth-while literature and in arousing an enduring interest in history.

Similarly, the history of Latin America and Canada may be better understood and enjoyed by the use of suitable and interesting biographical materials. Pertinent information about the exploration and growth of these regions abounds in these fascinating volumes. Biography is a definite part of history. Europe presents a comparable picture; rich in interesting study.

Social studies reading programs have expanded; the use of biography has increased in the secondary schools. Librarians are willing to provide reading lists of selected biographies to aid both teachers and pupils. All social studies teachers who direct reading programs will find it advantageous to read E. H. O'Neill's book, A History of American Biography, 1800-1935 (reprinted as a paperback by A. S. Barnes and Company, 1961). There are numerous such aids available for the selection of attractive biographies that will both show the personal elements in history and provide worth-while experiences. Among such aids for the librarian and teacher are the following:

1. Carpenter, H. M., Gateways to American History. New York: H. W. Wilson Company, 1942. (Out of print; rev. ed. in press.)
2. Eaton, A. T. Treasure for the Taking: A Book List for Boys and Girls, rev. ed. New York: The Viking Press, Inc., 1957.
3. Logasa, H., Historical Non-Fiction, 7th rev. and enl. ed. Philadelphia: McKinley Publishing Company, 1960.

The success or failure of any attempt to make extensive use of biography in the history course, like other phases of the teaching-learning situation, depends largely upon the personality, knowledge, and skill of the teacher. In most situations, time is too limited to permit the devotion of class time to adequate discussion of the lives of even a brief list of representative personalities. The problem, then, becomes concerned with the techniques and procedures of stimulating a program of outside reading. Social Studies instruction that focuses attention upon reading for pleasure and leisure will also utilize biographical materials in the learning process.

Historical fiction

Historical fiction, like biography, contributes to the understanding of history. Good fiction with factual, authentic background has great institutional value because the lively narrative attracts and then sustains the pupil's interest. Historical fiction gives depth and meaning to events and adds color, warmth, and reality to the various phases of life in the past. It may well serve as the starting point for a genuine interest in history.

Fortunately for the teacher of history there has been a notable increase recently in the number of books appearing in both fields: for example, the *American Landmark Series* featuring such titles as *Lee and Grant at Appomattox, The Monitor and the Merrimac,* and *Gettysburg.*

Titles cover a wide range of reading interests and abilities. The books are attractive, interesting, and very readable. It has been customary to warn teachers to be critical in their evaluation of historical fiction and of biographies. This caution is no longer imperative. The number of authors of stature who are writing in the field for young people is steadily increasing, and in general the accuracy and reliability of both biography and historical fiction are very dependable. Careful study and meticulous research are conducted into past events and their backgrounds, including scenery, costumes, and habits of people.

To bring bygone years to a spirit of the contemporary and to make history read like an accurate report chronicled in a newspaper today, the office of the historiographer, the historical novelist, and the classroom teacher are employed. Each brings in noted characters of history and holds the interest of the young person both in the plot development and in the stream of events. James Boyd and Carl L. Carmer have written about the legend and lore of the Mohawk Valley and the efforts of the pioneers to change a wilderness, infested with savages, into a garden country—for example, the stirring descriptions by Carmer in *Listen for a Lonesome Drum, The Hudson, Dark Trees to the Wind,* and the captivating story of *Drums* by Boyd. The extraordinary exploits of Washington have filled and will continue to fill novels in succeeding generations.

Among others, Cooper, in *The Spy* (1821), started the vogue for native American instead of English romances. *The Spy* has a good story, throws the glamor of romance over the men and women of the Revolution, and creates one original character, Harvey Birch, whose patriotism appeals powerfully to men of every nation, because he is a patriot who serves without hope or possibility of reward. The American Puritan period of New England is reflected in Hawthorne's generally gloomy romances. Although Hawthorne's historical knowledge may be open to question, he was a skillful writer.

The reading of historical fiction may be encouraged by recognizing the pupil's contribution through epochal projects organized by personal initiation. Such credit may be based on the pupil's report on each novel, developing the historical background, the personalities delineated, the events of historical interest described, an epitome of the plot, and an evaluation of the merits of the book as history. The best of these papers may be read aloud to the class. On the bulletin board may be posted lists of books read by pupils, giving each pupil status for the leisure-time effort. Likewise passages on definite epochal events may be read by the teacher from vivid historical novels. Recognition in both history and English may be accorded the conscientious pupil.

Through definite graphic illustrations, the tackboard may portray the progressive movement of a story, and each day some pupil can develop his part of the tale. To illustrate: for *Northwest Passage* by Kenneth Roberts, one might use miniature cut-outs showing all movements of this segment of the American Revolution—the British Redcoats in glowing crimson uniforms against a blue background, the drab Colonials, in contrast, portraying the story for the class and exciting their daily interest. The same could be done for the strategies of the Civil War with such books as *Richard Carvel* or the *Virginian*. Teachers should make a special effort to find stories to answer the drives and urges of their students. Some such aids for the teacher are the following:

1. *Fiction Catalog*. New York: H. W. Wilson Company, 1950. Annual supplements.
2. Dickinson, A. T. Jr., *American Historical Fiction*. New York: Scarecrow Press, 1958.
3. *Harvard Guide to American History*. The Harvard University Press, 1960.
4. Logasa, H., *Historical Fiction*, 7th rev. and enl. ed. Philadelphia: McKinley Publishing Company, 1960.

Poetry

Poetry is also an important supplement in history. The rhythms and lyric qualities have a natural appeal for all ages and bring to life the colorful words and ringing phrases that add much to easy understanding and visualizing of a scene. Poetry is an excellent means of depicting man's existence and place in a generation. Of course, some historical poems need classroom discussion for clarification and fuller understanding. For example, Walt Whitman's poem, *O Captain! My Captain!*, probably one of the best poems about Lincoln, is full of metaphor and poetical imagery that stimulate lively class discussion and development. "Captain," "ships," "voyages," and so on take on new meaning in this poem.

Ballads and narrative poetry are easily understood by all groups. The pupil lives the poem and the event. The experience gained from reading poetry is delightful. Through reading, studying, and discussing these poems, the pupil learns qualities that constitute good poetry. Both oral and silent reading have their place in the educational scheme: skills developed in oral reading give a richer, fuller appreciation of the poetry and make the group practice in active and attentive listening more significant.

Poetry relating to American history usually presents a phase or movement in our development and growth written by contemporaries or by later poets. Burton Egbert Stevenson in his excellent anthology, *Poems of American History*, has collected both kinds. The material is well organized for reference and class use. Each chapter presents a particular epoch; "The Discovery of America," "Independence," "The West and the New Nations" are typical of this organization.

Songs of the Cattle Trail and Cow Camp by John A. Lomax is popular, and the various songs and lyrics furnish an enthusiastic appreciation for the audacious spirit and life of the Old West. Such poems as *The Old Mackenzie Trail* and *The Call of the Plains* give the true atmosphere of the portrait of the land and of the men and women.

The culture of any country is brilliantly reflected in its poetry. When studying a particular region—for example, Canada—materials gathered from the library can readily be integrated with narrative poetry. The teacher may present several well-chosen poems that animate the delineation of the cultural pattern. *Paul Bunyan: Saga of the Woodsmen and the North* portrays the lonely vastness of the northern primeval forests and the emotional grip nature has on the imagination of their inhabitants. *Evangeline* reflects the culture of the French-Canadian community—its religious aspects, its political resentments. The teacher will find many other narrative and lyric poems of all times reflecting the cultural pattern of other countries.

Numerous approaches may be employed in the presentation of poetry. A poem effectively read by the teacher can engender interest and enthusiasm. Group reading of poetry can open the door to pleasurable class experiences. Choral reading opens another enjoyable avenue for group reading and appreciation of poetry. Poetry recordings, available with authoritative readings by the poet himself or an interpreter, are significant for use in the learning process. Such recorded poetry can be successfully used in the social studies classes if the teacher develops effective techniques to prepare the student to read and to listen intelligently.

Reading in the history courses

An effective supplementary or collateral reading program is an important aspect of any modern history curriculum. The study of history can do much to stimulate the growth of integrated reading interests. The organization of a program of reading for pleasure, leisure, and information should be a definite part of the planning of a history course. Such a program should include periodicals as well as books.

Most instructional guides for the social studies contain a supplementary reading list for the units studied. General references for teachers are also included. A good bibliography furnishes a mine of valuable sources for enriching the study of history. The teacher should make students aware of the sources from which they can gain additional knowledge and important information relating to a particular topic. He should also point out the value of reading for pleasure and for personal enjoyment. The skillful teacher in directing the learning in a history course can kindle the desire on the part of students to become confirmed readers of worthwhile materials. The following suggestions may provide helpful assistance in fostering a reading program in our history courses.

1. An adequate supply of reading materials should be made readily available in school and public library.
2. Each teacher should be a salesman in interesting students in the values derived from reading.
3. The reading of book reviews and new book lists tend to arouse interest and stimulate the student to obtain a book and explore its contents.
4. The utilization of book reports as a part of the instruction in each course.

To be completely effective, any program of collateral reading for the social studies should be instituted as a coordinated effort of the entire department and carried through in progressive sequence on each grade level. Much can be accomplished by any teacher in the course of a year's or a semester's work, particularly in the junior high school, since the reading habit, once begun, seems to gain momentum of its own accord. The following suggestions may help to stimulate a reading program:

Both the learning laboratory and the library can serve teachers and students in various ways through (a) tackboard displays, exhibits of books, and a display of book jackets; (b) talks by the teacher and librarian concerning books; (c) formation of a reading club; (d) planned summer reading; (e) reading lists including new books, and (f) reports and discussions concerning reading materials.

These ideas can supplement the teacher's planning and furnish directives for what could be done in a particular history course.

History through special devices

There are many devices and techniques for enlivening the study of history. The social studies teacher should be constantly on the alert for new ideas and for devices that may be adapted to add interest to phases of history. A section of the history file devoted to the systematic collection of simple aids collected and developed by the pupils themselves and for the teacher's potential ideas for vitalizing the teaching of history will prove a valuable source of suggestions in planning classroom activities.

A history fair

A history fair is a unique way of seeing history in action. The fair is aimed at stimulating historical interest on the part of the students and the citizens in the community. Such an event usually brings about a strong public reaction that should "popularize" history in the community. The people are informed and made aware of the historical heritage of the nation.

Students, through their many exhibits and projects, present a varied view of information available in the social sciences. They are encouraged to go out into the field and actually experience remnants of the past. Secondary school students, under the guidance of their teachers, establish the list of categories for the entries which are scaled reproductions of scenes and institutions in American and European periods of history.

A special criterion is formulated for the rating and the judging of each entry. Such items as creativity, originality, construction, authenticity, informative value, and research depth are considered in the evaluation process. This type of experience is productive from the standpoint of research and of acquiring new knowledge from the social sciences and the humanities.

Cartoons

Boundless possibilities may be found for the application of cartoons to the teaching of history. Many of the important issues in American history were depicted freely in contemporary cartoons; in some cases, the cartoon has been instrumental in affecting the course of history. A series of cartoons by Thomas Nast aided in exposing the Tweed Ring and were largely instrumental in alerting the people of New York City to arise and overthrow Boss Tweed. Cartoons have played an important part in many a political campaign and have been used as a protest agent to mold public opinion during war and peace.

A collection of cartoons of historical significance can be utilized in many ways to create interest and throw light on our history. The cultural value in connection with the consideration of cartoons has been somewhat neglected. Through the use of cartoons in history classes, pupils may become familiar with cartoon symbols and their meaning—Uncle Sam, John Bull, John Q. Public, the elephant and the donkey (Thomas Nast created these); Mars, the olive branch, the dove, the tiger, the bear, the eagle, the bulls and the bears—and learn to interpret correctly the cartoons in daily newspapers.

Slogans and sayings

A wealth of historical slogans and famous sayings are a part of our heritage from the past. These should be directly related to the events and times whose spirit they represent. Slogans may be used as a means of introduction, as interesting and valuable sidelights, or—since we certainly need a little levity in the classroom—as the basis for games and quiz contests. Pupils should be encouraged to make a collection of the sayings and slogans of each historical period from "No taxation without representation" to "Blood, sweat, and tears." A single slogan that has been adequately taught may enable the pupil to recall a whole series of events.

Songs and music

Playing much the same part in American history as slogans and sayings, folk songs, war songs, patriotic songs, and campaign songs reflect the sentiments of the people. The stories behind the origin and importance of our national music and songs are an important part of our heritage, but all too frequently the pupils' only knowledge of them is limited to the singing of *America, The Star Spangled Banner,* and perhaps their own state song in the school assembly. *Yankee Doodle* of the Revolution and the great songs of the Civil War period, such as *The Battle Cry of Freedom, Tenting on the Old Camp Ground,* or *Maryland, My Maryland,* are seldom heard and still more seldom explained historically. The songs of World War I, *Over There, Keep the Home Fires Burning,* and others are known only to the older generation. Many excellent popular songs that were born of World War II illustrate the temper and spirit of the people and signs of the period.

Conclusion

History has long been a major subject in the secondary school curriculum. It assumes an important role serving as a sort of core in the modern social studies program. History, including American and World, unfolds the past and develops a knowledge of our contemporary civilization. The story of history carries great significance and should be made to live and become realistic so that the student can grasp the stream of events that are enacted as a drama before his eyes. History—people, places, and events—presents the teacher with many rich opportunities to stimulate the student in acquiring information and much worthwhile knowledge. Interest is the key to competent research, selective reading, fuller understanding, and greater student growth. Many materials, activities, and experiences should be provided for the student in order to assist him in acquiring a finer appreciation of history. Instruction in every history course should be effective in producing an informed and enlightened, democratic American citizen for living in our age.

Bibliography

Cartwright, W. H. and R. L. Watson, Jr., co-eds., *Interpreting and Teaching American History,* Thirty-first Yearbook of the National Council for the Social Studies. Washington, D.C.: National Education Association, 1961.

Cartwright, W. H., "Role of History Teaching in Citizenship Education," *High School Journal,* 44 (December 1960), 112-117.

Johnson, H., *The Teaching of History,* rev. ed. New York: The Macmillan Company, 1940.

Moffatt, M. P. and S. G. Rich, "The Place of Local History in Modern Education," *The Journal of Educational Sociology,* 26 (October 1952), 79-88.

Steinberg, S., "Teaching History in a Rapidly Changing World," *Social Education,* 24 (November 1960), 298-300.

Stoler, M. C., ed., *World History in the Curriculum,* Vol. 57, Annual Proceedings of the Middle States Council for the Social Studies. Washington, D.C.: Middle States Council for the Social Studies, 1960.

West, E., ed., *Improving the Teaching of World History,* Twentieth Yearbook of the National Council for the Social Studies. Washington, D.C.: National Education Association, 1949.

Chapter Twelve

Geographic Knowledge–
A Global View

The study of geography provides essential knowledge for a better understanding of the modern world. This subject is assuming a more significant role in our educational structure. The space age together with global happenings over the recent past necessitate our having some information concerning geography. Today's vehicles of mass media, especially television and radio, have revolutionized the flow of first-hand information. The events of the global world are paraded as they occur to a vast audience. Such experiences are vastly educational because they arouse interest, stimulate thinking, provoke discussion, and encourage reading for acquiring further knowledge. Mass communication is a powerful force and has a definite influence on American culture.

Geography is concerned with the development of meaningful generalizations concerning the areal arrangement and association of things on the earth. Since no two points on the face of the earth are identical, it is necessary to formulate generalizations that illuminate problems of real relationships. When the sociologist or the anthropologist studies people, he defines groups or classes, for he cannot deal only with individuals. The geographic, similarly, seeks to generalize the characteristics of area, to define regions.[1]

---

[1] R. A. Price, ed., *New Viewpoints in the Social Sciences*, The National Council for the Social Studies, 28th Yearbook (Washington, D.C.: 1958), p. 48.

Geography

Geography is an old as well as a new science. Civilization is geographic: world events are tied to specific places on the globe. Geography is the study and interpretation of the distribution of the physical and cultural features on the surface of the earth. This subject may be considered both a natural and a social science because it is based upon the natural and the social factors and their relationships. Modern geography also presents us with an understanding of the world in which we live. It furnishes an opportunity for genuine exploration and research. In analyzing man's pursuits in the various parts of the world, we must understand and appreciate the influence of climate, weather, natural resources, transportation facilities, and the general characteristics of the specific areas.

General purposes of geography

The following *purposes* should be kept clearly in mind throughout the study of geography:

1. To establish the understanding that to a large extent man patterns his living socially, economically, and politically to fit his natural environment by a process of adjustment to changing natural and cultural conditions
2. To recognize the relationship of the natural environmental conditions throughout the world to the living patterns of the inhabitants, which results in specialization in their work and courses the interdependence of peoples
3. To recognize the responsibility that the United States has as a world leader and understand its relationship in the family of nations
4. To understand the close relationship between man's activities of the past and the development of his culture with the natural forces of his environment
5. To emphasize the importance of a world-wide program of conservation of resources for present and future generations
6. To show how the knowledge of geography may make living more enjoyable and satisfying through a wiser use of leisure time[2]

The development of geographic concepts and essential skills is important at each stage in the secondary social studies program. In this manner students gain a better understanding of their immediate world and gradually see the relationship of people to the broader world view. The geographical concepts of a state, our country, and the world are developed as a group of students expand their study of geography.

---

[2] *World Geography Grades 9 and 10*, Curriculum Bulletin No. 13 (Cincinnati, Ohio: Cincinnati Public Schools, 1958), p. 31.

The significance of geographic studies

The importance of geography upon the prevailing economic condition of any given area must be given careful consideration before the region can be fully understood.

A basic understanding of the physical environment remains an essential condition for a correct appreciation of the economic and social superstructure, notwithstanding the highly developed technical skills of modern man—in final analysis he still must live off and with Nature.

Modern geography is in part a physical science, in part a social science. As, among other things, it attempts to relate facts of the physical environment to those of the social environment, it is one of the few sciences that tries to bridge the apparently widening gap between the two great groups of the physical and the social science. Its position is a difficult one, but an extremely important one.

Physical geography embraces studies of cartography, the elements of weather, climatology, land forms or morphology of the land, water bodies and drainage, soils, natural vegetation, and animal life. *Social* or *human geography* embraces economic geography, social geography, in the strict sense of the word, political geography, historical geography, and certain other phases of geography.

Economic geography investigates the diversity in basic resources of the different parts of the world. It tries to evaluate the effects that differences in the physical environment have upon the utilization of these resources. It studies differences in economic development in different regions or countries of the world. It studies transportation, trade routes, and trade resulting from this differential development and as affected by the physical environment.[3]

Economic geography is related to trade and commerce and shows the effect of the material resources of a region upon the economic activities of a people. It considers the provision made for producing and distributing all kinds of goods from the geographic viewpoint. It considers the environments and the relation between different areas and their exchanges of goods and material resources.

Geographic setting and scope

Geography is dynamic and is vitally concerned with the rapid changes in our contemporary age. The scope of geography is broad in terms of the earth and the modern world. Land formations, bodies of water, and the climate embrace some of the natural features of the earth. The economic aspects include communication, production, consumption,

---

[3] N. A. Bengston and W. Van Royer, *Fundamentals of Economic Geography* (4th ed.; Englewood Cliffs, N.J.: Prentice-Hall, Inc., 1956), p. 53.

distribution, and the financial means which foster the occupations of people in the industrial sphere—agriculture, lumbering, fishing, mining and manufacturing. The means of transportation is a most important consideration in terms of economic activity. Mineral resources, including those of vital importance for the production of nuclear energy, have a marked influence upon industrialization.

Agricultural geography as such relates to the farmer's activities, the choice of crops, and the use of soil to the best advantage. All these factors are in some way interwoven into the study of man's location, his activities, and his problems. The cultural features are achieved and developed in his constructive daily pursuits on the earth. The influences of rivers, mountains, plains, oceans, and climate conditions upon people is important to learn in order to gain a better understanding of the patterns of civilization wherever located.

The geography of the world is no longer a far-away dream. The space-age, with its jets, has lifted former barriers, and modern communication has promoted an interest in world affairs.

Natural and cultural landscape

It is essential that the teacher have a clear understanding of the meaning of the natural landscape and its relationship to the cultural landscape. The following is an excellent discussion of these topics:[4]

> The natural environment in any given area is usually well reflected in the features of the *natural landscape.* By that term we refer to the land as it is with its various kinds of surface forms, its streams and lakes, its natural vegetation, and its native fauna. Through man's activities, changes are brought about, such as plowing up the sod, cutting down the forests, planting various crops, straightening or deepening stream channels, constructing irrigation projects, preparing grades for roads and railroads, and constructing houses, barns, factories, villages, towns and cities. In these and other ways the natural landscape is changed in its details and rendered more adaptable for use by man. By these means a *cultural landscape* is created.
>
> A cultural landscape in its fullest sense would imply a complete fade-out of the features of the original, natural landscape and its replacement by cultural features to such an extent as to hide even the fundament upon which they stand. There are relatively few areas that may be considered "pure" cultural landscapes. Areas of pure natural landscape, that is, regions where man has caused no changes, still exist in different parts of the world, but their extent is shrinking every year. The only really large area of natural landscape is Antarctica. Even in the deserts and in the northern wilderness of Canada and Siberia man is beginning to leave some imprints.
>
> Usually the landscape before us is a combination of both: the cultural

---

4 *Ibid.,* pp. 65-66.

features have been superimposed upon the natural in varying proportions. In grazing areas such as those of the southwest or in parts of the Great Plains the principal cultural features are the fences, widely spaced houses, and a few trails and roads. In farming areas man's imprint upon the natural landscape is more effective—there, cultivated crops have replaced grass and forest; farmsteads are close together and connected by telephone and perhaps by power lines; and roads lead to near-by towns. With all these changes in detail, the general topography remains virtually unchanged as to flat lands, hills, and valleys. In the cities, however, man's structural activities are generally dominant. Hills have been reduced, grades lessened, and streets and buildings conceal much of the original landscape.

The principal aspects of the natural landscape may be listed as: (1) location, (2) landforms, (3) water bodies, (4) climate, (5) land content, or soils and mineral resources, (6) native vegetation, and (7) animal life.

Physical geography

Physical geography presents the lay of the land as its structural characteristics, its mountain ranges, rivers, lakes, and like features, including climate and soil characteristics. Some boundaries are defined by nature, as for example, the island of Cuba or the Danish peninsula, whereas other boundaries may be marked by man-made straight lines, as the western borders between Canada and the United States.

In general, this study covers the various elements of the natural environment—location, climate, surface or relief, soil, minerals, water supply, native vegetation, animals, and oceans. Location leads naturally to a view of how people live, whether they have a maritime outlet, whether the lands are too cold for agriculture, and how these lands are related to contiguous areas. Important in this study is the surface or relief of that region, which gives a clue to the distribution of population and their occupations. Differences in soil fertility make for the differences in living; compare the areas of the Nile Valley and the adjacent Sahara. Mineral resources and the extent to which they are produced account for the progress of a people. Many a potentially rich country is neglected because, for example, the inhabitants are ignorant of technology and lack the ability to transform the riches of the valleys and hills into things of service.

When the physical geographer studies physical factors, he analyses them with reference to their possible application to commerce and industry and other projects. These physical factors are basic forces in shaping human affairs, especially industrially and agriculturally. Professionally trained geographers in such government bureaus as the Geologic Survey, the Forest Service, and Mapping Agencies emphasize the significance of physical geography in the making of a prosperous nation.

An earth science course

A new phase of instruction embracing science and physical geography is called earth science. This subject has become increasingly important especially at the ninth-grade level. Earth Science offers learning and practical experience in such areas as geology, weather, oceanography, astronomy, and map reading. This course is especially well suited for laboratory work, field trips, and experience in using simple scientific instruments. Resulting especially from the work that was started with the International Geophysical Year, there is now a greater realization of the necessity for man to understand his physical environment and to fill newly found gaps in his knowledge. Much information is readily available through mass-media, films, newspapers and periodicals. Such a course should emphasize its practical aspects of the physical world through functional and everyday experiences.

In the process of establishing such an earth science course, the faculty should be selected from individuals who have a strong background in the physical sciences and who are competent in applying their skills in an effective manner. This entails a challenge to one's imagination, combined with a technological knowledge of the subject. An evaluation of the interests and ability of the teachers for such a specialized course is also necessary. Finally, the school administrators must be willing to encourage teachers to improve their professional qualifications and to supply them with the essential tools for instruction.

Earth and space science

With man's success in orbiting the earth, the study of earth science as related to space has become an increasingly absorbing study. Every student has an impelling motivation to learn how the men of science have made these feats possible and what the effect will be on man's daily life. He can derive from such a study increased knowledge and a broader understanding of his physical environment both on earth and in space.

The student should be introduced to Earth and Space science as a distinct meaningful pursuit of learning. He should comprehend that in this discipline he will be studying the Earth, the Atmosphere, and Space. He should not study these as separate unrelated subjects with distinct boundaries but instead as closely related parts of Man's total physical environment in the Universe.[5]

---

[5] *A Suggested Teaching Guide for the Earth and Space Science Course* (Harrisburg, Pa.: Pennsylvania Dept. of Public Instruction, 1959), p. 3.

Pennsylvania has developed an instructional guide so that the student can learn the elements of geology, astronomy, meteorology, and oceanography. The major units for study include: Introduction (Background for the Teacher), The Changing Earth, The Earth in Space, Weather and Climate, and The Oceans.

It is with the total 'physical' Earth that this course is concerned; the Earth's physical setting and its major physical characteristics provide the frame of reference for the more detailed, analytic studies to follow.[6]

It might be wise to define oceanography.

It is the study of the oceans and the basins containing them. It is not a separate science but draws on other fields, such as biology, chemistry, physics, geology, geography, astronomy and mathematics. This course deals principally with physical oceanography and is only indirectly concerned with marine biology.[7]

Earth science is the study of the physical forces which influence and shape the surface of the earth. The domain of the earth scientist encompasses such realms as geomorphology, or the study of land forms, the oceans, weather, such phases of astronomy that pertain to earth and sun relations. The tools of the earth scientist include such items as land-form models, topographic maps, hydrographic charts, aerial photographs, daily weather maps, rock and minerals identification sets, weather instruments, and field trips to areas of interest and museums.

In geographical instruction at the secondary level, many students are introduced to the basic facts of earth science by showing them the areal distribution of peoples and economies over a diverse planet. The diversities are attributable directly or indirectly to the elements making up the study of earth science. Since geography is a combination of the physical sciences and the social sciences, the interrelations between man and his environment are ofter major topics of concern with respect to the geographic peculiarities of the regions.

Human geography

There are many human items of interest to the geographer in contrast to natural ones such as climate, minerals, and surface features. The human elements one may consider are farming and land utilization, population distribution, and various uses of available mineral resources. The cultural aspects are assets consisting of acquired knowledge and skills as well as ability to use machinery and equipment. The density of population in New England is not explained entirely by the resources at hand

---

[6] *Ibid.*

[7] *Ibid.*, p. 63.

there but by such historical circumstances as early settlement, nearness to the sea, and nearness to Europe. In effect, relationships between specific groups of population and their natural environment are studies, although general environment is not to be regarded as a cause of cultural values. The relationship between the resources and cultural assets is surveyed. Much depends upon the energy and culture of peoples involved, and often less on the physical features, for man by his own activity can make even the desert bloom. Cultural or human geography serves to show how the kinds of people who inhabit certain areas of the globe live and develop certain ways of life on a background of the physical environment.

Such a study is not merely descriptive but seeks to explain human items in a scientific manner how people . . . have adjusted themselves to their environments. The main emphasis on cultural geography as a social science is upon man-made features and how and why population is distributed as it is. Such a study gives pupils an understanding of different kinds of people and their ways and offers some explanation of the shaping forces at work.

Modern geography

The modern approach to the teaching of geography is the global framework of society. We no longer think of the continents as isolated by the vast expanses of the Atlantic and Pacific Oceans but as neighbors around a common inland sea. The old geography was concerned with an Eastern and a Western Hemisphere in which the continents were subdivided nto more or less self-sufficient political units. Modern geography is concerned with the world as a unit and stresses an intelligent appreciation of the people in every land.

Today, geography is coming to the fore in the study of international relations. In order to understand our own country and its problems, it is necessary to know something about the location and the problems of other nations.

Because of the events of World War I and II, the basic content of geographic studies has been expanded. Although there is a shifting emphasis on various topical additions to the curriculum from time to time, a new world background has come into view.

Units dealing with "How Can We Help to Promote a Better Understanding and Appreciation of Other Peoples?" and "What Factors Influence the International Activities of Our Nation?" have brought a world viewpoint to the classroom. Certain concepts are being replaced with a more accurate picture of the world's areas and distances. For example, the distances across the North Pole often represent short cuts between the principal cities of Europe, Asia, Africa, and North America, which may be the future chief routes of aerial transportation because of the shorter flying time.

Geography at the secondary level

The study of geography in the secondary school program should serve to review previous knowledge of the subject and to open new and broader avenues of interest and understanding. Contemporary world affairs, current events, and area problems have a geographical significance that is important in providing further knowledge. A functional study of geography can contribute in guiding the growth and development of youth. Such instruction aids in meeting their needs, problems, goals, and responsibilities in our contemporary society. The following offerings in geography are typical of what can be done in developing courses at the secondary level.

World Geography[8]

Purposes and Goals

1. To develop the vocabulary, skills, and tools basic to a study of geography
2. To understand the kind of environment in which man lives
3. To understand why and how man has adapted to or changed his environment to meet his needs
4. To understand how and why the world is becoming more interdependent
5. To understand how and why the United States and its citizens are involved in and concerned with world affairs
6. To develop abilities to think critically and objectively about related world problems and ways of working toward their solutions

Areas of Study

I. World Physical Geography
An overview and introduction to the study of geography
II. The U.S.S.R.
Physical aspects; economic, cultural, and political geography; relationships and problems with other areas
III. The Far East
Physical, economic, cultural, and political geography of China, Japan, Southeast Asia, India, and Indonesia; problems and relationships to other areas

---

[8] *A Guide for World Geography in the Senior High School,* Soc. Stud., 1958-61 (Oakland, Calif., Oakland Public Schools, 1958), p. 35.

IV. The Mediterranean Basin
Physical, economic, cultural, and political geography of the Middle East, North Africa, and Southern Europe; problems and relationships with other areas

V. Western and Central Europe
Geographical aspects of various key countries; problems and relationships with other areas

VI. Underdeveloped Areas
Physical, economic, cultural, and political geography of Africa, Australia, Latin America, and the Polar Regions; problems and relationships with other areas

VII. The United States and Canada
A consideration of all important geographical factors and a summarization of the position of the United States and Canada in relation to all other areas

In the process of planning, organizing, and teaching a course in world geography, flexibility should always prevail. The materials of instruction and the areas for study should be adapted to the ability level of the particular group. The immediate interests and needs of the students are of major importance. Considerable thought should be given to the development of those essential geographical skills and concepts so essential for effective learning. The techniques of problem solving, library skills, research skills, and study procedures should be re-enforced. The enlargement of a geographic vocabulary is important. The process of critical thinking should be fostered and contemporary materials utilized whenever they are related to particular problems. Appropriate supplementary reading content and audiovisual materials serves as enrichment for the study.

Campbell Union High School District[9]

Course of Study for World Geography

I. Objectives
The study of World Geography should aid each student:
A. To develop an appreciation and knowledge of the major physical characteristics of the earth
B. To comprehend the effects of physical geography on population
C. To develop an understanding of the difference in cultural, economic, and social factors contributing to the development of the countries of the world
D. To develop an understanding of geography and its influence relating to political entries
E. To locate his own geographic position and relate it to the major land masses of the world

---

[9] *Curriculum Guide 9-12*, Campbell Union High School District (Campbell, Calif.: Board of Education, 1960), pp. 66-69.

F. To develop a conception of the world as a single family of nations

G. To gain greater insight into history through a study of geography

H. To improve his skill in interpreting and constructing maps and charts

II. Major Divisions of Subject Matter
   A. Learning about our earth
      1. Man's geographical accomplishments before the Age of Discovery
         a. The Mediterranean area
         b. Measurements and the early maps
         c. Post-Roman geographical problems
      2. Man's geographical accomplishments after the Age of Discovery
         a. Initial discoveries
         b. Expansion of man's knowledge of continents and oceans and the beginnings of modern geography
         c. Study of the earth
            (1) Surface
            (2) Atmosphere
            (3) Water
            (4) Plants and animals
            (5) Man
   B. Cultural study of the world
      1. Man and his relationship to geographical setting
         a. Culture as affected by race, population, and history
      2. European cultural area
         a. The Scandinavian countries and Finland
            (1) Material culture
            (2) Social institutions
               (a) Family and community
               (b) Education
               (c) Political institutions
            (3) Attitudes toward the unknown
               (a) Religion
               (b) Morals
         b. The countries of Western Europe
            (1) Material cultures
               (a) Tools and skills
               (b) Economic or ways of making a living
            (2) Social institutions
               (a) Political parties
               (b) Medicine
               (c) Social organizations
               (d) Religious beliefs
            (3) Art
               (a) Folklore
               (b) Drama
            (4) Language
      3. The Mediterranean Countries
         a. Material culture
            (1) Economics

        (2) Natural resources
- b. Social institutions
  - (1) Family
  - (2) Politics
- c. Attitude toward the unknown
  - (1) Religion
- d. Art
  - (1) Folklore
4. American culture area
   - a. Anglo-American
     - (1) Material culture
       - (a) Tools and skills
       - (b) Economics, or ways of making a living
   - b. Latin America
     - (1) Material culture
       - (a) Economics, or ways of making a living
     - (2) Social institutions
       - (a) Social organization (tribes, etc.)
       - (b) Administrative agencies (government)
       - (c) Language
5. North African and Eastern Border countries
   - a. Material culture
     - (1) Economics, or ways of making a living
   - b. Social organization
     - (1) Social organization
     - (2) Government (administrative agencies)
   - c. Attitude toward the unknown
     - (1) Religious beliefs
   - d. Language
6. Oriental cultural area
   - a. India
     - (1) Material culture
       - (a) Economics, or ways of making a living
     - (2) Social institutions
       - (a) Education
       - (b) Politics
       - (c) Social organization
     - (3) Attitudes toward the unknown
       - (a) Religious beliefs
       - (b) Magic
   - b. The mainland countries of Southeast Asia
     - (1) Material culture
       - (a) Economics
     - (2) Social institutions
       - (a) Social organizations
   - c. The island countries of Southeast Asia
     - (1) Material culture
       - (a) Economics
       - (b) Tools and skills
     - (2) Social institutions
       - (a) Social organizations

(b) Politics
(c) Education
(3) Language
d. China
(1) Material culture
(a) Economics
(2) Social institutions
(a) Social organizations
(b) Administrative agencies
(c) Politics
(3) Attitude toward unknown
(a) Religion
7. Soviet culture area
a. Natural resources and their development
b. Communist economic policies
(1) Commercial, farming, and industrial
c. Political administration and organization
d. Establishment of satellite countries and controls
(1) Political and economic position of the Iron Curtain Countries
8. African culture area
a. Union of South Africa
(1) Population and the land
(2) Settlement and control of government
(3) Mining, agriculture, and industry
b. Tropical Africa
(1) Climatic restrictions
(2) Division into colonial areas

World Geography[10]

Grades 9 and 10

First Semester

Part I. Geography and its Effects on the People of the United States and Other Parts of the World
1. Basic understandings of geography
2. Geography and its effect on sources of food
3. Geography and its effect on sources of clothing
4. Geography and its effect on resources for heavy industry

Second Semester

Part II. A Survey of the Geographic Areas outside the United States
5. Neighbors of the United States
6. The countries of Europe
7. The Middle East and Africa
8. Eastern Asia and the Pacific

---

[10] *World Geography Grades 9 and 10*, Bulletin No. 10 (Cincinnati, Ohio: Cincinnati Public Schools, 1958), p. 35.

Correlation with history content

The content of history can be correlated with the study of geography. In fact, world history and geography are essential for a comprehensive understanding of the global picture. A unit in a particular course can be devoted to the presentation of geographic concepts. The study of geography can be enriched with current events as well as with the consideration of history. For example, at the eighth grade level when studying our United States history and government, usage can be made of geography. The inclusion of geography gives emphasis whenever it can be related to the content. In the study of state history materials, geography can readily be correlated with the state's physical landscape. This type of correlation places special emphasis upon geography when deemed desirable. The correlation of content areas with geography provides the student with rich learning opportunities and profitable experiences.

Some of the most important elements of the physical environment are the location of an area, climate, natural vegetation, soil, topography, and drainage, mineral deposits, animal life, and population. It should be emphasized that, while these factors influence the development of a nation, they do not determine it. These elements are not exclusive, but are interrelated in patterns consisting of combinations both advantageous and adverse to human welfare. By permitting or denying, they may encourage or discourage specific economic, social, cultural, and political developments.[11]

For proper interpretation, current events depend upon a knowledge of modern geography. In the discussion of world news events, we must be ready and able to draw upon geographic detail for clarification. News items should be located geographically and regional implications noted.

Geography and our own community

The student as well as the adult should be well informed about the geography of his own community, county, and state. The neighborhood community is an excellent point of departure for the study of geography on all levels of instruction. The teacher should arouse the student's interest in knowing the community better by listing its chief features of interest and by pointing out the origin of the name and first site of the town. The early history of the area often presents a fascinating story for any group of students. How do the natural resources of the community influence the way the people live? What influence has geography had upon the location of industries? The geographic setting where they live

---

[11] *Course of Study United States History Eleventh Grade,* Bulletin No. 145 (Maryland: Public Schools Montgomery County, 1959), p. 9.

and work is an important interest in their everyday life. The familiar landscape of valleys, rivers, forests, and hills begins to hold new meaning. The industries and natural resources furnish an insight to occupational opportunities in a particular community. Environmental material is abundant and should be utilized in teaching. By knowing his own community better, a student can more fully understand state, national, and world situations. Such information about his own community and state provides a personal identification for the student. It reveals to him the relation of his community to the rest of the world and increases his appreciation of the efforts of the people in building the country. It should further the growth of a democratic society and the place of the student in his society. The growing knowledge of and relationship to the community will make him more capable of assuming his responsibilities as a citizen.

Land Use maps provide an interesting and practical activity for students wishing to learn about maps and their relation to the community. Large scale maps such as topographic maps from the United States Geologic Survey can provide a suitable base for learning about the land in the immediate community. Students indicate the various uses of the land by filling in, with colored pencils, such areas as farm land, businesses, vacant lots, and other areas.

Some Geographical Tools

Geography, like history and the other subject-matter fields, has specific tools and various devices applicable for reasearch and instructional purposes. Each of these tools or aids is essential for effective instruction. Each serves a definite purpose in clarifying learning, amplifying knowledge, and providing insight to specific information. Each aids in showing the relationship of the natural or physical elements to the cultural elements of the various areas. These tools aid the student in acquiring a wider understanding of the complexities of a world in which we are living.

These tools of geography include globes, maps, charts, models, and diagrams of various kinds of relating to specific information.

Maps

Ancient as well as modern maps have served the needs and spurred the imagination of men. Maps have multiple uses and are employed for many special purposes. Cartography, or the art of map making, requires skill and the accurate application of knowledge. The activities and events of the twentieth century have been clarified and enhanced by the use of especially designed maps. World geography has been made familiar to the masses through the use of maps illustrating current events.

Maps are an indispensable part of all social studies instruction. Historical data relating to all phases of civilization may be more clearly interpreted by maps. One of the primary uses of the map in the social studies is to enable the pupil to locate the site of both past and present events. This is particularly desirable in the study of current history. The pupils should become accustomed to locating geographically the scenes of world happenings. Maps showing population, products, and industries should be studied in connection with units on crime, housing, agricultural problems, unemployment, and labor-management. The problem of conservation should be interpreted through maps dealing with natural resources, production, and population. In fact, there is scarcely a topic discussed in the social studies class that cannot be made more realistic and meaningful through the use of an appropriate map. Maps may be obtained in three general forms: the globe, the relief model, and the flat map.

Globes. The most accurate map is the globe. Since the globe is a scale model of the earth, it presents land and water areas in their relative size and position without the distortion that is inevitable on a flat map. The use of the globe in teaching basic geographic facts and principles such as change of seasons, zones, and time belts is essential for effective understanding. The study of flat maps should constantly be supplemented by reference to the globe.

In studying geography, separate countries and regions do not receive the same degree of attention today. The relations of all regions of the world is of prime importance. Our ideas of distance and direction can be appreciated only by study of the world as a globe.

Relief Models. These models attempt to show actual surface elevations and depressions in relief. If well made, they are valuable teaching adjuncts, but they are not inexpensive.

Flat Maps. Because a globe is too bulky and cumbersome to be practical for a detailed study of its various divisions, flat maps, or projections of the earth's surface into two dimension, must also be used. Flat maps may be made to show many different types of information and are frequently classified according to the data shown.

Types of Flat Maps. Those that show the physical features of the area, such as mountains, valleys, plains, plateaus, rivers, and lakes are *physical maps.* Differences in elevation are most commonly shown by contour color layers, ranging from deep blue for deeper parts of the ocean, to green for lowlands, to brown and red for the highest mountains. Elevations may also be shown by contour lines, by hachures, or by shading to produce the effect of the photograph of a relief map.

Political maps depict political divisions and their boundaries. The countries or states are distinguished by color. The political map usually includes such physical features as rivers and lakes but does not usually show elevation.

A *physical-political map* combines both types or information on one map and is probably the most practical of the several types of flat maps. This is usually done by expressing the physical features in contour color layers on a background which clearly marks the political boundaries. Another but less effective kind of physical-political map is made by using hachures to show elevations on a political map as described above.

Outline maps are also available in different sizes for class use. Large wall outline maps are of two general types: the outlines may be drawn in yellow or white on a black background or the background may be white and the outlines black. Chalk is used on the former and colored crayon on the latter. Small desk-size outline maps may be obtained for individual pupil use. These usually show the outlines of the political divisions as well as rivers and other bodies of water.

There are numerous other types of maps which furnish data for specific purposes: population maps, weather maps, products maps, rainfall maps, temperature maps, vegetation maps, industrial maps, and road maps.

Map construction. Outline maps of desk-size may be purchased very economically or they may be mimeographed. Large outline maps may be drawn in colored chalk or painted on the blackboard. *Flat maps* of the large, wall variety may be made for specific purposes either by the teacher or by individuals in the class under the guidance of the teacher. These, if well-planned, can be very attractive, interesting, and meaningful to the study.

The opaque projector may be used to construct maps. To do this, place any small map (not to exceed 10 inches by 10 inches) in the opaque projector, and an enlarged image may be projected on the blackboard or large paper tacked on the bulletin board. Trace the projected image.

There are available today sets of 2 x 2 slides which have outline maps of countries of the world on them. These may be projected with a 2 x 2 slide projector or combination film-strip-slide projector on either the blackboard or large paper and traced.

Common window shades can be used to make permanent wall maps. The outline of the map should be sketched first in pencil and retraced with black paint or drawing ink. Next, boundaries, rivers, and other details are drawn. If different states or countries are included, it is best to use different colors. Tempera colors, water colors, or colored drawing inks all work very well for this. Any names should be printed in black. General maps, political maps, economic maps, and historical maps can be made this way and are serviceable and effective.

Pictorial maps are especially effective in the junior high school and are easily constructed. The general outline of the map should be drawn on a large, heavy sheet of paper or cardboard. Calcimine, water colors, or tempera colors can be used for the large areas of land and water. Pictures that have been drawn, painted, or cut beforehand can then be put on the map in the appropriate places. The final step is the printing of names and descriptions.

Relief maps of specific areas can be constructed by members of the class. The area to be represented should be thoroughly studied beforehand and the map should be carefully planned. The relief map may be built on a sand table or modeled of clay, putty, plaster of Paris, or other materials. Two economical sources of materials for making relief maps are papier-mâché and salt-and-flour mixtures.

Papier-mâché can be used to make durable relief maps easily and inexpensively. Newspapers torn into tiny bits and placed in a large bucket should be covered with water and left to stand for several days. At the end of this time, the water can be drained off and the mixture worked or kneaded until it is like a thick paste or dough. A piece of wood or heavy cardboard is needed for the backing. On this, a clear outline should be drawn as a guide for the application of the papier-mâché which is easily worked into the desired contours. When the shaping is completed, the map should be left to dry for a day or two. Water and other features can be represented with water colors or crayons. Varnishing or shellacking the whole thing will add to its durability.

Salt-and-flour maps are also excellent relief maps. The method is simple. Mix two parts of common salt with one part of flour. Add enough water to give the mixture the consistency of wet sand. Using a spatula or knife, apply the mixture to a heavy cardboard on which an outline has been drawn. Shape the elevations and contours and finish the map by coloring and coating with varnish or shellac.

These are a few examples of what students can do in the way of map construction. Student-constructed maps provide the opportunity for individual as well as committee work.

Individual map work as carried on in the social studies laboratory may fall into two specific categories: the drawing of original maps of a particular state, country, region, or continent, and the filling in of specific informational details on individual desk-size outline maps. A valuable introductory technique is the drawing of individual maps of the particular area to be studied. This provides a physical basis for the study and adds meaning and interest to it. Pupils of all ages and all levels of ability like to draw maps. Map-making provides an opportunity to engage in constructive activity, allows for individual initiative and planning, and presents a challenge to creative instincts.

Specific materials are essential for map work. These include rulers, colored pencils, crayons, erasers, compasses, protractors, pens, various colored inks, and large sheets of white or colored drawing paper. For best results, pupils need plenty of desk or table space. Sometimes maps can be effectively traced against a window pane with the light from outdoors being used as a substitute for a cartographer's light table. Student cannot be expected to draw satisfactory maps on small desks or crowded tables. Instead they should be allowed freedom of movement. Pupils frequently become so engrossed in their task that they kneel on their chairs or stand on their feet in order to reach further. On occasion, they also like to walk around the room in order to compare their progress with that of their classmates, to seek help, or to exhibit their own accomplishment. The teacher who is wise enough to relax customary restraints to the point where pupils can do their best work without getting too noisy or boisterous is likely to achieve the most satisfactory results.

Although the drawing of original maps is an effective instructional technique, it can be overdone. Pupils naturally lose interest in drawing the same maps over and over. For this reason, work on prepared outline maps should be substituted whenever the chief emphasis is upon the location of specific details.

Definite instructions should be given for all map work if results are to be effective. Pupils should be told the approximate size of the map, since this may vary with the area being depicted and the purpose for which the map is drawn. They should also be informed at the outset, or be led to list for themselves, the exact types of physical features that are to be shown and labeled. This list, and all other specific instructions, should be written on the blackboard so that pupils can refer to it from time to time. Other things to be stressed may include the following points:

1. It is better to sketch first in very light pencil and then overlay pencil outlines in ink.
2. Simplicity, neatness, and accuracy are important.
3. Labels should be printed, spaced carefully, and spelled correctly.
4. For effective use of color, try out the various colors and color combinations first on a scrap paper of similar texture.
5. Every map should have a title, properly spaced and clearly printed at the top.
6. Every map should have a legend. For uniformity and emphasis, a definite place for the legend—a direction arrow and a simple scale bar—should be established at the lower left-hand corner.

7. Each pupil should place his name on his map soon after beginning his work. Frequently maps are not completed during a single class period. Much time will be saved for both teacher and pupils if all names are placed in the same relative position, preferably in the lower right-hand corner.

Map projections

Because the earth is a sphere, the only exact scale representation of its entire surface is a globe. However, a globe of the size necessary to show any single country large enough for detailed study would be expensive, enormous, and unwieldy. A map on a flat piece of paper can be rolled or folded and stored away when not in use. For practical purposes, therefore, map makers have attempted to devise some method of making a flat map that would be reasonably accurate in physical detail. This involves the process of "projecting" a curved surface upon a flat surface or plane, and for this reason flat maps are often termed *projections*. Since it is impossible to change the curved surface of a sphere to a plane surface without distorting some part of it, various types of maps have evolved in an attempt to minimize this distortion.

One projection in quite common use is the *Mercator projection* which was first applied to a world map for use in navigation in 1569. This was worked out by Gerhard Kramer who used the pseudonym of Mercator, meaning *trader* or *merchant*. The Mercator projection is a modification of the cylindrical projection. It is accurate at the equator but becomes increasingly distorted as it nears the poles. The disadvantages of the Mercator projection are that the meridians appear as parallel straight lines instead of great circles meeting at the poles; the poles cannot be represented on the map; and land and water areas near the poles are highly distorted, making scales inaccurate.

Despite these shortcomings, however, the Mercator projection is still an excellent map for many purposes since compass directions are true and are shown as straight lines. East and west are at right angles from north and south, as they are naturally on the earth's surface. This makes the Mercator projection especially useful for place location and for surface navigation. Also, the shapes of the land and water bodies are relatively true, although the areas are distorted.

Another type of the flat map, commonly but inaccurately called the *polar projection*, has come into greater prominence during recent years. Actually, there are several types of *polar projections*, but the one generally referred to is really an *azimuthal equidistant projection*, which is centered on one of the poles, usually the North Pole because the Northern Hemisphere contains two-thirds of the land surface and nine-tenths of the population of the earth. Since the term *Azimuth* is just another word for "direction," a projection preserving the true directions of all lines drawn from some central point (center of map) to any other point on the globe is called an *azimuthal projection.* Such a projection, having equidistant parallels of latitude and centered on either the North or the South Pole, is correctly termed a *polar azimuthal equidistant projection.*

On some polar projection maps the parallels appear as concentric circles and the meridians as straight lines radiating from the pole like the spokes of a wheel. Since the parallels are equidistant, they cross these "spokes" at equal intervals and thus furnish a reliable scale for measuring distance from the center. There is relatively little distortion of land shapes and areas in the Northern Hemisphere. South of the equator, how-ever, the distortion greatly increases, a disadvantage which can be over-come by supplementing it with a similar map centered on the South Pole. A straight line connecting the center of the map with any other point on its surface is actually a great circle route and is true to scale. Other air or great circle routes, though not appearing as absolutely straight lines, can be more nearly shown in their proper perspective than on the Mercator projection. Because the meridians radiate in all direc-tions from the poles, the maps retain a desirable resemblance to a globe when viewed from above. Thus, the polar azimuthal equidistant projec-tion presents a good picture for studying air-age geography.

Other types of projection include the following:

1. Cylindrical projection; Examples: the Mercator Navigational Charts and many world wall maps.
2. Conic projection (Many atlas maps especially of the United States)
3. Polyconic projection (The U.S.G.S. Topographic map)
4. Lambert's conformal conic projection (Air navigation charts)
5. Gnomonic projection (special purposes, great sailing chart)
6. Stereographic projection (Polar Navigation charts)
7. Orthographic projection (Impressionistic)
8. Lambert's azimuthal equal-area projection
9. Mollweide's homolographic projection
10. Aitoff's equal-area projection
11. Goode's interrupted homolographic projection
12. Goode's interrupted homolosine projection
13. Fuller's "Dymaxion World"

These thirteen are not all the types of map-making, but they are the principal techniques of representing the global areas on a plane in order to show a fairly correct size and area relationship of continents and oceans. The conical projection named after Lambert, its inventor, uses a piece of paper shaped like a conical hat over the tope of a globe and projects the lines upward. This form does not distort the polar areas so much. What is called *orthographic projection* shows half the earth's surface as it is seen from far above space at infinity as though one were standing on the moon. In the azimuthal equidistant projection, the whole globe centered on the North Pole is peeled out to show the southern half around the rim, including Australia and South America, with north in the center and the spokes radiating like umbrella ribs southward. Any other point on the globe may be taken as the center of this diagrammatic representation. The airplane companies issue maps of this sort. Aerial photography takes in many miles of global area, and when many of these photos are taken from different points and pieced together, they give a large continuous photomap. However, no projection can show the whole truth in respect to size, shape, and direction as shown by the globe.

Location— Latitude and Longitude

Maps and globes are useful aids in locating the areas of and the places on the earth's surface. After learning the basic concepts of the globe, students can use this background knowledge in determining the location of any place shown in terms of latitude and longitude. Such instruction usually begins earlier in the student's education. It is always advisable to review the location of the equator, the tropics, the poles, and the cardinal principles of direction in order to establish guide posts. In teaching the concept of latitude, the learning should proceed slowly so the student can establish the real meaning of this new information.

Latitude

Latitude is the distance in a north or south direction from the equator and is measured in degrees. The lines running around the globe parallel to the equator are called *parallels of latitude*. These east-west lines are numbered on a map or globe. For example, the units may be expressed as 10, 20, and 30 degrees. There are 90 degrees between the equator, or 0 degree latitude, and each pole. Although expressed in degrees, latitude can be converted into a distance measurement of miles. One degree is equal to about 70 miles in length.

The author has found it very advantageous during the process of developing the concept of latitude to mention something about the thermometer, the compass, and the ruler in terms of measurement. In examining the globe or a map, a student may find a parallel north or south of the equator marked 20 degrees. Later the student may find the 60 degree parallel and may explain whether it is nearer or farther from the equator.

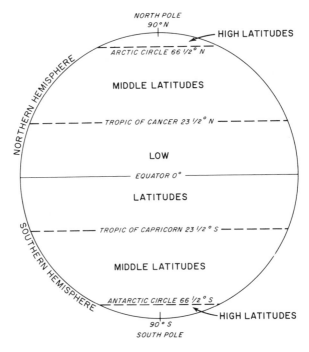

LATITUDE BELTS

A city can be selected for determining its latitudinal location. Each student should have the experience of finding the latitude of a given place. Cities, islands, and other areas can also be located for practice. Frequent reference to such concepts and skills in the study of geography builds competence in map reading and appreciation of the idea of location.

Longitude

Turning again to the globe, we observe lines running north and south around the globe and passing through the north and south poles. These lines are called meridians and form the basis for determining the longitudinal location of a place. Longitude may be defined as the distance east or west of a selected meridian, namely the prime meridian. The prime meridian is the meridian passing through the Greenwich Observatory near London, England.

Since there are 360° in a circle, measuring from either east or west from the Greenwich meridian, one may go as far as 180° longitude and be half way around the earth at or near the International Date Line. If one continues in the *same* direction beyond the 180th meridian, the value of longitude decreases until one returns to the prime meridian.

Students can enjoy locating the longitude of a place on the globe, but in many cases the less complicated latitude concepts are more easily understood at first.

Time concepts

In developing time concepts, we again turn to our globe and maps. Time on the earth is determined by the sun and the earth's rotation on its axis counterclockwise when seen from above the North Pole. The earth in this rotation process moves 360 degrees of longitude at a rate of 15 degrees of longitude each hour; thus, about twenty-four hours is required for a complete rotation. Time varies east and west from one's location; it is one hour earlier 15 degrees to one's west and one hour later 15 degrees to one's east. Many years ago it was decided by international

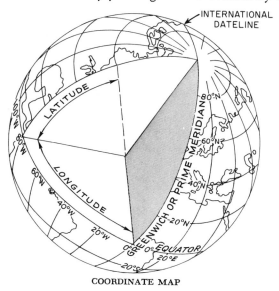

COORDINATE MAP

agreement that the 180th meridian would be called the International Date Line. At this selected meridian, opposite the Greenwich meridian, yesterday ends and tomorrow begins at midnight. Thus, in traveling eastward across the International Date Line, the calendar is turned back a day and in going westward it is moved ahead a full day. Therefore, one can see that time, distance, and longitude have a very close relationship.

We generally think of only two kinds of time; standard time and daylight saving time during the warmer months. However, we have four standard time zones based on 15° apart meridians in the United States excluding Alaska and Hawaii: Pacific Time 120° west longitude, Mountain Time 105° west longitude, Central Time 90° west longitude, and

Eastern Time 75° west longitude are our four standard time zones. A traveler changes his watch when moving from one time zone to another. In addition, with Alaska and Hawaii, we now include Yukon Time, Alaska Time, and Bering Time. Developing the concept of time for students entails concrete learning experience. The use of the calendar helps to extend our understanding of time. It is interesting to compute the difference in time between cities on our east and west coasts and between our cities and other parts of the world on the globe. Such time problems and study are directed more to the junior or seventh and eighth grade level.

Map-reading

The ability to read many kinds of maps is essential for intelligent living in the modern world. A good map tells a story, but pupils must be taught how to interpret each kind of map so that its story is clearly revealed. Pupils must learn to identify the kind of map, to find and use the scale and the legend, and to relate the flat map correctly to the globe and thereby to the earth's surface. They must acquire a map vocabulary, including such words as *equator, meridians, parallels, time zones, tropics, longitude, latitude, altitude, poles,* and *scale,* etc. Pupils must also develop skill in interpreting symbols of various kinds and in using letter and number location guides in the margins. It should not be expected that all this specialized knowledge can be imparted to pupils in a few lessons in a single grade or subject. Skill in the interpretation of maps is built up slowly and gradually over a considerable period of time and with constant use.

Maps are the foundation for studying geography and for interpreting history. Pupils should be taught to read and interpret at least three types of maps: the globe, the Mercator projection, and the polar azimuthal equidistant projection. Many secondary school pupils already have a reasonable facility in interpreting the globe and the Mercator projection. The social studies teacher should ascertain their difficulties and seek to remedy any deficiencies.

The pupils are probably not familiar with the pole-centered map. The social studies teacher should explain it by comparison with the globe and the Mercator projection. All three types of maps should be placed before the pupils at the same time.

The polar map might be introduced by rotating the globe so that the North Pole is directly toward the observers, giving them a clear view of the Northern Hemisphere. A point of departure in contrasting the pole-centered map with the Mercator projection might be the concept of direction. Pupils may be accustomed to think that north is always at the top

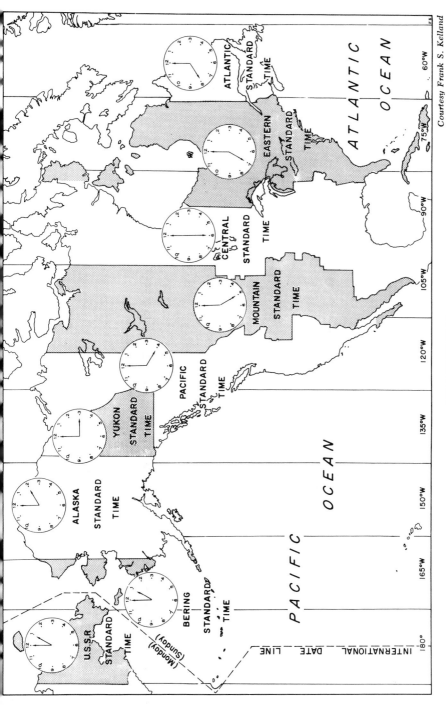

TIME BELT MAP

of the map and east toward the right. New methods of determining direction must be applied for the polar map. As an aid in understanding and remembering directions, a clock face should be drawn on the blackboard with an arrow indicating west.

If the South Pole centered map is to be considered, after these directions have been mastered, a second clock can be placed beside the first with the words "east" and "west" interchanged.

An azimuthal equidistant projection centered on the United States may also be advisable for studying global relationships in reference to the United States. This may be more easily understood after the pole-centered maps have been studied.

Pictures

Pictures are as essential as maps in the study of geography. The teacher of geography will find that the picture collection is one of his most important sources of instructional materials. Pictures not only arouse interest, stimulate discussion, and induce exploration but also furnish the best means of presenting in concrete form phases that would otherwise remain outside the pupils' comprehension or imagination. Such concepts as land formations, tropical areas, arctic regions, deserts, glaciers, swamps, erosion, tidal waves, floods, industries, and occupations can be far more easily and adequately understood through the use of appropriate pictures than by means of the spoken or printed word alone. Pictures should also be used for the representation of unfamiliar vegetation and animals and phases of human life and customs which differ from our own.

The teacher of geography should take every precaution to make sure that the pupils actually understand all pertinent implications of the information shown. When the pictures are being shown to clarify conceptions of unfamiliar objects, processes, or customs, nothing should be taken for granted. Even in the senior high school if pupils are shown a picture depicting foreign customs and dress, for example, insufficient discussion or explanation may result in their understanding the picture only and not the facts behind it. The teacher should assume that erroneous impressions are likely to occur and should take whatever steps may be necessary to insure complete understanding.

Stamps in geography

Postage stamps can provide a fertile source of pertinent visual-aid material for the teaching of both geography and history. Stamps are symbols and recorders of events. Stamps of varied denominations with various designs and inscriptions interweave adventure and achievement with their teaching. Suitable stamps depict history of geographical locations, exploration and discovery, new lands and ports, transportation and communication, agricultural progress, scientific achievement, areas of countries, scenes of cities and regions, significant personalities and their contributions, expeditions and routes followed, and the commemoration of events. Factual information abounds in a stamp collection.

Vitalizing geography instruction

Methods of presenting geographical materials will vary with the needs, interests, and abilities of the class. Much of the desired content in geography can be effectively taught by the use of problems, and many other methods of instruction will be employed from time to time. A lesson in geography can be alive, rich, and stimulating for each student; on the other hand, it can be the dullest, most uninteresting, and boring class session. The difference depends almost entirely upon the teacher, his own interest in, and knowledge of, geography, and his skill in applying appropriate methods and techniques to arouse student interest.

Considerable laboratory work is desirable, and students should have ample opportunity to become familiar with various geographic tools and references. The teacher has an excellent opportunity to capitalize upon the creative abilities of all the students. He will find this one of the best ways to challenge student interest and to provide for individual differences. Students can best learn to understand and use such tools as maps, charts, and graphs by making originals. Each student should be inspired to attempt and carry out an original project suited to his abilities and interests. The informality of the laboratory environment is ideally suited to inspire creative ability. At the same time, the laboratory atmosphere enables the teacher to become better acquainted with his students and better able to adapt phases of his program to meet their needs and capacities.

Suggested student activities

A well-planned program of varied, interesting, and constructive student activities is necessary. These activities should grow out of the topic under consideration; directly because of a definite need or indirectly because of the inspiration of a motion picture, a field trip, or a bulletin board display. Many student activities stress map work.

Outline Map Work. Outline maps may be used as a basis for many different kinds of geographical and historical interpretation. Information to be supplied may include physical and political features, rainfall, natural resources, industries, and population centers. This type of activity may be used to supplement or summarize the study of a particular topic, or, occasionally, for testing purposes.

Map Projects. Making a large wall relief or pictorial map as a group project provides excellent training in research, organization, and cooperation. Increased interest and enthusiasm can be secured if the finished product is to be a permanent contribution to the school. Such work may be correlated with the activities of the art department.

Community Maps. County, township, or other local areas may be included. Local maps supply geographical as well as historical information. A chronological series of community maps should be simple, accurate, and complete. Community maps are valuable for spotlighting local changes, problems, and issues. Descriptive slides may display this information through opaque projection. Secondary school teachers should explore the possibilities of using a community map in preparing a group for field trips. An aerial photograph of a community, in addition to supplying geographical knowledge, can also show the advantages and disadvantages of maps. The examination of community maps and the story that they tell will make geography more functional.

Three-dimensional maps

Another activity closely related to map making has been the introduction of a method of terrain representation which is not on a single plane. Items of this type are referred to as a *relief model.* They are usually constructed from papier-mâché or clay. Commercial and government mapping agencies have perfected such relief models from plastic which are molded to represent ridges and valleys and other landforms. Maps of this type are difficult to store and transport, but if designed as a permanent display, they will give a realistic view of the physical landscape.

For areas of small extent, the relief model can be especially meaningful to the student because he can actually sense by touching and seeing the surface irregularities. In relief models, the vertical scale has to be exaggerated. Without exaggeration of the vertical scale, hills and mountains become practically flat.

In the learning activities, experience can be gained in building this type of terrain representation because the construction procedure may consist of building up contours from enlarged topographic maps. A material such as clay or plastic can be molded into the space between the contours. By smoothing and filling in the actual slopes and ridges of the topography of a selected area, these materials can be quite accurately reproduced in miniature. After the model has become firm, it is possible to paint or place materials to represent roads, small buildings, and vegetation.

Tack Board Display. The responsibility for collecting and arranging tack board materials fosters and maintains interest in the work being done in the classroom. Excellent pictures can be obtained from periodicals of foreign countries and foreign peoples. By using these and maps, geography can be brought vividly to life.

Let us say, for instance, that the class is studying France. Maps can be used, giving a picture of France's physical appearance. Pictures showing the country's main products can be mounted around another map by strings to points of the picture to indicate which parts of the country produced these products. Transportation can be shown with other pictures, as well as raw materials and minerals. A realistic way of illustrating raw materials produced in a particular country would be to use small samples of these materials to decorate the tack board or display table.

Booklets. Original booklets may be made as individual activities or as the cooperative achievements of small groups within the class. In general, the teacher should endeavor to encourage group responsibility for this type of activity in order to minimize any possible sense of failure on the part of students who are less gifted or less able to carry out a project on their own. These booklets may include scrapbooks on different industries or occupation, guide books for a specific country or region, or a geography of the local community or area.

Quiz Contests and Games. Geographical games and contests of various types may be used to review basic facts, furnish vocabulary drill, and aid in stimulating interest and critical thinking.

Discussion Activities. The teacher of geography should endeavor to correlate discussion activities with instructional procedures wherever possible. Forums, debates, or panel discussions on current events relating to the particular topic can be prepared and presented by students committees. Individual or committee reports may be prepared by the students and followed by group discussion. Preparation for these activities should be made under the guidance of the teacher in the social studies laboratory where there is ready access to needed materials.

Miscellaneous Activities. There are other activities and experiences which the students, guided by the teacher, may plan and execute during the process of studying a geography unit. Students may work independently, in small groups, or as a complete class. Some of the work may include correlation of geography with other content fields; students may read supplementary materials and stories, report on topics, go on field trips, interview people, listen to radio programs, view television programs and films, exhibit materials, write term papers, write letters to business firms and exchange letters with students in other states and countries. They may conduct surveys, investigate specific problems, listen to recordings, make studies of climate, rainfall, and weather, collect articles, dramatize events and the lives of people, keep notebooks, make new-word lists, make posters, plan assembly programs, organize a geography club, use community resources, plan special topics, assemble bibliographies, collect clippings, and build various geographical models.

Evaluating in geography

Evaluation is considered a part of the learning process and is continuous throughout the study of a geography unit. Frequent evaluation sometimes may change and enrich the general outline of the work. We are concerned with the general growth of the student. A group should benefit from geographical knowledge. They want to see the functional values derived from their efforts. A list of well-stated objectives must be achieved in whole or at least partially if evaluation is to be significant. Students and teacher should evaluate their own work in terms of the objectives of the particular unit. Students who are allowed to establish goals for themselves generally show an interest and are motivated in the learning process. They see the results of their planning, experiences, and success—a gratifying experience.

Conclusion

Geographic education has an important role to play in meeting the needs of youth in our secondary school. Courses are developed with functional and meaningful units that furnish valuable knowledge for the student. The problem-solving approach challenges the student and develops competence for meeting life situations as an individual citizen. Geography can be correlated with other subjects, thus enriching learning. With the wide variety of activities and an active imagination, the teacher can stimulate student interest and enrich learning for the group. The study of geography can reveal the interrelations between the local community and the state, nation, and world. The student's development through functional experience is important. Evaluation has a significant role to play in the growth of each student.

Bibliography

Bengtson, N. A. and W. Van Royen, *Fundamentals of Economic Geography*, 4th ed. Englewood Cliffs, N.J.: Prentice-Hall, Inc., 1956.

James, P. E., ed., *New Viewpoints in Geography*, Twenty-ninth Yearbook of the National Council for the Social Studies. Washington, D.C.: National Education Association, 1959.

Kohn, C. F., ed., *Geographic Approaches to Social Education*, Nineteenth Yearbook of the National Council for the Social Studies. Washington, D.C.: National Education Association, 1948.

Price, R. A., ed., *New Viewpoints in the Social Sciences*, Twenty-eighth Yearbook of the National Council for the Social Studies. Washington, D.C.: National Education Association, 1958.

Smith, V. A., "Material for a One Year Course in High School Geography," *The Journal of Geography*, 60 (September 1961), 262-268.

Thralls, Z. A., *The Teaching of Geography*. New York: Appleton-Century-Crofts, Inc., 1958.

Wilson, R. C., "Using News to Teach Geography," *Social Education*, 24 (February 1960), 56-57.

Chapter Thirteen

Developing Economic Competence

There is a recognized need for instruction in economic education for students in our secondary schools. Effective citizenship requires that each individual acquire some knowledge and understanding of our contemporary economic society. Modern society and especially effective community living assumes that individuals have an intelligent approach to meeting their specific everyday needs in adult life. It is through some basic knowledge of economics that new insights or understandings of our economy may be acquired. Such a study describes basic concepts and some of the analytical processes characteristic to the subject. Many of the occurring events relating to our nation and the world carry some economic significance. Agriculture, manufacturing, trade, and commerce may have a wide influence upon the activities of the population in a particular community, state, and even an entire region.

Each student today must have the educational opportunity to learn how to manage his own economic affairs intelligently, understand certain basic economic principles, and know the general economic structure of the United States and its role in world affairs. He should:
1. Prepare himself to assume the financial responsibilities of establishing a home and become realistic about the obligations necessary to maintain a happy and self-sufficient home before marriage.

2. Know how to budget his own finances and keep accurate personal accounts.
3. Learn how to buy wisely and ascertain where he may secure reliable information on personal business transactions.
4. Understand the workings, benefits and costs of insurance, social security, taxation, loans, mortgages, banking, transportation, and ordinary business procedures.
5. Develop a sense of individual responsibility as a producer as well as a consumer.
6. Study some of the basic principles and problems relating to the exchange of goods and services.
7. Understand the general economic structure of our nation and the basic problems and principles involved in our economic relationships with other countries.
8. Remain cognizant of the relation of human values to economic values.
9. Develop a sense of personal responsibility and integrity in managing his own economic affairs.
10. Understand the basic principles relating to the interdependence of government, politics, economics, and culture.
11. Know the contributions and responsibilities to our economy of labor and management.
12. Study and discuss intelligently from known facts the probable impact of present and future automation of our economic and social relationships.[1]

Economics

Economics like history is one of the earliest of the social science disciplines. In turning back the pages of time and space, it is interesting to see how the growth of commerce, exploration, and colonization in various parts of the world brought new economic problems and relationships. The history of growth in the American economy is, on a small scale, a reproduction of the story of economic growth in the Old World, when commodities were used in business transactions and for the payment of debts. Money economy and credit economy succeeded this early stage of exchange. The present development of the complicated banking system and international economy followed.

In the adolescent days of Western capitalism, rigorous thrift stood, with much reason, as the cardinal economic virtue. Capital was desperately needed to make nature's resources and the labor supply more fruitful. The catalytic powers of credit were imperfectly understood and credit institutions both crude and meager. The farm family pinched pennies to enlarge flocks and improve land and buildings. The artisan denied himself to get a "nest egg" and set up a small shop of his own. But with the expansion of the factory system and growth of a wage-earning population, "cash money" was more in evidence,

---

[1] M. S. Olson, "Educating for Economic Competence," *California Journal of Secondary Education,* XXXI, No. 4 (March 1956), 175-176.

salesmanship became more aggressive, and a quicker tempo of trade kept step with the rising efficiency of manufacturing.[2]

Economics is an organized body of knowledge dealing with man's activities in satisfying his wants for scarce goods. It is a social science which deals primarily with production, distribution, and exchange.

Production is the creation of utility by economic goods. To produce goods, one must properly organize the factors of production: land, labor, enterprise, and capital. Economics also includes the study of both the movement of goods from their point of production to their point of consumption, and the ways that goods are exchanged.

Economic instruction and courses

Economic materials are presented chiefly in the social studies, home economics, and the business education departments at the secondary level. The courses may generally include such titles as Economics, Consumer Education, and Consumer Economics. Economic content may be presented as a unit or as topics in the twelfth-grade Problems of American Democracy course or a similarly titled course. In the treatment of contemporary materials and current events, there is considerable opportunity to emphasize the economic analysis and significance of the event or topic. Many items such as automation and technological change, agriculture, and taxes are significant items in which the student may acquire new knowledge.

Economics can take its place in the social studies curriculum under either of two possible arrangements. A major unit dealing with economic materials can be included in the Problems of American Democracy course or an elective course in economics can be offered for high school students. It is most essential that economic understanding be a part of the knowledge required for equipping young people to participate as effective citizens in our democratic society. It is therefore recommended to curriculum builders that, if possible, a full year's course be devoted to the study of economics as a separate subject, so that it be given systematic treatment.

It is presupposed that a thorough introduction to the meaning and concepts of the social science discipline, economics, is to be provided for students enrolled in such a course. In this manner students will be more capable of effectively exploring selected economic problems with the group.

---

[2] Edwin G. Nourse, "New Viewpoints in the Economic Area," in *New Viewpoints in the Social Sciences*, R. A. Price, ed., The National Council for the Social Studies, 28th Yearbook (Washington, D.C., 1958), p. 91.

Economics instruction at the secondary level should provide functional learning experiences for the students. This requires that the teacher and group have an adequate supply of resources including audio-visual materials and current literature. In the discussion that follows excellent examples of course arrangements for the study of economics will be found. Selected problems are helpful; however, the teacher should be ever alert for current and timely topics.

What is economics?

The following material presents an enlightening treatment of economics.

Economics has been described as the science of choice. To economize in the area of political economy is to choose an action that the chooser regards as best in accordance with the criteria or values he wishes to attain and that he believes will maximize his welfare.

Economics has also been defined as the social science that is concerned with the allocation of scarce resources among competing uses. *The economic problem* is the problem of choice that is forced upon us because our wants exceed our ability to satisfy these wants. Human and material resources are scarce in the sense that not enough resources exist to satisfy all the wants of all the members of our society.

One of the major reasons for studying economics is to learn how we organize our society with a view toward deciding *what* goods or services are going to be produced, *how* these goods and services will be produced, and *for whom* these goods and services will be produced.[3]

Economics Course of Study[4]
(New York City)

Scope and Suggested Time Allotment

Unit I.   Economic Systems (7-8 periods)
    Economic Systems, Activities, and Institutions
    Capitalism versus Communism
Unit II.   The Development of American Business (13-17 periods)
    The Contribution of Management
    The Growth of American Business
    The Effects of Big Business on American Life
    The Corporation: Characteristics and Problems
    Stock Exchanges
    Government and Business

---

[3] M. C. Olson and E. L. Swearingen, eds., *Business And Economic Education for the Academically Talented Student* (Washington, D.C.: National Education Association and United Business Education Association, 1961), p. 28.

[4] *American History and Economics* (Regents), Curriculum Bulletin 1961-62 Series No. 10 (New York, N.Y.: Board of Education, 1962), pp. 67-69. Reprinted by permission of the Board of Education of the City of New York.

The Place and Responsibility of Big Business in the American Economy Today

Unit III.   Labor (8-10 periods)
The Labor Force
Wage Determination
Development of the Labor Movement
The Government and Labor
The Place and Responsibility of Labor in the American Economy Today

Unit IV.   Agriculture (7-8 periods)
Significance of Agriculture for the American Economy
Historical Survey of Farm Problems
Government and the Farmer
Impact of Technology on the Farmer
Current Problems

Unit V.   Money, Credit, and Banking (5-8 periods)
The Need for a Medium of Exchange
Credit: Creation, Types, and Controls
Inflation and Deflation

Unit VI.   Promoting Economic Stability and Growth (3 periods)
The Business Cycle: Nature and Factors
Keeping the Economy Healthy and Growing

Unit VII.   Public Finance (7-10 periods)
Government Spending and Income
Tax Programs and Policies
Criteria of a Good Tax Program
Government Borrowing and Debt
Federal-State-City Fiscal Relationships

Unit VIII.   International Trade (5 periods)
The Need for Foreign Trade
Changing Trends in American Trade
Payments in International Trade
Efforts to Increase International Economic Cooperation

Unit IX.   The Consumer (optional)
Problems of the Consumer
The Consumer and Ways of Getting Value for his Money
Special Problems in the Management of Income

Points to be Emphasized Throughout the Course

1. The free enterprise system has achieved one of the highest living standards in the world, while affording maximum individual freedom.

2. While our system is a mixed economy with both private and public activity the most characteristic feature is that of individual initiative and enterprise.

3. Our economic system has become so complex and inter-related that changes in any one aspect of our economic operations may have repercussions in many other aspects of our economy.

4. Both American business and American labor have contributed materially to our standard of living and industrial leadership. Both in turn have continuing responsibilities to the public welfare.

5. While the role of agriculture in our American economy has become relatively less significant, it is still of primary importance, and the

problems of this sector of our economy must receive careful and sympathetic consideration.

6. Money and credit are major factors in facilitating the smooth operation of our productive machine and market operations.

7. It is now generally accepted that the government has a major responsibility for curbing extremes of the business cycle, promoting economic health and growth, encouraging full employment, and acting as an umpire in balancing the countervailing forces of industry, labor, agriculture, and other special interests.

8. The economic well being of the United States is related to the economic health of other regions of the world. Our nation must accordingly concern itself with such matters as foreign trade, the advancement of underdeveloped nations, and international economic stability.

9. Responsibilities of world leadership require the American economy to maintain high living standards at home and, if necessary, to provide technological and economic assistance to other nations abroad.

10. The many services of government necessitate the payment of taxes by our citizens for the general interest. Contributions to the development of sound economic policies wherever possible and a readiness to render appropriate support even at some personal financial sacrifice are hallmarks of good citizenship.

11. The challenge of communism and other rival political and economic systems makes it crucial that we point up our ability to maintain a superior productive system without sacrificing individual freedom in contrast to systems which offer some economic gain at the price of totalitarian regimentation.

12. The many economic choices confronted by every American citizen in consumption, job selection, business decisions, and in making judgments on public policy require a high degree of economic literacy.

Economics and economic history

A knowledge of the role of history and the geographical influences or natural environment in a region undoubtedly aids in providing background for the understanding of economics and contemporary economic problems. This is particularly important when we study the factors of production, distribution, and the processes of exchange. The resources of a particular area play a significant role in the everyday life of a people.

The economic history of the United States is concerned with the economic accomplishments of the United States, with the factors that accelerated economic progress, and with the effects of economic development on the nation's individual citizens and on its political, social, and economic institutions. . . . Economic history is . . . the study that ties in economic events with changes in the level of living and explains those events in terms of their causes and effects.[5]

It may be possible to include some economic aspects of history in

---

[5] H. E. Krooss, *American Economic Development* (Englewood Cliffs, N.J.: Prentice-Hall, Inc., 1955), p. 4.

American as well as in world history courses—for example, in discussing the growth of the tariff, industry, business, agriculture, and labor. Some mention could be made of the economic aspect as it shaped the destinies of history and society. From these studies the student should gain an economic understanding as well as a historical perspective. In the organization of units dealing with specific materials, effort should be made to interweave economic aspects as it relates to over-all economy in the total culture.

Economics[6]

(Houston Public Schools)

Unit 1   Economic Factors Involved in the Educational Opportunities Provided by the Houston Public Schools
Unit 2   The Fundamental Principles of Economics
Unit 3   The American Economic System: Its "Roots" and its "Fruits"
Unit 4   The American Economic System: How it is Organized and How it Operates
Unit 5   What Young Americans Should Know about Other Economic Systems
Unit 6   The American Economic System: Current Problems and Trends
Unit 7   The American Economic System as it Operates in Houston and the Surrounding Area

Major Objectives

1. To encourage objective and logical analysis of economic problems, by helping students to recognize and understand that:[7]
    Intelligent judgment is dependent upon clearly defined objectives and accurate factual information.
    The best choice among several alternative ways of achieving objectives can be made only after careful analysis of the consequences of choosing each possible alternative.
2. To develop a thorough understanding of the principles upon which the American economic system is based, by showing that:
    The Constitution of the United States guarantees the right of all Americans to engage in private business, to own private property, to make enforceable contracts, to seek private employments, and to maintain other private rights.
    These principles, though imperfectly applied, have preserved in the United States a greater degree of freedom for the individual and a greater degree of opportunity for all citizens than have ever been available under any other system, at any other time.
3. To develop a good understanding of how the American economic system is organized and how it functions, by showing that:
    Productive capacity is dependent upon quantity and quality of tools

---

[6] *Economics,* Curriculum Bulletin No. 61CBM63 (Houston, Texas: Houston Independent School District, 1961), p. iii.
    [7] *Ibid.,* pp. 3-5.

(capital goods), availability of basic natural resources, and effective application of human effort in utilizing these tools and resources.

Capital goods are made available by individuals who through the exercise of their own free initiative have saved part of their production in the hope of profits.

Productive capacity has continued to increase in the United States, resulting in an increasingly higher standard of living for all, through continuous improvement in the utilization of tools, resources, and human effort.

4. To impress students with the fact that the American system of private enterprise affords a greater degree of opportunity for the individual, and at the same time imposes a greater responsibility upon the individual, than does any other type of economic system, by pointing out that:

One of the most important factors in American economic development has been the willingness of Americans to work hard and undertake risks; there is no other "magic formula" by which real progress may be achieved.

Each one of us, as American citizens, must be willing to accept our economic responsibilities and discharge our economic obligations intelligently and ethically, in full appreciation of our heritage and of our duty to future Americans yet unborn.

Suggested Teaching Procedures

Since a major purpose of this course is to help students understand the basic principles of economic life and to appreciate more fully the American economic system of private enterprise, a large portion of the class time should be devoted to carefully planned discussion and thoughtfully prepared written assignments based upon the content outlined in this course of study. Discussion activities may include:

1. *Formal recitation periods,* in which the teacher raises questions to draw out facts, develop understandings, stimulate thinking, and encourage further study and investigation.
2. *Panel discussions,* in which small groups of students present varying points of view and class members join in a general discussion following the presentation.
3. *Symposiums,* in which several students present prepared speeches, each developing a special topic or a particular part of a given subject. A symposium may or may not be followed by questions or comments from the rest of the class members.
4. *Lectures,* either formal or informal, which may be presented by the teacher, by an invited guest speaker, or by a member of the class. The lecture should be well-prepared and should be pertinent to the topic under general study at the time. Students should be required to make notes on such lectures.

Written activities may include:

1. *Written reports* (including a properly prepared bibliography) on special topics. One or more such reports are recommended for each six weeks.
2. *Longer themes,* or *essays* (including a properly prepared bibliography) on some special problem of particular importance in the study of economics. One such essay per term is recommended.
3. A *notebook,* which should include:
   a. Data called for in the "Outline of Content" in this course of study.

This material may be presented in the form of questions and answers, or as a completion of the outline.

b. A record of any reading done by the student from sources other than the textbook (*Economics for Our Times*). This record should include full bibliographical data and a few brief notes on the material read. Newspaper articles *should not* be accepted unless they comply with the above-mentioned procedures.

c. Notes on lectures, films or filmstrips, panel discussions, oral reports, and symposiums. These should be brief, but should follow a definite form.

d. Any other material that the teacher may wish to require or agree to accept from the student.

Other activities may include:

1. Use of *audio-visual materials* such as tape recordings, disc records, films, and filmstrips.

2. *Class excursions*, if circumstances permit. In a city the size of Houston, however, physical conditions often make the use of this device highly impractical. Before any such project is suggested to students, the teacher should explore the idea thoroughly with the principal of the school.

3. Any *projects* that may be assigned. For example, a bulletinboard display on events of current economic interest may be maintained by class committees.

Economics[8]

(Pennsylvania)

The following is a prepared guide with suggestions for instructions in economics. It provides a source for teachers and supervisors who are in the process of including economic materials in a social studies program.

Minimum economic literacy is the aim of the program; but the time allocated toward achieving this goal in many cases is limited to 36 hours or about nine weeks. On the basis of rather extensive and responsible evidence, six units have been designated as most essential.

In addition to the six units selected as fundamentals, eight others which might be included in a general course in economics are suggested. Those classes which have sufficient time for additional units should choose from among them according to the general interests of the students and the socio-economic nature of the community.

For those schools which intend to teach economics on the basis of the minimum mandated time allocation of 36 hours, the following schedule is suggested:

Unit   I An Introduction to Economics; 1-2 hours
Unit   II The American Economy; Prices, Profits, and Markets; 5-8 hours
Unit III Economic Growth; 5-7 hours

---

[8] *Suggested Procedures And Resources For A Minimum Course In Economics,* Curriculum Development Series No. 4 (Harrisburg, Pa.: State Dept. of Public Instruction, 1962), pp. 2-3.

Unit IV Causes and Effects of Business Cycles and the Problem of Maintaining a Prosperous Economy Without Inflation; 5-7 hours
Unit   V The Role of Government in Our Economy; 5 hours
Unit VI A Comparison of Capitalistic and Communistic Economic System; 6 hours
Testing and Evaluation; 3 hours

Objectives

To provide fundamental literacy about economic concepts and problems of our times

To develop the ability to make economic judgments by objective, rational analysis

To understand the common instruments of everyday economic life

To apply economic principles to specific problems

To understand the nature and methods of our own and other economic systems

Consumer Education[9]

Consumer Education is offered to meet the needs of high school graduates in their practical participation in everyday economic life. A basic understanding of money management, prices, consumer goods, advertising, buying habits, credit, taxation, savings, and insurance is included. The student should also be made aware of his importance as a consumer in the world economy of his community and nation. This course is primarily for noncollege and business students in grade eleven, though others may elect it.

General objectives

1. To assist the students to understand the role they play as consumers in our economic system and to realize that the consumer is the key individual in demand. This is the prime motive which keeps our economic system functioning.
2. To enable the student, as a consumer, to make intelligent decisions.
3. To acquaint the student with government regulations of our economic life.
4. To inform the student, as a consumer-citizen, of the operation of consumer organizations.
5. To teach the student basic understanding and adequate information gaining techniques to assist him in finding solutions for himself.
6. To provide the student with training and practice in the evaluation of skillful propaganda devices designed to influence consumers.
7. Since good consuming depends upon social relations, consumer education aims to cultivate in the student habits of realistic thinking in relation to the problems of consumption, and a courteous yet discerning approach to other individuals.

---

[9] *Curriculum Guide Social Studies Stoneham High and Junior High Schools* (Stoneham, Mass.: Stoneham Public Schools, 1961), pp. 70-75.

Specific Objectives

1. To help the pupil know the three fundamental processes of an economic system; production, consumption, and exchange.
2. To teach the pupil how the law of supply and demand affects the prices of goods.

Suggested topical sequence

  I. General Economic Information Essential for Background
 II. Financial Planning and the Consumer
III. Credit and the Consumer
 IV. Investments and the Consumer
  V. How Prices Affect the Consumer
 VI. Buying Problems of the Consumer
VII. Review and Mid-year Examinations
VIII. Using Sources of Information
 IX. Insurance and the Consumer
  X. Taxes and the Consumer
 XI. Housing and the Consumer
XII. Transportation and the Consumer
XIII. Legal Relationships of Buyer and Seller
XIV. Frauds, Swindles, and the Consumer
 XV. Consumer, Producer, and Labor Relationships
XVI. Review and Final Examinations

Training in intelligent purchasing will make students better consumers of goods and services, thus improving the status of the consumer in our modern social and economic society. A consumer must be an inquisitive and thoughtful purchaser if he expects to balance his budget. Most persons do not spend their income equitably. It is difficult for the consumer to judge in advance of his year's outlay the kinds and quantities of articles and services he may require. Consumer education is a subject that should be approached earnestly, as a straightforward introduction to practical economics.

Consumption, the goal of economic effort—desires and wants satisfied through the process of earning a living—represents the final stage in the economic process. It deals with real wealth, the actualities of goods, articles, and satisfactions that can be purchased. Profit alone is not the ultimate result of economic activity until it is put to use or liquidated by purchase. To this end, the consumer has to think straight—to measure and restrict his desires—to live within his means.

Our economy operates on an income and exchange basis. Since incomes vary as individuals and their tastes vary, we find a variety of methods of expenditure and consumption. If the consumer is well informed, he will know how and when to make his purchases, how to resist the desire to buy when it is to his ultimate disadvantage, and how to have a responsibility for savings and security. This requires wisdom in budgeting—knowledge of prices, values, and the proper markets—and intelligent selection. If all these goals are attained, the citizen has his income adjusted to his needs, plus a surplus for his aims and goals. He will not be misled by improper advertising, and he will have the technical information necessary to choose and select goods and services.

Social Economics[10]

The initial objective of this course is to present the basic concepts of sociology and economics as revealed in the historical, cultural, and biological backgrounds of our society.

The practical aspects derived from the theory of sociology and economics are accomplished by the use of current audio-visual materials and resources persons versed in particular fields, such as labor and management. The range of material presentations and the scope of the course offer much opportunity to employ people who work in the practical aspects of both sociology and economics.

Emphasis in this course is placed upon the nature of change in society. One of the ideal ways of studying change is to take contemporary society and work back in time to discover how far we have departed from the past in mores, customs, ideas, values, institutions, and social roles.

Course Outline

I. Backgrounds of Society
  A. Historical
    1. Development of Man
    2. Contributions of American Indians
    3. Contributions of European Cultures
  B. Cultural
    1. Cultural building of Man—Revolutions
    2. Material Ages of Civilization
    3. Social Progress
  C. Biological Foundations
    1. Races of Man
    2. Superiority of Man
    3. Social Progress
    4. Characteristics Influencing Social Development
II. Social Roles
  A. Concept of Personality
    1. Influences of Society
    2. Development in Society
  B. Institution of the Family
  C. Relations with Peer Groups
  D. Citizen Roles
  E. Religion
III. Social-Economic World

---

[10] *Instructional Guide: Social Economics,* Northern Valley Regional High School (Demarest N.J.: 1962), pp. 1-2.

A. Industry and Labor in Our Culture
B. Patterns of Consumption, Distribution, and Production
  1. Development of Wants and Needs
  2. Social Influence
C. Vocational Opportunities
D. Rural Life
E. Urban Life
IV. Contemporary Problems of Society
  A. Population Problems
  B. Natural Resources
    1. Conservation
    2. Utilization
  C. Regional Studies
    1. Social Development
    2. National Unity
  D. Health
    1. Physical
    2. Mental
  E. Education
  F. The Handicapped—Rehabilitation
  G. Safety
    1. Driving
    2. Traffic
    3. Home
    4. Industry
  H. Welfare—Social Security
  I. Crime and Delinquency
  J. Minority Groups
  K. Immigration and Assimilation Problems
  L. National Ideals
  M. Social Controls
  N. Public Opinion and Mass Media
V. Evaluation—Critique

Vitalizing economics instruction

Planning, organizing, and teaching economic problems and topics requires considerable knowledge of the content and of the skill in directing the instruction. The study of economics should be made realistic, interesting, and functional for the students in order to furnish some self direction for effective learning. Many of the methods, techniques, and procedures applicable for teaching other social studies courses can be utilized in economic education. The teacher should employ all available resources for the enrichment of instruction. The enthusiasm of the instructor can make economics vitally exciting for the students. For example, the utility aspect should be employed when studying the techniques of modern banking and the mechanics of money and credit. The audio-visual materials such as films, recordings, film strips, radio, and television should be employed when deemed advisable. Films can be used to furnish background material depicting different stages of economic development and showing the methods of exchange, production, and distribution of different periods.

Care should be given to the proper selection and application of realistic films that have a practical value to the study of economics. The harnessing of rivers for the use of industry, the numerous dams and power projects in our country, the role of steam, oil, coal, and electricity of the present and past, show the rapid rise of the industrial revolution and the accelerated progress of current scientific advances. Films that deal specifically with separate units are valuable—development of agriculture, railroads, aviation, or mass manufacture through machine tools and technology. Besides the pictorial effects, field trips to the actual sites of these developments provide interest and practical information. These represent an important phase of the study of economics.

The local community can serve as a most profitable laboratory for the study of economic problems. Whatever the type of community, industrial or agricultural, excursions should be planned to tie in local resources with the realistic interpretation of economic principles. The utilization of resource people who are authorities in their fields from the various business concerns, industries, and financial agencies will supply firsthand knowledge. Visits to the commercial centers of nearby communities can furnish valuable information for students and the teachers. Projects of the local county or state that have economic significance for the citizen should be considered for functional learning experiences. It is through knowing one's economic community better that effective citizenship will be fostered. The importance of developing competence in economic understanding of an individual so that he may have a more productive life in his community, his state, and in the nation cannot be underestimated.

The tackboard should be utilized for displaying material that will foster economics instruction. Student committees will find current, pertinent material for displays that will enliven and vivify economics discussions. Specific materials related to a particular problem being studied has value. Current event material dealing with economic topics aid in furnishing background knowledge. Information giving charts, graphs, diagrams, and maps are an indispensable part of the study. Students should become proficient in interpretation and construction of such materials and in their application as a means of clarifying and disseminating information. Such activities as panel discussions and debates relative to selected questions and problems may also find visual aids helpful.

A wide variety of pamphlets, booklets, and periodicals will provide a generous supply of reference material. The financial, business, and real estate sections of the daily and weekly newspaper should be studied until the students are able to read and interpret them correctly. Both teachers and students should become familiar with the various types of pamphlets, magazines, and bulletins dealing with economics and consumer research. Supplementary reading materials are more essential in the study of economics at the secondary level.

The teacher

Knowledge of the community is essential to effective planning for economics instruction. In order to achieve good organization and planning of materials, it is important that the teacher recognize the economic problems, past and present, of a given area. With this approach the students are gaining an understanding of our own American economic system. Appropriate methods and procedures that are flexible and adaptable to changes and research findings should be evaluated frequently. The use of democratic procedures when investigating problems is essential for creating a proper atmosphere for economics instruction.

The teacher must read extensively to acquire background knowledge. Also, he must become an alert student of contemporary materials that are available in pamphlets, bulletins, and newspapers. Students should be made aware that each problem or unit can be expanded or enriched by the application of current problems and events whenever it is practical. The learning activities must be dynamic; effective pupil-teacher planning should stir the imagination, arouse creative thinking, and cultivate further discussion.

Too often a course in economics is descriptive only and devoid of stimulating thought. When an economic problem is raised, the "belief" of the teacher is represented as the "answer." This does not develop economic understanding or objectivity.

The only approach to economic understanding is to analyze the subject objectively. The most important result of the study of economics is to develop in the pupils a way of thinking about economic problems. When a problem is raised, alternate solutions based upon reason and values should be examined.[11]

The Problems Course

In the Problems of American Democracy course or Modern Problems units, a block of time can be allotted to economic education. Most problems courses include some topics of an economic nature. For example, conservation, labor and management, money and banking, agriculture, or the farm situation are considered for study. When such a course is planned, other areas of content including sociology and government also

---

[11] Pennsylvania, *op. cit.*, p. 3.

are considered. The intelligent explanation of selected topics, utilizing a problem-solving approach, should provide insights with which to attack future problems as citizens in modern society.

The author is suggesting the following ideas for consideration resulting from his own experiences in teaching these materials at the twelfth grade level. Students are interested in acquiring a knowledge of our American economic system as well as some knowledge of consumer education. Such instruction assists students in becoming familiar with basic laws and principles of economics.

The introduction of the study should include the meaning of economics in our everyday life. A definition of economics serves a helpful purpose. The terminology or vocabulary employed by economists should be defined and understood. The nature, types, and phases of American business provide foundation information. Economic activities should be elaborated upon and clarified to provide understanding. In the organizational structure of the unit or study, Banks and Banking, Money and Credit, Taxation, Commodities and Securities, Insurance, Investments, Consumer Problems, and Looking Ahead Together at Current Economic Problems could be listed. These are but a few of the ideas that can be explained in an outline. Various activities can be engaged in by the group to functionalize such a study. Students should be encouraged to read widely and to employ a variety of supplementary materials. Since this course is the capstone of the social studies program, it should be productive and informative for the senior students.

Economics instruction in the problems course should help students to prepare for both their future employment in adult society and their education at the college level. Therefore, instruction in the problems course should consider some of the following for student development.

To interpret and analyze charts, graphs, diagrams, symbols, and figures

To construct charts, diagrams, graphs, and outlines for presenting pertinent information

To summarize various articles, statements, and reports found in sources

To prepare research materials for oral and written reports

To provide for vocabulary growth relating to economic terminology

To become aware of the industrial, commercial, and financial structure of the immediate community, county, and state

To comprehend the availability of resource materials in the school, private and public libraries in the local area

To understand the importance of human, natural, and material resources in the local community

To develop skill in problem-solving techniques as an aid to meeting challenges and problems in the instructional process and in society

To become aware of the rapid scientific and technical changes occurring and their impact upon contemporary society

To foster the growth of those essential traits for active and effective citizenship

Conclusion

The development of economic competence for life in our modern technological society is an essential phase of the student's education. This entails the growth of effective skills, constructive attitudes, and understandings for working and living in a changing society and complex world. A knowledge of the workings of our free American economy is important information in our times. In the instructional process various units are employed which relate to problems and timely topics for helping to meet the needs and interests of the students. The teacher and students employ a variety of educational resources, current literature, and audiovisual materials in the gaining of worthwhile information. Instruction in economics and other courses in the social studies curriculum help materially to build the basic foundation for competent citizenship.

Bibliography

Baker, G. D., "Educating Citizens for Economic Effectiveness; 1960-1980," *Citizenship and a Free Society: Education for the Future*, Thirtieth Yearbook of the National Council for the Social Studies. Washington D.C.: National Education Association, 1960.

Economic Education in the Schools, a report of the National Task Force on Economic Education. New York: Committee for Economic Development, 1961.

Heilbroner, R. L., *The Making of Economic Society*. Englewood Cliffs, N.J.: Prentice-Hall, Inc., 1962.

High, J., *Teaching Secondary School Social Studies*. New York: John Wiley & Sons, Inc., 1962.

Hurwitz, H. L. and F. Shaw, *Economics in a Free Society*. New York: Oxford Book Company, 1962.

Johnson, E. A. J. and H. E. Krooss, *The American Economy: Its Origins, Development and Transformations*. Englewood Cliffs, N.J.: Prentice-Hall, Inc., 1960.

Chapter Fourteen

Modern Problems and the Social Science Disciplines

At the twelfth-grade level the modern secondary curriculum for the social studies usually includes a course in contemporary problems, modern problems, or problems of American democracy. However, some of these courses may have a theme specifically stating the nature of the content and the educational area; for example: the theme of the course, Living Together Under Our Democratic Government, Government in the United States and Problems in American Life. Whatever the nature or name of such a course, the purpose and structure frequently follows a similar pattern and is the culminating course or the capstone of the social studies program.

Modern problems, therefore, is a course of major importance. The materials included draw heavily upon the social science disciplines—history, sociology, economics, and political science. The problems course or any elective course in the social studies generally follows the study of American history. It provides the student with the opportunity to examine the prevailing problems in our democratic society. The problems course includes an awareness of current questions as well as many problems of an economic, social, and political nature that have their roots in the past.

Any type of problems course should be the most flexible and functional of all the social studies offerings. Units or problems to be included should be selected on the basis of needs and interests of the students.

These problems for study may vary from time to time as changing conditions in the local, state, national, and international scene make it advisable. Since the content material is both flexible and functional, no general principles for course organization can be laid down. It may be of value to examine and compare some course organizations in modern programs.

Modern Problems

Oregon

The following outline is suggested for the organization of the subject content. It consists of eight required units. (Except for Unit 1, which should be presented first, there is no recommended sequence.)

Content for modern problems includes:[1]

Unit 1. Helping Individuals Make Intelligent Decisions
Unit 2. Providing an Adequate Education for all Our People
Unit 3. Understanding and Improving Our Economic System
Unit 4. Improving Industrial Relations
Unit 5. Advancing Human Rights—Opportunities Offered by Various Political-Economic Systems
Unit 6. Maintaining World Peace
Unit 7. Helping Divergent Groups to Live Together in Harmony
Unit 8. Achieving a Happy and Successful Personal Life

California

Government in the United States and Problems of Democracy[2]

A. The Constitution, its Expanding Meaning, and How it Meets the Problems of a Rapidly Changing Civilization
B. The Processes of Governmental Budget-building and Taxation
C. Activities of Government Affecting Our Daily Lives
D. State and Local History and Government
E. Intelligent, Active Participation as Citizens of the United States in Local, State, National, and World Affairs
F. The American Economy; Capitalism and the Free Enterprise System; Wise Use of Human and Natural Resources
G. Influence of Individuals upon the Stability and Effectiveness of Social, Political, and Economic Institutions
H. United States and International Affairs: Strengthening of the Free World

Introductory Statement

Young people in their senior year of high school tend to become serious about problems and events that touch upon their lives. They are interested in the practical problems they will face after leaving high school. They seek a

---

[1] *Guide to Secondary Education in Oregon—1961-1963* (Salem, Oregon: State Dept. of Education, 1961), p. 211.
[2] *Social Studies Framework for the Public Schools of California*, State Curriculum Commission, (Sacramento, California: State Department of Education, 1962), p. 82.

greater degree of economic and social independence, often with more awareness of the factors involved, particularly if they have had work experience in
part-time and summer employment. Many seniors are acquainted with youth
who are no longer in high school and thus they gain insight into some of the
adjustments that are ahead after graduation. Students in the twelfth grade
recognize the significant citizenship responsibilities they will be assuming. It
is important to provide them with a thorough study of government and social
and economic problems. Since not all the important problems in American life
can be studied in the time available and since these problems are constantly
changing, an underlying emphasis in the social studies program needs to be
placed upon methods by which problems in American life can be studied and
understood through the application of knowledge that is derived from a variety
of sources, including the social science disciplines.

Anticipated Outcomes

Becoming better prepared for the responsibilities of adult citizenship
through learning about current and immediate problems of the life of the nation and the adults in it
Studying thoroughly the government of the United States, its relations
with other nations, and important aspects of local and state government
Realizing the need for citizens to be informed and to participate in political
affairs
Understanding the complexities of social institutions and of economic
enterprise
Learning about the basic contemporary issues facing American society
and how these problems touch their own lives
Recognizing the international aspects of most modern problems
Realizing the individual's responsibility for high levels of constructive
thought and action in the achievement of our national aspirations and goals

Campbell Union High School District[3]

Course of Study for Senior Social Studies

I. *Objectives*
 To develop an understanding of the individual, his immediate environment,
 society, and his position in national and world affairs.
 A. The individual in local, state, and national problems.
 B. The individual and the world in which he lives.
II. *Major Divisions of Subject Matter*
 A. Interrelationship of the individual and society
  1. Introduction
  2. Continual need for adjustment to change
  3. The family
  4. Minorities and their rights
  5. Youth and crime
 B. The individual in local, state, and national problems
  1. State and federal interest in education
  2. The individual pays the bill for carelessness

---

[3] *Curriculum Guide 9-12,* Campbell Union High Schools (Campbell, Calif.: Board
of Education), pp. 60-62.

3. Planning or chaos?
   a. Civic planning
   b. Citizens' obligations and benefits
      (1) Old age
      (2) Health
      (3) Military obligations and benefits
      (4) Civil obligations and benefits
4. Conservation of natural resources
   a. Mineral resources
   b. Watershed and timber resources
   c. Power resources
5. Our American Economy
   a. Agriculture
   b. Transportation
   c. Big business and free enterprise
   d. Labor and industry
   e. Business cycles
6. American politics
7. Government finances
C. The individual and the world in which he lives
   1. Modern weapons of war and control of them
   2. Economic interdependence
   3. Efforts toward world peace and security
      a. United Nations
      b. Regional arrangements
         (1) NATO
         (2) SEATO
         (3) Warsaw Pact
         (4) Monroe Doctrine and IAS
         (5) Neutralist blocs

Specific objectives and purposes of a problems course

This type of one-year course relating to political science, economics, sociology, and other social science disciplines deals with problems of our democracy. It attempts to integrate the area of study through a problem-solving approach. Opportunity is provided for gaining a greater insight into the nature, organization, and function of our government, the workings of our modern economy, and the various problems that develop in our democracy. Problems pertaining to the United States in relation to the world or international scene are also considered. In a world of dynamic change new problems will arise as we move ahead in time and history. Such a course that furnishes an understanding of our free democratic way of life has specific objectives; they are framed around understandings, skills, and attitudes. As teachers and students plan, work, study, and discuss together selected topics using democratic procedures the best kind of citizenship training is fostered.

The course builds a foundation for constructive planning, critical thinking, and direct action for those students who are completing their terminal education. Each student enrolled is about to face new responsibilities in tomorrow's society. Many of these new challenges are growing out of our changing society and complex world. This requires that we explore new frontiers and interesting problems which will prove functional by providing new knowledge and by building competence in the group. In this manner youth should gain a deep appreciation of democracy as a way of life. The skills acquired or strengthened should kindle a continuous interest in community, state, and national affairs. The student also becomes aware of the fact that study, research, investigation, and education are continuous processes down the road of life.

The effective modern problems course should provide for flexibility in organization of problems for investigation. Students should be provided with the opportunity to apply skills and gain experience in the basic techniques of cooperative and individual problem-solving. It is in this manner that the student will continue his interest and active curiosity about problems that will confront society. Students who pursue an independent line of investigation can utilize supplementary materials and formulate constructive ideas about selected topics which were investigated by the individual or group.

A list of possible topics that are pertinent to the trends of society, the nature of the community, and the welfare of the individual should be presented. Both teacher and pupils should spend sufficient time in thoughtful consideration of these topics. If, at any time in their high school career, pupils are to gain experience in doing an effective job of investigation, the problems course should furnish that opportunity. Some students will receive very little additional formal education and will soon be faced with the problems of adult life. For those reasons, they should have experience in studying current problems. Guide sheets or study outlines can be used in conjunction with a textbook and supplementary references, and students should be responsible for all phases of the course from its planning to its final summarization. The course should be directed toward the acquiring of knowledge and the building of intelligent, active, and democratic citizenship.

A sequence arrangement

Some school systems may provide for a two-year sequence in grades 11 and 12. In this manner American history can follow a two-year pattern. However, another combined arrangement would include United States History, Government, and Modern Problems. The latter type of pattern would include the treatment of United States History, Government, and Modern Problems:[4]

This course has been included in the social studies program for the use of those schools which wish to secure a more complete integration of United States history and government, and the study of problems whose solutions are vital to the continued health and welfare of our democracy. By utilizing this two-year sequence, more effective use may be made of the problems approach in teaching; a greater variety of instructional materials may be employed; research may become more intensive and fundamental; and functional activities can be made to yield genuine understandings and appreciations of American citizenship.

The following units for study:

Unit 1. The People of the United States Establish a Nation Under the Constitution

Unit 2. Our Government Evolves as the Constitution is Applied and Interpreted Through the Course of Our History

Unit 3. Partisanship Becomes a Tradition

Unit 4. Westward Growth Intensifies Our Sectional Differences and Results in Conflict

Unit 5. Helping Individuals Make Intelligent Decisions

Unit 6. Providing an Adequate Education for all our People

Unit 7. Practicing Democratic Theory in the United States

Unit 8. Understanding and Improving our Economic System

Unit 9. Improving Industrial Relations

Unit 10. Advancing Human Rights-Opportunities Offered by Various Political-Economic Systems

Unit 11. Maintaining World Peace

Unit 12. Helping Divergent Groups to Live Together in Harmony

Unit 13. Achieving a Happy and Successful Personal Life

Economics in the modern problems course

The study of economics as organized units and as specific problems or topics is a part of the modern problems course. Students learn about such topics as taxation, labor-management relations, and business and industry which are all a part of the workings of our economic system. To meet the needs and interests of a particular group, various topics of an economic nature can be included in the course.

The imaginative teacher who uses a creative approach can generate much interest when discussing economic problems that challenge the students. Guided research, oral and written reports, readings, and discussions allow the students an opportunity to delve into the subject. Productive experiences and functional activities furnish opportunities to learn about the business cycle, investments, stocks and bonds, insurance, advertising, marketing, tariff, budgeting, and many other phases of eco-

---

4 *Guide to Secondary Education in Oregon—1961-1963* (Salem, Oregon: State Dept. of Education, 1961), pp. 211-212.

nomics required for educational understanding. For further study see the chapter dealing with economics.

Political science and government

Political science is considered to be the study of government. A knowledge of the organization, structure, and function of our American government is the responsibility of every citizen. Knowing the features of the national constitution and one's own state constitution is most essential for today's living. The political or administrative units of each state all carry a major responsibility in today's changing society. The knowledge of the legislative, executive, and judicial divisions of our government and their specific functions in the over-all structure is important. The study of government assists the individual to become more aware of his privileges, responsibilities, and obligations as a citizen in our democracy. The place and function of political parties and interest groups in the governing process should be comprehended. Each citizen should keep well informed regarding current affairs in his own community, county, and state. National and world happenings should also be followed and interpreted in the light of our times. Courses in civics and government are both found in the instructional program at the secondary level.

Government[5]

Unit 1.	Heritage, Foundations and Fundamentals
Unit 2.	The Legislative Department
Unit 3.	The Executive Branch
Unit 4.	The Judicial Branch
Unit 5.	Political Rights and Practices
Unit 6.	The States
Unit 7.	The Betterment of Society through an Educated Citizenry
Unit 8.	Local Governments
Unit 9.	Territories and Other Dependencies
Unit 10.	Governments and Political Ideas in the World Today

In the modern problems course through the study of units dealing with government, students gain a broader understanding of our democracy. Learning about the development of our government through the framework of the constitution is important. Students acquire a knowledge of the many services provided by the government and the role of the various agencies operating as regulatory units. They understand the need for and purpose of conservation. They learn to analyze information concerning the activities and special services performed by their own state as

---

[5] *Emphasis Upon Citizenship and Patriotism, Grades, Ten, Eleven, and Twelve,* Curriculum Bulletin, No. 113 (Fort Worth, Texas: Fort Worth Public Schools, 1961), pp. 101-129.

well as by the national government. They learn the relationship of government to business, labor and management, transportation, and communication activities. They learn the meaning of such agencies as Health, Education and Welfare as it relates to individuals in our society. Students acquire information pertaining to government and public issues through alert reading, inquiry, and the channels of mass media. They learn about our relationship with the nations of the world and about international trade. Through these experiences and new knowledge they are building a framework for competent citizenship with its opportunities and responsibilities.

Recommendation 21: Twelfth-grade Social Studies
In the twelfth grade a course on American problems or American government should be required. This course should include as much material on economics as the students can effectively handle at this point in their development. Each class in this course should be a cross section of the school: the class should be heterogeneously grouped. Teachers should encourage all students to participate in discussions. This course should develop not only an understanding of the American form of government and of the economic basis of our free society, but also mutual respect and understanding between different types of students. Current topics should be included; free discussion of controversial issues should be encouraged. This approach is one significant way in which our schools distinguish themselves from those in totalitarian nations. This course, as well as well-organized homerooms and certain student activities, can contribute a great deal to the development of future citizens of our democracy who will be intelligent voters, stand firm under trying national conditions, and not be beguiled by the oratory of those who appeal to special interests.[6]

It is through the study of American history and government that the student acquires a fuller knowledge of our democracy. Today's youth, who are the informed citizens and voters of tomorrow, should comprehend the nature and structure of their own local and state governments. A wider understanding of the functioning of the national government is essential for living in modern society.

A Sociological Unit

Sociology, another of the social science disciplines, has a part in the modern problems course and contributes directly to the social studies program. It may be an elective course and should provide the individual with a better understanding of human society and of his own personality in relationship with others in his contemporary society. The student should become aware that, in adult life, he must work effectively with

---

[6] J. B. Conant, *The American High School Today* (New York: McGraw-Hill Book Company, Inc., 1959), pp. 75-76.

an individual as well as in a group. He may have the occasion to serve as a leader, but he must also be able to serve as a follower in a group endeavor.

Some units in the modern problems course or other twelfth grade courses usually allot time to explore institutions in our society. A knowledge of home and family living is of major importance to the individual if he is to contribute his share to the establishment and maintenance of a stable society in today's world. The following is an example of an excellent sociological unit.

The Importance of the Family[7]

I. The family as a social institution
   A. Definition of a family
   B. Functions of the family unit in society
      1. Continuation of the human race
      2. Services as basic social group
         a. Provision for emotional satisfaction and security
         b. Provision of standards for social behavior
         c. Transmission of social heritage
         d. Degree of economic, religious, protective, and recreation functions
II. Changes in family life with growth of Industrial America
   A. Usual pattern of family life in early nineteenth century
      1. Size of family circle
      2. Functions of living performed within family circle
         a. Economic
         b. Social
         c. Religious
         d. Educational
      3. Roles of various members
      4. Stability of family unit
   B. Pattern of family life in the twentieth century, rural and urban
      1. Size of family unit
         a. Effect of occupational status and amount of education of parents
         b. Relation of size of community to size of family
      2. Functions of living performed within family circle
         a. Economic
         b. Social
         c. Religious
         d. Educational
      3. Role of various members
   C. Reasons for changes in family life during the last 150 years
      1. Decrease in size of family
      2. Effects of industrialization
         a. Rise in standard of living
         b. Decline in economic functions within household
         c. Growing independence of women

---

[7] *Course of Study Social Studies Grades 10-12* (West Orange, N.J.: West Orange Public Schools, 1960), pp. 26-27.

        d. Increase in inventions
          (1) Radio and television
          (2) Automobile and movies
      3. Effects of urbanization
      4. Advances in medical science
    D. Effects of changes
      1. On family stability
      2. On individual members
      3. On society
III. Success and failure in family life
    A. Social causes of tension in family life
      1. Factors related in part to social conditions
        a. Economic insecurity
          (1) Poverty
          (2) Unemployment
          (3) Child labor
        b. Inadequate housing
        c. Juvenile delinquency and crime
        d. Inadequate medical care
        e. Alcoholism
        f. Emotional instability
        g. Physical and mental health

Sociology

Sociology deals directly with the origin, structure, development, and function of social institutions. It also deals with the interrelations between the individual and these social institutions. As a science, sociology seeks to provide guidance for these institutions and individuals for the general advantage of the individuals. Sociology, although one of the newer of the social sciences, has for some time been an important offering in our colleges and universities. Despite the fact that all social studies contain sociological materials in varying degrees, sociology, as such, has until recently received little attention in secondary schools. The amount, complexity, and extent of social problems at the present time, and the degree to which they affect the life of the average American citizen, have resulted in a greater emphasis on the teaching of sociological principles in secondary schools. More and more of these schools are offering courses in sociology or in social problems as a means of preparing pupils for intelligent citizenship. Such courses are usually limited to one semester in the senior or junior year, either as a separate course or as one-half of the problems course.

Although economics is directed mainly toward showing how the world earns its living through agriculture, industry, and service, sociology indicates how our present customs and habits of living grew out of primitive beginnings and gradually became standard for the group and the nation. For example, there are different ways of holding and transmitting property; so, different kinds of family organization developed within the social structure. Socially approved methods of satisfying human needs give rise to those institutions that make up our society. This represents more than social philosophy and discussion; it is a science for study in the high school advanced classes. Although there is an obvious lack of synthesis in this field, owing to the various schools of thought, a definite correlation exists in the social studies.

Social Change. Those social changes that are to be observed in our world of the present moment occur by almost imperceptible stages but are manifest and taken for granted. There are many of our older institutions that have been forced to change to meet newer demands. Although many changes of the twentieth century came slowly, one must remember the old adage "progress means change"; so, today we witness the transition from the old to the new. To one who looks and studies the flow of happenings, there are a number of natural and social factors to be seen operating on the structure of society which give it a new appearance from generation to generation.

A definite source of social change is the progress of invention—for instance, the automobile, railroads, sewing machines, radios, and hundreds of other devices. Vast numbers of persons are employed in fabricating these inventions and operating them. With technological changes, new needs arise to keep people employed. Social change witnesses alterations in many aspects of society despite the desire of a large element to conserve old ways.

Organization of Materials. Sociological materials may be organized and presented either as sociology or as social problems. Whatever course arrangement is followed, certain basic sociological principles and terms must be taught if pupils are to be prepared to assume responsibility as adults. Like all other subjects, sociology has a specialized vocabulary that must be understood if pupils are to proceed to intelligent discussion of social problems. None of these sociological terms is too difficult for the secondary school pupil if it is analyzed and clearly explained.

Sociology, or social problems, can be taught with or without a textbook. If a text is to be used, the teacher or supervisor should give careful consideration to its selection. Some difficulty may be encountered in the selection of a completely satisfactory textbook, since most sociology texts are intended for college use. Although it is possible to use an elementary college text in some classes, it is not to be generally recommended. A vital and realistic course must be founded on material that is too current to be found in any textbook. Pamphlets, periodicals, and the daily newspaper furnish essential and pertinent information. With a few copies of several sociology texts in the library and with carefully planned and coordinated guide sheets, sociology instruction can become interesting and challenging.

The Community as a Basis for Organization.   The local community is the best starting point for the study of sociology. By definition, sociology deals with the origin, structure, development, and function of human institutions and with relations of individuals to these institutions. If instruction is to begin with the known and proceed to the unknown, the community should be the textbook from which sociology is studied. The community itself is one of our basic institutions; examples of all the other institutions with which sociology is concerned will be found within its bounds. The only textbook that can present a true picture of the interrelationships of people is the community in which they work, play, and live together.

An essential phase of the sociology course is the consideration of social problems. Among the most pertinent problems commonly found in modern society are the changing family, housing, crime, social security, unemployment, health, juvenile delinquency, population trends, conservation of human resources, pressure groups. leisure, recreation, public opinion, and propaganda. Generally speaking, the impact of these problems is felt in the local community as much as in the whole society. It is impossible for a high school class to study all of these problems adequately in one semester. The course organization involves the selection of only the most important problems.

Vitalizing Sociology Instruction.   The basic sociological principles and terms should be so presented, so interwoven with current affairs and problems, that they have realistic meaning for pupils. This method of presentation is logical and feasible since, as each problem is analyzed and investigated, pupils will naturally come to see its existence in the past as well as in the present. The teacher has also an exceptional advantage in maintaining interest since the investigation and discussion of one problem frequently leads directly into the discussion of other problems. For example, an analysis of the problem of juvenile delinquency will lead the class to a recognition of such problems as the changing family, housing conditions, slum clearance, health, and recreational facilities.

The teacher will find an effective approach to the study of sociology or social problems if he spends the first class period discussing the subject informally with his pupils and allowing them to suggest problems in which they are interested. A list of such problems can be submitted by each pupil at the next class meeting. From these lists, the class can be led to select a definite schedule of topics to be investigated throughout the semester. This approach is calculated to create the maximum amount of pupil interest in the subject.

As in other phases of the social studies, variety in method, careful selection, and use of appropriate teaching aids are essential. The library is a highly important element in sociology instruction. To the degree that pupils gain experiences in analyzing social problems, in using the library and community resources, in discussing their findings, in summarizing and drawing valid conclusions, sociology has contributed to their growth.

The Individuals in Society. Social activity revolves about groups of individuals that make up society. This complex society is composed of two basic groups of individuals who form primary and secondary relationships. A primary group specifies immediate association—the family, the children's play group, and the closely knitted neighborhood groups. The individual, through direct contact, is receiving a considerable amount of socialization. In the primary group, the individual acquires, through training and association, definite attitudes that influence his future life. The secondary group is composed of individuals having the same interest or purpose. It may be an outgrowth of a primary group as it becomes "of age." The individual may carry many of his early interests, attitudes, and ideas to this more advanced yet permanent group. He has learned the advantages of group affiliations.

Social institutions have a significant influence upon group life. The physical (geographical) environment has a definite effect upon the individual, for it determines the nature of his group life. The type of industries and occupations engaged in by members of that community will determine their habits, customs, and institutions. Natural resources have been a potent force in the development of our industrial activities. Similarly, the social heritage of a group has both an economic and social influence upon the individual. The folkways, customs, and mores, although somewhat broadened, are the basis for social living in our nation.

Communities are more or less in a state of transition; this is characteristic of the modern age where changes come very rapidly in industry, business, and agriculture. Changes directly influence our social institutions and breed new social and economic problems. Group life is also in a state of transition as the result of technological changes, new opportunities for employment, and transportation and communication advances. The increased specialization in modern society has made group life more interdependent. Similarly, individuals must depend upon one another to a greater degree.

Social change is apparent in a dynamic society. Many times, such rapid change leaves the individual in a quandary, challenging his initiative and sense of direction. Social progress on the other hand, means better group living, since the individual's status is improved by the attainment of desirable goals. Changes in contemporary society, however, necessitate some means of regulation so that individuals may make the necessary adjustments. Social control is the means by which many social problems are restricted or even eliminated in a dynamic society. Frequently, social institutions are unable to cope with the rapid changes in a community, and new agencies are born to perform functional tasks in the socialization process.

Social organization is essential for desirable group life. Social disorganization can result in chaos. The state of society caused by cultural lag necessitates definite changes in the life of the community. Social reorganization is the force necessary for progressive community growth.

Modern society is faced with many complex problems; some are long-standing whereas others are of recent origin; however, all are a challenge. Desirable recreational activities and educational opportunities will do much to build a desirable and pleasant personality in the individuals who will make up future society.

Elective and Seminar Courses

The foregoing discussion and course outlines provided an opportunity to examine social studies offerings primarily for the twelfth grade. However, today's youth need proficiency in becoming effective citizens and in coping with problems. Learning experiences that broaden the student's horizons of the world in which we are living are growing in importance in the social studies. We should like to point out that elective and seminar courses are increasing and may include such offerings as economics, sociology, contemporary affairs, government, international relations, and world geography. Experimentation is being encouraged in units and course offerings for senior high school students. This is especially common where there is a need for an additional social studies course or subject for those students with an interest in gaining greater insights into the social sciences. Disciplines such as sociology and economics necessitate that the students draw upon other social sciences such as history, political science, and anthropology.

At the secondary level a combined two-year sequence alternative arrangement for the eleventh and twelfth level in United States History, Government and Modern Problems is suggested. A two-year alternative course combination for the ninth and tenth grades is also another approach for world culture.

Conclusion

The culminating course or capstone of the social studies program permeates many areas of knowledge. Together with the elective course offerings, the student should gain a greater knowledge of the social sciences. The problems course especially is an important subject for every student, since it challenges him to think critically about problems. The student is gaining a more mature appreciation of the rights and responsibilities of our democratic way of life. The many valuable learning experiences should enhance his ability to understand better the local community and the contemporary world. His experiences in studying problems will furnish a broader insight into the problems that will be faced in the path of life. He will be helped somewhat in the selection of a career. He will have a better picture of our economic order and culture, in which he will be a producer, consumer, and citizen. He will gain a greater knowledge of the organization of business and industry. The privileges and responsibilities of suffrage will become more realistic, and the functions of government will be clarified. One will agree that intelligent citizenship must be based upon a knowledge of democracy's political, social, economic, and cultural aspects. This terminal education for many students at the secondary school level helps to lay the groundwork for our future generations and for the growing heritage of America.

Bibliography

Biesanz, J. and M. Biesanz, *Modern Society: An Introduction to Social Science*, 2nd ed. Englewood Cliffs, N.J.: Prentice-Hall Inc., 1959.

Gross, R. E., R. H. Muessig, and G. L. Fersh, *The Problems Approach and the Social Studies*, Curriculum Series No. IX, rev. ed. Washington, D.C.: National Education Association, 1960.

National Society for the Study of Education, *The Dynamics of Instructional Groups Sociopsychological Aspects of Teaching and Learning*, Fifty-ninth Yearbook, Part II. Chicago: University of Chicago Press, 1960.

Paterson, F., ed., *Citizenship and a Free Society: Education for the Future*, Thirtieth Yearbook of the National Council for the Social Studies. Washington, D.C.: National Education Association, 1960.

Price, R. A., ed., *New Viewpoints in the Social Sciences*, Twenty-eighth Yearbook of the National Council for the Social Studies. Washington, D.C.: National Education Association, 1958.

Problems of Democracy, Curriculum Bulletin, 1960-61 Series, No. 9. New York: Board of Education, City of New York, 1960.

Trump, J. L., *Images of the Future: A New Approach to the Secondary School.* Urbana Illinois: Commission on the Experimental Study of the Utilization of the Staff in the Secondary School, appointed by the National Association of Secondary School Principals, 1959.

Chapter Fifteen

The Process of Culture

A knowledge of the cultures of the world should be a significant aspect of every modern social studies curriculum. The very nature of the contemporary world with its many different characteristics necessitates a greater understanding of the various peoples and their society in today's world setting. A study of the cultures of the nations should include their past, present, and a view of the future in the processes of continuous change. A greater insight into the geographical as well as the historical aspects of the lands and the everyday life of the peoples in the varying culture areas is of major importance for students as they look ahead. The space age with its new knowledge, ideas, and technology has and will bring strong impacts upon the patterns of life for all people.

Defining culture

A discussion of the meaning and understanding of the term *culture* should be helpful and should assist in the clarification of the terminology.

Culture—All that which is nonbiological and socially transmitted in a society, including artistic, social, ideological, and religious patterns of behavior, and the techniques for mastering the environment.[1]

---

[1] C. Winick, *Dictionary of Anthropology* (New York: Littlefield Adams and Co., 1958), p. 144.

What is a culture area? . . . It includes what has been described as the attitudes, objectives, and technical skills of people, their way of living, their systems of value, their language.[2]

Culture, therefore: (a) is the characteristically human product of social interaction; (b) provides socially acceptable patterns for meeting biological and social needs; (c) is cumulative as it is handed down from generation to generation in a given society; (d) is meaningful to human beings because of its symbolic quality; (e) is learned by each person in the course of his development in a particular society; (f) is therefore a basic determinant of personality; and (g) depends for its existence upon the continued functioning of the society but is independent of any individual or group.[3]

A world that features rapid transportation and equally swift communication requires that we learn more about the daily culture of a people. With greater opportunities for travel and educational experiences, the individual can learn more about the daily interests of a people; these include economic pursuits, agricultural as well as industrial, family patterns, recreational activities, education, and religion. Furthermore, the political structure, the scientific progress through research, and the nature of the literature are all included in the better understanding of a particular culture. The future gives promise of steady progress or change in centers of the world that may become more industrialized.

Patterns of culture

All cultures have characteristic patterns. These patterns reveal themselves in the day-to-day lives of the people who follow them.

Culture patterns vary with respect to the degree of standardization and the social media involved in the learning process. In a primitive society, regularity of behavior results from word-of-mouth learning and example, as the child learns the expected way of thought and action proper to his status. He has before him the example of his elders, and he learns the basic patterns of the group by observation, conscious training, and unconscious imitation. The elementary patterns of the culture are present in the behavior of persons in his immediate environment. Under such conditions, the learning process is simple, direct, and strong. The raw material of personality is there for all to see.

In a large and amorphous society such as our own, regularity of behavior is also the result of mass media of communication, in addition to the more intimate efforts of the primary group. Radio, television, the comics, and the movies play an important part in cultural patterning. Many of the behavior

---

[2] P. E. James, "New Viewpoints in Geography," in *New Viewpoints in the Social Sciences,* ed. Roy A. Price, National Council for the Social Studies, 28th Yearbook (Washington, D.C., 1958), p. 56.

[3] F. E. Merrill, *Society and Culture: An Introduction to Sociology* (2nd ed.; Englewood Cliffs, N.J.: Prentice-Hall, Inc., 1961), p. 116. © 1961 by Prentice-Hall, Inc. Reprinted by permission.

PHYSICAL ELEMENTS   CULTURE ELEMENTS

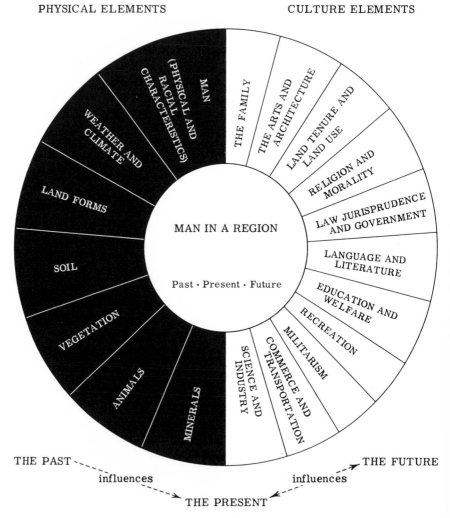

THE PAST   THE FUTURE
    influences   influences
              THE PRESENT

Courtesy Department of Public Instruction, Harrisburg, Penna.

patterns of the adolescent generation directly reflect the mass media. The adolescent peer group assumes many of its attitudes and behavior patterns from these forms of communication. The adolescent learns how to dress, talk, dance, and amuse himself from these sources. As localized patterns have broken down, culture patterning has become increasingly standardized under the impact of mass communication.[4]

A thorough understanding of the ways in which these standardizations are brought about is important if we are to communicate effectively what these patterns are and why they are as they are.

---

[4] *Ibid.*, p. 133.

Culture and the Individual

Culture tends to serve the individual in a number of significant ways. It is important that we review again the definition of culture in terms of the individual.

Culture, man's characteristic adaptation to his physical environment, his biological nature, and his group life, arises out of language communication within a social group and is a configuration of shared understandings concerning the meaning and value of things, ideas, emotions, and actions.[5]

Let us focus our attention upon some of the ways that culture does serve the individual.

1. Culture provides the individual with a blueprint for behavior, thought, and feeling in almost any situation.
2. Culture provides the individual with ready-made explanations of the origin of man, the nature of the universe, and man's role in that universe.
3. Culture defines situations for its participants.
4. Culture gives men a conscience.
5. Culture provides for the satisfaction of the individual's biological needs.
6. Culture is the nourishing milieu for personality.

In a broader sense, culture gives meaning to life, purpose to existence. It provides the individual with values and goals, hopes and aspirations, "something to live for." In one culture, men may strive for material possessions, in another for spiritual salvation, in a third for pleasant enjoyment of the passing moment.

A common culture gives men a sense of belonging or identification. It binds men together into a "we-group" that sets them off from people of another culture.[6]

In view of the individual's position in his culture, the impact of that culture upon him, and, in turn, his impact on the culture, to fully comprehend the complexities of the interrelatedness of culture and the individual it is necessary to understand cultural laws, tendencies, and processes.

Culture as social control

The system of social control is a major aspect of a particular culture.

Culture fulfills its third function—ensuring the unity and survival of society by (1) providing patterns for the behavior of individuals and groups in the

---

[5] J. Biesanz and M. Biesanz, *Modern Society: An Introduction to Social Science* (2nd ed.; Englewood Cliffs, N.J.: Prentice-Hall, Inc., 1959), p. 46.
[6] *Ibid.*, pp. 48-50.

society, (2) providing means of teaching individuals to behave according to these patterns or "rules of the game," and (3) providing means of enforcing correct behavior. The patterns are the customs or norms, the process of teaching them is called *enculturation* or *socialization,* and *enforcement* is carried out through a system of sanctions or rewards and punishments. (You will notice we have not said, "Culture teaches the individual to behave and enforces his correct behavior." Culture is the pattern; groups and individuals put the patterns into action.)

All these three very closely related functions of culture are aspects of social control, the means by which society establishes and maintains order. Social control can refer to something as elaborate as our system of government, with its vast machinery of law enforcement; but here we shall consider it in a more fundamental and inclusive sense as the network of mutual expectations that create order in a society and the sanctions that keep these expectations in force. Social control boils down essentially to people who, as individual members of society and as members of groups, influence one another to behave according to cultural patterns.

Obviously the system of social control is different from culture to culture. The patterns vary, the methods of indoctrinating the individual vary, and the methods of enforcing adherence to the patterns vary. In some cultures all the life situations are defined for the individual; in others only crucial ones are defined, and a person is left free to make a number of choices.[7]

Social controls are arrived at by a common concensus of what people think is "right," and are based on their interpretation of their own experiences. These generalized ideas are known as perceptions and eventually become the guides and bases for their idea of "right" social control.

The anthropologist studies culture

The study of culture is a most significant process. The following explanation can provide an insight into the work of the anthropologist.

Partial and specialized studies of modern culture are modeled, more or less explicitly, upon studies of whole living societies in which the anthropologist observes the life of a people, witnesses birth and death, participates in ceremonials, visits individual households, and establishes relationships with many members of the community within which he is working. In the course of such observation and participation—participation in which his role as interested observer from another culture is conspicuously defined—he also uses the verbal accounts and explanations which can be given by individuals who are willing to talk, to translate, to interpret, and to explain. One not only attends ceremonies but also obtains accounts of other ceremonies, writes down from dictation myths about the ceremony, and discusses with informants, within interview situations, the traditional interpretation and rationale of details of the ceremony. Furthermore, in a living culture there are always artifacts, cultural products of one sort or another—houses, carvings, costumes, masks and offerings, pictorial representations of religious and magical ideas, charms constructed of fur and feathers or leaves and flowers, and the play constructions of children. When a whole culture is being studied, the observed

---

[7]*Ibid.,* pp. 51-52.

style of architecture, the ways in which a house form differs from the house forms in adjacent or related cultures, the ways in which people use a house, who sits where and when, the meaning of the screen across a Balinese court-yard gate (to outwit devils who do not know how to go around corners) are all materials for the anthropologist. By observation of living behavior, by question-ing and listening to verbal statements, and by analysis of physical objects, he arrives at a rounded presentation of the cultural whole.[8]

The anthropologist through fruitful studies has shed much light upon the cultures of the world. This valuable knowledge has provided a clearer concept of the life of people living under diverse environmental condi-tions and in different moments in time and space. The patterns of culture are revealed and a particular society is better understood. This compre-hension furnishes the student who studies world cultures with a greater insight into the people and their way of life.

Cultural dynamics

Growth, development, and change are the dynamic aspects of cul-ture, i.e., the processes by which cultures adjust to changing environ-mental, technical, scientific, and historical conditions, and, as such, are also cultural "constants." One anthropologist has stated that, "The most constant thing about culture is constant change." Cross-cultural data and comparative studies have, since the earliest beginnings of the science of anthropology, tended to prove over and over again that even in the most traditionally oriented societies, culture change, albeit slow, has been pres-ent always. For today's *rapidly* changing world perhaps few areas of study offer more pertinent data for social studies curricula than the area of cultural dynamics. In the following section a brief summary of the basic principles of culture change is presented as a guide to this expand-ing and often poorly understood field of inquiry:

1. Every society experiences an interplay of those forces making for stability and those making for change. Culture is never really static.
2. Culture changes in either of two ways: by borrowing cultural items from another society or by invention or discovery of new cultural elements within a given society.
3. All discoveries and inventions derive from the culture of a given time and place.
4. Inventions may be classified as primary or secondary; the former are basic and fundamental, the latter derived or "improving."
5. Invention is influenced by attitudes, values, and run of attention.
6. While high ability or special talent are positively correlated with highly significant discoveries and inventions, the cumulation of in-

---

[8] M. Mead and M. Wolfenstein, *Childhood in Contemporary Culture* (Chicago: The University of Chicago Press, 1955), p. 37. Copyright 1955 by the University of Chicago.

ventions and discoveries depends on the day-to-day detailed work of
the whole body of scientists, artists, and other contributors.

7. The importance of social-cultural foundations for discoveries and inventions is clearly indicated in the duplication of many discoveries and
inventions throughout the course of history.

8. Diffusion of culture is the spread or borrowing and acceptance of
cultural elements. It may be direct, that is, from person to person or
group to group, or indirect, that is, without personal contact.

9. A wide variety of factors influence the rates of diffusion. Among them
are availability of transportation and communication, resistance or
readiness to accept new items, need, and the power or prestige of the
giving and the receiving groups.

10. Cultural lag occurs when some parts of a culture are changing more
rapidly than other, related parts. Lag tends to induce strain and mal-
adjustment, at least temporarily.

11. Technology is the totality of means or techniques used by a society or
group in their efforts to adapt themselves to the material environment.

12. The rate and extent of technological change are influenced by attitudes and values of owners, experts, workers, and the general
public.[9]

Discovery, invention, diffusion

The role of the foregoing in terms of the growth of culture are significant. In our space age we are bewildered at times with the rapid progress
in science and technology.

The role of inventions in terms of the growth of culture is significant. In our contemporary age we are bewildered at times with the rapid
progress in science and technology. However, in terms of the study of
world cultures we should ponder over the following:

> Invention is a combination of previously existent cultural elements that
> produces something new. This combination may involve ideas about the world
> of nature, the world of man, or human control of any part of these worlds.
> Artistic ideas are combined to produce an invention in aesthetics, either in the
> form of technics (oil painting) or subject matter (abstract painting). Ideas may
> be combined in moral or ethical standards, with such great religions as Chris-
> tianity or Mohammedanism serving as examples. Ideas may involve technics
> for dealing with the physical universe and the production of new goods and
> services. The latter combination of cultural elements is the only one usually
> considered under the heading of inventions.[10]

Major inventions in any culture, either borrowed or developed, are
certain to bring about some type of change. This important factor of

---

[9] Kimball Young and Raymond W. Mack, *Sociology and Social Life* (New York:
American Book Company, 1959), p. 105.

[10] F. E. Merrill, *Society and Culture: An Introduction to Sociology,* (2nd ed.;
Englewood Cliffs, N.J.: Prentice-Hall, Inc., 1961), pp. 463-464.

change resulting from invention has long had a marked influence upon man and his daily activities. The greater the inventiveness of a people, the more pronounced the eventual social changes.

Technological progress and discovery have and will continue to be a dominant factor in shaping human society and will call for varying degrees of adjustment on the part of individuals involved in a specific culture.

Cultures reflect the inventions that helped to shape them, and in the formative process, changes both bring deviations from past activities, and, in turn, many foster additional changes. We must also recall that the diffusion of new ideas into a culture brings about change based upon the extent of their usage by the people involved.

Emphasis

It cannot be overstressed that men everywhere are molded to their cultures. Change which strikes at fundamental value systems tend to be resisted even in our own society where change for the sake of change alone is highly valued. Among the more traditionally oriented peoples of the world the desire for technological improvement may emerge second to the stronger desire to preserve aspects of the past. It becomes increasingly imperative in our shrinking world that we understand that (1) the cultures of all men contain elements worth preserving, (2) where change is imperative, change be introduced through existing mores and values to prevent cultural impoverishment, and (3) we all share in the responsibility of cultural salvage and support.

When studying, reading, and learning about the growth of the world's nations, we focus considerable attention upon the lands and the people. We are naturally interested in their everyday life pursuits as well as their past heritage. In the space age with its growing web of technology, we must also take a view of the future with its many new visions, activities, and contributions to culture.

Suggested Objectives and Outline

The following list of objectives and course outlines is intended to provide assistance for those who plan courses in world cultures. The selection and planning of units becomes an important aspect in building the framework for such a course. Much will depend upon whether such a course is to be studied for one year or for a two-year sequence. Some units may be selected for a greater or more intensive study than others.

Such a course should aim to provide students with some knowledge, understanding, and appreciation of the cultures of peoples in different areas of the world. It should be remembered that all cultures have some more or less basic patterns. The modern scientific surge is bringing the peoples of the world in closer contact with our nation. It must be remembered that new ideas are often slow to be accepted and inculcated into older patterns of culture.

The outline should be sufficiently flexible to allow for any alterations. When the course is in actual operation any changes can be readily made to fit the established objectives. It should be remembered that such a course will need to be constantly evaluated in terms of new materials available for instructional purposes. A certain amount of experimentation, exploration, and evaluation is needed for the establishment of a solid framework for such a course.

World Cultures[11]

(*Semester Course, Required Grade Twelve*)
Abington, Pennsylvania

General Objectives

Information and Understandings
1. To become oriented in basic patterns of culture, its variations, and the factors which influence change and growth
2. To understand that culture, because it is learned, can be changed
3. To understand that other cultures cannot be judged on the basis of our own standards and values alone
4. To understand the effect of physical environment on the development of cultures
5. To understand the variety of ways of living and the variety in institutions common to all societies
6. To gain an elementary understanding of the political systems and governments of other culture areas
7. To gain some understanding of the major religions in the culture areas
8. To understand the role of economic factors in human life and in world affairs
9. To understand the conflicts which may develop between traditional and contemporary values in culture groups
10. To understand the problems and aspirations of other peoples
11. To understand the interdependence and vulnerability of all peoples in the atomic age
12. To recognize trends which may influence the future of world relations

---

[11] Florence O. Benjamin, Coordinator of Social Studies, School District of Abington Township, Abington, Penna. *Curriculum Guide World Cultures* (Abington, Penna.: School District of Abington Township, 1962), pp. 7-9.

Appreciations, Behaviors, Skills
1. To develop attitudes and behavior of respect for all cultures and races
2. To become more informed and effective citizens of U.S. world affairs
3. To appreciate that the differences in culture groups do not connote inferiority
4. To recognize that prejudice may be an obstacle to both better human relations and to world relations
5. To appreciate the differences within culture groups, that people do not conform to sterotypes
6. To appreciate the creative abilities, the hopes, the aspirations of all peoples
7. To develop an interest in the language and literature of other peoples
8. To judge the reliability of sources of material and information
9. To think critically
10. To use materials from many sources effectively
11. To evaluate individual and group work

Units in World Cultures

I. Orientation Unit (5 days)
   What Is Culture?
   What Is Race?
   What Is Civilization?
II. Russia and S.E. Europe (18 days)
III. Sino-Japanese Area (15 days)
IV. India, Pakistan, and S.E. Asia (18 days)
V. The Middle East (15 days)
VI. Africa (15 days)

The foregoing materials provide an excellent guide for a course in world cultures.

Oregon[12]

1. World Cultures (A Two-Year Alternative Course Combining Ninth- and Tenth-Grade Social Studies)
2. World Cultures (A One-Year Alternative Course for Grade 9 or 10)

This world-cultures approach represents an attempt to make the study of world peoples more functional, more interesting, and more comprehensive through the fusion of geography, history, and cultures. The emphasis is upon understanding the people of the world today, the formal subjects (history, geography, etc.) becoming tools by which people are studied and understood rather than disciplines to be learned. By focusing all of the various disciplines making up the social studies on a people at one time in an organized manner, it is believed that students will know more about those people as they are now, and the forces causing them to be as they are. In seeking to understand each national or ethnic group the class will delve into its historical development, plan of government, philosophy, ethics, religions, racial backgrounds, physical geography, economy, cultural traditions, expressions in art, literature, music, and recreation, its modern problems, and any other forces which may be help-

---

[12] *Guide to Secondary Education in Oregon—1961-1963* (Salem, Oregon: State Department of Education, 1961), pp. 205-207.

ful in gaining an understanding of the people's present status and aspirations for the future. Such a study should result in the students' realizing that all peoples possess many common characteristics and that any recognized dissimilarities are not necessarily barriers that would prevent interdependence and mutual help toward the common goals of peace, richer cultures, and a higher standard of living for all. Also, if the student understands and appreciates the differences, similarities, and richness of world cultures, his understanding of his own contemporary life which is involved in world problems today should be promoted. The course will help develop standards of reference for appreciation of democratic values and will offer a broader scope for development of individual potentialities along lines of better citizenship both within the nation and the world.

The basic units suggested include:

1. What is culture?
2. Primitive cultures
3. Mediterranean peoples
4. Peoples of the Far East: India and Pakistan; China; Japan
5. Union of Soviet Socialist Republics
6. United Kingdom and British Commonwealth of Nations
7. Nations of Western Europe: France, Germany, peoples of Northern Europe
8. Africa
9. Slavic peoples
10. Peoples of Southeast Asia
11. European cultures in the New World
12. An independent project
13. Geography of the world
14. Patterns in World History
15. World cooperation

Materials for Instruction

Resource materials

Such a course as world cultures should and does require and utilize a considerable amount of resource materials. A great deal of information is essential to acquire a high quality of functional knowledge. It should be remembered that this type of course represents a wide variation from the usual materials used in a course in world history. The nature of the content needed for this course also differs considerably from traditional history.

One essential tool will be a mimeographed list of suitable up-to-date references. This is imperative and the listings should be supplemented with other pertinent resources. Each unit will require specific information and this selected knowledge will come from many sources found in the library files.

The background materials dealing with the past may be more readily found in the school library. However, newer source materials will have to be made available for studying the more recent as well as tomorrow's culture. Textbook materials, supplementary volumes, magazines, pamphlets, newspapers, and current events as they happen around the global scene will have to be used. Furthermore, private library collections in the community, the resource of the public library, museum resources, and easily acquired newer literature can prove very productive for learning.

Audio-visual materials and others

Use should be made of available audio-visual materials when deemed advisable. A file of suitable pictures, charts, and articles for tackboard displays and for use in the teaching-learning process will prove helpful. Films, filmstrips, recordings, and slide collections should be wisely selected, since they provide for a greater understanding of the culture under consideration. Television programs and radio broadcasts may contain a wealth of current as well as past information that can be applicable to some particular unit or topic.

Guest speakers or visiting resource personnel, when available, can also be called upon for information-giving purposes. Logs, picture collections, and accounts that are recorded by individuals when traveling in various areas of the world can prove beneficial for students to see and study.

Procedures and techniques

The methods, procedures, and techniques for instruction in such a course might include a telling procedure or a role-playing technique along with other methods deemed essential by the teacher. A brief lecture or telling procedure as well as a question and discussion period can be used occasionally along with the application of audio-visual materials. Students should receive some basic instruction in the skill of outlining, note-taking, recording of data, simple research, and evaluation.

The very nature of this instruction no doubt will entail the study of productive units and interesting topics. This in turn should foster discussion and a wide use of supplementary materials along with the presentation of reports. In this manner the student can share with the group the results of his findings. The application of problem-solving techniques and the selection of suitable individual and group activities are apparent to every social studies teacher.

Conclusion

In conclusion it might be stated that the nature of a course in world cultures is most essential for individuals growing up in the modern complex world, especially as we note the changing patterns of everyday life in various cultural areas. This type of course should provide the general understanding and meaning of cultures. It connotes the story of the past, the growth of cultures, the development stages, the apparent changes, the variance among cultures, the present status, and the probable future status.

Bibliography

Merrill, F. E., *Society and Culture: An Introduction to Sociology*, 2nd ed. Englewood Cliffs, N.J.: Prentice-Hall, Inc., 1961.

Miller, S. N., "World Cultures Course," *Social Education,* **26** (February 1962), 69-70.

Price, R. A., ed., *New Viewpoints in the Social Sciences,* Twenty-eighth Yearbook of the National Council for the Social Studies. Washington, D.C.: National Education Association, 1958.

Young, K. and R. W. Mack, *Sociology and Social Life.* New York: American Book Company, 1959.

Titiev, M., *The Science of Man: An Introduction to Anthropology.* New York: Holt, Rinehart & Winston, Inc., 1954.

Chapter Sixteen

Current Affairs in the Program

The study of current affairs and contemporary world happenings is an important and essential part of the social studies curriculum. At the secondary level it should receive a comprehensive treatment so that students are assisted in gaining a better understanding of our changing society and a growing awareness of the complexities of the world. Students soon become alert and sensitive to the current news reports. They are developing a need for intelligent reading and a desire for critical thinking about specific topics. Students gradually build the habit of following events as they occur around the world. The interest generated in contemporary affairs should be encouraged in the learning process. The many events of today resulting from activities throughout the world are shaping tomorrow's history. In reality, it is current history amplified and going through the process of being recorded. Today's history is evaluated in terms of its importance to the nation and to the world as we look ahead.

An introduction to the study

An introduction to the study of current affairs carries importance similar to that of a content course (problem or topic). The teacher should clarify the very nature of current affairs for the students and should point out the value derived from this learning in the social studies units. Students soon become aware of current events and world happenings occurring in their daily lives. Furthermore, they understand the meaning of these events in terms of opening the door of history. The channels for obtaining firsthand knowledge of current affairs should be explained and clearly understood. A good orientation or overview to a study of current affairs especially at the junior high school level will be rewarding for students when they reach the senior high school and later in college.

The study and knowledge of current affairs requires an awareness of the steady flow of new information in contemporary society. The major task is the selection of pertinent topics that lend significance to a particular course. Does the item, issue, or topic fit a particular need and is it relevant to the prevailing study or unit? Has it significance for the future or will it be an ephemeral topic with little meaning for present or future learning.

It should be pointed out that major events of world and national importance can be of consequence as a lesson in itself. Today's space age, characterized by scientific achievements and momentous decisions which affect the future civilization, should receive immediate attention. The planning of any social studies lesson should allow for some flexibility to explore events that have real meaning for students. Isolated topics should be avoided, since they lack interest and help defeat the general purpose of the program. Teachers should be ever alert to select only those problems or topics in our contemporary life that are geared to the group's abilities.

The following examples are related to programs that deal with current affairs and current events:

Current Affairs

Current affairs is a more inclusive term than current events. Current events is frequently a simple reporting of news happenings, whereas the term current affairs includes not only the events in the news but the issues behind the events upon which there are conflicting points of view. Current affairs is a vital part of the social studies program and should be included regularly at every grade level.[1]

Objectives of the Current Affairs Program

All of the objectives of a good current affairs program are applicable in teaching the academically talented. However, the objectives listed below are particularly suited to the needs and abilities of these pupils.

1. To develop critical or reflective and projective thinking; that is, greater

---

[1] *A Curriculum Supplement, The History of Our America, Grade Eleven, Superior and Gifted Students* (Towsen, Maryland: Baltimore County Public Schools, 1959), pp. 12-16.

competency in arriving at valid opinions on vital questions that confront our society
2. To encourage an intense interest, a feeling of responsibility, and active participation in those activities in the school and widening community which are necessary to the orderly functioning of a democratic society
3. To foster the principles that judgments and decisions should be based on the moral values undergirding our democracy
4. To help pupils recognize the revolutionary and inter-related character of the world today in politics, technology, science, and society in general, and the necessity of the international cooperation
5. To develop the habit of reconsidering a problem when new evidence appears and revising conclusions accordingly
6. To encourage pupils to adopt points of view which are free from prejudice and superstition

Suggested Procedures

A current affairs program may be organized in many ways, no one of which should be used to the exclusion of the others. The interests and needs of the pupils, their maturity, the teacher's preference and background, and the availability of materials and equipment points up the necessity for the use of a variety of approaches. Three possible approaches are suggested below:
1. Isolated topic approach. The study of a topic which had immediate and urgent interest for the pupils
2. Correlated approach. The study of topics that are pertinent to the social studies unit under consideration
3. Persistent issue approach. The study of significant topics which have been and seem likely to continue to be in the news over an extended period of time

Current Events

A study of history is essential to a proper understanding of the present. Such a study, however, is not sufficient to equip students with the knowledge and attitudes they must gain in order to develop an understanding of the complex world in which they live. In order to achieve this goal, the social studies teacher must guide his students in a direct and purposeful study of current events.[2]

Objectives

1. To acquaint students with important current affairs
2. To develop the ability to appraise information obtained from mass media
3. To help students identify important problems and issues, to see how these affect their lives, and to sense what they can do about them
4. To stimulate a lively and continuing interest in local, state, national, and international affairs
5. To become better acquainted with newspapers, news magazines, and other sources of information

---

[2] *Course of Study, United States History, Eleventh Grade,* Bulletin No. 145 (Montgomery County, Maryland: Montgomery County Public Schools, 1959), pp. 36-39.

Suggested methods

1. Provide a few minutes daily for consideration of current events
2. A class discussion led by the teacher as students report on news items
3. Continuing committees studying selected problems of current interest
4. The preparation by the class of a weekly glossary of names, places, and events for a bulletin board display
5. Panel discussions on current issues
6. The collecting of clippings or making of a scrapbook on a variety of current topics to be used as resource material
7. The use of current event films, news maps, or other visual aids to emphasize present happenings
8. The analysis of newspapers, radio and television news programs, and cartoons by the teachers and students
9. The correlation of school affairs with events occurring on the local, state, or national level

Developing essential skills

The following skills can be valuable and essential in the study of current affairs and current events. The student should develop the ability to read and interpret charts, graphs, diagrams, tables, and statistical data; he should be able to read and interpret the real meaning behind cartoons and similar illustrations; he should read, understand, and interpret the materials furnished by various types of maps and the globe; he should develop skill in critical and creative thinking; he should develop skill in the art of research, locating, gathering, organizing, and evaluating new knowledge and important information; he should develop skill in speaking, discussion, and respecting the opinion of other members of a group; he should cultivate the skill and habit of exploring several sources for further information; and he should develop skill in grasping the main points developed by a resource speaker and the current materials presented by radio and television news commentators. Keeping up with the news is a lifelong process, and the student should always remain aware of the events occurring in our rapidly changing society and complex world.

The place of contemporary affairs

Students at all levels of social studies instruction should have the opportunity to study contemporary affairs. A wide sweep of topics is interwoven with the events occurring in the world scene. With a clearer understanding of these issues, the individual will be helped in developing greater competency in dealing with the problems of current society.

A planned program in the teaching of contemporary affairs will require approximately one-fifth of the total time devoted to social studies instruction. A program is needed in which pupils are guided carefully in their study of a wide range of contemporary affairs over a period of time. Their study should enable them to recognize how events in the current scene affect the present and future welfare of people; how current developments stem from decisions made earlier; how current happenings reflect the basic values held by people; how changing circumstances lead to modifications in policy; how local, state, national, and world news reflects the beliefs of various groups of people; how study of current affairs can improve the skills of analysis, interpretation, and judgment; how current happenings in the arts, science, technology, politics, and government reveal changes throughout the world; and how important it is for citizens in a democracy to be alert always to their civic responsibilities.

Use of approximately one-fifth of the total social studies time for instruction in current affairs should not result in arbitrary decisions to devote one day per week to such instruction. Rather, instruction in contemporary affairs should be incorporated into the on-going social studies program at times and placed where it will be most effective.[3]

Resource materials

Appropriate materials in sufficient supply are essential for teaching current affairs. The very nature of these materials change as the student moves up the educational ladder and through the eighth grade. Upon reaching the sixth grade, students begin to broaden their research into international problems. Students are capable of doing research into the background or past history of a specific topic. Therefore, it is important that they have access to productive sources. It is through individual searching and through sharing work with the group that the students' sphere of knowledge grows.

Some suggested sources of information both in and outside of school include:

1. Library (school and public)—current books, reference books, bulletins, pamphlets, reports, and magazines
2. Mass media—rapid communication through radio and television
3. Press—daily and weekly newspapers including both local and large municipal issues
4. Classroom periodicals—graded weekly papers and magazines for student study
5. Community—resource persons, lectures, conferences, and programs suitable for acquiring information
6. Audio-visual materials—films, slides, news films, filmstrips, transcriptions, maps, graphs, and charts for clarifying information
7. Agencies—local, state, and national for acquiring significant data

---

[3] *Report of the State Control Committee on Social Studies* (Sacramento, Calif.: California State Department of Education, 1959), pp. 17-18.

Mass media and audio-visual materials

The channels of mass media, especially television and radio, are valuable aids in following and reviewing current topics in the news. The world events are surveyed and valuable knowledge that relates to various global areas can be readily acquired.

Television provides the opportunity for viewing significant events that help to make history. The social studies teacher should utilize this aid when deemed helpful in the learning process. Programs that have educational and learning value can be employed in the lesson. Students should also be encouraged to be selective in the choice of programs relating to current events. Many worthwhile panels, discussions, and speeches by important authorities in various areas of society present information that is valuable to the student of current affairs.

In addition to the advantages inherent in the programs themselves, the students are developing skills of program selection. Moreover, the students' ability to discriminate between informative and purely entertaining programs lays a foundation for lifelong habits.

Radio presents many programs that have value for the student, since discussion by news experts furnish much current information. It might prove profitable to have certain programs recorded and played in the lesson with a follow-up discussion of the question or topic presented. Radio, through news reports, assists the student and teacher in keeping informed on current events.

Films and filmstrips, tapes, and records can also serve a real purpose in studying contemporary affairs. Students can learn much about the location and physical landscape of a particular region. Many times such a procedure leads the group to become interested in the study of key developments around the world. Learning to spot the geographical region where problems and significant events are developing is of major importance to the group. By combining information and ideas brought out through audio-visual materials and the follow-up discussion, the teacher stimulates the students to read for further information and to embark on a research project.

Newspapers, weeklies, and monthly periodicals

Newspapers, weeklies, and monthly periodicals reflect or serve as mirrors for life in the immediate and world scene. Such materials are a part of the mass media communication which gives the student a vast mine of information on diverse topics. Many interesting articles relating to human activities in the far-flung corners of the globe may be read and discussed with interest by teachers and the group. In this manner students are building the foundation for becoming well-informed individuals. The teacher should point out the value derived from reading information-giving periodicals and the importance of being informed on current issues and problems in today's world.

The student should become acquainted with at least one good daily newspaper. Since current affairs are generally associated with the press, this study provides an excellent opportunity to learn *how* to read a newspaper. The type of information found in newspapers and periodicals should also be pointed out. Students should analyze and evaluate the influence of the press upon society and acquire the habit of reading a newspaper intelligently. An examination of several newspapers will provide an opportunity to compare the difference in treatment of a given item and the difference in emphasis of the materials or current information presented.

A study of the newspaper and periodicals should provide a starting point in the examination of current affairs. By this method students learn to look for pertinent articles that specifically relate to the problem being currently studied. Learning how to locate information in current literature is a valuable asset for the learner.

Current events periodicals also have a place in the study of current affairs. They have several advantages.

1. They usually appear weekly and thus give balance and perspective to the events of the week.
2. They are frequently supplied in graded series; so they may be selected to suit the students' level of understanding and vocabulary.
3. They usually supply much of the geographical and historical background necessary for understanding the news.
4. They are authoritatively written and are considered reliable.
5. They provide both an interpretation of issues and a presentation of facts.

At the junior and senior high school levels, these periodicals can be read and studied to furnish current information. However, in most senior high school classes, these graded periodicals should not be used as the sole source of material for the current affairs discussion, but should supplement the newspapers, the news periodicals, and other sources. Senior high school groups particularly should become familiar with as many news-giving publications as possible and should be encouraged to read widely on contemporary affairs.

Teachers and students alike might also utilize the following sources for informative, supplementary, and timely reading: *Time, Newsweek, Fortune, Life, United States News, National Geographic, Current His-*

tory, Survey Graphic, Saturday Evening Post, and the *New York Times Magazine.* Some of these suggested magazines may be found on the magazine rack in the classroom library or in the instructional materials center.

The role of current affairs in the program

A study and knowledge of current affairs is an essential phase of social studies instruction. The modern age calls for an informed and alert citizenry. This in turn calls for due consideration of current affairs at the secondary level.

In the past as well as in the present, various approaches were employed by supervisors and teachers in utilizing current event materials in the social studies curriculum. Placing the study in a special course was considered. Also some thinking prevailed that all or at least certain courses should consider including current events. The time allotment for adequately presenting current events for the students posed a problem. In many cases either a definite part (perhaps the first ten minutes) of each lesson or one entire period a week had been set aside for this discussion. Some students were responsible for presenting news items to the group; others were responsible for studying and reviewing pertinent materials from current literature.

The teacher is the important cog in directing current affairs instruction. He must be enthusiastic and competent in handling the various news topics and the issues of the times. He helps in selecting those current affairs materials that are essential for students at the secondary level. It is the teacher who alerts the students to the necessity of reading and understanding the important topics of the day and the trends of the times. The following materials present some preferred ways of handling current affairs in the teaching-learning process

Presenting Current Affairs Materials

Creative techniques

The modern teacher is creative and always seeks new approaches for enriching the current affairs instruction. Helping students to understand better the happenings of the world in which they live is a challenging responsibility. Selecting the best sources for supplying information related to current affairs is an important task. Utilizing those techniques and procedures that are productive for learning holds a high priority. The study of current affairs helps the student to relate his understanding of academic social studies to his everyday life. Students in the cooperative planning process frequently arrive at interesting approaches for exploring and presenting the news developments selected for study and discussion. What are some of the various methods and procedures applicable to learning experiences in current affairs?

Informal discussion provides students with the opportunity to discuss selected items of importance. The students exchange ideas, listen to various viewpoints, learn to respect the opinions of others, and reach some conclusions within the group.

Panel discussion calls for students to assume some leadership in the planning and presentation of selected topics or questions. A modern touch with a radio or television type of program encourages the students to select and discuss their information with improved skill. Such a procedure necessitates effective speaking and requires attentive listening in order to answer questions and present a summary. Occasionally it may be wise for the teacher to conclude the discussion in such a manner as to stimulate further study. The panel groups may also be responsible for a compatible display on the tackboard.

A chairman usually directs the activity of the panel. A brief introductory statement relating to the question is the point of departure; each panelist is allotted time to present his viewpoint on the issue. Some brief interchange of discussion between the panelists is generally the pattern followed. The entire group is later given an opportunity to question the statements of any member of the panel. To assure smoothness of procedure, pre-planning is most essential. A guide sheet listing essential information relating to the problem is profitable. An evaluation sheet completed by members of the group indicates the success of the discussion and insures their attention. It may be wise on some occasions to employ co-chairmen to act as directors in regulating the time, recognizing individuals, listing materials on the chalkboard, guiding the questions, and assisting in bringing the discussion to a final conclusion.

Round table discussion is an approach for a committee or an entire class. A group can arrange their seating in a circle, so that each student who has questions or information is included as a contributor in the discussion. However, some pupils can act as experts and present materials or state a question related to a topic as a means of orientation. The teacher usually takes his place in the discussion and can act as a resource person and keep the discussion moving by thought-provoking questions. Students learn to think critically, discuss intelligently, and present materials in a logical manner. It is always important to select timely issues and topics that are of interest and that are challenging to the group.

Attempts should be made to relate this information to some phase of the students' present knowledge.

News reporting is an effective procedure by which learning of current affairs and events fosters understanding of history in the making. Interests are kindled and aroused; thinking tends to encourage further independent research as it relates to an interesting topic. Reporting may be the responsibility of an individual or of a committee.

Frequently, some specific topic of importance will continue in the news. If this should be the case, an individual student may wish to continue this particular study and periodically report developments to the group. If there are various world topics that arouse sufficient interest, the group through committees can continue research and report their findings. Students should be encouraged to use graphic materials in presenting data relating to current affairs.

Seminars is another recent approach being utilized by some social studies teachers. Interested students devote a portion of their free time during the school scheduled program once or twice a week to meet and investigate current affairs. Under the guidance of the teacher, they attempt to analyze the significant and underlying world events occurring throughout the academic year. The students have a greater opportunity to penetrate geographical areas which are prominent in the news and which could not be as broadly covered in the prevailing program.

Controversial issues

The beginning as well as the experienced teacher should keep in mind that a few of the topics, issues, and problems studied in the social studies may be of a controversial nature. Every effort should be made to develop the scientific approach to problem-solving of various issues. The social studies teacher should not avoid material likely to lead to controversial issues. Sometimes topics do arise naturally out of the experiences in a teaching-learning situation. He should attempt to develop skill in handling such topics, utilizing the proper procedures, and employing adequate source materials. Teachers acting as impartial leaders may be guided in the development and evaluation of problems for group study and discussion by the following criteria: 1. Can the group handle the topic adequately or is it beyond their comprehension? 2. Is the problem related to the material studied in the course; has it any direct value to the learning situation? 3. Will there be adequate source materials available in the library for a worthwhile study of this issue? 4. Does the issue relate only to the community or does it have a wider significance? 5. Will the experiences derived from this study provide growth and development for the individual? 6. Is the issue current and interesting to the majority; does it challenge the interest of the group? 7. Does the issue relate to the secondary school curriculum and will the group acquire desired learning experiences through discussion of the problem? 8. Will such a study lead to the development of individual citizenship?

Teachers have to approach such problems in a spirit of reasonableness. They should guide any group discussion in a common-sense manner. An objective point of view, sound judgment, and proper guidance are most essential in any discussion. The competent teacher considers the rights of the student and his responsibility for building democratic citizenship.

The teacher who is new in a community should inquire about the policy of the school toward controversial issues. The public should understand clearly the objectives of the program and the place of the teacher in the educational scheme. If a common-sense approach is applied to the teaching of material that may prove controversial, unpleasant situations may be averted. A sound and intelligent policy formulated by both faculty and administration should be established and adhered to at all times.

For the public schools, policy on controversial issues is defined in terms of the rights of pupils rather than in terms of the rights of teachers. In the study of controversial issues in the public schools, the pupil has four rights to be recognized:

    a. The right to study any controversial issue which has political, economic, or social significance and concerning which (at his level) he should begin to have an opinion.

    b. The right to have free access to all relevant information, including the materials that circulate freely in the community.

    c. The right to study under competent instruction in an atmosphere free from bias and prejudice.

    d. The right to form and express his own opinions on controversial issues without thereby jeopardizing his relations with his teacher or the school.

The study of controversial issues is objective and scholarly, with a minimum emphasis on opinion. The teacher approaches controversial issues in the classroom in an impartial and unprejudiced manner, and must refrain from using his classroom privileges and prestige to promote a partisan point of view. Good teaching of subjects containing controversial issues requires more skill than most other kinds of teaching, and, so far as possible, only teachers of superior ability are assigned subjects in which a large body of material involves controversy.

Instructional policy on controversial issues should be defined by constituted authority in order to protect teachers and school administrators from unwarranted attack by pressure groups and to insure youth a well-balanced preparation for American citizenship.[4]

---

[4] Claude V. Courter, chairman, *An Educational Platform for the Public Schools, Some Phases of Instructional Policy* (Chicago: Inland Press, Inc., 1952), p. 10. Developed and indorsed by school superintendents of cities in the U.S. and Canada with population over 200,000.

Current practices indicate that some school systems and state departments of education have established guiding policies that govern the teaching of controversial subjects.

The following examples can provide a directive for handling the problem of controversial questions:[5]

The consideration of controversial questions has a legitimate place in the work of the public schools.

Sooner or later young people must meet and face such questions. It is important that they have experience with such questions under circumstances which promote consideration of all pertinent factors.

School treatment of such questions should not only promote fair and many-sided study of those questions; it should also help the student develop techniques for considering controversial questions—techniques which he will habitually use in later life.

The handling of a controversial question in school should be free from the assumption that there is one correct answer which should emerge from the discussion and be taught authoritatively to the student.

Indoctrination is not the purpose; rather, the purpose is to have the student see as fully as possible all sides of the question.

A controversial question should be handled in an appropriate setting by a teacher prepared for such a responsibility. Such a question is always related to many things in the past and the present, which are important to any profitable study of it.

The wise teacher avoids going into a controversial question beyond his own depth. A student would better be uninformed about a question than misinformed about it.

The decision as to whether a controversial question shall become a matter for school study should be based on such considerations as the timeliness of the question, the maturity of the students, the needs of the students, and the purposes of the school.

The school must determine how much time and how much emphasis shall be given the question.

In addition to the planned discussions of controversial questions, there are occasions when such a question arises unexpectedly. The teacher has the responsibility of discerning its controversial nature and handling it accordingly.

The local board of education should go on record with a declaration of policies for handling controversial questions in the schools. Having done so, it should protect the teaching and administrative personnel from partisan pressures. . . .

Correlated Activities
and Experiences

The study and teaching of current affairs and important news items should, whenever desirable, become a part of the units being studied. In this manner the geographical setting and the historical background can be stressed. Such a continuous study provides many opportunities

[5] "New Jersey—New Jersey State Board of Education," *Controversial Issues in the Classroom* (Washington, D.C.: National Education Association, 1961), pp. 27-28.

for student activities in terms of the issues and topics studied. At the same time the practical skills of reading, interpretation, analyzation, research, organization, and evaluation are becoming more effective. Concepts are also being acquired as well as the development of a useful and functional vocabulary.

Tackboard displays

It is surprising the amount of interest which can be generated in current events and global affairs through worthwhile displays on the tackboard. Significant personalities in government and people from all walks of life who are in the news can be spotlighted through their various activities and travels. An attractive and stimulating display becomes a broad window for viewing the parade of events and happenings throughout the global scene. A major section of the available tackboard area should be devoted to the treatment of current affairs. Students should be made aware of the importance of observation in acquiring knowledge. When discussing issues and in planning committee reports, students should consider the utilization of an effective display to clarify the question or problem being studied. Reference should always be directed to the active and current display in the learning process. The general responsibility for an active tackboard display can be shared by both the teacher and the students.

A current affairs map

Another effective aid in helping to keep abreast of world events is an active news map. In this way students can pinpoint the area where the event occurred or where the problem is centered. A map also provides the student with a picture of the physical landscape and the geographical setting of an area. This should aid the reader in better understanding the complete news story. Students should be encouraged to use graphic materials when investigating current affairs.

A continuous learning activity can be fostered by placing a large world map on the tackboard, allowing for adequate space around it to post news items, pictures, graphs, and so on. Each of these items is connected by means of colored string or ribbon and a map tack with the exact geographical location of the site where the event originated.

The sports world

Sports of various types hold some interest for a large segment of the population in modern society. The interest that students display in sports, along with other phases of the news, is most revealing. In fact, some major sports events tend to push other items to the background for the time being. Materials relating to sports can serve as a valuable aid for learning more about modern society. A tackboard display and the store of knowledge that students have of sports can be utilized by the skillful teacher in better understanding the dynamics of society and the current affairs of the world. Students should also develop the habit of using the tackboard to display things that are of interest to them. Eventually, this will lead to their acceptance of other displays which are of secondary importance to them.

Knowing one's own state

Effective citizenship calls for knowing the political, social, and economic features of one's own state. What happens specifically in a state can be expanded to better understanding of what is happening generally in the nation. A tackboard display depicting the current affairs and news items relating to a state arouses student interest. This activity tends to stimulate investigation and furnishes an incentive for intelligent reading about specific issues. State laws currently enacted and pertaining to some aspect of society are studied. Election and party platforms are considered with much interest. These and other experiences help to make government more understandable as it functions in everyday life.

Knowing the local community

Community news holds much interest for all groups whether they live in a county or a city. Like any state, the local unit of government is also confronted with problems, issues, and questions that stir the citizen. Many times a local event holds both state and national significance. Most Americans have their only direct experiences with government on a local level; so it is profitable for them to be aware of the patterns of community events. Students should be encouraged to read materials pertaining to all phases of society in the immediate community and region; an active tackboard display therefore becomes a learning feature.

Growth in vocabulary

Vocabulary development is a specific phase of all current affairs instruction in the social studies. Contemporary affairs provides us with many new words, phrases, slogans, terms, and expressions. Certain words, used in news stories as well as in radio and television programs, may present barriers to understanding for a group of learners. Current history has a vocabulary that is economic, historical, political, geographical, and social in nature. Selections from periodicals and newspapers embody words in current use and furnish an excellent source for vocabulary study. Students in the learning process are steadily acquiring a useful vocabulary in addition to new information. However, the teacher must be alert to clarify the meanings of words, and in this way students can gain a better comprehension of current affairs and news items.

Students especially at the junior high school level are encouraged to list all new words in their notebooks. The teacher should clarify the meaning and application of new words found in materials. These words should then be used in daily class assignments and in discussion.

Notebooks and a scrapbook

A notebook may be used to good advantage by students in the study of current affairs. The student may wish to write news summaries and record notes taken from reading feature news articles and reference materials pertaining to a specific issue. He can collect and organize pictures, graphs, and charts related to the problem being studied. These materials when properly arranged can serve as firsthand resources and as an aid for future discussion. Examination of these notebooks by the teacher and credit given for them tends to stimulate interest in the work. Before the collection of the notebooks starts, the criteria and purpose for them should be decided cooperatively by the teacher and the students. This should help prevent the indiscriminate collection of useless articles.

A group can also compile a scrapbook with materials pertaining to issues and problems studied in connection with the units in a particular course. These compilations contain much valuable knowledge gained from study and research of various sources.

The community and current affairs

Each community, large or small, agricultural or industrial, is the center of events, incidents, and stories that may be of deep interest to students. Many times a local community becomes nationally known because of some special event or problem which has general public appeal.

News in one's own community is a part of the life and culture of the community. It alerts the student to his own surroundings and reveals to him history in the making. Local news of current issues and happenings become the theme of the day for many people in the small towns or rural areas.

Students and teacher working cooperatively may build a unit around current affairs in their own community. Such a project might include the geography, history, industries, people, leaders, opportunities, and problems of the immediate area. The student who studies the problems of his own town learns about its people and the role he plays in its present and future status. Every community is rich in both past and current material. It·will reveal much to the student who will take the time to do research.

Evaluating the teaching of current affairs

Evaluation is an important phase of the teaching of current affairs. Teachers and students can both share in and benefit from an inventory of their findings and accomplishments. The acquisition of and growth in special skills are valuable assets for our youth. The progress in ability to select and evaluate materials and to think critically about problems and issues builds competence. Growth should be measured in terms of using and interpreting of such aids as globes, maps, tables, diagrams, and charts. The development of good study habits and interests in reading informative newspapers and periodicals and in selecting constructive television and radio programs is a necessary contribution to the student's learning. The teacher may evaluate the student's growth by the use of standardized tests published by some of the mass news media and by follow-up quizzes and tests based upon the group's interests and discussions. Progressive testing that begins early in the year may allow the student the rewarding experience of seeing his knowledge grow. Self-evaluations allow the youth to develop the ability to criticize himself and his peers and to build upon the critique for a more selective learning process for the future. The skillful teacher through observation and informal discussion can judge to some degree the growth of his students. By sharing this judgment, the student is given a standard which he must strive for. The teacher is also interested in the importance and value of the issues, problems, and materials incorporated in the teaching of current affairs. The attainment of the established objectives is an important aspect of the evaluation process.

Conclusion

Modern secondary education considers current affairs as a part of the instruction included in the various courses of the social studies curriculum. Current materials pertaining to important issues and problems should be included in the study of contemporary affairs. Many resources are drawn from the library, community, and the avenues of mass media. Newspapers, periodicals, reference books, maps, and charts are examined and evaluated. The methods, procedures, techniques, and approaches are usually varied and selected in terms of group needs. Committee reports and group discussions are built around a desirable climate that fosters critical thinking and effective learning. Various evaluation devices are employed in determining the growth and behavior changes in our youth.

The role of the teacher is significant in directing students in those activities and experiences relating to the study of current affairs. Students under teacher guidance are developing effective skills and establishing lifelong habits that aid in the analysis of current issues. They are learning to consult a variety of productive resources available in the school and community when gathering information. Alert observation and intelligent listening arouses curiosity and student interest in acquiring knowledge. Students are learning new words in their reading and research. These words are clarified by the teacher in the learning process. Appropriate citizenship for living in a democratic society is an important goal for students in the study of current affairs.

Bibliography

Anderson, H. R., ed., *Approaches to an Understanding of World Affairs*, Twenty-fifth Yearbook of the National Council for the Social Studies. Washington, D.C.: National Education Association, 1954.

Cascioli, A. R., "Motivating Current Events Discussions," *High School Journal*, 44 (December 1960), 112-117.

Kinney, L. and K. Dresden, *Better Learning through Current Materials*. Stanford, Calif.: Stanford University Press, 1952.

National Education Association of the United States, *Controversial Issues in the Classroom*. Washington, D.C.: National Education Association, 1961.

Payne, J. C., ed., *The Teaching of Contemporary Affairs*, Twenty-first Yearbook of the National Council for the Social Studies. Washington, D.C.: National Education Association, 1950.

Wass, P. B., "Improving Current Events Instruction," *Social Education*, 25 (February 1961), 79-81.

Chapter Seventeen

The Central Library—A Resource Center in the Instructional Program

The modern secondary school library is an instructional materials center. It has a vital role to play in supplying a variety of resources for the effective functioning of the modern curriculum. In fact, the library is the "pulse" for aiding both the students and teachers in the learning process. It is a central clearinghouse for all the instructional materials necessary to fulfill the instructional program. The growing importance of the library services is recognized by teachers, since the application of newer tools, methods, and techniques have become essential for creative and imaginative teaching.

It is important that social studies teachers have a knowledge of the objectives of a school library.

The general objectives of dynamic school library service are common to all schools. They apply to elementary and secondary schools alike, to independent and parochial schools as well as to public schools, to small and large schools, to rural schools and to urban. They are in harmony with the over-all objectives of education which they serve.

The purposes of the school library are to:
1. Participate effectively in the school program as it strives to meet the needs of pupils, teachers, parents, and other community members
2. Provide boys and girls with the library materials and services most appropriate and most meaningful in their growth and development as individuals
3. Stimulate and guide pupils in all phases of their reading so that they

    may find increasing enjoyment and satisfaction and may grow in critical judgment and appreciation

4. Provide an opportunity through library experiences for boys and girls to develop helpful interests, to make satisfactory personal adjustments, and to acquire desirable social attitudes

5. Help children and young people to become skillful and discriminating users of libraries and of printed and audio-visual materials

6. Introduce pupils to community libraries as early as possible and cooperate with those libraries in their efforts to encourage continuing education and cultural growth

7. Work with teachers in the selection and use of all types of library materials which contribute to the teaching program

8. Participate with teachers and administrators in programs for continuing professional and cultural growth of the school staff

9. Cooperate with other librarians and community leaders in planning and developing an over-all library program for the community or area[1]

    The library provides needed guidance to teachers in curriculum development and to students in reading and research. A plentiful supply of stimulating and appropriate materials are essential for meeting the interests and needs of our youth. The library becomes a laboratory for students doing research and investigating the available resources when studying a problem or preparing a written report. The high school student should have acquired adequate skill and essential knowledge to make constant and profitable use of the library.

    The library as an instructional materials center must be ready to meet the many demands of the school community. To organize, maintain, control, circulate, and provide for utilization of the many varieties of instructional materials called for requires a trained librarian with teaching skill who will also function as a resource person.

An Instructional Materials Center

    The modern secondary school program, which is geared to the demands of the space-atomic age, requires a dynamic curricula and a fully equipped library serving as the instructional materials center. The effective instructional program and the experimentation with new methods and procedures utilizes a wide variety of materials, resources, and audio-visual materials in the teaching-learning process. The library services in today's secondary school must assist in meeting the demands of the curricula as well as the growing needs and changing interests of all students. The needs of the teachers for a wider supply of resources and

[1] American Association of School Librarians, *Standards for School Library Programs* (Chicago: American Library Association, 1960), pp. 8-9.

different types of materials is most evident, and this calls for greater assistance from the library.

One of the current major recommendations for the further development of school libraries, including those in high schools, is that they be made into instructional materials centers. Those who support this recommendation believe school libraries should be depositories of all types of materials and resources for teaching and learning. They maintain that school libraries should develop collections of pictorial and graphic materials, maps, globes, films, filmstrips, slides, tape and disc recordings, and three-dimensional materials as well as collections of books and other printed materials. They contend that the role of school librarians is to provide teachers and pupils with expert professional advice and assistance in the location, selection, and use of all these materials. And they make the point that library materials and services should be organized so that they are easily and readily available to those who use them.[2]

A good school library program

The modern educational program, instructional procedure, and newer techniques in the teaching-learning process require that both teachers and students understand a good school library program. The following criteria provides a basis for comprehending the functional and practical aspects of such a program.

The program of a good school library is the sum total of the ways in which wide and varied collections of materials are provided and used to enrich and vitalize the curriculum, to offer stimulation and guidance in the reading program, to develop library skills and habits, and to contribute to the personal growth and development of the individual. In this program the work with students and teachers is the unique contribution of the school librarian.[3]

1. Accessibility. By accessibility is meant the degree to which materials and facilities in the school are easy to use. This involves convenient, adequate, and attractive location, length of the library day, scheduling procedures, and organization of materials.
2. Instruction. One of the prime responsibilities of the school library program is to teach children to become independent users of libraries. This instructional aspect involves both the teaching of library skills according to a sequential plan from primary grades through secondary school, and the supervision of the development of these skills as they are applied in a laboratory-type environment.
3. Guidance. Of paramount importance in the school library program is guidance in reading, listening, and viewing. Personal, social, and vocational aspects of guidance are also important and can be fostered through informal contacts with individual students as well as with student assistants and other groups.

---

[2] Paul W. F. Witt, "High School Libraries as Instructional Materials Centers," *The Bulletin of the National Association of Secondary School Principals,* XLIII, No. 250 (November 1959), 112.

[3] American Association of School Librarians, *Standards for School Library Programs, Discussion Guide* (Chicago: American Library Association, 1960), pp. 7-9.

4. Service to Students and Teachers. An alert librarian continuously seeks ways to improve and expand the program of services to students and teachers. He provides information about materials for curricular, professional, and personal use. Through contacts with students and teachers and participation on curriculum committees and in faculty meetings and in-service training activities, he lends his special skills and is informed of the school's needs.
5. Publicity and Public Relations. The success of the school library program largely depends on the ability of the library staff to maintain lines of communication with classroom teachers and school administrators, as well as with lay groups, in order to make known the services and needs of the school library program.

The librarian and teacher as co-teachers

There are many avenues in the education of students where the teacher-librarian team could cooperate in providing for individual differences to enrich the students' learning experiences. The librarian as a professional leader-teacher and as a co-teacher who utilizes the library facilities can contribute much to the instructional program. In the process of providing guidance for teachers through the wider use of the library, the librarian becomes a co-teacher in improving instruction. In a friendly manner students are provided guidance and direction in the selection of suitable reading materials. The librarian as an outgoing individual makes teachers and students feel welcome in the stimulating atmosphere of the library as they seek assistance in the solution of problems. At the same time the librarian can evaluate the library facilities in terms of the program and the methods followed in the learning process.

The central library

The modern secondary school library is an instructional materials center. It has a vital role to play in supplying a variety of resources for the effective functioning of the modern curriculum. In fact, the library is the "pulse" for aiding both the students and teachers in the learning process. It is a central clearinghouse for all the instructional materials necessary to fulfill the instructional program.

The librarian provides guidance to teaching in curriculum development and to students in reading and research. A plentiful supply of stimulating and appropriate materials are essential for meeting the interests and needs of our youth. The library is a laboratory for students doing research and investigating the available resources when studying a problem or preparing a written report dealing with a special topic.

Courtesy Hanover Park High School, Hanover, N.J.

A MODERN LIBRARY

The librarian and others work together

The librarian can furnish much valuable assistance to teachers in the instructional process. This aid follows many avenues and is productive in the development of the curriculum. It should be remembered that the services of the library extends to the teachers, the individual student, and groups of students grappling with a solution for various learning problems. The well-informed teacher, who is seriously concerned with the many sciences and the increasing supply of new materials available in the library, can do much to enrich instruction for the learners. The librarian functions as a resource person for the ent're school community and in this way furnishes available materials from outside sources and through loan from other libraries.

The librarian realizes the importance acquainting teachers with the available resources of the school. Some of the ways a librarian works with the instructional staff follow: (1) bulletins are distributed to teachers noting additional new books, specific publications, and any exhibits or displays being featured, (2) bibliographies are made readily available, listing materials pertinent to a particular unit or topic, (3) conferences are held with a teacher in preparation for assembling materials dealing with a problem or topic about to be studied by a group of students, and

(4) collections of books, pamphlets, and pictures to be used in the classroom by a teacher are made available for planning and developing a unit of work. Teachers and students are encouraged to utilize the library for a laboratory lesson in doing research for the later presentation of materials to a group. The librarian works with the individual student and a committee in securing essential contemporary information and adequate background knowledge through the research facilities when the occasion arises. Students are assisted in developing proper library habits, effective skills, and research techniques that can be a continuous asset in education. Whenever the need arises teachers and subject supervisors are helped in the selection of textbook purchases and adoptions, reference sources, and other instructional tools for use in a specific subject-matter area. Classroom visits and department or committee meetings are attended by the librarian to furnish professional assistance when needed. The librarian works with the administration and community to provide the best possible education for the youth of the area.

The library and the teacher

The classroom as a learning laboratory must have a close affiliation with the library activities. It is the responsibility of the teacher to become famil'ar with the available resources of the school and local community libraries. If more fruitful learning experiences are to be acquired, the teacher has a responsibility to teach the values derived from using the resources of the library to the students. It should prove profitable for the teacher at the beginning of the school year to take classes to the library for a "refresher" given by the librarian, and at the same time to be permitted to browse through the inviting collections. Teaching students proper library habits and skills as well as the need for constant reading in the contemporary age is training for effective citizenship. Sharing the rich treasures of books is a cooperative venture. The teacher should make students aware of new materials and books available for library usage. This can be done by planning and developing new units and by special assignments.

The teacher and librarian who work on a cooperative basis can do much to make life and learning more enjoyable and functional for the students. The student in turn will develop his power of thinking effectively by becoming more discriminating in his choice of materials and by deriving greater satisfaction from his reading. Learning will be constantly extended to new horizons for those who cultivate the library-usage habit.

It might prove timely in our discussion to list the goals of the library services for the student and teacher. These goals may be listed as follows:

1. Providing a broad collection of materials spanning many subject areas and varied reading levels. . . .
2. Providing assistance to pupils and teachers in locating materials. . . .
3. Providing space for reading and research by class groups and individuals. . . .
4. Guiding students to develop effective study skills. . . .
5. Promoting lifetime habits of reading and using libraries. . . .[4]

Using the library

The modern educational program for students at the secondary level calls for the constant use of the library. The role of the librarian calls for adequate functional planning and providing essential services throughout the facilities of the library. The atmosphere of the library is a significant factor in today's educational scheme.

Educational literature generally and library literature specifically expound the philosophy that the school library is the house of knowledge; unfurling the feats of the past; interpreting the world of today; opening new intellectual frontiers; pointing out unexplored scientific horizons; ever helping the pupils to move forward to a richer personal, school, and community life. But does the administrator, teacher, pupil, visitor detect this as he walks past or through the library in your school?

The climate in the school library must be conducive to the accomplishment of these goals. It must provide a welcoming, congenial, restful atmosphere that contributes to inquiry; assists research; stimulates pleasure reading; encourages browsing; furthers magazine reading; promotes frequent questions; favors patronage at all school hours; advocates that all library materials are tools to be used not hoarded; subscribes to independent exploration of files, catalogs, bound volumes, reference materials; and permits circulation of reference materials to classrooms and all types of materials during holidays; thus always helping the pupils toward a happier and more meaningful school and everyday life. If your library climate is to be regarded as radiant, an affirmative answer to each of the above goals is necessary.[5]

The modern secondary library is in fact an extension of the learning laboratory. This in turn brings the social studies teacher and the librarian into a closer working arrangement. The social studies courses lend themselves to extensive library work. The proper use of the library is particularly important to the study of units in the modern problems course. The very nature of the courses in the senior high school necessitate that the students utilize references and current periodicals. Students bring guide sheets for a particular course to the library that contain selected references pertaining to a specific unit. Reference work has become im-

---

[4] M. F. Kennon, "Library Science in the Twelve Grade School," *The Bulletin of the National Association of Secondary-School Principals,* XLIII, No. 250 (November 1959), 43-44.

[5] J. L. Woodward, "What Type of Atmosphere Radiates from Your School Library?" *The Bulletin of the National Association of Secondary-School Principals,* XLV, No. 268 (November 1961), 134.

portant in today's social studies instruction. In this manner students take notes accurately from productive sources and properly record the pertinent references. At the same time the student is developing skill in research, organization, and evaluation of materials.

When beginning the study of a new unit, the teacher usually takes the group to the library. The teacher needs to prepare the group for the library visit by clarifying what is to be accomplished and by making sure that the assignments are understood. The teacher and librarian can both assist the group in a laboratory setting with the selection of materials suitable for individual and committee reports. The librarian can furnish displays of additional new books and recent literature pertaining to the topic under consideration. After conferring with the librarian and the teacher, the group can use the library as a materials resource center for previews and selections of films, recordings, and other materials for their particular usage. The library program, as we can see, should be an integral part of the social studies curriculum.

A copy of the outline for each social studies course presently being taught should be filed in the library. The teacher should also give the librarian a copy of each unit outline to be studied in sufficient time in order to prepare materials in advance for the particular study.

Library and the community

The community by its very nature has many resources that can be catalogued for reference materials in the school library. The community with its many opportunities for learning is actually a laboratory for social studies instruction. Some communities may have in addition to the public or municipal library resources a private collection of books dealing with some specific resource materials. All such available sources have value for reference work in addition for furnishing interesting reading material.

The school librarians may wish to correlate the activities of the public library whenever deemed advisable and profitable for students. The school and public library personnel can work cooperatively in permitting individual students to utilize the available services and resources. The teacher may also wish to take a group of students to the public library to view interesting exhibits and book displays. The public librarian can also help a committee of students who are engaged in a research project pertaining to the local community and county. Many times a local author or an authority on books may give a talk on some particular writing to which students may be invited as guests.

If the community has a radio or television station, surely the librarian can use their facilities to good advantage to keep the local community well-informed about new resources. Later in the chapter the author will list the variety of community resources available for educational purposes. The following list of worthwhile suggestions for reading and reading guidance should be studied by the social studies teacher. Reading is a most essential skill for gathering information in social studies instruction.

1. The pupil's growth in reading ability and interest is a joint responsibility of the teachers, the librarians, and the parents. . . .
2. The warm and friendly atmosphere, the range of reading materials, and the expert reading guidance of the staff encourage every boy and girl to pursue his reading interests in the school library.
3. The combined efforts of librarians and teachers are necessary for an effective reading guidance program. This implies an exchange of information regarding the interests, needs, and abilities of students and the materials to satisfy these demands.
4. The librarian works with all teachers responsible for the developmental, corrective, and individualized reading programs. . . .
5. The librarian contributes to the accelerated learning program by co-operating with the teachers in providing challenging reading experiences for the maximum development of gifted students.
6. Reading guidance in the library can be more meaningful when the librarian has access to and makes use of reading scores, intelligence quotients, and other pertinent information about the characteristics of individual students.
7. Information reported by the librarian concerning the reading behavior, library use, and attitudes of students, especially those having reading difficulties and high school students trying for scholarships and other awards, make useful additions to the reports of classroom teachers in the school records.
8. Reading guidance is implicit in almost every contact the student has with the librarian. . . . The initiative and creative ability of the librarian shape the approaches used.
9. Reading guidance in the school library . . . involves the use of recordings, television and radio programs, films, and the theater. It includes book displays, book reviews by students in school publications, assembly programs, book talks. story-telling, reading aloud, and many other techniques that are also effective.
10. Reading guidance in reference services and research and in instruction in the use of materials is also an important aspect of the program.[6]

Library personnel

A trained school librarian is needed to maintain the instructional materials center. But beyond mere maintenance, the librarian must provide planned, expert service reaching out to all teachers so that the

---

[6] American Association of School Librarians, *Standards for School Library Programs* (Chicago: American Library Association, 1960), pp. 15-17.

curriculum materials will be constantly in use in order that the collection does not become static.

The modern librarian has a significant role to play while working with teachers and students. As a teacher of teachers, she provides guidance in attacking the problem of curriculum development. As a teacher of students, she foresees the needs of youth and hastens to provide materials to meet them.

Such a concept of a school librarian is coming into being. But it cannot be realized until the librarian is released from the shackles of custodial and technical processes and is given an adequate staff to develop curricula which provide individual reading guidance both for pleasure and for correction. The library of today which employs one librarian and several student assistants is totally inadequate for the new activity programs coming over the horizon. At least two full-time librarians with additional secretarial help will be needed. They will require a large workroom and adequate office space in order to function effectively.

Then and only then can the librarian function as a coordinator of materials. Free to act in her truly professional capacity, she will be able to create in the library an atmosphere of friendliness, self-control, and self-direction. Her ability to develop such a favorable climate will stem from her sharing equal responsibility with the entire faculty in helping students to acquire good study habits and in guiding them to develop a love of books, a regard for them, and proper care of them. Her responsibility will also include the planning of a well-directed program of reading.

In addition, the librarian will be able to work with teachers in the proper use of the library as a resource center in conjunction with the classroom learning situations. The librarian would spend most of her time in cooperation with teachers and students in keeping the resource center a "live" agency. Vitality would be preserved by selecting books because of review and choice of students' editorial boards; by encouraging student assistants to organize and circulate library materials by properly assessing reading competencies and past reading experiences; by encouraging faculty and student evaluations of book reviews, book talks, group discussions, and authors' lectures; by evaluating the materials on hand after class use; by eliminating book duplication and imbalance; by encouraging student evaluation of actual needs; by discarding materials whose usefulness is outworn; by discussing and weighing materials to be discarded against the ability to replace it; by indexing and classifying materials for ready availability; by providing students with lessons in library organization; by providing catalogs of materials wherever located in the school; by cooperating with other subject areas or with the Student Council.

Finally, the librarian would then be free, also, to work with parents and adults in the community, especially in the area of book selection for the student's personal collection of books and in guiding his out-of-school reading experiences.

The Library and Guidance Service

The school library has an essential relationship to the guidance service, and the librarian is the official agent in the instructional scheme. She realizes that "close to the source of many world events is a fact that a boy and a book got together," and she guides the stimulus for worthwhile reading. Through individual conferences the librarian determines the pupil's preference for a specific type of reading material. A record is kept of his reading as a means of determining the selection of desirable books. Students are systematically exposed to interesting books and good literature. Lists of books for all reading abilities are available, and in this way the librarian assists in a remedial program. Reading clubs are organized for those pupils low in reading ability, and mimeographed materials are furnished to the teachers directing remedial instruction. Furthermore, the librarian provides suitable materials that will aid groups in preparing for school activities, including assembly programs.

The librarian assists pupils in choosing a college or in selecting a vocation. She provides catalogs and vocational materials that will aid those who wish to attend evening classes for technical training. This service extends from advising on hobbies to selecting and pursuing worthy leisure-time activities. The librarian in some high schools, as a member of the guidance committee, interviews each member of the senior class and assists him in planning his future career. The library itself provides information and education by showing vocational films, by sponsoring talks on vocations, and by furnishing career materials. Vocational bibliographies may be prepared by the librarian or by a group of pupils interested in a number of fields. Readings, research, and experiences conducted through the library facilities furnish purposeful understanding of a contemplated career.

The librarian and the social studies teacher are both aware of providing for individual differences and at the same time improving the instructional program. Each student has a goal or ambition to enter a profession or some type of work upon entering adult life. The student is eager to learn more about his career choice through the avenue of books. The gifted student needs guidance in the selection of proper materials to serve his educational needs. Students are happy to have the counseling of the librarian to help widen their reading scope and to help them develop skills in the methods of inquiry. They can gather new knowledge, develop interests, and derive the pleasure from worthwhile reading. Students with a little encouragement will develop a desire to browse and to search the avenues of knowledge to satisfy interests and solve problems. We are living in the space age that will furnish many challenges and stir the imagination of the students in quest of an education through the services and resources of the library. The librarian can supply guide lines and book lists for enriching and expanding the scope of the thinking of youth.

School librarians in the smaller communities extend their guidance services to the citizens of the town. They help select reading and procure books and other periodicals for the local people. They assist community leaders in planning their activities and special programs. The librarian can also give pupils and adults points in buying books.

Librarians give service to the school faculty and assist teachers in professional growth. The library offers recent books, professional journals, commission reports, and pamphlet materials reporting the results of experiments in various fields; provides a loan service for teachers wanting or needing materials from local, county, and state libraries; publishes a monthly bulletin for teachers informing them of lectures, forums, radio programs, guidance conferences, and conventions. The preparation of bibliographies aids teachers in their research and specific projects or units. The librarian thus provides a professional guidance service for teachers in assisting them to solve their own professional problems.

The Resources

Books

For the library to function at its maximum capacity, it must provide adequate book resources for the school's needs. These include the following areas: (1) reference books, (2) supplementary books of information, about five to ten copies of each title being adequate, (3) a stack of reserve books, to insure fair distribution for student needs when the title is much in demand and the number of available copies is restricted, (4) recreational books, for leisure-time enjoyment, for browsing, and for developmental growth, and finally (5) professional books for teacher needs and interests.

The reference collection of a high school library is exceedingly important. In order to cover all phases of the curriculum, it will total approximately one-third the entire collection in size, and one-half of it in cost. The reference books necessary for the social studies field will be extensive in scope, size, expense, and maintenance, for all books containing statistical information will have to be replaced biennially, in order to keep the statistics reasonably current. New and revised editions of standard works will also have to be replaced frequently. At least one copy, and preferably two, of each of the major works of reference should be on the shelves.

Following is a list of the standard references in the field of the social studies with which all teachers in the field should be familiar. These will not be in every school library, because the cost is great and because many of the standard works are out of print and not replaceable.

I. Encyclopedias
    A. *Encyclopedia Americana; Americana Annual*
    B. *Encyclopedia Britannica; Britannica Book of the Year*
    C. *Collier's Encyclopedia; Collier's Yearbook*
    D. *Compton's Pictured Encyclopedia*
    E. *World Book Encyclopedia; Annual Supplement*
    F. *Columbia Encyclopedia*, 2nd ed. with *1959 Supplement*
    G. Abridged Columbia Encyclopedia: *Columbia-Viking Desk*
    H. *Lincoln Library of Essential Information*

II. Dictionaries
    A. Unabridged
        1. *Webster's New International Dictionary*, 3rd ed.
        2. *Funk and Wagnalls' New Standard Dictionary of the English* Language
    B. Abridged
        1. *American College Dictionary*
        2. *Webster's New Collegiate Dictionary*
        3. *Funk and Wagnalls' Comprehensive Standard Dictionary*
        4. *Thorndike-Barnhart High School Dictionary*
    C. Specialized
        1. *Dictionary of American Slang*
        2. *Dictionary of Americanisms*

III. Yearbooks
    A. *World Almanac and Book of Facts*
    B. *Information Please Almanac*
    C. *Statesman's Yearbook*
    D. *South American Handbook*
    E. *Minerals Yearbook*
    F. *Municipal Yearbook*

IV. Atlases and Gazetteers
    A. Adams, J. T., *Atlas of American History*
    B. Bartholomew, J., *Advanced Atlas of Modern Geography*

     C. Boyd, Andrew, *Atlas of World Affairs*, rev. ed.
     D. *Encyclopedia Britannica*, XXIV, Atlas
     E. *Encyclopedia Britannica World Atlas*
     F. Goode, J. P., *Goode's School Atlas*
     G. Lord, C. L. and E. H. Lord, *Historical Atlas of the United States*
     H. *Rand-McNally Cosmopolitan World Atlas*
     I. Shepherd, W. R., *Atlas of Medieval and Modern History*
     J. ———, *Historical Atlas*
     K. *Webster's Geographical Dictionary*
  V. Histories, Source Books, and Special References
     A. Adams, J. T., *Album of American History*
     B. ———, *Dictionary of American History*
     C. *American Nation Series*
     D. *Cambridge Modern History*
     E. Campbell, Gordon and I. O. Evans, *Book of Flags*, 3rd ed.
     F. Commager's *Documents of American History*
     G. Douglas, G. W., *American Books of Days*
     H. Durant, William J., *Story of Civilization*, 6 vols.
     I. *Everyman's United Nations*
     J. Fairchild, Henry P., *Dictionary of Sociology and Related Sciences*
     K. Hart, A. B., *American History Told by Contemporaries*, 5 vols.
     L. Hazeltine, M. E., *Anniversaries and Holidays*, 2nd ed.
     M. *Heritage of America*
     N. *Encyclopedia of the Social Sciences*
     O. Kane, J. N., *Facts about the Presidents*
     P. ———, *Famous First Facts*
     Q. *Langer's Encyclopedia of World History*
     R. MacDonald, W., *Documentary Source Book of American History, 1606-1926*, 3rd ed. rev.
     S. Morris, Richard B., *Encyclopedia of American History*
     T. *Oxford Classical Dictionary*
     U. Peck, H. T., *Harper's Dictionary of Classical Literature and Antiquities*
     V. Shankle, G. E., *American Nicknames: Their Origin and Significance*
     W. ———, *State names, flags, seals* . . .
     X. Smith, E. C. and A. J. Zurcher, eds., *Dictionary of American Politics*, rev. ed., 1955
     Y. State Legislative Manual (Annual)
     Z. Statistical Abstracts of the U.S. (Annual)
     A_1. United States Bureau of the Census, *Historical Statistics of the United States, 1789-1945*
     B_1. *United States Government Manual* (Annual)
  VI. Biographies
     A. *Biography Index*
     B. *Current Biography*
     C. *Dictionary of American Biography*
     D. *New Century Cyclopedia of Names*
     E. *Webster's Biographical Dictionary*
     F. *Who's Who*
     G. *Who's Who in America*
     H. *Who Was When*
     I. *Who Was Who in America*

VII. Bibliographies
   A. Beers, H. P., *Bibliographies in American History*
   B. Howe, P. F., et al., *Guide to Historical Literature*
   C. *Key to the Past*, American Historical Assoc.
   D. Logasa, H., *Historical Fiction . . . for Junior and Senior High Schools*
   E. *Richer By Asia*, A.L.A., 1959
   F. United States Superintendent of Documents, *Selected Publications of the United States Government* (Bi-weekly)
   G. *World History Book List for High Schools*, Nat'l. Council for Social Studies
VIII. Parliamentary Practice
   A. Card, M. W. and Emma M. Wine, *Come to Order. Essentials of Parliamentary Practice*, rev. ed.
   B. Roberts, H. M., *Roberts' Rules of Order*
 IX. Periodicals Indexes
   A. Cundiff, Ruby Ethel, *101 Magazines for Schools. Grades 1-12*, 3rd ed.
   B. *New York Times Index*
   C. *Readers' Guide to Periodical Literature*
  X. Pamphlets and Serials
   A. *Headline Series*
   B. *Junior Life Adjustment Series*
   C. *Life Adjustment Series*
   D. *Oxford Social Studies Series*
   E. *Public Affairs Pamphlets*
 XI. Some Pertinent Sources
   A. *Chronicles of America Series*
   B. *Everyday Life Series*
   C. *Famous Biographies for Young People*
   D. *History of American Life* (Series)
   E. *Lands and Peoples Series*
   F. *Mainstream of America Series*
   G. *New American Series*
   H. *Pageant of America Series*
   I. *Portraits of the Nations Series*
   J. *Reference Shelf Series*
   K. *Rivers of America Series*
   L. *Teach Yourself History Series*
   M. *World in Color Series*
   N. Writers Project, *American Guide Series*

For proper ways to approach using these tools of reference, teacher and pupils might consult Rossoff's, *Using Your High School Library*,[7] or Rossoff's, *The Library in High School Teaching*, 2nd ed.[8] These manuals are based upon typical classroom situations and problems and are useful because they are readable and practical.

Supplementary books of information, taken from the regular social

---

[7] M. Rossoff, *Using Your High School Library* (New York: The H. W. Wilson Company, 1952).

[8] M. Rossoff, *The Library in High School Teaching* (2nd ed.; New York: The H. W. Wilson Company, 1961).

science collection, may be purchased in quantities from five to ten copies by the librarian to answer demands for more detailed information than can be ascertained from reference books. These may include titles of general data, perhaps from high school and college textbooks.

The reserve book collection is, of course, an administrative device to insure that books for specific needs shall be available within the library to all pupils at the time of need. Certain restrictions relative to hours of withdrawal from the library necessitate that the books shall be "reserved" for student use until a stated hour at which they may be withdrawn.

By far the most popular books in the school library will be those which provide reading for enjoyment. These will include books of historical fiction, sports, travel, adventure, and hero stories for the boys and historical fiction, romance, careers, drama, and poetry for the girls. Besides producing leisure-time enjoyment, these books will provide occasions for developmental growth when the student learns about human relationships, family living, and the customs of other nationalities, as well as standards of etiquette, modes of conduct, and ethical, moral, and spiritual values that are depicted in the lives of storybook characters.

For the teacher interested in wise counseling of youth in their developmental reading, certain bibliographies might prove helpful. These include:

Logasa, H., *Historical Fiction*, McKinley, 1960.

——, *Historical Non-Fiction*, 7th ed., McKinley, 1960.

Munson, A., *An Ample Field: Books and Young People*, American Library Association, 1950.

McAllister, M., *A Basic Book Collection for High Schools*, 6th ed., American Library Association, 1957.

Spengler, Margaret V., ed., *A Basic Book Collection for Junior High Schools*, 3rd ed., American Library Association, 1960.

Carpenter, H. M., *Gateways to American History*, H. W. Wilson Co. New ed. in preparation.

Strang, R. M., S. E. Phelp, and D. Winthrop, *Gateways to Readable Books*, 3rd ed., H. W. Wilson Co., 1958.

Heaton, Margaret M. and H. B. Lewis, *Reading Ladders for Human Relations*, rev. and enl. ed., American Council on Education, 1954.

Standard Catalog for High School Libraries, 1957 and Supplements, H. W. Wilson Co.

Hoselitz, Bert F., ed., *A Reader's Guide to the Social Sciences*, Free Press, 1959.

3,000 Books for Secondary School Libraries, R. R. Bowker Company, 1961.

Coan, Otis W. and Richard G. Lillard, *America in Fiction*, Stanford Univ. Press, 1956 (paper).

Dickinson, A. T. Jr., *American Historical Fiction*, Scarecrow Press, 1958.

Books for You, National Council of Teachers of English, 1959.

Your Reading, National Council of Teachers of English, 1960. A list for junior high schools.

Good Reading, 18th ed., R. R. Bowker, 1960.

Fadiman, Clifton, *The Lifetime Reading Plan,* World Pub., 1960.

Books for the Teen Age, N.Y. Public Library.

The collection of professional books for teachers in the field of the social studies will include the yearbooks and other publications of the National Council for the Social Studies; books in methods and techniques; bibliographies; periodicals like *Social Education, The Journal of Educational Sociology, The Social Studies;* pamphlets and brochures from institutions and commercial agencies as well as associations; courses of study, curriculum bulletins, and publications of state and local boards of education; publications from the state university about state and local history, economics, and government; leading newspaper indexes, clippings, and publications.

Periodicals

Student needs for periodicals in the social studies will vary from school to school according to the socio-economic levels, environment, cultural backgrounds, interests, and reading abilities of the pupils. Size of the periodical collection of the school library will depend upon the curriculum of the school, the budget, and the availability of materials from other sources such as the public or county library. The collection will be enhanced in its accessibility if it follows the list indexed in the *Readers' Guide.*

Not only current events periodicals like *Time, Life, Newsweek, U. S. News and World Report, American Observer,* and *Senior Scholastic* will serve the social studies program, but also magazines of every facet of American life, including literature, art, music, and the dance, because these too reflect the social trends of the period.

Pamphlets

Pamphlet materials are very helpful because (1) they are inexpensive and can be reproduced in large quantities, so that almost all the pupils can have a copy, (2) they are usually written about one specific topic, (3) they are generally very profusely illustrated with photographs of cartoon drawings, and (4) they are extremely valuable for the adolescent reader who does not care to probe for facts.

The social studies teacher should keep abreast of the sources of currently published pamphlets. The best index to publications of commercial agencies is the *Vertical File Service,* published monthly by The H. W. Wilson Company of New York City. It lists free and inexpensive materials, one-page sheets, and any brochure or circular not in serials. It is classified by subject, so that it can be readily scanned by the teacher or pupil. It appears immediately after the publication of the pamphlets, so one can obtain the materials before their stock is exhausted.

The largest number of pamphlets is published by the United States Government Printing Office, the largest publishing house in the world. Its pamphlets are invaluable for social studies use because they are written by governmental agencies and bureaus for specialized services. Also, they are a primary source material, since their contents are factual and unbiased. In addition, they are extremely low-priced publications. The Superintendent of Documents for the United States Government publishes a small, semi-monthly brochure entitled, *Selected United States Government Publications.* This is a free service which lists, without classification or analysis, various governmental pamphlets on a wide variety of subjects. For each pamphlet the following information is given: title, type of publication, summary of contents, scope, purposes, uses, limitations, the agency publishing it, and the price. To purchase these pamphlets, one must pay in advance. The Printing Office has developed a system of coupons. Enclose a postal money order with the request for coupons. Then, as orders for pamphlets are placed, the requisite number of coupons to cover the cost can be enclosed.

Pamphlets are usually filed in the school library in the "Information File" or the "Vertical File" or the "Pamphlet File." These are varied names for the four-drawer, metal or wood filing cabinet. Filing is usually done alphabetically in folders by subject headings. The headings are determined by the curriculum needs of the school.

Newspapers

The modern concept of American journalism—the responsible reporter of every phase of American life—makes the daily newspaper a documentary of inestimable value. The library collection should house a file for one newspaper of major importance as well as a newspaper index. The one newspaper of primary national significance and scope is the *New York Times.* This newspaper maintains its own index. Although the cost of this service is high, it can be most valuable in a school library. For various regions of the country the St. Louis *Post-Dispatch,* the Cleveland *Plain Dealer,* and the Milwaukee *Journal* would be of comparable value.

If the library cannot afford the daily issue, the Sunday issue of a large newspaper will be a volume of weekly happenings as well as a treatise on the arts, gardening, home economics, literature, radio, television, and travel. The Sunday magazine section of a state-wide newspaper will include serial articles on state and local history, the panorama of American life, folk arts and crafts, indigenous cultures, biographies of local figures of eminence, histories of local industries, institutions, and corporations, and inventions and artistry of local persons. It will feature the activities of the local libraries and museums. Its editorials and columns, syndicated or local, will promote thinking and will encourage analyzing issues of every consequence.

County newspapers emphasize the role of the county seat, county activities, and county government, especially judicial proceedings.

Regional or area newspapers may cover a section of common political interest—a tri-county area—or one of economic interdependence—a shopping center and its outlying rural area—or a summer resort area with similar natural resources of lakes, forests, and fish and game preserves. Newspapers published for such areas feature common interests.

Local newspapers, of course, highlight purely local history, events, issues, personalities, and developments.

The problems of the library in relation to newspaper files are these: (1) the cost of purchasing the materials, (2) the storage of the files, and (3) provision of facilities for consulting the papers. Microfilm may be one answer, but a projector would be needed. When these are beyond the budget of the school, the materials in the public or county library will have to serve. Here, inaccessibility may necessitate the restriction of the investigation to one pupil who will then report to the class.

Special documents, publications, programs

The school library, in its integration with the curriculum, must assume the responsibility for preserving and filing rare items of special local importance such as unusual program folders for special festivities or anniversaries. Particularly if the event occurs only once—opening to the public a great estate or an historical home or an auction or rare items from a private home—these programs are of tremendous value.

Today, state and local Chambers of Commerce are depending upon the local citizen's pride in the community to enhance business by "advertising" the advantages of the town, region, or state. These folders frequently include photographs and art work of memorable value. To stem population migrations, or to invite it, state governments now publish brochures showing economic advantages of the state. Some states publish yearly "calendars" or "date books" of activities within the state. The library's collections of such items can be a valuable resource of primary source materials.

Auditory and visual materials

In addition to the collections filed outside the book shelves, the library may house large maps, globes, models, museum cases, display cases, and dioramas. This is particularly true if a teaching aid is very expensive and transcends the curriculum of any one subject-area department.

Auditory and visual equipment, such as projectors, recorders, radios, and television receivers, may also be housed in the library if the number is limited, if it is not available to the school at large because of inadequate facilities, or if it is to be used by individuals or groups rather than by classes. School-owned materials such as a library of films, film strips, slides, kodachromes, recordings and transcriptions, radio and television scripts, tape recordings, materials for opaque projection—whether these are commercially or intraschool produced—should definitely be housed in the library's files for use by the entire school.

Community resources

The library must also include files of community resources, as well as publications of community import and origin. These files should include the following:

A card file of resource persons from the community, whose abilities, interests, hobbies, achievements can be of service to the school's curriculum. These must be persons who are available at school time, and who are willing to aid students.

An information file of the environment of the community—physical, economic, cultural, social—which will indicate the industries, businesses, products, institutions, agencies, welfare facilities, historical roots, and their relationship to the region, county, or state is involuable.

A file of the sources of primary source materials might include: the local municipal clerk, the county clerk, the historical association, and the local and county librarians whose offices include the development of special local collections; the local businessmen of long standing whose business history is tied up with the community and whose offices have influenced the development of the community; the files of local or regional newspapers which contain serial articles on local history and development; the local clergymen whose offices include the creation of a primary center of activity for the community; the school records in the office of the superintendent of schools or the clerk of the school board; the offices of local colleges and schools which may have been granted huge amounts of land; the local railroads' historical collections; the library collections of old and wealthy families; family Bibles and photographs and documents.

The librarian as a resource person

Because she must maintain extensive files of resource materials, the librarian becomes acquainted with all sources of materials in the area. She knows where they can be obtained. She makes contacts to permit the opening of private or special collections to the school group desiring access to them. She can, through interlibrary loan, make available to pupils the resources of great collections throughout the nation. Since she covers all areas of the curriculum, she is able to develop an over-all view of the resources in order to meet the need for a classroom problem of any scope. By knowing the interests of all the faculty members, she can inform interested groups of special talents or activities or hobbies of all school personnel from the superintendent of schools down. Her professional relationships to other librarians in the area and in the state enhance and widen the scope of this knowledge. The same can be said of dealings with museums, private collections, and business interests. She can be very helpful in the organizing of field trips. The librarian can prove to be a surprising resource for developing a classroom project.

The student and library usage

The student has many occasions for using the facilities of the library. The skill of using the major resources of the library is important for all students. Since the social studies field lends itself to many types of research projects concerning the community and state, some students may wish to examine old maps, photographs, newspapers, diaries, records, and books. Students should develop skill in cataloging the information obtained from primary sources. They should acquire an ability to make a good, comprehensive bibliography on a particular subject. The pupil who learns to collect and arrange his sources of information efficiently will be better equipped to organize his thoughts and knowledge. By carefully listing the sources and by making his notes exclusively on cards or slips of paper, the student can save much valuable time and gain working efficiency. The size usually used for this purpose is 3 by 5 in., the same size as library catalog cards. A separate card should be used for each source of information. This method allows sufficient space for brief notes about the value of each source and provides for flexibility in rearrangement of items and the addition or elimination of sources at any stage in the work. The material collected should challenge critical judgment, so that the student is given a real opportunity for making wise evaluations.

Teaching the use of the library

At the secondary level it is very important that students be able to locate materials and to use them effectively.

School librarians must assume responsibility, with the cooperation of teachers, for seeing that all pupils have instruction in this important phase of library work.[9]

There seems to be general agreement as to what topics relating to library use need to be taught. They are roughly as follows:

1. Library regulations and procedures, such as circulation routines
2. Parts of a book, especially with reference to how each may serve the reader, with emphasis on the index and its use
3. Arrangement of books on the shelves, a brief account of the ten main classes of the Dewey Decimal Classification, and the letters used to indicate certain groups of books, such as biography, fiction, and short stories
4. The card catalog as an index to books on the shelves and how to use it
5. The use of dictionaries
6. The use of encyclopedias, the types of information to be found in them, and the arrangement of different encyclopedias
7. Other reference books in the collection: biographical dictionaries, handbooks, statistical abstracts, etc.
8. Periodical indexes as a key to material in current publications useful for references purposes
9. Other indexes, such as those to fairy tales, poetry, short stories, etc.
10. How to use atlases, globes, maps, and other geographical materials
11. Types of materials in the picture collection and vertical file and how they may be used
12. How to take usable notes on and outline material as read
13. Simple form for making a bibliography of materials consulted

The last two points have to do with using materials after they have been located; they are too often ignored in programs of teaching the use of the library.

Collateral reading and the library

The resources of the school library can furnish a rich supply of books for collateral reading in the social studies program. The teacher and librarian should cooperate in providing many opportunities for the

[9] A. Wofford, *The School Library at Work* (New York: The H. W. Wilson Company, 1959), pp. 176-177. Reprinted by permission of the publisher and the author.

student to enrich his learning through the printed page. They can work together in building a desirable and current collection of materials to meet the needs of the social studies curriculum. The selection of books should be made in terms of the student's needs and interests and should be geared to the times.

Among the important purposes of reading in the social studies is the interest that is stimulated through the addition of full and accurate information and illustrations. The materials outside the ordinary data in the textbooks acquaint the students with a range of important knowledge that can be put to use in many ways. Independent thinking and sound judgment come from enlarging the range of information and lead to reading the books and periodicals of a worthwhile nature.

Reference reading is a definite part of the work because it supplies adequate background and the information for studying a topic. Some textbook material is inadequate and must be supplemented by additional reference reading. Much collateral reading is also desirable. Students should be encouraged to read widely and consistently on topics that interest them. The habit of reading is seldom acquired by chance. Most students need to be stimulated and guided in order that they may form the habit of looking to the printed page for both information and entertainment. For this reason it is essential that the social studies department inaugurate a definite program for fostering reading habits and broadening reading interests.

Students should be taught to form good reading habits along with proper study procedures. They should be shown how to select, read, and apply the knowledge obtained from books. Much of the reading should be for pleasure as well as for the acquisition of information. Teachers should require a variety of reading materials but they should use discretion in assigning outside reading. The materials may be read for oral reports, class talks, discussions, outlines, written reports, or simply for enjoyment. Students should be encouraged to take notes and to keep a record of their readings. If written book reports are to be submitted at stated intervals as a part of the course requirement, a definite plan should be followed. These reports need not be long, but the summary should be sufficient to indicate a knowledge of the book's content. All written reports should be in ink or typewritten. The following form is suggested for written reports:

Student . . . . Subject . . . . Teacher . . . .

Title . . . . Author . . . .

Publisher . . . . Publication Date . . . . Number of Pages . . . . .

    1. Summary (general theme or high points)

2. Personal evaluation and opinion (why did you select this book and would you recommend it to others?)

Every effort should be made, however, to avoid overemphasizing reading, since this course of action may be detrimental to the original purposes of the program. For some students, the reading habit is a delicate growth that must be coaxed, nurtured, and cultivated to full fruition. The social studies teacher should consider carefully individual differences in this respect, since too rigid requirements in the matter of selection of books or of written reports may stifle reading interests.

Cooperation between teacher and librarian

The individual social studies teacher is in an advantageous position to cooperate with the librarian in directing the students' attention to nearly every type of printed material found in the library and at the same time in teaching them how to use these materials effectively. Students must be systematically exposed to interesting books and good literature. The teacher should keep in mind that example is the best precept. If he, himself, visits the library frequently, uses its resources freely, and follows its procedures, he does much to "sell" the library to the students. If he, himself, is a confirmed and omnivorous reader and frequently mentions specific books he has enjoyed, he can interest students in reading.

There are many ways in which the social studies teacher, with little effort on his part, can help the librarian. If he feels that his classroom work will be enriched by the addition of a specific book or books to the library, he should suggest this purchase to the librarian. When he prepares mimeographed guide sheets for the study of a topic, a copy should be given to the librarian, so that ample time is available for assembling the materials that will be needed. For the same reason, the librarian should always be notified in advance of any assignment that will require extensive student use of library resources. Many school libraries set aside for each teacher a special reserve shelf on which are placed the important books and other materials in current demand by his classes. The social studies teacher will make the best use of this service if he keeps the librarian informed in advance about topics being studied and furnishes a copy of any book lists being used by the class. The form for library requests should be used to clarify the teacher's wants. If all teachers are furnished with these request forms, the requests can be accurately dispatched from the library and easily filed for future reference. The teacher who is sponsoring a club or other extracurricular activity will find it profitable to confer with the librarian for information and suggestions.

The social studies teacher should be aware of the training and capabilities of those students who serve as student library assistants. They are a selective group who spend time and effort in learning routine library procedures in order to aid the librarian and augment library service to both students and faculty. They serve without pay or other reward (except in those few schools where additional academic credit is given) and, because of the excellent training they receive from the librarian, can assume a great measure of responsibility in supplying needed materials. These assistants deserve and should receive respect and cooperation from all teachers.

REQUEST TO LIBRARY

Date . . . .

From . . . . To . . . .

Date . . . . Room . . . . Period . . . .

Specific Items and Instructional Needs

Topic . . . . Grade Level . . . .

General Assignment . . . .

. . . .

Materials

    Books:

        Reserve . . . . Reference . . . .

        For use in Library . . . .

        For reserve shelf . . . .

        For classroom use . . . .

        Bibliography lists available . . . .

    Periodicals:

Title   *Date*

        Pamphlets . . . .

        Magazines . . . .

Audio-Visual Aids

    Scheduled in room . . . . or send to room . . . .

Type	Number
Slides	
Films	
Pictures	
Recordings	
Filmstrips	
Map	
Graphs	
Charts	
Instruments and machines	

Remarks:

Suggestions for the teacher

1. Inform the librarian in advance of any assignment that will draw heavily upon the resources of the library.
2. Warn students that library materials must not be mutilated.
3. Allow some leniency in following book lists for required reading. Allow reasonable substitutions.
4. Encourage reading and advertise the library by appropriate bulletin board displays.
5. Express your appreciation to the librarian for the services you are given.
6. Remember that the library may not contain a complete supply of everything you want to use. The library operates on a budget, and there are other departments to be served.
7. Stress the importance of returning all borrowed books on time.
8. Return at once any library materials which you or your pupils may find in classrooms, corridors, or similar places.
9. Assign a limited number of pupils to use the same book in a short period of time.
10. Request the librarian to buy only those books about which you know something and which have definite value for the course.
11. Make appropriate and constructive use of all books that the librarian has purchased at your specific suggestion. It is very discouraging to the librarian to stretch a limited budget to include materials requested by teachers but never used in their classes.
12. Respect library rules yourself. See that all library materials you remove from the library are properly charged by the librarian or her assistants.
13. Pupils should not be sent to the library for disciplinary reasons. Library passes should be given to pupils for work in the library.
14. Be ready to help pupils with reference work in the library.

15. Use every opportunity to recommend the library facilities to the new teacher. Accept the responsibility of helping him to orient himself to the library as well as to the department.

The Role of The Library in Meeting Youth's Needs

The modern school library as an instructional materials center does much to meet the needs of secondary school students. It contributes much to the functioning of the curriculum and in meeting the individual interests of all youth. It serves as a laboratory for research where students may work individually or in groups.

In the education of all youth, from the slowest learner in kindergarten to the most intelligent senior in high school, an abundance of printed and audio-visual materials is essential. These resources are the basic tools needed for the purposes of effective teaching and learning. That the achievement of the objectives of a good school program requires the resources and services of a school library has been recognized and demonstrated for many years by school board members, administrators, teachers, parents, and other people in communities having such schools. These individuals, too, have long realized that the school library program contributes something more to the over-all education of youth than materials and services geared to curricular needs. The scope of knowledge has become too vast to be covered extensively within the boundaries of classroom instruction, superior though that instruction may be. Through the school library, these boundaries can be extended immeasureably in all areas of knowledge and in all forms of creative expression, and the means provided to meet and to stimulate the many interests, appreciations, and curiosities of youth.

The school library thus stands as a symbol for the truthful expression of man's knowledge and experiences. The extent to which many children and young people of today will be creative, informed, knowledgeable, and within their own years, wise, will be shaped by the boundaries of the content of the library resources available within their schools.[10]

By helping to meet the needs of youth in the instructional scheme, the library carries a major responsibility for the social studies curriculum at the secondary level. The student is expected to follow an active reading program that includes biographies, histories, historical novels, and related works.

The social studies classroom as well as the library are considered as laboratories for learning, study, and active research. Both contribute much in developing proper attitudes, understanding, skills, and interests. It is through the application of the modern techniques of guidance and instructional procedures that students are developing effective citizen-

---

[10] American Association of School Librarians, *Standards for School Library Programs* (Chicago: American Library Association, 1960), pp. 3-4.

ship. In the all important teaching-learning process the teacher and librarian furnish the essential guidance that fosters growth in the use of printed materials and audio-visual aids. This dual cooperation assists in many ways to promote student growth, development, and progress in the total educational program.

The school library with its many facilities, resources, and services contributes much to the total education of youth. It is in this inviting setting that many of his immediate needs and growing interests are met through reading, viewing, listening, researching, and discussing. Individual differences have always been apparent to the school librarian who could never recommend books en masse, but who knows that individual students have specific needs which must be met properly. Reading, counseling, and guidance have always been fruitful on an individual basis. Book selection for libraries has always taken into consideration the interests and needs of many kinds of readers and users. The book collection of the school library has been set up to satisfy these needs. Records of individual students' reading achievements have been maintained for purposes of reading guidance as well as for direction in utilizing materials that present a challenge.

The library environment provides students with many opportunities for developing democratic citizenship. It tends to foster a spirit of cooperation, to promote assuming and sharing of responsibilities, to encourage respect for property, and to kindle appreciation for the facilities provided for student use.

Conclusion

The secondary school library contributes much to the social studies curriculum as well as to the total educational program. It is also an important force in helping to meet the needs and interests of youth in their all-important growth process. It aids in the socialization of students and tends to promote the qualities of responsible citizenship. It provides the momentum for students to continue to use the library facilities when they enter adult life. The library with its many facets can materially help the social studies teacher and students to achieve established goals in the learning process. The experiences gained and the skills acquired through the avenues of the library should assist youth in meeting and solving problems faced later in adult society. In the process of having students, teacher, and librarian work as a team in the library and social studies learning laboratory, the essentials for fostering cooperation and the framework for democratic living in a free society are being steadily developed.

Bibliography

American Association of School Librarians, *Standards for School Library Programs*. Chicago: American Library Association, 1960.

Berner, E. R., *Integrating Library Instruction with Classroom Teaching at Plainview Junior High School*. Chicago: American Library Association, 1958.

Hook, L. and M. Gaver, *The Research Paper*, 3rd ed. Englewood Cliffs, N.J.: Prentice-Hall, Inc., 1962.

Rossoff, M., *The Library in High School Teaching*, 2nd ed. New York: H. W. Wilson Company, 1961.

Shores, L., *Instructional Materials: An Introduction for Teachers*. New York: The Ronald Press Company, 1960.

Wofford, A., *The School Library at Work*. New York: H. W. Wilson Company, 1959.

Chapter Eighteen

Audio-visual Materials

Audio-visual materials are used widely in teaching and learning social studies in order to bring new experiences to students. They help to reveal the past, illuminate the present, give meaning to content, and clarify experiences. The use of such tools of instruction is ever expanding, since television has become the most recent vehicle to invade the learning laboratory. The newer communication techniques are helpful to the skillful teacher in directing effective learning for students.

Real skill in teaching involves an insight into the teaching-learning relationship in the context of that which is to be learned. This requires a thorough knowledge and appreciation of what materials and techniques are needed for given learning tasks. Materials and techniques are means to an end—instruments to be placed in the hands of the well-informed teacher.

Learning, it is generally agreed, is effective to the degree in which the learner is involved. This participation is neither purely intellectual nor entirely overt. Ideally, it consists in the solution of a real problem by the learner himself. The implication follows that method cannot exist in a vacuum. From the teacher education point-of-view, it also follows that visual and sensory techniques can be learned best in association with the problems of the learner.[1]

---

[1] *Suggested Materials: A Guide for Planning a Course in Visual and Other Sensory Aids for Teachers,* Curriculum Services Series No. 1 (Harrisburg, Pa.: Pennsylvania Department of Public Instruction, 1958), pp. 2-3.

Learnings are enriched and interests are kindled by embarking upon new and living experiences through activities relating to a unit in progress. Many times, considerable background knowledge is needed to provide meaning for the present study. During the process of learning pupils need concrete experiences which can be made readily available. For example, a film dealing with canals may completely change the students' original ideas on the subject. With this experience the student can compare transportation of the modern age with that of the canal era. The individual and group findings and reports in conjunction with the study of a problem can be supplemented by student-made and other audio-visual materials. Even when evaluating the work and activities in progress, the teacher will find suitable films and slides especially helpful.

Some types of audio-visual materials

There are many types of audio-visual materials, old and new, for use in modern instructional process. Their use should be followed by functional activities. Visual aids comprise by far the larger proportion of those devices now included in the classification: chalkboards, tackboards, maps, globes, charts, graphs, diagrams, pictures, posters, cartoons, exhibits, models, specimens, sand tables, films, filmstrips, and slides. The chief auditory aids are radio and recordings and transcriptions; those that are both auditory and visual are sound motion pictures, sound slide-films, dramatizations, and television.

An effective teaching aid need not necessarily be limited in its appeal to the two senses of sight and hearing; the employment of as many as possible of the five senses is desirable for a complete understanding. In studying objects, specimens, models, and some exhibits, the sense of touch can also be employed to advantage. One very important type of audio-visual aid—the field trip—does frequently utilize all five senses, as pupils view scenes, hear on-the-spot explanations as well as the sounds characteristic of the setting, sniff typical odors, and touch and taste samples of products. We have a variety of combinations of these perceptions in teaching aids.

Guides for using audio-visual materials

Audio-visual materials effectively used by good teachers should improve instruction in the social studies. There are numerous applications for visual aids in the study of units and problems. However, teachers should be alert to the function of such devices in the instructional process.

The following guiding principles should govern the selection and use of audio-visual materials.

Audio-visual materials are merely aids to learning. They are not a substitute for the experience gained from an activity. They are a supplement to, rather than a substitute for, an activity. They aid materially in the development and evaluation of a problem. Modern audio-visual materials may also constitute a source of content material and may be used to enrich, clarify, or interpret content material. The teacher is still responsible for the organization of content material, the planning of instructional procedures, and the direction of student activities. However, in the intelligent use of audio-visual materials, he has at his disposal a wealth of resources to aid him in accomplishing more effectively the various phases of his work.

A definite purpose must attend the use of any type of audio-visual aid. All types of audio-visual materials are interesting to students. However, this interest factor, itself, constitutes a danger. Audio-visual materials that are used merely for their entertainment value contribute nothing to learning and can scarcely be considered as teaching aids. A definite purpose must characterize every application of audio-visual materials in the classroom. The teacher must have this purpose clearly in mind and must plan his procedures so that his purpose is accomplished most effectively.

Audio-visual materials must be carefully selected. Numerous types of audio-visual aids are available for use in connection with social studies materials. With so wide an opportunity for choice, the teacher must exercise judicious care in selecting the aid that best suits his purpose. He should learn how to evaluate each different type of audio-visual aid so that, for example, he knows a good still picture or a good motion picture from a poor one. In addition, he must learn how to balance the respective merits of each type, so that he does not waste time or befog the issue by showing a motion picture when a still picture would accomplish the same purpose. Since the selection of audio-visual aids should be made on the basis of their fulfillment of a definite need, the grade level and maturity of the students is an important factor.

Effective techniques must accompany the use of aids. Audio-visual aids are valuable tools in the hands of the social studies teacher, but they must be skillfully used. A hammer is an important aid in building a house, but no carpenter lays a hammer among the boards and nails and expects it to accomplish work while he stands idly by. The extent to which audio-visual materials are effective in the classroom is determined by the skill of the teacher in relating them to the learning activities.

The use of audio-visual materials should stimulate further learning activity. The teacher who finds that any teaching aid does not contribute effectively to the learning process should revise his procedures. Audio-visual aids should be broadening rather than narrow; students should be stimulated to further learning activity. Aids that are geared to a lower level of instruction should not be used. Too frequent or too abundant use of audio-visual aids, particularly in the senior high school, will tend to defeat their real purpose, since students may be led to rely upon aids although they are perfectly capable of conducting independent investigation. Teaching aids that arouse curiosity, stimulate new interests, and challenge students to furnish research should be substituted for those that merely satisfy.

Some purposes for using audio-visual materials

The specific instructional techniques that the social studies teacher should employ in connection with audio-visual materials will depend upon the purpose for which he is using the aid. The chief purposes may be classified as follows:

Introducing. Audio-visual materials constitute an exceptionally effective means for introducing a unit, a problem, or an activity. Through the effective use of such aids, the problem of motivation takes care of itself as students study and discuss materials that attract their attention, arouse their curiosity and form the basis or directive for future activities.

Clarifying, Supplementing, and Enriching. Audio-visual materials should be used to clarify instruction either for the entire group or for the individual student at any point in the work where such clarification is needed. Skillful teachers become adept at foreseeing the exact difficulties students may encounter in the learning process and take steps to provide the needed audio-visual aids. They should frequently be used to supplement and enrich learning activities. Variety is essential for effective learning. Students need many kinds of experiences, emotional as well as intellectual, in order to develop. They should engage in field trips and dramatizations, study maps and pictures, examine models and specimens, and participate in every type of desirable experience that the social studies can furnish.

Concluding and Summarizing. Many times during the learning process—at the end of the planning period or an activity, and at various stages within the study of a problem or a unit—conclusions should be drawn and summaries made. The teacher will attempt to visualize the progress and concluding achievement of all group activities in order to clarify learning and insure understanding. Various individual problems must be correlated with each other and with the larger theme; activities must be correlated and unified with the general topic or unit; and each topic or unit must be properly related to those that precede and follow.

For the sake of continuity and perspective, the process of summarizing must usually proceed on a group rather than on an individual basis. Audio-visual materials of all types should be employed in the summary or conclusion of a unit.

Evaluating. Audio-visual materials may be utilized in many ways to evaluate the outcomes of learning in the social studies. In fact, students can evaluate the various types of visual aids used in teaching the unit. How did the information supplied by the types of audio-visual materials used help us with the problem studied? Some teachers use maps as a means of effectively evaluating the students' understanding of geography, history, and current events. For example, a projected map on which specific areas, geographic locations, and political divisions or cities are numbered can furnish the basis for identification purposes. An individual outline map in the hands of a student can evaluate his knowledge just as well as a piece of examination paper, provided the questions are carefully phrased. Graphs, charts, diagrams, and cartoons should also be used occasionally for evaluation purposes whenever the problem under consideration makes them appropriate. The social studies teacher may at first find difficulty in constructing evaluation devices around audio-visual materials; in fact, such a procedure may not always be feasible. However, such techniques can be developed with some experimentation and pioneering on the part of the teacher. The outcomes generally reveal increased student interest and enthusiasm for the work and learning in progress.

Providing pupil activity. In terms of modern usage pupils should be encouraged to utilize audio-visual materials by themselves in presenting projects, committee reports, and individual presentations. This usage would be pertinent to modern seminar groups on the high school level where students present their research findings.

Since effective materials often are teacher and pupil prepared, audio-visual materials afford pupils experience in the production of such materials. This is a definite learning situation for the pupil.

Good teaching and learning utilizes all types of creative materials in addition to commercially prepared items.

Some Basic Aids

The chalkboard

The chalkboard, a contrast from the old-style blackboard, is of modern design and may be black, white, yellow, or green. It serves as a functional aid in the instructional process, and the social studies teacher finds that the chalkboard has wide utility. It serves to illustrate ideas for giving directions, for outlining, for recording progress of work, for diagramming, for developing plans, and for summarizing.

Pupils use the chalkboard for many phases of their learning activities, including both individual and group work. Committees should use it to develop problems, to plan individual distribution of responsibility, to check on individual progress, to post notices, and to evaluate purposes.

A few suggestions for using the chalkboard are as follows: write legibly and sufficiently large, keep chalkboard and erasers clean, make drawings and sketches, have plenty of space to work, prevent overcrowding of material, employ color for emphasis, meaning, and variety, plan chalkboard work in advance, and strive for originality and creative techniques as they relate to the work.

The beginning teacher should not be afraid to draw or sketch on the chalkboard when the need arises. He should check on chalkboard legibility thoroughly and frequently. Experience and practice will aid the teacher in being more effective in using this teaching aid. Walk around and view your writing as it appears to pupils from all angles of the room. Make this helpful device an important instructional aid.

The tackboard

The tackboard (bulletin board or work display panel) is a valuable aid to the social studies teacher. As an instructional and motivating device, it should be utilized to stimulate and enrich a learning situation. The social studies tackboard should be one of the important centers of classroom activity and interest. The teacher should make frequent reference to the current display as it relates to work in progress, and students should be encouraged to contribute to its effectiveness.

Tackboard displays of graphic materials can aid the instructional process in many ways. Among the purposes which may be served by the tackboard display are: attracting attention, creating an interest in a specific topic or problem, furnishing an additional aid for learning, cultivating the habit of observation and evaluation, motivating pupil activities and discussions, stimulating exploration, critical thinking, and creative effort, and revealing the outcomes of probing into a problem or studying a unit. Displays should be attractive, appropriate, meaningful, timely, and interesting. They may include pictures, posters, pamphlets, cartoons, graphs, maps, news items, charts, book jackets, bulletins, magazine articles, and also samples of pupils' creative work, such as outlines, project booklets, book reports, and maps. Each tackboard display should tell a story. It should be a unit that clearly focuses attention on one central theme. The topic or theme for the display depends upon the classroom activity or discussion at the moment.

Displays should be simple and well balanced. A preliminary sketch will aid in planning an attractive and striking arrangement. As a general rule, pictorial materials should be consistent with the educational level of the group. A definite but short title should be chosen. All labeling should be simple and clearly discernible.

Different types of study displays should be used for variety and to create attention and interest. One arrangement which usually inspires much pupil interest is a "Who's Who" display featuring personalities prominent in current news or in the period of history being studied. The bulletin board can also motivate a program of supplementary reading. Such a display can include book reviews or interesting advertisements. Book jackets, borrowed from the library, will add color and attractiveness. An occasional display may be devoted to the major sport of seasonal interest with playing schedules, feature articles, pictures of players and teams, and statistics on batting averages, touchdowns, points scored, or league standings. If space permits, one bulletin board may well be allotted to the regular display of such materials.

The following suggestions may be helpful for the teacher in arranging a study display on a tackboard: avoid overloading and crowding materials, use short and interesting titles, arrange related items, trim the edges of all articles before posting, avoid sensational articles, give recognition to leisure-time activities, consider color, enlarge the study display with supplementary exhibits and materials, encourage pupils to share in the thinking and planning of displays, conserve materials for future use, discard useless and ephemeral articles, have an active display for all learning, and evaluate all displays in terms of their productivity for learning.

Pupil committees can accept responsibility for the arrangement and posting of materials and also for their removal and filing. These committees should be changed frequently, preferably every week. Both pupils and teacher should work in close cooperation with the librarian and the head of the art department. Such pupil activities aid in creative expression, exploration, and social training.

Modern versions of the tackboard such as magnetic boards and hook 'n' loop boards (for display of third-dimensional objects) widen the application of the display principle.

Textbooks and instructional materials

Textbooks and reference books, the basic tools for learning found in every learning laboratory, contain a wealth of valuable illustrations that should be drawn upon. These illustrations are directly related to the textual material which they accompany and constitute one of the best information sources of visual materials. The social studies teacher should especially consider the pictures and maps that are found in abundance among these illustrations, since they will excel in quality and will be appropriate for many purposes. Much thought and discrimination is applied to the illustration of modern texts and references. The social studies teacher who wishes to establish an efficient program that employs visual materials will do well to begin with the meaningful use of these illustrations.

Pamphlets, periodicals, and bulletins are also a valuable source of visual materials for social studies classes. They keep textbooks up to date by presenting contemporary topics, and, in general, the illustrations included are worthy of consideration. There are many instances where such materials form the best possible aid to effective instruction. It is frequently impossible to place individual copies of such material in the hands of pupils, but opaque projection allows the entire class to study the various illustrations selected or even whole paragraphs of essential information.

Pictures

A good picture must be accurate; if it portrays a period of history, for example, the details of costume, architecture, transportation, and the like must be faithfully reproduced. The picture must be sufficiently complete to give adequate meaning to the subject it is intended to illustrate. A picture of unfamiliar objects or geographical formations should include a familiar object, so that relative size is clearly shown. Whatever is displayed should be clearly discernible and unhampered by confusing details. Color adds attractiveness, but the social studies teacher should be very critical in evaluating a colored picture for classroom use. An accurate black-and-white picture should be used in preference to one in which color is applied too generously or inaccurately. Pictures should be of appropriate size for their intended use.

Techniques for using pictures

Social studies teachers should be cautious in the selection of pictures and in their application to classroom instruction. Pictures are interesting to pupils and serve to stimulate discussion and enliven the teaching-learning situation, but they may too easily become the end itself. The picture should be shown for a purpose. A definite need for illustration should exist, whether for recognition, comparison, or clarification. The picture should promote constructive thinking rather than serve merely as a means of entertainment.

Specific techniques for the presentation of pictures should be developed. If pictures are being used by the teacher as an aid to instruction, the attention of the entire class should be focused upon one picture at a time. The pictures should not be passed among the pupils, since pictures used in this manner immediately become a source of entertainment rather than an aid in achieving a common purpose. Instead, they should be thrown upon the screen by opaque projection or, if very large, may be exhibited from the front of the room. An approach or introduction should precede the showing of the picture to prepare the pupils. Discussion or summary should follow in order to make sure that all pupils have gained an adequate and complete understanding.

The social studies teacher who hopes to gain the maximum value from the classroom use of pictures should be systematic in collecting, analyzing, classifying, and filing them and in planning their appropriate application. He should analyze each picture in relation to its intended use and prepare a series of questions that will aid pupils to interpret and evaluate the information it furnishes. Once prepared, the questions may be written on the back of the picture or typewritten card. The card should be kept in a pocket attached to the picture where it will easily be available. A suitable pocket can always be made for this purpose by pasting a piece of wrapping or an envelope to the back of the mounting.

Posters

The poster is designed to convey a single idea or story both simply and clearly. Posters can be used to stimulate thought and interest and to provide for the general development of concepts and impressions. They are usually attractive and employ a few key words. Color, size, and design do much to make the poster a dynamic medium and an effective learning device. Good lettering helps to attract the eye and emphasize the basic idea. As a teaching aid the poster should be analyzed so that its message may be effective. Posters can be made by the pupils to illustrate or explain government activities, contemporary problems, geographical influences, and other phases of life in a democratic society. Posters can also be used to create interest and to arouse enthusiasm in conjunction with specific activities or programs such as a community survey, a field trip, or a pageant.

Pupils should be taught the techniques of poster making. They should be encouraged to employ originality and creativeness and to think in terms of appropriateness of design. Evaluation, as well as teacher guidance and direction, is important. The poster is a many-purpose aid and, in addition to the teaching and learning situation, can easily be used effectively throughout the entire school program.

Cartoons

Cartoons usually tell a story or express a particular idea in a simple and yet humorous manner. They are found in newspapers, periodicals, and even textbooks. They usually deal with current topics of the times in different phases of society. The cartoon has a special appeal, attracts attention, and has a natural interest for pupils. They are specifically constructed to emphasize a point or issue and convey an idea. The caption and symbols utilized are vivid, supply information, and require reflective thinking for the correct interpretation. Cartoons can be projected on a screen as the teacher explains their essential nature. They are symbols rather than accurate presentations and achieve their effect through caricature, exaggeration, and satire; however, they present only a single point of view. Pupils should acquire considerable familiarity with cartoons if the cartoon is to be used effectively as an aid to learning.

The selection, interpretation, and evaluation of a cartoon for instructional purposes is important. Cartoons are sometimes difficult for pupils to understand. By questioning and discussing, the skillful teacher can effectively teach the characteristics of the cartoon. These teaching aids can be used as a motivating device as well as for summarization. Pupils who understand cartoons like to work with them, to talk about them, and to draw them.

Cartoon drawing by pupils is desirable and can be a worthwhile activity. Producing good original cartoons is not an easy task. It will require practice, imagination, and the patience to achieve good results. The social studies teacher has many opportunities to use cartooning in teaching. He must guide and direct pupils in drawing cartoons in order to reveal the understanding, learning, and knowledge they have acquired through the work.

Globes and maps

Globes and maps are effective teaching aids for helping pupils to learn about the world. They are useful in showing locations, directions, distance, and relative size. The globe, which is a scale model of the earth in three dimensions, has on its surface the only kind of map that can give the pupils a true conception of geographical relationships. Globes are studied with a high degree of interest by young children. They furnish a basis for reading a physical-political map. In the study of geography, the globe is well adapted to help the pupil visualize man's relationship to his environment. The air-age globe is particularly helpful in demonstrating airplane distances between countries and in describing the dynamics of air transportation.

Maps used in conjunction with globes are valuable instructional materials in the social studies. They are valuable in providing us with important knowledge about geographic regions and political areas. Pictures provide a foundation for map reading and pupils soon understand that map symbols have meaning. Pupils should be taught to derive information from globes and maps. They should be able to locate countries, rivers, and mountains. To compare and contrast different areas of the world is very important for understanding modern society. Each social studies teacher should acquire a good supply of maps for instructional purposes. Some map projections are: physical, political, physical-political. Special-purpose maps include such items as weather, population, rainfall, climate, roads, and history. These information-giving devices should be of sufficient size, accurate, up to date, of good color, and yet simple enough for comprehension.

Charts

The word *chart* is the most inclusive of all the terms which have been applied as designations for audio-visual materials. Under charts may be included both maps and cartoons, diagrams, tables, and graphs. There are, however, other types of charts that do not fall entirely within these specific classifications. Most common among these are tree charts, stream charts, and flow-of-organization charts. Flow charts make use of rectangles or other geometric figures to represent separate steps or items, and connecting lines to indicate the flow of relationship. A flow chart is frequently used to show relationship between the various branches of government or other organizations. Tree charts and stream charts, although representing opposing concepts, have a striking resemblance; the former begins with a major source, the trunk of the tree, and depicts development in many directions, the branches. The stream chart begins with minor sources, the tributaries, and shows how the various sources converge into the main stream. A common example of a tree chart is the representation of a natural resource, such as oil, and its different by-products.

Diagrams

It is somewhat difficult to distinguish between a diagram and several other kinds of charts. Some writers use the term *diagram* to include area graphs; others prefer to limit the term by insisting that no pictorial elements may be present. Perhaps the best basis for determining what is and what is not a diagram is the fact that a diagram explains rather than represents. On this basis, a flow chart may, in some cases, also be considered a diagram. Diagrams aid the social studies teacher in explaining the various phases of man's natural environment, governmental processes, or the operation of mechanical devices. Examples of ways in which diagrams may be applied are: (1) to explain how coal is formed, how erosion takes place, or how a hurricane develops, (2) to show how a constitution may be amended, or how a bill becomes a law, or (3) to explain how Eli Whitney's cotton gin worked.

Tables

Many kinds of tables may be considered under the heading of charts; in fact, these have sometimes been designated as tabular charts, table charts, or time charts. The table which is, perhaps, most generally known to social studies teachers and found in the appendix of nearly every American history textbook is the chronological table of the Presidents of the United States, with separate columns listing the states from which they came, the dates of their births, deaths, and inaugurations, their party affiliations, and the Vice Presidents and Secretaries of State who served under them. Another well-known table is one of the states in alphabetical order, showing the date of admission to the Union, previous status, area, population, capital, and representation in Congress. Various kinds of chronological tables may be used in connection with the study of history. Statistical tables are indispensable in economics.

There is no precise limit to the number of columns that may be included in a table. Many chronological and statistical tables have but two columns; many others have as many as ten or twelve. The chief caution about tables is that columns of figures are difficult to read and interpret; therefore, if a table that is composed of figures alone is to be of help to pupils, it should contain very few columns. In this case, it is better and less confusing to use two or more separate tables or to use a graph instead of a table.

Graphs

Graphs are an excellent means of presenting quantitative data in a form that enables pupils to understand fundamental or specific relationships. There are several kinds of graphs that should be used in presenting statistical materials in the social studies. Students should become sufficiently familiar with these, so that they are able to interpret them correctly and to construct them accurately. In fact, the best method of learning how to interpret a graph is by learning how to construct it. When beginning instruction in the making of graphs, the social studies teacher should furnish simple sets of figures to be represented and should insist upon accuracy of representation. The understanding of graphs is encouraged in this way and will lead to intelligent handling of more complicated materials later.

The *bar graph* is an effective method of representing relative amounts or values, so that comparisons can be made at a glance. The bars may run either horizontally or vertically from a base representing zero. The horizontal type with the scale of values placed at the bottom is usually easier for pupils to construct and to interpret. Bars may be plain, colored, or crosshatched. Plain bars are easier and quicker to make, but since they do not show up very well, it may be advisable to paste in pieces of colored paper or strips of colored cellophane tapes. At any rate, pupils should not be asked to spend time in laboriously filling in or crosshatching when they are making graphs merely to learn graph construction. If the bar graph is used to represent quantities, so that accurate comparisons may be easily made, all bars must be of the same width, all bars must start on the same line, and the spaces between them should be equal. The graph should have a title, and each bar should be labeled, either within or at the base of the bar, so that it may be readily identified. Choice of scales is important. In dealing with large numbers, such as populations which run into millions, round numbers must be used. Graphs can be used to a much better advantage when the *number* of amounts to be compared is not too large and complicated.

The *circle graph*, or "pie" graph, is used to represent the relationship between a whole and its various parts. Circle graphs are readily interpreted and easy to make, although a certain degree of skill in mathematics is necessary to plot their construction. Since we are dealing with a whole and its parts, we let the entire circle represent 100 per cent. Then, since the sum of all the angles at the center of any circle is 360 degrees, we figure that 1 per cent will be represented by a central angle of 3.6 degrees. After determining the percentage of each of the separate parts to be shown, we multiply each percentage by 3.6 and, using a protractor, construct central angles of the required number of degrees, allowing each line drawn to extend to the circumference of the circle. A label should be placed inside each sector giving the name of the quantity and the percentage it represents. Some consideration should be given to the arrangement of the various angles according to size, since a circle graph looks better if small sectors are not scattered about among the larger ones. Circle graphs may be used in the social studies to show the various items in a family or in a government budget, how a single tax dollar is spent in a local community, the percentage of various crop totals produced by the different states, or any other kind of data in which a significant relationship exists between the whole and its parts.

The *line graph* is used to show fluctuations and trends in the value of one variable in relation to another variable. Line graphs can depict slight variations easily and accurately but are more difficult to read than the bar graph or the circle graph. However, since line graphs are so frequently found in textbooks, newspapers, and periodicals, it is very important that all pupils learn how to interpret them. The line graph is made on a grid marked off by horizontal and vertical lines. Two scales of values are needed: horizontal and vertical. These are written outside the graph at the bottom and left side, respectively. Since most line graphs are used to indicate the fluctuation of some quantity at different periods of time, the horizontal scale of values usually represents hours, days, months, years, or decades. The vertical scale represents the different values of the quantity and the fluctuations that are being charted. The title may be placed at the top or at the bottom of the graph.

Various types of *areal figures,* such as squares, circles, or triangles can be used to represent a limited number of quantities for the purpose of comparison. For example, two squares of different sizes can represent the number of automobiles in use in 1910 and in 1940. However, this type of graph has a number of disadvantages. Fewer items can be effectively represented in an areal graph than in a bar graph. Many areal graphs, even those found in printed materials, are inaccurate or at least susceptible to an inaccurate interpretation, since the figures may use height, area, or even volume as the ratio of comparison. Even if the ratio used is clearly explained, it is still difficult to interpret some graphs of this type since visual comparisons of solid figures or pictorial symbols are usually inaccurate.

If the social studies teacher wishes to use the areal graph accurately, he should use areal figures (squares and circles are best) rather than solids or pictorial symbols. He should also remember that, mathematically, the ratio of areas is the same as the squares of their dimensions. For example, if the second square is to represent a figure four times the size of the first, the side of the second square must be twice as long as the side of the first square, not four times as long. If the second circle is to be nine times the size of the first, the radius must be three times, not nine times, as long. Correct ratios between given sets of statistics are difficult for students to compute accurately and to apply to these areal figures. Therefore, although it may be advisable for students to construct two or three simple areal graphs in order to learn how to interpret them, as a general rule bar graphs, rather than areal graphs, are preferable in presenting original material.

The *pictorial graph* is valuable because it appeals to the interest and imagination of the student. In the most common form it resembles the bar graph except that comparisons are expressed by means of a varying number of symbols rather than by bars of varying lengths. Like the bar graph, the pictorial graph compares large numbers approximately rather than exactly. Since the symbols themselves are interesting, working with them, either in interpretation or construction, is usually more fun for students than working with lines, bars, or circles. For this reason, pictorial graphs are sometimes more effective visual aids than are graphs of other types.

When making pictorial graphs, pupils should be careful to choose symbols that are appropriate to the material, simple to construct, and easy to understand. For example, if a student is making a pictorial graph of the amount of wheat produced by the different states, he might appropriately use as his symbol a basket of wheat, a pile of wheat, a bag of wheat, a sheaf of wheat, or a head of wheat. He should not use a tiny map of the state, a figure of a human being, or a farm implement, since his symbol must suggest wheat and nothing else. After deciding upon his symbol, he should reduce it to its simplest form by removing all unnecessary details. Symbols that can be represented in silhouette are usually the most effective.

It is desirable for social studies students to make one or more of these graphs in order to understand them thoroughly. Perhaps pupils will wish to continue making pictorial graphs occasionally to present certain of their findings more effectively when submitting reports. However, considerably more time is required to construct an effective pictorial graph than an equally effective bar graph, and students, particularly in the senior high school, should not be allowed to concentrate upon this type of graph. They should not waste time in choosing, drawing, and coloring beautiful symbols when a good bar graph would serve the same purpose.

Exhibits

Exhibits can be used to trace the steps in the manufacturing processes from the raw material to the finished product, in the progressive developments in science and invention, in the history of transportation and communication, or in the growth of a state, community, or a local area. In geography, exhibits of such things as rocks and minerals or the products and industries of a region can do much to add interest and realism. Much of the material used in the various exhibits can be obtained directly from industries, museums, and similar sources that are frequently willing to lend it for relatively long periods of time. The social studies teacher should also be on the alert to capitalize upon any pertinent exhibits that may be displayed in the community or within reasonably accessible distance. Public libraries, museums, banks, industries, historical societies, and other institutions usually prepare social exhibits from time to time. Many of these can furnish a direct aid to social studies instruction and can be made the basis of a field trip, a committee report, or a specific assignment.

For many purposes, exhibits that are prepared in the classroom or in the school are more effective. The collection, preparation, and display of such an exhibit can be carried out by students of either the junior or the senior high school under the direction and supervision of the teacher. Whether the students are preparing the exhibit merely for their own satisfaction or to show others what they are doing in the classroom, they will gain many real experiences in the process. Frequently, an exhibit that was intended as a strictly private venture becomes such a success that the students discover occasions for displaying it to the school and community.

Like other teaching aids, the exhibit should tell a story. It should be built around a central theme directly related to the unit or topic being studied. Labels should be used whenever they are necessary for explanation, but all labels should be brief and concise. Written or printed material should be kept to a minimum. Much thought should be given to the arrangement of the separate items. If the story is to be told effectively, all unnecessary details should be eliminated and the exhibit should be so arranged that the eye is first attracted to the beginning of the story, then on to the other steps in progression. Crowded displays should be avoided. If insufficient space is available, it is better to limit the theme than to crowd the materials.

Some Activities

Murals

Murals can be planned and produced as a project by students in connection with the study of a selected problem or unit. This creatively designed picture or scene usually tells a story or stresses a definite idea. It can be drawn on the chalkboard, heavy construction paper, or placed upon the wall. Original sketches drawn by students may be enlarged through the opaque projector and then traced on walls, sheets of paper, or the chalkboard, thus becoming a scale-enlargement sketch for the mural. The mural may be done with paint, colored chalk, or crayon, and sometimes pasted paper is used for those murals placed on the tackboard.

Those that are made as a permanent fixture on a classroom wall are sprayed with shellac or "fix-it" to keep the colors brilliant. Murals are attractive and serve to decorate the learning laboratory.

Field trips

Field trips provide an excellent means for obtaining firsthand information and for studying the community. The resources of any community are many, and each can furnish rich learning experiences. The amount and variety of the experiences that may be productive for group learning will vary with each area. Definite planning, study, discussion, preparation, follow-up, and evaluation are essential if the full value and objectives of the field trip are to be achieved.

Dramatizations

Dramatizations are a type of activity that may be considered as both audio and visual. They can occasionally be applied to the social studies, particularly in the junior high school, to arouse interest and furnish variety. Students enjoy writing the dialogue, preparing costumes and scenery, and thoroughly investigating the event to be dramatized. Dramatizations should be simple, and the instructional values should be paramount. At the senior high school level the materials may be presented as a radio script or may assume the form of a town meeting, a debate, or a panel discussion.

School-made films

Students in a particular group, or the entire student body, can produce their own films. They can do the planning, prepare the script, do the photography, and furnish the narration. Such films may be the direct outgrowth of activities in a particular unit. They may also depict some historical event in the community or state. The project can be accomplished under the guidance of a competent teacher with some assistance from other members of the school staff. If the equipment is accessible, the expense need not be too great. The learning that is furnished by such a project is both interesting and stimulating. The educational experiences are numerous and the functional values derived from such a project are well worth the time and effort. A film provides a lasting record of some particular activity or event for the school.

Projection Equipment
and Materials

Many of the purposes of using visual aids in the social studies can be accomplished only if the entire class can study a single item at a time. If a lesson or an activity is to be introduced through the use of a picture, every student in the class must be able to see the picture clearly during the introductory procedure. Large pictures, large wall maps, or smaller maps and pictures in each student's textbook pose no problem in this connection. However, many other essential visual aids cannot be used effectively unless they are projected upon a screen, so that all students may focus attention upon the same item at the same time.

The opaque projector

The opaque projector provides an effective means for projecting on a screen materials for study. A picture, map, drawing, cartoon, chart, clipping, graph, diagram—even a flat object or a specimen—can be readily projected for group discussion. The social studies teacher with the opaque projector has many opportunities to use a wide variety of materials. In fact, for teaching purposes, practically any type of flat material up to a certain size can be accommodated in a projector. The new and improved projectors have an area of 10 by 10 in. for projection in contrast to the older 6 by 6 in. size on the platen.

Illustrations from the page of a textbook can be enlarged and even projected on a large piece of work paper or on the chalkboard. Students can easily trace the particular material in any size desired. When drawing a mural on the wall of the classroom, the opaque projector is also useful for the projection of students' work. Students themselves should be allowed and encouraged to use the opaque projector in connection with individual and group reports.

Opaque projection is economical. It saves time, and materials are abundant and easily obtained. After the original expense, the equipment itself is inexpensive to maintain, and good projectors—some of them with slide attachments—can be obtained. Some newer projectors are equipped with special ventilation devices so that materials are protected from heat. Since opaque projection operates on the principle of reflection, a darkened room is necessary for maximum effectiveness. However, a partially darkened room may sometimes be satisfactory if the projector is placed nearer the screen.

The slide projector

One of the oldest types of projection devices is the lantern slide projector, or stereopticon, that projects slides of standard size, 3¼ by 4 in. In recent years individual 2 by 2 in. slides have taken their place as teaching aids along with the 3¼ by 4 in. standard slide. Slide projection does not require so dark a room as does the filmstrip or opaque projection. Usually, if slides are clear, only the direct light from the windows need be excluded. An additional advantage of the stereopticon is that it can be used nearer the screen than other types of projectors. This enables the teacher or lecturer to operate the machine from the front of the room, where his explanations or comments are more easily heard and where he can reach the screen for demonstration. Slides are inexpensive, but proper filing and storage are essential for their care and availability. Slide production is a worthwhile learning activity.

Silhouette Slides. Silhouette slides can be made from freehand drawings or tracings on dark paper. The silhouette itself is cut out and either pasted to a single glass plate or fastened between the two plates.

Etched and Plain Glass Slides. The chief difficulty encountered in drawing directly on glass slide plates is that the smooth surface of the glass is not receptive to ink, pencil, or crayon. This difficulty may be overcome either by using glass that has been etched on one side (that is, roughened by means of acid or other agent) or by preparing plain glass, so that it will take the chosen medium. A plain glass slide that has been thoroughly cleaned with soap and water or with a dry-cleaning fluid, and then dried, will take India ink satisfactorily, providing a good pen point is used. If crayon, pencil, colored inks, or water colors are to be used, further preparation of the surface will be needed. The surface may be painted with a coat of thinned clear lacquer or washed with a gelatin solution made by dissolving ordinary cooking gelatin in warm water in the ratio of one-half teaspoonful of gelatin to five tablespoonfuls of water. The drawing should be first prepared upon good drawing paper and then traced onto the glass slide. Care must be taken to prevent either dust or natural oils from the hand from spoiling the surface on the slide. Many of these slides will be short-lived, and, in this case, a cover glass will not be needed. However, there are many possibilities for making excellent slides of maps, charts, and other drawings that will prove valuable as a permanent part of the collection, especially if some of the students have some artistic ability.

Cellophane Slides. Excellent slides may be made on either clear or amber cellophane. A typewritten slide of this type should be made with fresh sheets of carbon paper. The typing is done directly on the carbon paper with the ribbon removed as in making a stencil. If the cellophane is placed between two pieces of the carbon paper, the slide will be better, since the impression is made on both sides of the cellophane. A flexible mask made from heavy paper may be used for keeping the margin, or the margin may be indicated by making pencil marks on the first piece of carbon paper. By allowing a ½ in. margin on all sides of a 3¼ by 4 in. slide, the maximum number of typewritten lines will be fourteen and the maximum number of letter spaces in each line will be thirty-six for elite type and thirty for pica type. The cellophane should be placed between two glass plates. Cellophane slides of drawing, maps, graphs, and similar materials may be made with India ink if great care is taken. Slides with striking color effects can be produced by combining pieces of different colored cellophane with drawings made on slide glass.

Plastic Slides. Several types of plastic materials can be used for slides instead of glass. These include Plastacele and Lumarith. Both of these come in sheets that can readily be cut to size and, when frosted or etched on one side, are very satisfactory for the purpose. Slidecraft, another plastic material, has been developed for the specific purpose of making slides. It comes already cut and masked for margins, in both the standard sizes, 3¼ by 4 in- and the smaller 2 by 2 in. It is unbreakable and light in weight. The slides may be drawn with pencil, ink, or crayons, or they may be typed or printed.

The Photographic Slide. A photographic slide is obtained from an original negative by making a positive print directly upon a piece of sensitized slide glass or by using a direct positive film. Photographic slides are the type most commonly supplied by commercial firms and most frequently purchased or rented for use in schools. The Polaroid Corporation through its camera and film now provides a simple means for the teacher and pupil to prepare photographic 3¼ by 4 in. and 2¼ by 2¼ in. transparent slides which may be projected immediately and require no additional laboratory processing or developing. Original photographic slides may be made by teachers and by the more advanced students who have the equipment and a natural bent for photography. Either black-and-white or color film may be used. Slides made from the former may be hand colored, if desired.

Filmstrips or Filmslides. The filmstrip (also called filmslide, slide-film, stripfilm) consists of a series of still pictures printed on strips of 35mm motion-picture film. Each of the individual pictures is known as a frame. Filmstrips come in either the single frame or the double frame. The pictures on the single-frame filmstrip are 1 by ¾ in, placed one above the other on the film, and projected vertically. On the double frame film-strip, the pictures appear side by side, are twice the size of the single frame pictures (1 by 1½ in), and are projected horizontally. Filmstrips vary in length from about one foot to three or four feet. The pictures are arranged in fixed sequence but the filmstrip, unlike the motion picture, can be stopped and held with a single picture on the screen as long as needed.

Stereographs and stereoscopes

The stereograph is superior to an ordinary flat picture or photograph because it achieves a more vivid and realistic effect. The ordinary photo-graph is somewhat limited in creating a complete impression, since it must present three-dimensional objects in two-dimensional form. The stereograph is composed of two photographs of the same object or scene taken from a slightly different angle and mounted side by side upon a card. When viewed through a stereoscope or telebinocular, the stereo-graph appears as a single picture in three dimensions. The stereograph is the most realistic still picture available, but it has the disadvantage of being strictly an individual aid and is not applicable to group work. Nevertheless, the stereograph can be used effectively in the elementary grades and the junior high school if techniques similar to those for other types of pictures are applied. For the teacher who wishes to take photo-graphs in order to make his own stereographs, there are several types of special equipment available. Two cameras with matched lenses placed side by side can also be used satisfactorily.

Overhead transparency projector

The overhead projector is another valuable asset for instructional purposes. The entire group under the guidance of the teacher can derive much benefit from this effective teaching medium. Like the opaque pro-jector it reflects images on a screen for study. A roll of acetate, upon which material may be drawn, diagrammed, or outlined with a special ink pen before class and which illustrates the speaker's report, can be a very effective teaching device. Charts, maps, graphs, outlines, and pictures may be transferred to plastic sheets for use in the projector. The projector is portable and is easily operated by the teacher as he speaks. The teacher may use a series of individual transparent sheets to build up a concept through overlapping a series of sheets. The size of the projection will vary with the type or model of projector.

Recordings and transcriptions

Recordings make it possible to enrich and supplement classroom procedures. Phonograph records illustrating the songs and music of a specific period in history, as well as dramatizations, speeches, literary works of famous persons, interviews, and panel discussions contribute to the understanding of that phase of the work. Transcriptions of radio broadcasts of outstanding merit can be more easily used than the original broadcasts to integrate instructional materials. Many suitable radio programs are broadcast at times that are inconvenient or out of the question for direct classroom listening. Transcriptions of these broadcasts can be played whenever they best fit into the instructional procedure, and they may be stopped at any point for discussion. They may also be used again and again for different classes. In addition, they may be previewed by the teacher, so that he can make definite plans for their use. The most recent development, and one which seems to hold the most promise for use in schools, is the magnetic recorder, recording on tape. These provide for instantaneous recordings and immediate playback of programs. The tape can be edited with a pair of scissors, using splicing tape to join desired segments. Tapes can be stored in a small space and will remain permanent indefinitely. Tape may be reused.

The social studies department that is equipped with a recorder will find innumerable possibilities for it. The tape recorder can be taken to civic meetings or outstanding events to make on-the-spot records of speeches and discussions. Recordings that are so easily made will provide invaluable teaching materials. A definite program should be adopted to record special broadcasts for future use. The recorder can be used for improving discussion techniques, group activities, diction, and oral reports and for providing a record of special school programs.

Television

Television as a medium of communication furnishes many avenues for rich learning experiences in the social studies. It reveals history in the making and unfolds a realistic story of events as they happen. Telecasts make available a wide range of materials for instructional purposes. Current events and contemporary affairs, as a part of the work in the social studies, can be further enriched by classroom observation of a program. A group studying government can observe, as though they were actually present, Congress and the State Legislature in session. The skillful teacher will study the value of television and learn how to utilize a telecast to its best advantage in the learning situation. He will select a program with the same thought he gives other audio-visual materials. Every teacher should follow the listed and available television programs with the view of enriching instruction. Any program should be selected on the basis of its value and contribution to the immediate learning situation. Does it fit the needs and interests of the group at a particular learning level? Will it reveal new horizons and further the experiences and thinking of the pupils? Can another teaching aid serve the particular purpose better? If it is possible, the teacher should prepare the group for a telecast in the same manner he does before showing a film. He must follow up the telecast with the proper interpretation and evaluation techniques if it is to furnish productive learning. He must employ supplementary activities that further group learning and relate new with past experiences.

Educationally speaking, television has unlimited possibilities for bringing rich learning experiences into the classroom. It reaches far beyond the local area and into the world environment for numerous resources that could never otherwise be readily accessible. Television has some advantages over all other audio-visual materials in the vividness and completeness of its many presentations.

Television, like radio, will not replace the classroom teacher, but it will aid in enriching instruction. It will aid the teacher in pioneering and experimenting with new procedures through the use of this new equipment. Society has accepted the age of television in a very encouraging manner. New fields are constantly finding practical usage for this audio-visual device. The advent of noncommercial educational television channels promises to furnish much additional worthwhile television programming for the social studies teacher.

Radio

The radio supplements learning activities by bringing to the students immediate, live, and realistic information. The social studies teacher should include radio listening whenever feasible. In addition to educational programs specifically prepared for school use, other types of broadcasts, such as news reports, interviews, round-table discussions, and significant speeches, can furnish desirable materials for group instruction. The teacher may record a broadcast on a tape recorder for use at school. These broadcasts, if carefully selected, will prove valuable in current events and the problems course, and history will be enriched by "on the scene" broadcasts of historical events and other programs celebrating special holidays or events.

Many modern schools are equipped with a centralized sound system capable of reproducing recordings and radio broadcasts through loud-speakers in the classrooms. The central control cabinet is generally located in the principal's office. In schools equipped with this type of public address system, broadcasts of significant importance can be presented to the social studies classes if the necessary arrangements are made in advance. Where these facilities are lacking, it may be possible to obtain an individual radio for classroom use.

As with other types of teaching aids, effective use of the radio in the classroom involves careful planning on the part of both teacher and students. Definite purposes must be established before listening to any program to insure that students obtain the desired information. Adequate supplementary materials will be helpful in giving the students the necessary basic information for intelligent listening. Students must be taught how to listen and how to interpret the broadcast in relation to the topic under discussion. A receptive atmosphere should be created, and all interruptions should be avoided, so that students may give their undivided attention to the broadcast. An all-inclusive summarization, through some form of follow-up procedure, is essential for desirable results. Additional values in terms of leisure-time activities and cultural growth may be derived from the effective use of radio in the classroom. Students are not only encouraged to listen to news broadcasts as preparation for their current events discussions but are taught how to listen to these and other broadcasts intelligently.

Motion pictures

The motion picture is an effective aid in presenting information and factual knowledge. It furnishes the teacher with many opportunities to build the proper background for understanding the main currents in the stream of history. The motion picture holds the attention and at the same time accelerates the learning process by telling a complete story in a brief period of time. Through a learning experience, it can provide authentic, firsthand information that could not be easily acquired otherwise. A good film uses action, continuity, and suspense to make learning more vivid. The motion picture is not a substitute for the teacher but a helpful tool in the hands of a skillful teacher to enrich and contribute to the permanence of learning.

The social studies teacher should wisely select a film and proper follow-up activities if the students are to benefit from its use. Films, educationally speaking, may be classified as documentary and instructive or as teaching films.

Selecting the Film. Every film should be previewed by the teacher before it is shown to the class. This preview has a twofold purpose: to determine suitability and to plan the method of presentation and follow-up. The teacher should note the length of time needed for showing, the quality of the photography, and the extent of its contribution to the learning situation. A good film should be authentic and accurate both as to pictorial content and as to theme; it should not be one-sided or biased and should not contain extraneous materials.

Presenting the Film. Specific *preparation* should be made before showing the film so that the students will have definite objectives in mind. The teacher should always explain to the group the definite purpose for showing the film. The nature and amount of preparation will depend upon the film itself and upon the type of contribution it is intended to make to the learning process. A film that is to furnish the introduction to a unit will require less class preparation than a film being used to provide a basis for group discussion. The preparation should give the students a common basis of knowledge for understanding the motion picture and should bring out clearly the significant features to be noted. A series of well-phrased guide questions discussed with the students can be used both to prepare them for the showing of the film and to provide a basis for follow-up procedures.

Adequate time should be allotted for preparating the group and also for making the mechanical preparations for showing the film: checking the projector, the screen, and the source of current, as well as darkening the room. Arrangements should be made for proper seating of the class during the showing of the film. Classes should not be combined unless adequate seating space is available.

Follow-up. Effective follow-up procedures are essential if maximum benefit is to be derived from the motion picture. Class discussion should bring out all important details of the film and should answer the guide questions previously given. Vocabulary enrichment will result as the new words are explained and new usages applied. The summarization should encourage various other desirable activities. Through the discussion and other follow-up procedures, the motion picture should be integrated with the larger unit under consideration. A second showing of the film (with or without sound if the teacher wishes to comment) is often desirable. Repetition will clarify misunderstanding, furnish fuller information, and stimulate interest. All activities should be the outgrowth of the discussion, and students should be permitted to select an activity of their own choosing. The teacher may suggest an activity from his prepared list. However, film follow-up work should never be teacher-dominated. Evaluation of the films used furnishes another avenue for learning. This realistic instruction tends to make learning more enjoyable and meaningful to the group.

The museum

The museum is a growing educational force in our modern society. It contains a valuable collection of materials that serve as visual aids for the learners in our secondary schools. This agency can act as an educational link with our schools and furnish much worthwhile learning materials.

The social studies teacher realizes the importance of a field trip to the museum or the value of a loan of prepared materials for use in the learning process. Current stress in education places a premium upon concrete experiences for effective learning. The resources of the museum can aid tremendously in clarifying history and making it more interesting for students.

Every secondary school should build its own museum to meet the newer demands of modern education. Students and teachers can collect many articles suitable for the school museum. All objects, specimens, and models should be carefully labeled. Articles made during the instructional process in various classes might be considered for the collection. All exhibits and relia should be readily accessible for immediate use in the classrooms. From the examination of objects, students develop a fuller understanding of the particular study and are stimulated to do research in numerous related topics.

The social studies teacher and audio-visual materials

The social studies teacher is aware of the value of audio-visual materials for effective learning. He keeps informed about the trends and new materials available for use in the instructional program. He scans the catalogs, periodicals, professional literature, and bulletins for new and productive aids that will make his teaching more effective. The teacher will examine the files of all available materials in his own particular school.

Every school should have a well-organized audio-visual program for supplying teachers with both equipment and instructional materials. The teacher should have made readily available for his use the resources of the local school system. An effective distribution system should be established and maintained to furnish the teacher with needed audio-visual materials. Considerable freedom should be allowed the teacher in selecting audio-visual materials that will assist in developing realistic learning situations.

The administration of a program

The administration of the audio-visual program in a school may be under the direction of the principal, a teacher assigned to the task, the librarian, or a director or specialist in the field. The execution of the program is usually under the direction of one individual. He may be a teacher as well as the director; however, the particular situation may call for a full-time director. The director should work cooperatively with the administration, librarian, the visual-aids committee, and the teachers. Some of the duties of the director are the following: selling the program to the teachers, students, and friends of the school as an all-inclusive community service, assisting in curriculum and program planning, planning an effective audio-visual program, assisting teachers with instructional programs involving audio-visual materials for particular units of study, familiarizing teachers, new to the system, with the facilities available and the nature of the local program, assisting teachers in learning to operate new equipment, conducting study groups for teachers should the need arise, demonstrating new techniques, displaying for faculty inspection new materials, maintaining a collection of catalogs, periodicals, books, and bulletins to be used as guides for teachers in selecting aids, compiling bibliographies and preparing bulletins for the teachers, informing the teachers of new developments and experimentation in the field, organizing a core of student assistants to help in the work of the program, maintaining the equipment in good repair in order to prevent an unneccessary delay in the service offered, and functioning as a consultant with the audio-visual center serving as a clearinghouse for providing the best possible materials in the instructional program. A capable core of students serving as projectionists is a part of the service provided by the audio-visual program. A form of in-service program is maintained to alert the experienced teacher to significant changes in the methods of audio-visual instruction.

The value of any audio-visual program rests primarily upon the leadership provided by the director. His effectiveness will depend upon ability, training, teaching experience, initiative, and interest in directing the work. He must be alert to new developments in the field. He must be sympathetic to the problems of the faculty and must assist teachers whenever possible in the effort of improving instruction. He must strive to better his service for the benefit of the supervisors, teachers, and students.

The social studies teacher and the materials center

Where an audio-visual coordinator is not available to provide assistance to the teacher in this field, it has been suggested that the
librarian should be the coordinator of the audio-visual program in the
secondary school. The library as the resource center for audio-visual
materials can be very advantageous. The librarian can introduce audio-
visual materials into an already functional agency without any difficulty.
The selection, ordering, cataloging, housing, and distributing of maps,
charts, films, records, slides, and mounted pictures are a part of the
service offered by the library.

Librarians as consultants can suggest to the faculty effective instructional materials and work with the visual-aids committee. They can explore the field of audio-visual materials and compile lists of numerous
sources available to teachers as avenues for enriching learning.

In many school systems, films, filmstrips, and other types of audio-visual
materials are provided to schools from a centralized collection where circulation
methods are different from those of the individual school library. But every
school library will probably own some audio-visual materials which are circu-
lated directly from the library. Or the library may serve as the distribution
center, borrowing audio-visual materials from the centralized collection, then
lending them to teachers in the school. It is well, therefore, to establish a
definite routine for the circulation of audio-visual materials, whether they are
the property of the school library or have been borrowed from a centralized
collection.[2]

Conclusion

The effective use of audio-visual materials in the teaching-learning
process can contribute much to social studies instruction. The supervision of an audio-visual program, if properly planned and executed, can
help both teachers and students. The coordinator can contribute much
by assisting the teachers in evaluating, selecting, and applying audio-
visual materials in such a manner as to improve learning. He should, if
the need arises, be able to demonstrate the newer audio-visual techniques
in an actual teaching situation. He will emphasize to teachers the need
for selecting materials in terms of their needs. The coordinator as a
student, alert to changes in the field, will provide an in-service program
for the teachers.

The social studies teacher must select materials for activities in the

---

[2] A. Wofford, *The School Library at Work* (New York: The H. W. Wilson Company, 1959), p. 125.

learning laboratory with a definite purpose in view and correlate the experiences with the work. The teacher is interested in developing an environment where learning becomes realistic and experiences produce functional learning for the entire group. Social studies with the use of the proper learning tools can be made a living and functional study.

Bibliography

Brown, J. W., R. B. Lewis, and F. F. Harclerod, *A-V Instruction Materials and Methods.* New York: McGraw-Hill Book Company, Inc., 1959.

Cross, A. J. and J. F. Cypher, *Audio-Visual Education.* New York: Thomas Y. Crowell Company, 1961.

Dale, E., *Audio-Visual Methods in Teaching,* rev. ed. New York: The Dryden Press, Inc., 1954.

De Kieffer, R. and L. W. Cochran, *Manual of Audio Visual Techniques,* 2nd ed. Englewood Cliffs, N.J.: Prentice-Hall, Inc., 1961.

Haas, K. B. and H. Q. Parker, *Preparation and Use of Audio-Visual Aids,* 3rd ed. Englewood Cliffs, N.J.: Prentice-Hall, Inc., 1955.

Kinder, J. S., *Audio-Visual Materials and Techniques,* 2nd ed. New York: American Book Company, 1959.

Sands, L. B., *Audio-Visual Procedures In Teaching.* New York: The Ronald Press Company, 1956.

Wittich, W. A. and C. F. Schuller, *Audio-Visual Materials, Their Nature and Use,* 2nd ed. New York: Harper & Row, Publishers, 1957.

Chapter Nineteen

Utilizing Community Resources

The study of a modern community is an education in itself. Like the world, some communities are undergoing rapid change, which presents new challenges. A community can serve as a social science laboratory for acquiring firsthand knowledge about the immediate environment. Its historic past, present, and projected future are all a part of the local story. Each community has its population features, physical and cultural landscape, traditions, economic pattern, agencies, and institutions. A wealth of community resources are available for utilization in the social studies curriculum. Experiences that are both interesting and functional can be acquired through knowing the community. Rich learning results from educational field trips that penetrate the local community. Students steadily learn about living in their expanding communities and this knowledge multiplies rapidly in the senior high school. Such education helps to lay the foundation for effective citizenship in later life.

The school as an agency

The school as a significant agency has a definite relationship to the community. In the expanding educative process this social institution assumes a major responsibility. The school shares its resources and derives assistance from the other agencies in the local area in shaping the instructional program. The influence of the home, the community, and the student himself are always felt in the secondary school curriculum. Communication thus becomes an important factor in today's school and community relationships. As a unique sociological unit the secondary school serves as a center for the communicating process. The press, radio, and television are avenues for informing the citizens about their educational system.

Modern education geared to a highly technological society should be made most interesting and challenging to the student in every community. This requires the teacher to select effectively content, learning materials, instructional aids, and community resources. In this manner the students are helped to better understand life as it relates to any community. By educational planning, the school helps to meet the basic needs and aspirations of students through study of community life. This information becomes a key to a better comprehension of the broader community when developing the instructional scope of a total program. The role of the secondary school and its curriculum in an age marked by rapid change is one of vital importance in our democratic society.

The schools have long played their role as trainers for democratic living. Because of that role, stress has traditionally been placed on our national history and political structure for the purpose of inculcating in students the attitudes, knowledge, and skills required for good citizenship.

It is to be expected that the schools will continue to play this role. But more must be expected. Despite its obligations to society as a whole, the educational system faces perhaps its most meaningful challenge in dealing with the individual lives of those it touches. Good citizenship involves more than merely understanding the workings of government. To be effective and constructive, citizens must be intelligent and aware. The nation, therefore, will be served best by the fostering of a citizenry that is highly trained, and at the same time devoted to standards of excellence and integrity in all the various areas in which the individuals function.

Because our national life has grown to be so complex and so far-reaching, it must be recognized that no degree of excellence or creativity can ever be too great. Our schools, therefore, must prepare our young people to preserve individuality, initiative, and creativity in a highly organized, intricately meshed, society.[1]

Some community school propositions

Literature concerning the modern community school is available for study. The topic is pertinent for educators, teachers, and local community citizens alike in implementing a program.

---

[1] Association of School Administrators, *Educational Administration in a Changing Community,* Thirty-seventh Yearbook (Washington, D.C.: National Education Association, 1959), p. 109. Used by permission of the American Association of School Administrators.

The following propositions are by no means the only ones that may be formulated in support of the community school. Moreover as presented here, they are seriously inadequate as definitive statements of fact. In some respects they are statements of ideal conditions and ideal outcomes.

1. The community school is a demonstration of the law of increasing returns.
2. Increased use of facilities by the community school leads to better support of the school by the community.
3. The community school is an agent of cohesiveness in both the neighborhood and the larger community.
4. The community school may be a center for the assessment and management, if not solution, of problems unique to the neighborhood in which the school is located.
5. The community school is a major and indispensable characteristic of the educative community.
6. The community school helps create a set of common values which contribute to the intellectual and spiritual health of the community.
7. The community school is an educational ideal greatly respected by many other nations and, because of this fact, gives the U.S.A. a basis of meaningful communication with people and their leaders in different sections of the world.
8. The educative community is the ultimate test of the validity of American ideals. Democracy must be a living reality in the home community where people have most of their primary experience.[2]

The school is seen as an integral part of the community, sharing in its objectives and responding to community needs and pressures. At the same time the community reacts to the influences exercised by the school. With the school and community bearing such vital relationships to each other, it is a logical development in educational leadership to provide a social orientation to the educational process. It is recognized that community study, understanding and participation are prerequisites for effective participation in the individual's role as citizen in his community and in his society.

We suggest eight ways by which schools can develop a community approach to education:

1. Evolve a program based on the needs and interests of people in the community
2. Provide and develop leadership for servicing community needs
3. Build a curriculum around the major processes of community living
4. Provide the facilities for community forums, recreation, adult education, and other activities of a community nature
5. Utilize community resources in every phase of the school program
6. Engage in continuous research and study of the community so that its problems can be located and identified
7. Serve as a repository of community information
8. Serve as an agency of coordination in the community's educational efforts[3]

---

[2] H. Y. McClusky, "Some Propositions in Support of the Community School—A Summary," *The Journal of Educational Sociology*, XXIII (December 1959), 179-183.

[3] O. C. Smucker, "What Is a Community," *Educational Leadership*, XVII (February 1960), 278.

These points represent a notion of education which regards the educational process as a community-wide function.

The following is an excellent outline for the study of a community. It can easily be adapted to a particular community and can be fitted to the learning needs of students.

Our Community and State[4]

(New York)

Grade 7

I. Geography and Growth of Our Local Community
   A. Geographic influences affecting our community
      1. Location in the State and in the United States
      2. Surface
      3. Climate
      4. Natural resources
   B. Settlement and development of our community
      1. Founding of the community
      2. Growth of the community
II. Our Community Today
   A. General character of our community
      1. Description and general type
      2. Area and population
   B. The people
      1. Racial, national, and religious groups
      2. Influence of the various groups on community life, their cultural contributions
      3. Social groups
   C. The economic life of our community
      1. Leading industries
      2. Wholesale and retail business
      3. Service industries
      4. Transportation and communication
      5. Relation of community economy to regional economy to State and national economies and to the international economy
   D. Comparison with other communities of New York State
      1. Different types of communities in the State; folklore and tales of various regions
      2. Large number of urban communities
      3. New York City
      4. Distinctive communities in the State
      5. Contrasts and similarities in home and community life in urban, suburban, and rural areas
      6. Increasing interdependence of all the State's communities
   E. Community government
      1. Services the individual citizen cannot perform for himself
      2. Community governments

---

[4] *Social Studies 7-8-9, A Syllabus for Junior High Schools* (Albany, N.Y.: State Department of Education, 1961), pp. 18-22.

3. Structure and services of the government of the pupil's community
4. Community finances
5. Relation of the community's government to county government and to State and national governments
6. The adult citizen's part in his community government
7. The junior citizen's part

F. Special features of community life
1. Civil defense
2. Historic landmarks
3. Famous citizens of the community
4. Schools and libraries
5. Other educational agencies in the community and their relation to the schools
6. Homes and homelife

G. Improvement of the community
1. Improvements needed in connection with appearance, housing, recreational facilities, transportation and communication facilities, and other features
2. The community's planning commission and the responsibility of the individual citizen for community improvement
3. Work of civic groups for community improvement
4. Recognition of the widening role of the citizen and his community
5. Study of one typical project for community improvement with emphasis upon the process

Problems in Community Living[5]

Grade 9

Community problems are not those of any one social science. Rather, these problems need the insights taken from several of the social sciences—the political scientist, the economist, the geographer, the sociologist, and perhaps the anthropologist, and many other specialists. This final year of work in the junior high school is designed to be an introduction to these kinds of skills and insights.

Unit   I The Adolescent and his Future
Unit   II Public Leadership in Community Affairs
Unit III Problems in Community Government and Living in Home Town
Unit IV New Conditions in Connecticut Bring New Problems to its Cities
Unit   V Connecticut Citizens Secure Many Services through Their State Government
Unit VI Our National Government
Unit VII The United Nations' Role in International Affairs

The teacher and the community

The social studies teacher needs to acquire a knowledge of the educational resources and opportunities readily available in his particular community. This entails a study of the historical background and

---

[5] *Social Studies Grades 7-12*, Curriculum Bulletin Series No. XIII (tentative) (Hartford, Conn.: State Dept. of Education, 1959), pp. 20-22.

cultural aspects of the immediate area, the nature of the economy, the industrial activities and occupational pursuits, the major natural resources as they help to shape the everyday life, the recreational opportunities, and a sufficient background knowledge to understand clearly the educational structure.

Some school systems have established an orientation program for new teachers. This might include a tour of the community and a visit to the chief agencies such as museums, libraries, newspapers, government, communications, and social agencies. Prepared manuals by various agencies of the community serve as guides to obtaining resources. A faculty handbook is frequently a helpful source. The particular school may have a file pertaining to field trips and educational resources.

It is good for teachers to reach out beyond the confines of the school and participate actively in community efforts. Residents welcome the support of the schools in fund raising and membership drives of the Red Cross, Community Chest, YMCA and YWCA and other civic enterprises—Memorial Day programs, centennial celebrations, and parades. For the teacher, these personal contacts mean a broadening of interests and a widening of his world. At the same time, the layman comes to recognize the teacher as a fellow citizen who is sharing the problems of the community and earnestly trying to help in their solutions.[6]

Students as explorers

Today's youth as explorers can reveal a mine of information through planned educational experiences in the community. Modern society has its roots in the past and each community has an interesting story. Problems arise in the learning process that focus upon the community, county, and state. A group of students can study community problems, conduct surveys, and engage in local activities. They can attend a school board meeting, a city government meeting, and any special gathering dealing with a pertinent issue involving the local area.

Student groups can do research for and assist in the planning of celebrations depicting some historic event in the immediate area. Students may undertake a project dealing with a newspaper listing of historical accounts of bygone days in the community. In metropolitan areas students in the social studies department under the guidance of their teachers may establish a model United Nations with foreign students representing the culture of their countries. Current issues may be discussed and debated with local students representing views of different nations. This involves extensive research and evaluation of differing points of view.

Frequently, social studies students will re-enact a day in local govern-

[6] F. E. Morhous, "The Community—Includes Many Publics," *The Bulletin of The National Association of Secondary School Principals*, XLIV, No. 257 (September 1960), 56.

ment or in state government. These activities broaden the horizons and serve as a basis for continued study.

Today's youth participate as members of the community in many ways. Such activities offer wider social experience than would be possible within the school and encourage the adolescent's growth toward mature responsibility. The young people not only receive and gain, but also become able to give and share.

In some communities, for instance, high school youth serve as volunteer helpers in social and church agencies for younger and underprivileged children. Youth representation on the planning boards of many service organizations is increasing. United Fund and similar drives have found that the participation and leadership of youth add greatly to their success. In several communities, youth councils have formulated and published behavior codes and have taken an advisory role in Youth Traffic Courts for accidents involving juvenile drivers. Teenage driver clubs, often sponsored by adult groups or organizations, have rules and awards to control their own members.[7]

Problems relating to community health, safety, and fire prevention particularly call for the active participation of young people. The control of these problems cannot be left to individual choice. The illness of one person, for instance, may affect the health of many. This is why the school was early given responsibility for preventive immunization and direct teaching of health practices. Community agencies reinforce these efforts. Today, accident prevention and safety are crucial community problems requiring similar cooperation. In such programs, youth have proved that they can meet community problems with intelligence and ingenuity.[8]

The community as a laboratory

The modern community with its vast stockpile of available resources becomes a laboratory for learning. The teacher who turns learning into a challenging adventure can utilize effectively the resources for providing functional learning experiences for our youth. The knowledge acquired from direct observation and study of the everyday activities and life of a community is indispensable and basic to the education of youth living in our complex society. This type of practical information supplements the learning in the classroom while a specific unit is being studied. The materials in the curriculum should be related to the problems encountered in the community. The student learns about people and their occupations and the businesses and industries that comprise the society of the community. He has the opportunity to speak with individuals in various walks of life. When a group of students is conducting a survey or study, each should have the opportunity to interview people and to experience the real flavor of daily living in the community. The knowledge gained by the

---

[7] From *Guiding Today's Youth* by the Los Angeles County Superintendent of Schools Office, p. 275. Copyright © 1961 by California Test Bureau. Reprinted by permission of California Test Bureau, Del Monte Research Park, Monterey, California.
[8] *Ibid.*, p. 276.

students gives meaning to the information found in the resources of the library and in other educational materials. The experiences that youth encounter in their own community helps to build competence and to provide greater insights to life in the contemporary age.

Resources of the community on file

Community resources for effective instructional purposes should be accurately and systematically filed in the individual school. The cataloging of these educational materials requires the addition of new listings and the deletion of unproductive materials. We should take an inventory of our community resource file occasionally. The resources for securing information found in a growing community are bound to change. By periodically surveying the research materials that are available, sources suitable for a variety of learning experiences in or out of schools are revealed. In this way teachers can quickly evaluate these sources in terms of their instructional needs.

The information included on each alphabetical file card should be as complete as possible. The data includes name of resource, location or distance, telephone, contact, extent of materials, learning values, experiences previously derived from them, and the evaluation ratings. Those available resource persons who can make a contribution in their own particular way should be listed according to their specialties. Films, exhibits, tape recordings, and picture collections pertaining to a particular community that are available for use when studying such units should also be added to the file. A good school utilizes the resource people and other resources available in the community in carrying out the instructional program.

Each community is unique in terms of its resources. We should consider museums, libraries, art galleries, shrines, centers of transportation and communication, recreation and amusement, and business and industry. The listings may be extended to include the county and state government buildings and agencies, museums, libraries, shrines, monuments, institutions of various types, agriculture in its many phases, manufacturing and its allied branches, specific state and national projects, and important experimental sites such as agricultural and scientific experimental stations.

Social studies instruction presents many opportunities for the systematic instruction of resource people. Teachers and students alike should obtain the assistance of resource people to acquire firsthand knowledge and accurate information about specific problems and topics. Resource persons may be directly associated with the various institutions, agencies, factories, branches of government, newspapers, and museums that are visited. Learning opportunities and sources of new materials are provided through planned talks, discussions, demonstrations, and displays presented by such resource people. For example, a city manager can discuss questions and problems which may be confronting a particular community or citizens and professional people can share their experiences about choosing a career or selecting a particular profession with a group of students. The human and material resources of any community when properly utilized can help meet the growing needs and interests of our youth. They are available for rich learning experiences when needed in the program.

Field trips for securing information

Field trips are planned community exploratory experiences for acquiring information from various firsthand sources. The knowledge gained from these cooperative educational activities should be used in the organized learning process and analyzed in terms of the problem studied. Some units contain topics especially suited for direct study and observation by means of a field trip. The creative social studies teacher should plan field trips that will be productive and informative. Such excursions may encompass the local community, county, and state.

1. The planning process consists of determining or selecting desirable sites or places to visit, briefing the students for the visitation in terms of discovering more about our problem. It becomes the important process of relating the students' present learning with those direct experiences that are acquired on the specific field trip. Students should have a definite knowledge of what is to be viewed if the experience is to prove worthwhile. In this manner constructive contributions can be made most rewarding when problems are studied through community resources outside of the school.

2. By sharing their experiences of the field trips, the students are encouraged to exchange ideas. A discussion gives them an opportunity to answer previously prepared questions. Interests are kindled and skills are sharpened through correlated or related experiences. Tackboard displays, murals, construction projects, booklets, student reports, resource speakers, and films can further supplement the learning through a field trip. It is wise to write a record of the trip including any photographs or films taken. Students should write a thank-you letter to the proper officials for the courtesy extended through a field trip. Excellent citizenship training evolves around field trips as the students are brought closer to community life through an extension of the school's instructional program.

Community resources come to the school

Productive resources of any community can enrich the curriculum. As part of citizenship growth and practice, students should learn about the activities and problems of their respective communities. Because communities differ in resources, one community should not be isolated and studied to the exclusion of others. The study of other communities and their resources may be of value in later years, since, upon reaching maturity, students often find employment in areas other than that in which they attended school. The following procedure may be employed to study a community.

Interviews and surveys are also convenient means of obtaining information when field trips are not possible and of contributing to learning about one's community. Various techniques can be applied to the process of gathering data from a particular source. The nature of the study and investigation may be determined by the actual needs or by the problems that have meaning for the students. Teachers may wish to compile materials that relate to the community for future instructional planning through surveys, questionnaires, and the study of available literature.

Interviews are the basis for acquiring knowledge in a firsthand manner. Students may interview community personnel and obtain various types of information. Many resource people are most willing to furnish the student with valuable information, printed literature, and even audiovisual materials.

Surveys are another measure for conducting explorations or excursions into a community. In the case of high school students, a survey may include studying a topic that reaches beyond the community and into the county and state. It could be related to the economy or some phase of society in the area. Research and study of findings could reveal interesting information about these features and how they have an impact upon the life of the community.

Visits to the School. The modern secondary school has the occasion to have as great speakers an important personality, a businessman, or a government official. They may speak to an interested group on a subject-matter area or they may address the entire student body. The guests usually allot time for answering questions and for describing certain functions or aspects of their work. In this way students have a chance to hear and meet the leaders of the community and people from different parts of the world.

Many times parents can act as resource persons and supply valuable information for a group studying some phase of a problem. Students like to hear the accounts of travel experience and any type of occupation or work that may seem new or different in today's society.

The community and the curriculum

The curriculum or planned educational program of the secondary school should be geared to serve youth living in an expanding community and world today. It should be flexible and functional and should be evaluated in terms of change and improvement. Curriculum study can be a cooperative process with administrators, consultants, teachers, students, parents, and interested citizens engaged in the work. A fresh approach with thought given to the needs and problems of the community can be productive. Identifying community resources that can be used effectively in developing materials is important when organizing a framework for the social studies program. Study, research, and experimentation are essential avenues for instituting successful curriculum change.

Parents and lay people have an insight into many phases of our modern society. They realize that social change resulting from scientific and technological progress has influenced the lives of people in their own community. The population explosion and urbanization are important factors in many areas. The education for modern living is an important consideration involving both local individuals and groups.

Educational improvement is a constant process; the end result is a better education for the youth of the community. Too frequently in the past we have overlooked valuable assistance from competent people. Through skilled leadership that is both democratic and cooperative, curriculum improvement is achieved.

Curriculum improvement is a responsibility for educators and lay persons alike if the best possible education is to be provided for our children and youth. Today's pupils are the nucleus for tomorrow's society of competent citizens.

Other experiences and contributing resources

By having elaborated upon the informational aspect of community resources, we now will refer to experience—contributing resources useful in the social studies program. The activities listed provide students with realistic experiences in everyday living and contribute immeasurably to educational growth. They require student participation and are thus deemed by many to be more valuable than the types of situations in which the student is a listener.

Work experience opportunities

Some school systems have tried work experience programs relating to various occupational opportunities in the local community. In this manner the curriculum is related to the community's industrial and employment activities. Such a program provides direct experiences in some form of active participation with people and employers in the area. It opens the door for vocational and personel guidance when deemed essential. Students are thus having opportunities in a kind of work that is geared to their abilities and that gives insight to a specific type of employment. They are challenged and at the same time motivated to do a good job. These experiences provide the student with the opportunities for exploration and a look ahead. They have the chance to do some serious planning and evaluating. Learning of this nature is most valuable if the individual experiences a measure of success and accomplishment. The student has been in direct contact with adult life and has had the opportunity to appraise his own skills, interests, and understandings of what work experience is like. The guidance factor is most important in relating classroom instruction to the occupational training in the field. The experience is a type of citizenship training in terms of what the school and community are doing in helping students to achieve their objectives and to build proper attitudes and understandings.

Community agencies

Each community has specific institutions, agencies, and organizations that are most helpful in the process of fostering community-school relationships. They cooperate in many ways and are most generous in helping to meet the needs and interests of youth through the provision of educational and recreational opportunities. Students are members of such agencies as the YMCA, YWCA, 4-H Clubs, Boy Scouts, and Girl Scouts; all of these agencies make a contribution in the process of character development. The work of science clubs is encouraged by contributions from Kiwanis, Rotary, Lions, and others. Fraternal orders are also productive in aiding young people in their respective communities. These are only some of the agencies that contribute to furthering the education of our youth in most communities. It is to be expected that many communities have other means and facilities that are productive supplements to education.

The parents contribute

Today's secondary school program, which is geared to meeting the needs of youth, requires a close working relationship between the home and school. The parent-teacher association sponsors meetings to bring the parents, teachers, and students closer together. In such meetings the parents and teachers can discuss matter of mutual concern. The parents in this manner obtain a better view of the student's learning patterns and the nature of the instructional program. Parents should be encouraged to participate in the life of the school and at the same time be made to understand that their assistance is both needed and appreciated.

Parents can be helpful in the solution of problems as they participate in study and discussion groups. They can survey topics of general interest to both school and community. Special committees or small study groups may investigate topics pertaining to youth and report their findings to the entire organization at some future meeting. The PTA serves as a "clearinghouse" by keeping the channels of information and communication open. The parents are informed about the activities, problems, contemplated changes, and the general program of a particular school. We hear of such activities as "Family Night," "Open House," "Back-to-School Night," "Visiting Days for the Community," "Mother-and-Daughter Dinner," "Father-and-Son Dinner," "Career Day," "All-Sports Night," and other activities that build friendship and good community relationships.

Parents have many occasions to use the facilities of the school. Recent trends indicate that the secondary school is becoming a community center and is the site for varied activities. The school plant is used for the PTA meetings, special forums or lectures, civic affairs, and adult education classes. The shops and laboratories are frequently used by the parents and students working together on a project. The auditorium, gymnasium, and athletic field are frequently used by adult groups and students for various activities. Students, parents, and citizens are brought closer together and develop a sense of belonging and a spirit of interest through the facilities of the high school.

Local government and basic agencies

Local government and the basic or established agencies in the community are excellent resources from which knowledge valuable to students may be acquired. In fact, these resources may serve as a guidance factor for senior high school students.

Pupils may become better acquainted with the community government, its personnel, and the problems facing local administrators. The police, fire, street, and water departments should be studied and observed. Students should learn about the political aspects of the community government, the names of each department in their local government, and their functions. Organization for voting, the precinct system, and the use of voting machines should be included in the students' review of community resources as well as the hospitals, clinics, and welfare institutions.

Social studies classes at the secondary level frequently study the origin, development, and function of their own local government. A twelfth-grade class may divide itself into groups; the pupils of each group may study some specific agency. In this way the groups can visit many governmental departments to discuss with various officials matters which relate to and are of importance to the community. For example, at the City Hall the department heads can answer questions and explain the main function of their departments.

After returning to the classroom, the pupils engage in panel and forum discussions. They elaborate upon and consider further the material presented to them by officials. Such materials permit the students to view democratic government in action, and knowledge thus gained will prove valuable in planning their other activities.

The community and the school

Many communities have given considerable thought to the secondary school as a social agency that provides pupils with a type of program that would help them understand their community better. The school is in part a community center that utilizes many of the local resources in the curriculum. In addition, the school serves as a focal point for many adult and youth programs in which the emphasis is on educational, recreational, cultural, and social activities. Thus, many schools have moved toward making the school a center for much community activity.

The features and functions of the secondary school should be thoroughly reviewed by educators. The modern school attempts to meet the needs of youth through the use of its buildings, grounds, equipment, and program.

Individual schools in recent years have moved in the direction of building closer and better community relations. Both sound leadership and cooperation are essential to building effective school and community understanding. This entails the administrators, teachers, pupils, parents, and citizens working together as a team for the betterment of the educational program. Teachers extend the learning activities and procedures into the community and provide experiences that are functional and meaningful to a group of pupils. The teacher must realize that the important factor in home-school interaction centers around the interests and needs of each individual pupil. He must possess the qualities of leadership, initiative, resourcefulness, and responsibility to build community understanding for pupils. The very nature of our current secondary school curriculum and the social studies program lends itself toward building of a productive school-community affiliation.

Community public junior college

Many communities are experiencing demands to extend their educational opportunities to meet the needs of youth and adults.

The junior college serves its community through its offerings in general education, through its provision of preparation for advanced study, and through its program of vocational education, but this is not all.

It is natural to look to the public junior college for many and diverse types of service to groups and to individuals not enrolled in classes or courses. The junior college is a reservoir of distinctive and various talents and skills, knowledge and expertness, insights and understandings. Furthermore, the public junior college is a community-centered institution. Under these circumstances, the performance of service to the community becomes an important function of the junior college. Such service must not be limited to the meeting of requests made by citizens. The faculty has an opportunity and a responsibility to take leadership in identifying areas of community need to which the junior college can contribute.

The values of college service to the community are many and varied. They include increasing the productive efficiency of agriculture and industry, improving the functioning of communities and community organizations, contributing to the health and physical well-being of citizens, and enriching the cultural, aesthetic, and moral life of the community.[9]

Looking to the future this type of educational institution holds much promise in serving the needs of people in the community and country.

Youth and the community

The modern community, whatever its nature, holds much for the education of youth. The home and school share the responsibility for building the foundation for the student's early life. The school serving as a community center is the site of many of the educational, social, and recreational activities. The community is a natural laboratory for vitalizing and extending learning experiences of many types. It provides recreation and

---

[9] The Yearbook Committee, "The Role of the Public Junior College," *The Public Junior College,* National Society for the Study of Education, 55th Yearbook, Part I (Chicago: The University of Chicago Press, 1956), chap. IV, pp. 72-73. Quoted by permission of the Society.

leisure-time pursuits for the young people. Cultural agencies furnish opportunities for intellectual growth and development, while other local agencies provide desirable guidance toward effective living and citizenship. Part-time employment experiences provide a type of job training that is essential for entering the industrial and business world and starting a career. Thus educational and vocational guidance is functioning and students are developing skills.

Some communities have established recreation centers and junior colleges to further the education of youth in the area. Each community should develop the machinery to assist young people with problems through worthwhile measures and activities.

Conclusion

The modern community with its available resources can contribute much toward enriching the social studies curriculum and strengthening the total educational program. It serves as a natural laboratory for broadening instruction at the secondary level. This is particularly true when we consider the role of the social sciences in helping young people to gain a better understanding of a changing society. The total program of the school and community should help to build competence in the effective citizen of tomorrow who participates in the daily affairs of the community. It is through the cooperative efforts of the local citizens working with educators who consider the changing needs of youth that the process of effective program development in a community can be achieved. Youth benefit and develop through the many experiences engaged in within the community.

The secondary school is an important social agency and will play an even greater part in the future of the community. In some communities the public junior college will begin to serve the needs and interests of students and adults. Parents, civic leaders, resources people, and agencies can and will if given the opportunity assist in building a better educational program. An informed and interested public can assist in meeting the problems and needs of both our schools and the community. Students grow more appreciative of the value and importance of their own community through closer association with its people, industries, and history.

Bibliography

American Association of School Administrators, *Educational Administration in a Changing Community,* Thirty-seventh Yearbook, Washington, D.C.: National Education Association, 1959.

National Society for the Study of Education, *Community Education*, Fifty-eighth Yearbook, Part I. Chicago: University of Chicago Press, 1959.

Olsen, E. G., ed., *School and Community*, 2nd ed. Englewood Cliffs, N.J.: Prentice-Hall, Inc., 1954.

Pounds, R. L. and J. R. Bryner, *The School in American Society*. New York: The Macmillan Company, 1959.

Wiles, K. and F. Paterson for the Commission on the Education of Adolescents of the Association for Supervision and Curriculum Development, *The High School We Need*. Washington, D.C.: National Education Association, 1959.

Chapter Twenty

A Process of Evaluation

Modern evaluation in the social studies at the secondary level is a comprehensive process including many facets in the educational program. It plays a significant role in testing and measurement. A social studies teacher has many occasions to utilize the various techniques and methods of evaluation in planning and directing effective learning for students.

The purposes of educational evaluation are twofold: (1) educational evaluation helps the teacher to determine the degree to which educational objectives have been achieved, and (2) educational evaluation helps the teacher to know his pupils as individuals. The first purpose is basic; changes in pupil behavior are always evaluated in terms of the goals of education. The second purpose is subsidiary to the first, since, naturally, if the teacher is intimately familiar with his pupils, he will be better able to determine the degree to which educational objectives have been achieved.[1]

The teacher realizes that evaluation is a continuous process. This includes setting up definite objectives in the planning stages for the instruction to be accomplished, developing the instructional activities, and evaluating the educational experiences. The teacher is constantly aware of the established objectives. He evaluates the actual results of his instruc-

---

[1] J. S. Ahmann and M. D. Glock, *Evaluating Pupil Growth* (Boston: Allyn and Bacon, Inc., 1959), p. 6. Copyright 1959 by Allyn and Bacon, Inc. Reprinted by permission of the publisher.

tional procedures in terms of the established objectives to promote student growth.

The Social Studies teacher and evaluation

The social studies teacher is an important part of the process of evaluation. It is imperative that the teacher become aware of the various evaluative techniques employed in working with students in the educative process.

The task of utilizing modern evaluation practices in the social studies is somewhat more complex than in other content fields. All teachers are concerned with instruction in, and evaluation of, specific items of student knowledge and skills; in some fields these items comprise the greater portion of the outcomes to be evaluated. To the teacher of social studies, however, the development of understandings, attitudes, interests, behaviors, habits, and ideals is as important as the acquisition of information and skills, and some means of measuring such intangibles must be considered. Social studies teachers should therefore become familiar with the various techniques for evaluation and types of tests, both subjective, with criteria for determining when each should be used, and with efficient procedures for assigning, administering, and scoring tests. They should also strive for competence in the construction of tests and in the analysis and application of test results.

It is quite obvious that evaluation has become a significant factor in the daily lesson and the work of a larger unit of instruction. In either case the social studies teacher employs some new tools and devices as well as some older informal methods for evaluating the extent of learning or progress. Evaluation of this type tends to provide a conclusion or summary for the immediate study, appraises accomplishments, and points ahead to further study. It also offers a foundation for cooperative planning, new viewpoints, establishing goals, and a measure of constructive guidance and direction for the students. Evaluation thus becomes an active process in determining the measure of changes in the development of a student.

Educational evaluation is a process in which a teacher commonly uses information derived from many sources in order to arrive at a value judgment. The information might be obtained by using measuring instruments as well as other techniques that do not necessarily yield quantitative results, such as questionnaires, direct observation, and interviews. An evaluation may or may not be based upon measurement data, though appropriate measurement results are customarily used if they are available. Thus, evaluation includes not only measuring or in some way identifying the degree to which a pupil possesses a trait or the degree of which a pupil's behavior may have been modified as a result of an educational experience, but also judging the desirability and adequacy of these findings. Good measuring instruments can provide a sound basis for good evaluation.[2]

Measurement and evaluation

It might be well at this point in our discussion to identify and clarify terminology. This should prove helpful for a teacher planning and working with students. The following is an excellent example of the meaning of measurement and evaluation.

Evaluation and *measurement* are terms often used with little regard to their meanings. *Measurement* refers to observations that can be expressed quantitatively and answers the question "how much." *Evaluation* goes beyond the statement of how much, to concern itself with the question "what value." It seeks to answer the pupil's and teacher's question, "What progress am I making?" Evaluation, therefore, presupposes a definition of goals to be reached —objectives that have been set forth.[3]

Teaching and evaluation

Modern teaching involves the process and means in trying to understand groups better. The teacher has a significant role to play in organizing, guiding, and directing learning for each individual student.

Evaluation can guide teaching when they furnish a diagnosis of specific strengths and weaknesses in the pupil's achievements or capacities. The teacher may then seek either to eliminate the weaknesses by using special teaching methods and emphases, or to circumvent them by directing learning toward areas where the pupil's efforts will be more fruitful. The causes of weakness in a specific subject can be traced by tests to any one of the various pupil inadequacies underlying it. Weakness in a history or geography course may be found to be due to lack of either comprehension power or speed in reading, as revealed by a test in reading ability. Or it may be due to lack of general intelligence or to lack of the presupposed background material, a lack which could be revealed by tests designed to measure achievement at a lower level of the subject.[4]

The teacher should be alert to the fact that evaluation is a definite part of the daily learning activities and the variety of new experiences for each student. His task is to identify more or less those changes evidenced in the student behavior resulting from the actual learning taking place. No doubt motivation is a strong factor in the extent of this

---

[2] *Ibid.*, p. 13.

[3] *A Practical Introduction to Measurement and Evaluation* by H. H. Remmers, N. L. Gage, and J. Francis Rummel, pp. 7-8. Copyright 1943, 1955 by H. H. Remmers and N. L. Gage. Reprinted with permission of Harper & Row, Publishers.

[4] *Educational Measurement and Evaluation* by H. H. Remmers and N. L. Gage (New York: Harper & Row, Publishers, 1955), p. 15.

learning. In a sense evaluation becomes the means of weighing the effectiveness of the learning.

The teacher and evaluation of instruction

The modern social studies teacher understands that evaluation is a continuous process and appreciates its value for improving the instructional program. He utilizes in the process of instruction some formal as well as informal methods in the evaluating process. He also becomes a student of the techniques of measurement and evaluation as they become increasingly important in determining student development in the social studies curriculum.

In the process of planning and developing a unit of work or exploring a problem, the teacher establishes definite objectives. Considerable thought is given to the proper procedures to be employed in directing the learning experiences. The evaluation of the amount of progress and the outcomes to be achieved become an important consideration. The teacher naturally hopes for a high degree of achievement by the students in terms of the chosen objectives. This becomes an item of major importance in determining the value of the learning in terms of student growth. The function of evaluation for the teacher is to assist him in guiding the development of each student in the group. At the same time the teacher can make any change in the instructional program to meet the interests, needs, and abilities of the students in the particular groups.

Evaluation and good teaching go hand-in-hand. In fact, a description of the processes a good teacher tries to follow shows that evaluation is present throughout. Good teaching follows these five steps:

1. The teacher analyzes the individual pupil's capacities, knowledge, past experience, interests, and needs.
2. The teacher analyzes the pupil's goals and helps and encourages him to revise his goals in accordance with his capacities.
3. The teacher harmonizes the educational process with the pupil's capacities and goals.
4. The teacher evaluates the pupil's progress in terms of his capacities and goals.
5. The teacher and the pupil, working together, reconsider the revised goals in light of the progress achieved and strive to correct weaknesses which would interfere with the attainment of reasonable goals.[5]

The teacher and measurement

The teacher should have a considerable knowledge of the techniques of measurement. In fact each teacher must understand the general workings of measurement in an evaluation process—how results are interpreted

---

[5] Remmers, Gage, and Rummel, *A Practical Introduction to Measurement and Evaluation*, p. 12.

and applied to the school program. Some of the items a teacher should know about measurement are listed below:

1. Know how to construct an objective test with attention to the following details:
   a. Stating objectives of the course in terms of changes in behavior as well as knowledge, beliefs, and attitudes;
   b. Organizing subject matter and setting problems through which these objectives may be attained;
   c. The advantages and disadvantages of the various types of objective items, especially with regard to the mental processes required in answering them;
   d. The proper sampling of objectives and subject matter;
   e. The construction of an answer sheet;
   f. The construction of a scoring sheet.
2. Know how to construct an essay test with attention to:
   a. the mental processes involved in answering questions:
   b. the influence of the questions on study habits and skills:
   c. formulating directions for scoring the test:
   d. the relative merits of essay and objective tests.
3. Be able to analyze a standard test in the subject and at the grade level he teaches with reference to skills, subject matter and mental processes tested, ease of administration and scoring, and the nature and adequacy of the norms and scores provided.
4. Know the proper procedures and ethics of administering, reporting, and using teacher-made and standardized tests.
5. Know how to compute percentile ranks, percentile scores, and standard scores and interpret them with reference to equal units on the base line of the normal frequency curve, and how to convert raw scores to standard scores by either the linear or area method. (This will involve ability to use the following statistics: median, mean, standard deviation, and normal probability curve. Computation should be kept simple with emphasis on understanding the measures.)
6. Know how to interpret a test score with reference to the standard error of measurement.
7. Know how to construct individual and class educational profiles to show development over a period of years and to evaluate the adequacy of test batteries, testing programs, norms, scoring, and reporting.
8. Know how to prepare for and conduct an interview with a parent, analyzing the achievement and behavior characteristics of a pupil.
9. Know the relative value of so-called intelligence tests, different types of school marks, achievement tests, and prognostic tests in predicting pupil achievement in a given field.
10. Understand that the proper use of measurement makes possible the child development approach to education as opposed to the subject-matter-to-be-covered approach, relating this to school marking systems.
11. Understand that the purpose of measurement is to adjust instruction and teaching to the learning abilities of students, that the use of test scores for grouping, grading, and passing is always secondary to the adjustment of instruction to the needs of the pupil.
12. Understand that measurement and testing as a motivating device has

three functions in the learning process: (a) the energizing function to increase the general level of activity and effort; (b) the directive function to direct the activity of the learner into desirable channels; and (c) the selective function to determine the responses which will be fixated and responses which will be eliminated.[6]

The foregoing statements give the social studies teacher a broad overview of the many faces of measurement. It is to be understood that a teacher in the process of gaining teaching experience must learn much about measurement.

Developing an Evaluation Program

Secondary school administrations, social studies supervisors, and teachers are eager to have an effective evaluation program.

There are essentially four major steps in the development of a comprehensive evaluation program.[7]

1. *Formulating and classifying objectives of the school's curriculum.* For practical treatment, objectives need to be so grouped that those concerned with similar kinds of behavior are classified together. The kinds of objectives govern the selection of appraisal techniques.

2. *Defining the objectives of goals of education in terms of behavior.* Stating each objective in terms of specific pupil behaviors that can be recognized if achieved is an essential step in formulating the aims of the curriculum in such terms that the outcome can be readily evaluated. This is important because in many courses of study, objectives are so vague and general that the kind of behavior they imply is not clear. A common mistake is to have a great number of goals stated in broad generalities.

3. *Identifying situations in which students can be expected to display progress toward the objectives.* After a clear definition of the kind of behavior to be appraised has been established, the next task is to provide situations in which students can be expected to display these types of behavior. Planned learning experiences should be provided for students of many different levels of ability. All pupils should have opportunities to become proficient in the three R's as well as to develop those attitudes and behaviors that distinguish good citizens.

4. *Selecting instruments by which data for appraisal purposes can be obtained.* Certain curriculum objectives are directed toward academic areas of study while others are mainly concerned with the responsibilities of citizenship. Neither should be exploited at the expense of the other. Developing methods for identifying the presence of behaviors that are desired can be facilitated by adequate acquaintance with the

---

[6] W. W. Cook, "*What the Teacher Should Know About Measurement,*" National Council on Measurements Used in Education, Fifteenth Yearbook (New York, 1958), pp. 17-19.

[7] *Evaluating Pupil Progress,* Bulletin Vol. XXIX, No. 14 (Sacramento, Calif.: State Dept. of Education, 1960), pp. 5-7.

various kinds of evaluation instruments and techniques available for use. It may be that no tests are available to measure certain objectives. In such cases, it becomes necessary to develop new instruments of measurement.

Evaluation devices and techniques

Today's social studies teacher at the secondary level utilizes various devices, practices, and techniques in the process of evaluating student progress or growth. Evaluation is a cooperative, continual, and developing process and therefore is a definite part of the social studies curriculum. In selecting, planning, and developing problems and units of work the methods of evaluation are essential. Significant information for evaluation purposes is acquired from school and community sources.

The following are types of procedures that are employed in an evaluation program: Various types of tests, observations, conferences, samples of work, rating scales, anecdotal records, questionnaires, check lists, diaries and logs, and cumulative records.

Testing—A Part of Evaluation

Testing is an important phase of evaluation. It is a part of learning and has long been considered in the social studies curriculum. When teaching a particular course, the teacher is likely to employ several kinds of tests including the essay and objective types. The teacher is aware of the responsibility of measuring and evaluating the development of students. One of the specific purposes of testing is to furnish the teacher with information that will assist him to guide his students more fully. Tests have great value for the learner as well as for the teacher, both in evaluating and in guiding the learning process. The teacher thus explores his own methods and is able to see ahead and to plan wisely. Generally speaking, students are motivated in their study of a unit by the fact that they will be held responsible for the materials presented. In evaluating the worth of a unit, the students and teacher have an opportunity to review and to draw conclusions. Tests give the student practice in unifying and clarifying his thinking about a particular topic or problem. The vocational and educational values derived from tests are both practical and worthwhile for adult life in modern society. The teacher or the supervisor should carefully determine his purpose in testing and then should endeavor to select or construct the test that will be the most suitable for his purpose.

The terminology applicable to testing should be understood by the social studies teacher; especially the one who is new to the profession. For example, the term *validity* refers to actuality of values measured: the degree to which the test is true to its purpose. If the test is *reliable,* the test or examination can be depended upon to measure what it is planned to measure. The validity of a test refers to the objective or purpose as being the right kind of test, even if it is not actually accurate in results or percentages.

The kinds of tests utilized by the social studies teacher are generally related to the process of student learning. These include the essay, objective type, and the occasional few questions or quizzes for evaluating. Tests constructed by teachers relating to the immediate instruction are the pencil and paper variety and include both essay and objective questions. This type of test should always follow the good practices of modern test construction. In framing such tests it is wise to think in terms of the objectives to be achieved and to emphasize understanding in preference to memorized content. In classification of the types of teacher-made tests we should include variations of the essay, recall, recognition, and problem-solving. These tests have merit and are considered valuable in the educational scheme for busy teachers always striving for effective instruction.

The essay tests

The essay type of test has long been a definite means of evaluation in the social studies area. This type of test is helpful in appraising the student's ability to evaluate and similarly to recall and organize knowledge concisely. For example, a question asking for the causes of World War II requires the student to think and probe his memory of everything of related interest. An essay question dealing with the possible uses of atomic energy in our civilization would tax his general knowledge. This type of test aids in measuring the student's ability to express ideas in a logical and concise fashion.

In the social studies, the essay test has a definite role to serve as a supplement to objective-type tests. It may be true that the few questions included in such a test lack the breadth to cover the entire information presented in a course. The student is asked to express his knowledge of the special questions covering certain segments of the material presented or covered in the particular study. Even if this type of test lacks full objectivity, the value is apparent when well-framed questions arouse the full powers of the student. Among its advantages are its ease of preparation and administration. Students are led to express themselves more fully. It puts a premium on ability to organize and to express thoughts clearly;

besides being better adapted to certain types of materials, it tests a wide range of abilities. Critical capacity and reasoning ability are tested comprehensively. Essay questions may be used to a good advantage to measure the various objectives—attitudes toward some social, political, or economic phenomena or perhaps the question of compulsory arbitration of labor disputes. They may also determine the organization of facts and the evaluation of pertinent contemporary materials and events.

The essay test furnishes the student with a greater freedom of expression and response. He encompasses in his answers to questions a wide area of subject matter portraying his own specific ideas. He can present a narrative story or outline of some phase of history or geography in its proper stage setting. The student may be called upon to answer questions involving complex reasoning. It is general policy to introduce such questions with wording such as discuss, compare, or explain.

The beginning teacher will grow in competence in writing clear and effective essay questions. He will learn to be concise in framing each question and to estimate the proper number of questions to include in an examination. He will encourage the students to read and "think through" the meaning behind the question before starting to write their answers. This is a very important consideration when working with students at the secondary level.

Scoring the essay test

The teacher is also eager to develop techniques for scoring each essay question properly. One of the most valid criticisms of the essay test, as it was formerly used, was the degree of subjectivity possible and prevalent in scoring results. Social studies teachers who are aware of this factor, however, can apply objective procedures when scoring papers and thus eliminate somewhat this objection to the essay test. The following is an excellent discussion dealing with the all important topic the scoring of essay examinations.

A number of steps may be taken to mitigate the subjectivity and reduce some of the biases in evaluating the answers to an essay examination. These are mostly attempts to break up the process of evaluation into a series of more specific, fractionated judgments made upon a common base and applied to an anonymous product.

Decide in advance what factors are to be measured. If more than one distinct quality is to be appraised, make separate evaluations of each. If facts are considered important, score for facts. If organization is important, give a rating upon organization. If mechanics of English, sentence structure, spelling, punctuation, etc., are considered a significant outcome, give a rating upon mechanics. However, do not contaminate the rating for knowledge or understanding with appraisal of mechanics. It is hard to isolate quality of organization from extent of factual information, but if the essay question is to serve its distinctive purpose an attempt should be made to do so.

Prepare a model answer in advance, showing what points should be covered and how many credits are to be allowed for each. This will provide a common frame of reference for evaluating each paper. After the preliminary model has been prepared, it should be checked against a sample of student responses to the question. The model and the scoring scheme should be modified in the light of these answers. They can now be used as the yardstick for assigning credits to each paper in turn.

Read all answers to one question before going on to the next. A more uniform standard can be maintained for a single question and for a short period of time. There is more chance to compare one person's answer with another's and thus to build up a "feel" for the answers. There is less contamination of judgment by what that same examinee had written on the previous question.

Grade the papers as nearly anonymously as possible. The less you know about *who* wrote an answer, the more objectively you can grade *what* was written.

Greater reliability can be obtained by averaging independent ratings. If the importance of the test merits the expenditure of the extra effort, a more dependable appraisal can be obtained by having one or more additional raters each give an independent rating of the responses.[8]

Let us turn our discussion to another type of test that is constructed and commonly used by teachers in evaluating the student's achievement in a particular course-content area.

Objective tests

The objective type of test has an important place in the evaluation program at the secondary level. It can be used by teachers along with the essay type of examination. The informal objective type test is a teacher-made test formulated on objective principles to fit the particular instructional situation.

The objective test includes a variety of forms of test tasks having in common the characteristic that the correct answer, usually only one, is determined when the test item is written. The word "objective" in objective test refers only to the scoring of the answers; the choice of content and coverage of an objective test is probably as subjective as the choice of content and coverage of an essay test, and for some types of items there is subjective judgment involved in the original decision as to what is the correct answer.[9]

Since all social studies teachers will find it necessary to use objective tests in addition to the essay type on many occasions, their characteristics, forms, and advantages should be understood.

---

[8] R. L. Thorndike and E. Hagen, *Measurement and Evaluation in Psychology and Education* (2nd ed.; New York: John Wiley & Sons, Inc., 1961), p. 56.
[9] *Ibid.*, p. 47.

The objective tests seek a scientific and efficient method of probing the skill and knowledge of the student in the manner of a laboratory investigation seeking reliable and valid results. The objective tests in the main call for brief answers, check marks, or numbers. A wide range of information or knowledge can be tested this way. Only a small number of questions can be asked for each essay test, and much time is needed to develop the answers fully. In an average class period many items can be evaluated with the objective test, and the element of chance is reduced because of the wide range of topical matter to be scored. The students, who realize that there can be no bluffing, answer either "yes" or "no," "this" or "that." The scorer is not confused with outside matter or distracted from the marking of the essentials; the personal equation in marking is absent. The student is marked for what he knows and only that. The series of small units that were agreed upon by the examining teachers represent a fair sampling of the contents of the course. On the other hand, it is more difficult to prepare such blocks of short questions even if they can be more readily marked. Although it is harder for teachers to examine them, long questions and answers are easier to set up. Teachers have to use more ingenuity in devising short tests, but on the whole there is a saving of time.

Among the advantages of the objective tests may be noted that they are scored objectively and the results prove more reliable and valid. More comprehensive sampling is permitted in shorter time. The tests also are more quickly scored and administered. Students themselves are more interested in the short examination questions. The teacher can easily realize the gaps in students' knowledge and can prescribe remedial procedures with the aid of the short objective test.

Limitations of objective tests

The construction of good objective tests is more difficult and requires more time than the essay test. They must be printed, mimeographed, or reproduced in some similar way. In addition, these tests possess limitations that are of particular importance to the social studies teachers. The new test is essentially a measure of factual knowledge and, as such, puts a premium on the ability to remember. Social studies instruction is equally concerned with other types of abilities; organization, expression of ideas, reasoning, analysis, and problem-solving. For this reason, an adequate testing program for the social studies should combine both the essay and the objective test, either as separate tests or by the combination of both types.

Forms of objective questions

Questions used in objective tests are of two general types, classified according to the nature of response: *recognition*, which involves a choice among responses furnished by the test, and *recall*, in which the pupil supplies his answer from memory. The recall question may take either of two forms: completion, in which the pupil supplies a word to complete a sentence, and the simple answer, in which the pupil writes one word in answer to a direct question. A recognition question might require an answer to: "What is the capital of New Jersey?" a. Trenton, b. Paterson, c. Elizabeth. A recall question would require filling in the appropriate word or words, as "The time belt which encompasses most of New England is the —— belt." Recognition questions may take the following forms: true-false, multiple choice, matching, and arrangement or sequence.

True-False

This form of question is probably the most commonly known and widely used in the objective tests. However, it is open to criticism because guessing may be involved in responses and because of the inadvisability of placing incorrect statements before the students. If this type of test is used, however, the teacher should remember that vocabulary is a very important factor in the construction of the test.

The following are some excellent guides to be used when composing true-false items:

1. Have the number of true statements approximately equal to the number of false statements.
2. Avoid "tricking" the pupil by distracting his attention from the crucial part of the item.
3. Avoid "specific determiners," that is, words or modes of expression that are usually associated with a true statement or a false statement.
4. Reduce ambiguity by using quantitative rather than qualitative language whenever possible.
5. Avoid involved complex sentence structure with many dependent clauses, double negatives, or unfamiliar language.[10]

Sample[11]

23. Many of the pioneers built small houses or shelters on their flatboats.
$$T \text{——} \quad F \text{——}$$

---

[10] Remmers, Gage, and Rummel, *A Practical Introduction to Measurement and Evaluation*, pp. 229-230.

[11] Georgia Sachs Adams and John A. Sexson, *Survey Test in Introductory American History*, Form 1, Grades 7-8-9 (Monterey: California Test Bureau, 1959).

26. Cattle used to be driven hundreds of miles to be shipped on the first cross-country railroad.   T ——— F ———

Various methods are used in recording responses. The words "True–False" (or **T F**) may be printed before or after each question with directions to underline or circle the correct answer or to cross out the incorrect answer. A space may be provided before each question in which students are instructed to write *true* or *false*, T or F.

Multiple choice

This form of question includes a statement or a question and a group of three or more possible responses from which the pupil makes a selection to complete the statement or to answer the question. There are many variations of this form. The selection may be made on the basis of the "only correct answer" or the "best answer," in which case the student chooses only one answer; or the student may be supplied with a longer list of responses and instructed to choose a specified number of correct answers or all the correct answers. Selections may be made by underlining, by checking, or by writing the number of the correct answer in a space provided for that purpose. Multiple choice questions are frequently used in the social studies since they can be adapted for testing relationships, discrimination, and other elements as well as information.

Sample[12]

1. What was the most important large-scale change in control of the territory of the world from 1830 to 1930?
   (1) European nations gained almost complete possession of South America.
   (2) Asiatic nations led by Japan gained control over most of Africa.
   (3) European nations gained control over most of Africa and Asia.
   (4) Asiatic Nations gained control of large portions of Europe.

   ——— 1

2. Which of the following statements best describes the trends in general business conditions in this country between the end of the first World War (1918) and our entrance into the second World War (1941)?
   (1) A long period of depression followed immediately after World War I, and then quite suddenly a large-scale business boom developed as the second war began in Europe.
   (2) Business improved continually during the period between the two wars, although there were many slumps for short periods of time.

---

[12] Reprinted by permission of Science Research Associates, Inc. from ITED (Form Y-2). Copyright 1942, State University of Iowa.

(3) Business conditions were very good for a number of years following the first World War, but they rapidly became very poor and then gradually improved again.

(4) Business conditions grew steadily worse following the first World War, so that the government had to assume considerable control in order to secure the necessary production for the second war.

——— 2

Arrangement or Sequence

This form of question contains a list of items that the pupils are to rearrange in a specified order by writing the correct numbers in blanks before or after the question. Rearrangement may be made on the basis of chronology, size, or importance. However, these questions are difficult to score objectively unless the number of items is very small and questions are scored on the basis of completely right or completely wrong.

The incomplete sentence

Another effective technique requires the student to fill in blank spaces with the proper words and concepts so that the finished summary is complete, accurate, and with facts placed in proper sequence.

The preparation of such a test requires a concisely written paragraph or essay from which the major points are then deleted and replaced by blank lines.

The student will then fill in words and phrases to complete the thought. The teacher in grading such a test must bear in mind the variety of synonyms which may properly be used to convey the correct information.

Testing through audio-visual materials

Testing through the use of audio-visual materials is particularly applicable to some types of social studies materials. This method of testing should be used occasionally to provide variety and to motivate student interest in tests as well as in daily work.

One may test through the construction of maps, graphs, and charts, asking pupils to locate places referred to in the study of current problems. Ideas may be expressed by drawing or interpreting cartoons and pictures.

Map tests can be successfully applied in geography, history, and current affairs. A projected map on which specific areas, geographic locations, or political divisions are numbered can furnish a basis for an identification test either through matching or recall. The use of individual outline maps on which the pupils record their knowledge of specific facts can be adapted. For example, in American history, pupils may be asked to record on outline maps various steps in the expansion of the United States showing states, principal cities, frontiers, and territories acquired. Map tests have an added advantage for the teacher, since they can be readily scored. A series of pictures or slides can also be made the basis for an interesting, stimulating, and valid social studies test. Objective questions and pictures should be carefully selected. Graphs, charts, globes, and cartoons may also be made a part of testing. However, these aids should usually be made the basis for a number of single questions within a test rather than the entire test.

Classroom use of tests

Assigning the Test.   The test should be fully as much a part of the instructional procedure as the daily lesson. Students should be taught to realize the importance of a test in guiding their progress. They should learn to look upon it as a measuring device that will reveal to them, as well as to the teacher, their strength and weaknesses. Every possible step should be taken to encourage students to look forward to a test with eager interest rather than with fear and apprehension. If this goal is to be achieved, students must be taught how to take tests. They should be instructed to read each question or statement carefully and thoroughly for complete comprehension before starting to record the answer. This procedure will prevent many errors that occur from careless or hasty and incomplete reading of questions. Pupils who have been trained to take tests properly will learn to appreciate the satisfaction that comes with successful accomplishment. This, in turn, acts as an incentive toward better and more careful preparation of other phases of their schoolwork.

The procedure followed in assigning a test frequently has a direct bearing on the success or failure of the results. Pupils should be furnished with sufficient information to guide them toward intelligent and efficient preparation. Such information should include an explicit statement about the materials to be covered in the test and the kind of test to be given. In some situations it is desirable for the teacher to enumerate in greater detail the major items for which the pupils will be held responsible. This detailed preparation should usually be practiced with junior high school classes and with slower groups in the senior high school. It is also desirable in all classes where there has been a recent change of teachers and the group is therefore not familiar with the procedures of the teacher who is giving the test. In all cases, the test should be assigned sufficiently in advance to provide adequate time for pupil preparation. Sometimes it may be that a pupil has several tests on the same day. Students are only human, and they feel it unfair to spring a test on the group. As a general rule, students do not like to take tests. After a semester test is assigned and before it is given, the teacher should devote from three to five class periods reviewing. The types of test for which assignments are made in advance are based on time intervals or units of study and are known by the terms *periodic, unit, semester* or *quarter,* and *yearly* or *final* test. By using tests aids for evaluation, the teacher can appraise the effectiveness of teaching procedures and techniques. Tests also furnish the student with an overview of his own progress in learning and reveal the weaknesses and strengths of the group.

Types of tests commonly given

In general, the types of tests that the teacher will compose and administer fall into two divisions: those given chiefly for purposes of grading and those which are primarily instructional devices.

The *pretest* is given before the study of a new unit to create interest and to determine the extent of the pupils' knowledge of the unit. It serves as a basis for teacher planning. It is diagnostic and exploratory, for there is little value in going over already familiar ground or in touching on matters that are obscure and above the heads of the group. The results of the pretest will indicate which phases of the unit should be stressed and which are already sufficiently familiar to the pupils. The pretest should not be for purposes of grading.

The *unit test* is centered around some significant process in human affairs and relationships, such as the process of westward expansion or the development of transportation in the United States. The facts have to be known before generalizations may be expressed correctly, and the contents, materials, and exercises have to be familiar to the pupil before his attitudes and appreciations take form. The unit test is particularly applicable to the social studies. Since so much of the instructional material is organized into broad units, it is especially advantageous to plan for a series of tests, each of which serves to summarize the unit studied. The unit test should be planned to include all phases of the instructional material, including reports and supplementary readings.

The *periodic test* is one of a series of tests administered at regular intervals. The length of the interval usually depends to some extent upon the length of the "marking period" adopted by the school; for example, in schools using the six-weeks' marking period, teachers frequently prefer to schedule tests every three or six weeks. In this way, pupils learn to keep abreast of schedules, instead of making up for neglect by intensive efforts and memory cramming at the last minute.

The quiz is a short unannounced test that has been borrowed from the colleges for occasional use in the high school. It is usually about ten minutes long and may be used to test on outside readings as well as on the materials under discussion.

These four types of tests have value chiefly as instructional devices. The results, although in some cases used as an aid in determining grade, should be analyzed to evaluate and improve instructional procedures. The semester test and final test, on the other hand, are usually administered for the specific purpose of determining grades and promotions. But aside from their diagnostic value, these various tests have distinct worth in exercising the memory, if not imagination, and the power of attention in concentrating on a given detail of knowledge.

The *semester test* is designed to examine the pupil's knowledge of the important materials taught during the entire semester. Because of its broad scope, it is usually too long to be administered within the class period and is frequently given at a special time when two or more periods may be used. The procedure for administering the semester test is rather formal, and the test should be mimeographed, so that each pupil may be given a copy. If additional paper for outlining, answering essay questions, or other purposes is required, it should also be distributed at the beginning of the test. As an aid in facilitating the procedure and avoiding disturbance, each pupil should be instructed to bring to the examination several sharpened pencils and an eraser. If the size of the room permits, it may be advisable to change the usual seating arrangement of the pupils during this test. No pupil should be allowed to leave the room until he has finished the test, and a definite time should be set before which no pupil may hand in his paper. For one semester subjects, the semester test is also considered as the final examination.

The *final test* or examination is given at the culmination of the entire course. It usually covers the whole year's work but with greater emphasis on the materials covered during the second semester. In all other respects it duplicates the semester test described above.

Administering the test

The teacher should give definite instructions to his students at the beginning of every test in order to clear up any misunderstanding that may occur. When a test is written on the chalkboard, the questions should, if possible, be written before the arrival of the class. If this is not feasible, the first question can be dictated, and the entire test written while the class is working on the first question. Attention should be given to legibility, position, and size of the writing on the chalkboard, so that all pupils can see the questions clearly. When mimeographed tests are used, the teacher should immediately call the pupils' attention to any errors or omissions.

Since the pupils are more likely to be at ease in familiar surroundings, all tests should, if possible, be given in the regular classroom. If the usual seating arrangement is to be changed, this should be done before the questions are given to the class. In most cases, such a change is unnecessary. The teacher who is fair with his class in scheduling, assigning, and marking tests and who shows understanding in teaching his pupils how to take tests will have little trouble with students' copying or cheating. The teacher should warn his class occasionally (and briefly) of the passage of time, even though a clock may be in plain view. Otherwise, some students who concentrate intensely may not be aware of the time spent until too late. Every possible precaution should be taken to avoid distractions. At the end of the period, the teacher should remind students to see that names are on each sheet of paper, that the papers are in the proper order, and that no sheets have become detached.

Use and misuse of tests

It is essential that both teachers and students evaluate test results. The teacher should mark all papers carefully and thoughtfully, making note of any phase of the instructional material that should be retaught and also noting the strong points for pupil commendation. He should then return the test papers promptly, so that the pupils may examine them and determine their gaps in knowledge. Some part of the class period should be spent in discussion of test results, during which the teacher goes over the test, question by question if necessary, to make sure that each pupil has the correct answer thoroughly fixed in mind. If, for any reason, the teacher desires to keep the test papers on file, he may collect them at the end of this discussion period, but he should not dispense with this pupil-consideration of test results. It is necessary to have some objectives in giving tests—administrative organization, materials, and methods, or evaluating, recording, and reporting.

The beginning teacher should be extremely cautious about overtesting. Tests should have a definite instructional purpose. Too frequent use of tests is poor teaching, since no educational goal is achieved and valuable time is wasted. A test should never be assigned as a punishment. Neither should it be used as a means of avoiding supervision. Tests, in the last analysis, are valuable tools in the teaching-learning process and should be used as such. The occasional, informal group test has merit and may serve two significant purposes: measurement and motivation. Such a type of test is a phase of good instructional practice. The wise teacher will develop skill in all phases of testing and evaluation.

Reporting student progress

Evaluation in the social studies is a cooperative venture of the home and school, with the teacher, parent, and student playing on the same team. Good relationships are established and facilitated for all concerned through an effective report. Parents, through the report, are given a realistic review of how well the student is progressing according to his own ability. They also learn something about the teacher and his efforts in directing the various aspects of student growth. A good progress report serves as a powerful motivating force for the student. The parents derive a feeling of understanding and satisfaction for their part. And the teacher is given a gratifying directive for the efforts in his daily work. One must remember that the comprehensive evaluation of any student is not an easy task. Evaluation is a constructive and positive process that furnishes a directive for guiding youth successfully in learning experience.

Secondary education has been alerted to the need for a revision in evaluation practices. This is true in the case of reporting to parents. The report card has long been the established formal way of reporting to the parent. It is sent to the homes at stated intervals during the semester and carries the stated grades of A, B, C, D, and F—ranging from superior to not passing. In some school systems the scale has been modified: U, unsatisfactory; S, satisfactory; O, outstanding; D, doubtful; and N, needs to strive for improvement. An interesting departure from the more usual grading practice uses E for excellent; S for superior; M for medium; I for inferior, F for failure; and Z, a grade which permits the student to receive a certificate but not a diploma.

Some school systems indicate the teacher's reasons for low achievement. Some communities are using the informal yet friendly letter as a means of reporting to parents. Conferences with the parents—during which time teacher and parent meet on common ground and take a constructive inventory of the student's growth—are valuable and are extremely desirable. These changes are providing a clearer concept of the student and the teacher working together toward goals which provide functional and rich learning.

Parent-teacher conference

The parent-teacher conference at the secondary level is a significant part of reporting student progress. This means of communication tends to promote better understanding between the home and the school. The conference aids in clarifying the reporting system for the parents and tends to foster interest for all immediately concerned. Parents should be made to feel their importance in the education of youth. It is up to the school to make sure that they know and understand how teachers can work with them. As a general practice the conference is held in the evening, so that both parents can be present. However, other conferences can be so scheduled at the convenience of both parties. Both the teacher and parent have much to gain from the meeting, especially the teacher, who is gaining a clearer understanding of a student. The parents also are gaining insights into the nature of the school program through these informal and yet professional conferences. The teacher is gaining valuable knowledge about the student as he exchanges with the parents information about each student.

The teacher must plan and be adequately prepared to conduct such conferences. Sometimes it is very essential that this conference be held, especially in the case of a student new to the school or one who is having considerable difficulty in the educative scene. Many times the student together with the parent and teacher is included in a conference. In this way a program is formulated and plans are laid for the immediate future. These interviews should be conducted in a friendly and business-like manner. The essential information including records and materials should be at hand, so that any questions can be clarified with dispatch. Some school systems have developed excellent forms on which the student reports his own progress, and these along with samples of his work are helpful in a conference. Outlines or guides are frequently used in the interview. This essential information should be particularly helpful to the parent. Any productive discussion necessitates that parent and teacher understand the true meaning of growth and progress as it relates to the particular student. Some type of summary or evaluation is most helpful for planning the next conference. Any such meeting should conclude in a positive manner with a constructive view to the future. It is advisable to draft a written report resulting from the conference and to have a copy sent to the other teachers involved in the student's program.

The following guidelines may prove helpful for teachers in preparation for the parent-teacher conference:

1. Establish a friendly atmosphere free from interruptions
2. Be positive—begin and end the conference by enumerating favorable points
3. Be truthful, yet tactful
4. Be constructive in all suggestions to pupils and parents
5. Help parents to achieve better understanding of their child as an individual
6. Respect parents' and children's information as confidential
7. Remain poised throughout the conference
8. Be a good listener; let parents talk
9. Observe professional ethics at all times
10. Help parents find their own solutions to a problem
11. Keep vocabulary simple; explain new terminology
12. If you take notes during the conference, review them with parents
13. Invite parents to visit and participate in school functions
14. Base your judgments on all available facts and on actual situations
15. Offer more than one possible solution to a problem[13]

Student-teacher conference

Like the parent-teacher conference, the conference with the student can be a most profitable experience.

The social studies teacher may also employ the individual student conference or interview in evaluation. The student generally likes to know how satisfactorily he is progressing in the work. There are occasions in the learning laboratory when a pupil or small committee wants to discuss phases of the unit with the teacher. Students also have problems to discuss in terms of their daily life. The teacher should observe the pupil at work and record any pertinent data. When holding a conference with a student, the teacher should have available the individual's folder containing samples of his work. Evaluation reports that indicate the student's growth in attitudes, skills, and understanding are also useful. Through the friendly conference, the student can reveal his immediate needs, the interests and opinions he may have about the work under way in the group. A record should be kept of both the conference with the student and that with the parent.

Other informal evaluation techniques

Space will not permit a complete discussion of all the informal techniques in the evaluation process. Many are supplements to tests for gathering valuable information. The social studies teacher may have

---

13 National Education Assn., "The Parent-Teacher Conference," *NEA Journal,* XLVIII, No. 9 (December 1959), 21-22.

the occasion to employ one or more of these devices. The list may include the cummulative record, anecdotal record, questionnaires, diaries, logs, interviews, case studies, achievement lists, check lists, and rating scales.

Cumulative Records. The cumulative record provides considerable information related to the individual's history. The record should be complete and accessible to all teachers. Such material is helpful in understanding and guiding the pupil. The more complete knowledge a teacher has of each member of the class, the better able he will be to meet the specific needs.

Anecdotal Record. The anecdotal record is a recorded statement of an individual's behavior as observed by teachers. The anecdotes of behavior should be recorded accurately as observed in the learning laboratory or wherever the events occurred. Such records are cumulative by their very nature.

Logs and Diaries. Logs and diaries are useful devices for recording completed work, events, and activities. For example, a class might wish to record the activities and experiences relating to the study of a particular unit. A student may wish to list the books he has read, the mines he saw, the sport contests he attended, the projects he completed, the field trips taken, and the achievements in a particular individual project.

Teachers are becoming aware of the values derived from informal evaluation techniques. These devices are a part of the general evaluation and provide information not easily obtained otherwise. It is a way of knowing the student better in relation to the general aspects of his growth pattern. Some teachers have long used this informal type of appraisal in guiding the work of slow groups. It seems to be a more human approach in meeting the needs and problems of youth. We are concerned with each individual student in making his work functional, interesting, and successful.

Guideposts for evaluation

The social studies teacher in many school systems may have to follow an established policy of evaluation and testing. This is the common practice in the matter of the semester test and the final examination. Other aspects of evaluation are often left to the discretion of the individual teacher.

Although scholastic achievement in the basic subject matter remains a matter of utmost importance, the teacher must observe behavior patterns of students and evaluate such patterns objectively. With these points in mind, one must establish some common pattern or program for evaluating student growth. The following suggestions may aid the social studies teacher:

1. Understand the nature of the social sciences
2. Visualize the general pattern of the social studies organization and the type of programs in operation
3. Comprehend the basic objectives of the social studies
4. Appreciate the variety of evaluation materials available and the types of techniques used
5. Select tests, check lists, and inventories with a definite purpose in mind
6. Comprehend the specific outcomes of the social studies
7. Utilize informal evaluation procedures whenever desirable
8. Interpret and use evaluation results wisely and properly

We strive to develop intelligent individuals who can adjust readily to our modern democratic society. This achievement requires teachers in the social studies, when undertaking the selection and construction of evaluation devices, to direct their attention to the outcomes or goals of the learning process which include: the ability to locate, select, appraise, organize, synthesize and handle materials; desirable habits, interests, and attitudes; a spirit of tolerance, cooperation, and team work; a working vocabulary; an ability to understand and use maps, charts, tables, and graphs; the power of critical thinking and sound reasoning; and skill in reaching conclusions and expressing their significance forcefully.

Teachers must realize there is considerable difficulty in measuring all the objectives and outcomes of the social studies. The teacher must meet the challenge of evaluation through devising instruments for his own particular needs.

The Social Studies Teacher and Evaluation

The social studies teacher should develop skill in the process of evaluation. He can become alerted to the various aspects and techniques employed in modern evaluation practice. Each individual student should be studied, so that he can be helped to improve whenever needed. The teacher realizes that evaluation is a continuous process and a way of constantly employing the many phases of the learning situation. Evaluation is no longer a one-way street with only the teacher participating and a single test mark used for judgment; it has become a process involving other people and various techniques. The older method of testing and grading had many limitations. Today, evaluation reports are more complete, indicating the areas of strength as well as weakness and also the need for improvement on the part of the student. The parent, pupil, and teacher each have a better vision of the progress the individual is making in the social studies program.

Wiles[14] gives us some insights that are applicable to evaluation.

The judgment-making process can be applied successfully when: the teacher, parents, and students have agreed on goals sought; all persons involved understand and accept the criteria used; behavior about which judgments are made is adequately sampled and recorded. When these conditions exist, judgment-making has reached the level which produces self-directing students able to continue their education intelligently beyond formal education.

Do I:

Build mutual respect before introducing the evaluative process?

Utilize pupil-teacher planning as the first step in evaluation?

Seek agreement with pupils on desired goals for class activity?

Use the goals established as criteria for judging progress?

Discover a pupil's status as soon as possible after starting to work with him? Establish a baseline from which amount of change can be determined?

Help pupils discover and record the skills, knowledge, attitudes, and interests they possess as they begin work with me?

Take time to discuss with pupils the type of behavior which represents attainment of desired goals?

Collect and record samples of both individual and group change?

Secure evidence of pupil growth, where possible, in actual problem-solving situations?

Bring pupil and parents into the process of collecting, recording, and interpreting evidence?

Recognize that paper-and-pencil tests are only one way of collecting evidence, useful only when they measure the kind of growth sought?

Use many ways of sampling pupil growth—plans, products, diaries, and other records kept?

Provide space for pupils to file evidence of growth?

Make a pupil's records available to him?

Keep records of group progress and achievement—plans, minutes, and products?

Consider past progress and conditioning factors in the environment in making judgments concerning the quality of a pupil's growth?

Bring pupils, parents, and other persons concerned into the judgment-making.

Enter into an agreement to test judgments against future developments when judgments of parent or pupil disagree with my own?

Make judgments in such a way as to make possible continued evaluation?

Strive constantly to increase the amount of information shared with parents?

Invite parents to plan the reporting procedure with me?

Provide an opportunity for parents to join in making judgments about the changes reported?

Use evidence collected concerning pupil growth as evidence in judging the quality of the learning experience?

---

[14] K. Wiles, *Teaching for Better Schools* (2nd ed.; Englewood Cliffs, N.J.: Prentice-Hall, Inc., 1959), pp. 242-244.

Letters to parents

The letter to the parent can serve a definite purpose in the reporting process. This type of report provides another contact between the home and school and furnishes the basis for closer working relationships. Such letters are valuable and may be used occasionally in conjunction with other reporting devices. The letters should be friendly, courteous, sincerely written and yet present a fair analysis of the student's progress. They should contain basically good common-sense features such as a positive approach, the strong points in the student's work, the areas where satisfactory growth prevails, and, if necessary, the fields where guidance is essential for desirable improvement. If the weaknesses are glaring, the conference is a more desirable approach than the letter.

A letter might supplement the progress report card once each semester. It could also precede the first progress report or serve as a final supplement for the year's record.

The progress report

Satisfactory reporting of pupil progress to the home should be the goal of every school system. Administrators, teachers, parents, and students are all part of the modern evaluating process. The report must be understood by the individual student and his parents. Any report card or method of reporting can easily become outmoded and should be studied and re-evaluated at intervals.

Parents are interested in report cards which clearly describe the student's growth. They are concerned with his progress and want to know how they may help the school and the teachers. Evaluation has become a cooperative venture, with the home and school working for the good of each individual pupil. Parents, through friendly talks with teachers, can better understand what the school is trying to do for their students.

To find a perfect report card, as everyone knows, is a difficult task. One must reach some accord through experience, exploration, study, and compromise. All concerned must appreciate the true purpose of a reporting procedure and understand thoroughly what the card reveals.

Passaic Senior High School

PASSAIC, NEW JERSEY

PROGRESS REPORT

19 _____ - 19 _____

STUDENT_____ H.R._____

Grade Classification_____Sept. 19 _____
Grade Classification_____Feb. 19 _____

Dear Parents:

This is a report of our staff's evaluation of the progress being made by your son or daughter at Passaic Senior High School during the current year. Such a report will be issued each quarter.

The school's main interest is focused on the individual pupil and on his progress in relation to his ability. In cooperation with the home and other community influences, the school attempts to assist the pupil in developing to his full capacity. Regularity of attendance, punctuality, and application are important to this purpose. Necessary home study should take precedence over other out-of-school activities.

As partners in this effort, parents are cordially invited to confer with our teachers, guidance counselors, and principal in our mutual effort to assist pupils to make the best possible adjustment to life, both inside and outside the school.

Peter Cannici, Principal
Passaic Senior High School

Courtesy Passaic Senior High School, Passaic, N.J.

PROGRESS REPORT

Student _____ H.R. _____ H.R. Teacher _____

SUBJECT ACHIEVEMENT

SUBJECT	TEACHER	1st	2nd	3rd	4th	Final Mark	Crs.
English							
Physical Education							

QUARTER spans 1st, 2nd, 3rd, 4th columns.

MARK EXPLANATION

A - - - - - SUPERIOR

B - - - ABOVE AVERAGE

C - - - - - AVERAGE

D - - - - - PASSING

F - - - BELOW PASSING

INC. - CREDIT TO BE GIVEN UPON COMPLETION OF WORK.

FX - - - REPETITION NOT RECOMMENDED

PERSONAL AND SOCIAL GROWTH

The only items checked are those that call for special comment.

SUBJECT																																																		H. R.		
TEACHER																																																				
QUARTER	1	2	3	4	1	2	3	4	1	2	3	4	1	2	3	4	1	2	3	4	1	2	3	4	1	2	3	4	1	2	3	4	1	2	3	4	1	2	3	4	1	2	3	4	1	2	3	4	1	2	3	4
1. Is an unusually good, all-round citizen.																																																				
2. Is very cooperative.																																																				
3. Is considerate of others.																																																				
4. Accepts responsibility.																																																				
5. Makes great effort.																																																				
6. Shows improvement.																																																				
7. Can do better.																																																				
8. Needs more home study.																																																				
9. Is absent too frequently.																																																				
10. Should improve work habits.																																																				
11. Should have more respect for the rights of others.																																																				
12. Should exercise more self-control.																																																				

Courtesy Passaic Senior High School, Passaic, N.J.

Conclusion

Evaluation is a continuous and cooperative process. It is an integral part of the instructional program in which both teachers and students are active participants. Many devices are used to compile information that will reveal changes in the learner's behavior. Standardized tests, teacher-made tests, and informal techniques all serve to accomplish this purpose. Data gathered from the various channels should be used and interpreted in terms of the student's growth. The information acquired aids in the guidance of each pupil's program. The learner is the chief unit, and he should be made aware of his own growth in the various learning experiences. Complete exaluation of the individual, like the perfect report card, is a somewhat complicated task, although efforts have been made to improve the reporting of pupil progress. Some accord might be reached in secondary education relative to a more uniform and realistic marking system.

KALAMAZOO PUBLIC SCHOOLS

Secondary Department

Grades 7, 8 and 9

GROWTH IN SCHOOL SUBJECTS

Student's Name	Teacher	First Quarter			Second Quarter			Third Quarter			Fourth Quarter			Final Mark	
		Achievement Level	Effort Level	Habits and Attitudes	Achievement Level	Effort Level	Habits and Attitudes	Achievement Level	Effort Level	Habits and Attitudes	Achievement Level	Effort Level	Habits and Attitudes	Achievement Level	Effort Level
ENGLISH Grammar, Spelling, Writing															
Reading, Literature, Speaking															
SOCIAL STUDIES															
MATHEMATICS															
SCIENCE															
FOREIGN LANGUAGE															
TYPING															
ART															
MUSIC															
INDUSTRIAL ARTS															
HOMEMAKING															
PHYSICAL EDUCATION															
HEALTH AND SAFETY															
SPEECH AND DRAMATICS															

MARKING CODES FOR GROWTH IN SCHOOL SUBJECTS

ACHIEVEMENT LEVEL

In relation to the average for this age and grade level:

A Outstanding work — rapid progress

B Above average work — constant and consistent progress

C Work and progress about average for this grade

D Work below average for this grade — slow progress

F Unsatisfactory progress

EFFORT LEVEL

S Progressing satisfactorily for his ability

N Not working up to his ability

I Improved effort and progress

HABITS AND ATTITUDES

1. Satisfactory in regard to behavior and study habits.

2. See note enclosed.

3. Needs to improve study habits.

4. Needs to improve participation in class activities.

5. Needs to improve school conduct.

6. Needs to improve relations with other students.

Courtesy Kalamazoo Public Schools, Kalamazoo, Mich.

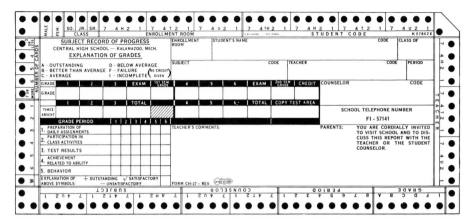

Courtesy Kalamazoo Public Schools, Kalamazoo, Mich.

Bibliography

Ahmann, J. S. and M. D. Glock, *Evaluating Pupil Growth*. Boston: Allyn and Bacon, Inc., 1959.

Green, H. A., A. N. Jorgensen, and J. R. Gerberich, *Measurement and Evaluation in the Secondary School*, 2nd ed., New York: Longmans, Green & Co., Inc., 1954.

Lindquist, E. F., *Educational Measurement*. Washington, D.C.: American Council on Education, 1951.

Lindvall, C. M., *Testing and Evaluation: An Introduction*. New York: Harcourt, Brace & World, Inc., 1961.

Noll, V. H., *Introduction to Educational Measurement*. Boston: Houghton Mifflin Company, 1957.

Remmers, H. H., N. L. Gage, and J. F. Rummel, *A Practical Introduction to Measurement and Evaluation*. New York: Harper & Row, Publishers, 1960.

Schwartz, A. and S. C. Tiedeman, *Evaluating Student Progress in the Secondary School*. New York: Longmans, Green & Co., Inc., 1957.

Thorndike, R. L. and E. Hagen, *Measurement and Evaluation in Psychology and Education*, 2nd ed. New York: John Wiley & Sons, Inc., 1961.

Wrightstone, J. W., J. Justman, and I. Robbins, *Evaluation in Modern Education*. New York: American Book Company, 1956.

Appendix

Textbook Publishers

Allyn and Bacon, Inc., 150 Tremont St., Boston, Mass.
American Book Company, 55 Fifth Ave., New York 3, N.Y.
Appleton-Century-Crofts, Inc., 35 West 32nd St., New York 1, N.Y.
Associated Press, 291 Broadway, New York 7, N.Y.
Barnes & Noble, Inc., 105 Fifth Ave., New York 3, N.Y.
Bobbs-Merrill Company, Inc., 1720 East 38th St., Indianapolis, Ind.
Bruce Publishing Co., 400 North Broadway, Milwaukee 1, Wisc.
Thomas Y. Crowell Company, 432 Park Ave., South, New York 16, N.Y.
Dodd, Mead & Co., 119 West 40th St., New York 18, N.Y.
E. P. Dutton & Co., Inc., 300 Fourth Ave., New York 10, N.Y.
Follett Publishing Company, 1010 West Washington Boulevard, Chicago 7, Ill.
Ginn & Company, Statler Building, Boston 17, Mass.
Globe Book Company, 175 Fifth Ave., New York 10, N.Y.
Harcourt, Brace & World, Inc., 750 Third Ave., New York 17, N.Y.
Harper & Row, Publishers, 49 East 33rd Street, New York 16, N.Y.
D. C. Heath & Company, 285 Columbus Ave., Boston 16, Mass.
Holt, Rinehart & Winston, Inc., 383 Madison Ave., New York 17, N.Y.
Houghton Mifflin Company, 2 Park St., Boston 7, Mass.
Iroquois Publishing Company, 1300 Alum Creek Drive, Columbus 16, Ohio
J. B. Lippincott Co., 333 West Lake St., Chicago 6, Ill.
Little, Brown & Co., 34 Beacon St., Boston 6, Mass.
Littlefield, Adams & Co., 128 Oliver St., Paterson 1, N.J.
Longmans, Green & Co., Inc., 119 West 40th St., New York 18, N.Y.
Lyons and Carnahan, 2500 Prairie Ave., Chicago 16, Ill.
McGraw-Hill Book Company, Inc., 300 West 42nd St., New York 36, N.Y.
McKnight and McKnight, Towanda Ave., Route 66, Bloomington, Ill.
The Macmillan Company, 60 Fifth Ave., New York 11, N.Y.
Charles E. Merrill Books, Inc., 1300 Alum Creek Drive, Columbus 16, Ohio
Oxford University Press, Inc., 417 Fifth Avenue, New York 16, N.Y.
Prentice-Hall, Inc., Englewood Cliffs, N.J.
Scott, Foresman & Company, 433 East Erie St., Chicago 11, Ill.
Charles Scribner's Sons, 597 Fifth Ave., New York 17, N.Y.
Silver Burdett Company, Morristown, N.J.

Stanford University Press, Stanford, Calif.
D. Van Nostrand Co., Inc., 120 Alexander St., Princeton, N.J.
John Wiley & Sons, Inc., 440 Park Ave., S., New York 16, N.Y.

Maps, Charts, Globes, Pictures, and Supplies

Air Age Education Research, 80 E. 42 St., New York 17, N.Y.
Charles Beseler Co., 219 S. 18th St., East Orange, N.J.
Clay-Adams Co., Inc., 141 E. 25th St., New York 10, N.Y.
George F. Cram Co., Inc., 750 E. Washington St., Indianapolis, 7, Ind.
Creative Education Society, 530 N. Front St., Mankato, Minn.
Denoyer-Geppert Co., 5235 Ravenswood Ave., Chicago 40, Ill.
Film Associates of California, 11014 Santa Monica Blvd., Los Angeles 25, Calif.
Hammett, Co., 290 Main St., Cambridge 42, Mass.
C. S. Hammond & Co., Inc., 515 Valley St., Maplewood, N.J.
Informative Classroom Pictures Association, 31 Ottawa Ave., Grand Rapids 2, Mich.
Keystone View Co., Meadville, Pa.
McKinley Publishing Co., 1021 Filbert St., Philadelphia 7, Pa.
National Geographic Society, 16 and M Sts., Washington 6, D.C.
A. J. Nystrom and Co., 3333 Elston Ave., Chicago 18, Ill.
Perry Pictures Co., Malden, Mass.
Rand McNally & Co., 536 S. Clark St., Chicago 5, Ill.
Weber-Costello Co., 12 and McKinley Sts., Chicago Heights, Ill.

Sources for Tests

California Test Bureau, Del Monte Research Park, Monterey, Calif.
Educational Testing Service, 20 Nassau Street, Princeton, N.J.
Harcourt, Brace & World, Inc., 750 Third Ave., New York 19, N.Y.
Science Research Associates, Inc., 259 East Erie Street, Chicago 11, Ill.

Sources for Films

Academy Films, 800 N. Seward St., Hollywood, Calif.
American Library Association, 50 E. Huron St., Chicago 11, Ill.
Association Films, Inc., 347 Madison Ave., New York 17, N.Y.
Avalon Daggett Productions, 441 N. Orange Dr., Los Angeles 36, Calif.
Bailey Films, Box 6509 De Longpre Ave., Hollywood 28, Calif.
Brandon Films, Inc., 200 W. 57th St., New York 19, N.Y.
British Information Services, 45 Rockefeller Plaza, New York 20, N.Y.
Churchill-Wexler Film Productions, 801 N. Seward St., Los Angeles 38, Calif.
Contemporary Films, Inc., 267 W. 25th St., New York 19, N.Y.

Coronet Films, 65 E. South Water St., Chicago 1, Ill.

Encyclopedia Brittannica Films, Inc., 1150 Wilmette Ave., Wilmette, Ill.

Films, Inc., 1150 Wilmette Ave., Wilmette, Ill.

Films of the Nations, Inc., 62 W. 45th St., New York, N.Y.

General Electric Co., 1 River Rd., Schenectady, N.Y.

General Motors Corp., General Motors Bldg., Detroit 2, Mich.

Ideal Pictures, Inc., 65 E. South Water St., Chicago 1, Ill.

Indiana University, Audio-Visual Center, Bloomington, Ind.

International Film Foundation, 1 E. 42d St., New York 17, N.Y.

Iowa State College, Visual Instruction Service, Ames, Iowa

National Audubon Society, 1130 Fifth Ave., New York 28, N.Y.

National Film Board of Canada, 650 Fifth Ave., New York 21, N.Y.

New York University Film Library, 26 Washington Pl., New York 3, N.Y.

Ohio State University, Columbus 10, Ohio

Princeton Film Center, Box 431, Princeton, N.J.

Syracuse University, Audio-Visual Center, 121 College Pl., Syracuse, N.Y.

United Nations, Film and Visual Information Division, New York, N.Y.

United World Films, Inc., 1445 Park Ave., New York 29, N.Y.

University of Colorado, Bureau of A-V Instruction, Boulder, Colo.

University of Minnesota, A-V Dept., Minneapolis 14, Minn.

University of Wisconsin, Bureau of Visual Instruction, Madison 6, Wis.

Wayne University, A-V Materials Bureau, Detroit 1, Mich.

Westinghouse Electric Corp., Film Division, Gateway Center, 401 Liberty Ave., Pittsburgh 30, Pa.

Young America Films, Inc., McGraw-Hill Book Co., Inc., 330 W. 42d St., New York 36, N.Y.

Sources for Free and Inexpensive Materials

Elementary Teachers Guide to Free Curriculum Materials. Educators Progress Service, Randolph, Wis.

Free and Inexpensive Learning Materials, Division of Surveys and Field Services, George Peabody College for Teachers, Nashville 5, Tenn.

Free and Inexpensive Materials on World Affairs. World Affairs Materials, Brooklyn College, Brooklyn 10, N.Y.

Monthly Catalog of United States Government Publications. United States Government Printing Office, Washington, D.C.

The Vertical File Index. The H. W. Wilson Co., 950 University Avenue, New York 52, N.Y.

Sources for Current Events

The American Observer, Junior Review, Young Citizen, and *Weekly News Review* are all planned for various grade levels and published weekly. They are published by the Civic Education Service, Inc., 1733 K Street, N.W., Washington 6, D.C.

Current Events, Every Week, and *Our Times* are graded series of school publications. They are published weekly by the American Education Publications, 1250 Fairwood Ave., Columbus 16, Ohio.

Current History, Current History, Inc., 1822 Ludlow St., Philadelphia 3, Pa. A monthly magazine of current affairs.

Newsweek, Weekly Publications, Inc., Newsweek Bldg., Broadway and 42d St., New York 36, N.Y. A weekly publication of current news items.

Reader's Digest, Reader's Digest Association, Inc., Pleasantville, N.Y. A monthly magazine of current news.

Senior and *Junior Scholastic* and *World Week* are published by Scholastic Corp., 33 West 42d St., New York 36, N.Y. *The Scholastic Teacher* is also helpful for the teaching of current materials. Published weekly.

Time, Time Inc., Educational Bureau, 9 Rockefeller Plaza, New York 20, N.Y. A weekly publication of current news items.

U.S. News and World Report, United States News Publishing Corporation, a weekly publication. Circulation Department, 437 Parker Ave., Dayton 1, Ohio.

Some Periodicals

California Journal of Secondary Education, California Association of Secondary School Administrators, 2220 Bancroft Way, Berkeley 4, Calif.

The Clearing House, Fairleigh Dickinson University, Teaneck, N.J.

Education, The Bobbs-Merrill Co., Inc., 4300 W. 62nd St., Indianapolis 6, Ind.

Educational Administration and Supervision, Warwick and York, Inc., 10 E. Centre St., Baltimore 2, Md.

Educational Leadership, Association for Supervision and Curriculum Development, National Education Association, 1201 16th St., N.W., Washington 6, D.C.

Educational Record, American Council on Education, 1785 Massachusetts Ave., N.W., Washington 6, D.C.

Educational Screen & Audio-Visual Guide, Educational Screen, Inc., 415 N. Dearborn, Chicago 10, Ill.

High Points, Board of Education, 110 Livingston St., Brooklyn, N.Y.

The High School Journal, University of North Carolina Press, Box 810, Chapel Hill, N.C.

The Journal of Educational Sociology, Payne Educational Sociology Foundation, Inc., New York University, Washington Sq., New York 3, N.Y.

The Journal of Geography, A. J. Nystrom and Co., 3333 Elston Ave., Chicago 18, Ill.

School and Society, Society for the Advancement of Education, 1834 Broadway, New York 23, N.Y.

The School Review, University of Chicago Press, 5750 Ellis Ave., Chicago 37, Ill.

Social Education, National Council for the Social Studies, 1201 16th St., N.W., Washington 6, D.C.

The Social Studies, McKinley Publishing Co., 809-811 N. 19th St., Philadelphia 30, Pa.

Wilson Library Bulletin, The H. W. Wilson Co., 950 University Ave., New York 52, N.Y.

Index

Ability:
  mental development, 52
  to think, 7
Achievement, of slow learner, 59
Activities:
  classroom, 151
  in core program, 45
  in planning, 95-96
Adams, Georgia Sachs, 368 n.
Administration:
  of audio-visual material, 337
  by department chairman, 84
Advanced placement, 31
Agencies, community, 351
Ahmann, J. S., 357 n.
Alberty, H., 41
American Assn. of School Librarians,
    283 n., 284 n., 290 n., 308 n.
American history:
  biography relating to, 180
  course structure, 166-168
  examples of themes in, 167-168
  fiction relating to, 181-182
  importance of, 165-166
  poetry relating to, 183
  program in, 20, 21-22
Anderson, V. E., 63 n.
Anecdotal record, 378
Anthropology (see also Culture):
  defined, 11
  work of, 256-257
Art related to social sciences, 11
Assignments, 121
Association for Supervision and Curricu-
    lum Development, 12 n., 17 n.,
    23 n.
Association of School Administrators,
    341 n.
Attention span, 52
Audio-visual materials (see also specific
      materials):
  administration of, 337
  cartoons, 185-186
  chalkboard, 315-316
  charts, 321
  in conclusions, 314-315
  in core program, 40
  in culture course, 263
  for current affairs, 270
  diagrams, 321-322
  dramatizations, 327
  in economics, 223
  enrichment by, 314
  evaluating, 315
  exhibits, 325-326
  field trips, 327
  globes, 320-321
  graphs, 322-325
  guides for, 312-314
  importance of, 158

Audio-visual materials (Cont.)
  increased use of, 31, 152
  instructional materials, 317-318
  in introducing unit, 314
  in laboratory method, 115, 116
  with lecture, 111
  library as center for, 301, 338
  maps, 320-321
  murals, 326-327
  objectives of, 311-312
  pictures, 214, 318-319
  posters, 319-320
  in problem method, 117
  projection equipment and materials,
      329-339
    motion pictures, 334-336
    the museum, 336
    opaque projector, 328
    overhead transparency projector, 331
    recordings and transcriptions, 332
    radio, 333-334
    room for, 153
    slide projector, 329-331
    stereographs and stereoscopes, 331
    television, 332-333
  purpose of, 313, 314-315
  role of teacher in, 336-337
  school-made films, 327
  selection of, 313
  as stimulus, 313-314
  tables, 322
  tackboard, 316-317
  in team teaching, 119
  testing through, 370-371
  textbooks, 317-318
  in unit planning, 93
  varieties of, 312
Authority, response to, by pupil, 53
Automation, impact of, 2, 30

Basic education (see Block-time studies;
      and Core curriculum)
Baughman, M. D., 35 n.
Behavior, illustrating skills, 128-130
Bengston, N. A., 190 n.
Benjamin, Florence O., 260 n.
Berman, L. M., 65 n.
Bibliographies:
  from library, 286
  making of, 145-146
  as study aid, 135
Biesanz, J. and M., 255 n.
Biography:
  history through, 179-180
  selection of, 180
Biology, related to social sciences, 11
Block-time classes (see also Core curricu-
      lum):

393